WE,
THE PEOPLE

Recent Titles in
Contributions in Sociology
SERIES EDITOR: Don Martindale

Sociology in Israel
Leonard Weller

The Revolutionary Party: Essays in the Sociology of Politics
Feliks Gross

Group Interaction as Therapy: The Use of the Small Group in Corrections
Richard Stephenson and Frank R. Scarpitti

Sociology of the Black Experience
Daniel Thompson

The Incomplete Adult: Social Class Constraints on Personality Development
Margaret J. Lundberg

Sociology in Australia and New Zealand: Theory and Methods
Cora V. Baldock and Jim Lally

Handbook of Contemporary Developments in World Sociology
Don Martindale and Raj P. Mohan (eds.)

The New Social Sciences
Baidya Nath Varma

The Population Challenge: A Handbook for Nonspecialists
Johannes Overbeek

Victims of Change: Juvenile Delinquents in American Society
Harold Finestone

The Fence: A New Look at the World of Property Theft
Marilyn E. Walsh

The Taming of the Troops: Social Control in the United States Army
Lawrence B. Radine

The Evolution of Population Theory: A Documentary Sourcebook
Johannes Overbeek

Contemporary Entrepreneurs: The Sociology of Residential Real Estate Agents
J. D. House

The Handwriting on the Wall: Toward a Sociology and Psychology of Graffiti
Ernest L. Abel and Barbara E. Buckley

WE, THE PEOPLE

American Character and Social Change

EDITED BY GORDON J. DiRENZO

Contributions in Sociology
Number 24

GREENWOOD PRESS
WESTPORT, CONNECTICUT • LONDON, ENGLAND

Library of Congress Cataloging in Publication Data
Main entry under title:

We, the people.

(Contributions in sociology ; no. 24)
"Product of a symposium . . . that was held at the University of Delaware in October 1974."
Bibliography: p.
Includes index.
1. Social change—Congresses. 2. Social values—Congresses. 3. National characteristics, American—Congresses. I. DiRenzo, Gordon J.
HN65.W38 301.29'73 76-51926
ISBN 0-8371-9481-4

Library of Congress Catalog Card Number: 76-51926
ISBN: 0-8371-9481-4
ISSN: 0084-9278

First published in 1977

Greenwood Press, Inc.
51 Riverside Avenue, Westport, Connecticut 06880

Printed in the United States of America

To those millions of Americans
who during the past two hundred years
have marked their character
on these United States

Contents

Tables

Chapter 3

Chapter 6

Preface

One of the central problems that confronts these United States today as we celebrate the bicentennial of our nation is to ascertain the effects of rapid and extensive social change on the character of the American people. Associated with this task is that of projecting the kind of national character that can be expected in the future generations for whom we are redesigning and building new sociopolitical systems. Particularly relevant in these considerations is the unparalleled expansion of personal and civic freedoms that took place during the past quarter of a century, especially in the 1960s. But if the efficiency and efficaciousness of our society is to be enhanced through greater democratic participation by the citizenry as well as through modernized structures, American government must more than ever fulfill its original design as a government *for* the people. Such a government requires social systems that are responsive to, and congruent with, the character and needs of the people it is intended to serve. Correspondingly, in order to function, particular social systems require certain kinds of people or personalities.

Contrary to the popular cliché, it may not take all kinds of people to make the world go around; rather, it may take certain kinds of people or personalities to make any particular sociopolitical world, or segment of it, go around. Accordingly, as we Americans embark on the third century of our democratic experience, and as we attempt not only to maintain but also to perfect our democracy, it is well for us to reflect on what manner of people we have become and might yet become. More importantly, we need to ponder what manner of men and women we *ought* to become in order to refine and strengthen our sociopolitical system. Our common endeavor in this volume is directed to this objective.

The specific focus of this volume is a multidisciplinary inquiry into the nature of American national character as influenced by sociocultural change during the post-World War II period. Emphases are given to changes in the dominant and variant systems of beliefs, values, motivations, psychodynamics, and social behavior that characterize the American people. The principal objectives of this inquiry are to assess the consequences of changes in the national modal character of the United States, and various sociocultural segments thereof, and to provide thereby an understanding of the directions that American society may take in the immediate future.

These deliberations should provide an appreciation for the types of sociocultural systems that need to be established and maintained in order to enable the United States of America, during the third century of its democratic experience, to become ever more responsive to the general needs and the specific character of its people. It is within these perspectives that we have undertaken this collaborative effort. Our expectations may be ambitious, but the opportunity provided by the bicentennial celebration of our nation is both an auspicious and an imperative one.

Gordon J. DiRenzo

Acknowledgments

This volume represents the product of a symposium on the topic of "Social Change and Social Character" that was held at the University of Delaware in October 1974 as a bicentennial assessment of the American people.

It seemed all too fitting to those of us participating, apart from our own professional interests in this question, that a work such as this should be generated in Delaware—the state that prides itself on being the one that started our nation. We had the good fortune to assemble on our podium, and now in these pages, a complement of distinguished scholars who addressed themselves keenly to the challenging issues of the symposium. To collaborate with them in this venture has been a most rewarding experience.

An undertaking of this magnitude necessarily involves the cooperation and good efforts of a number of people to whom I wish to express my sincere gratitude. First of all, the program was made possible by grants from the following segments of the University of Delaware: Office of Academic Affairs, College of Graduate Studies, College of Nursing, Division of Health Sciences, Department of Sociology, and the Committee on Cultural Activities and Public Events.

On the personal level, a host of people encouraged and supported us during the implementation of our symposium and the writing of these pages. In particular, we appreciate the personal assistance and generous contributions of the good offices of the following officials of the University: Dr. E. Arthur Trabant, President; Dr. L. Leon Campbell, Provost; Dr. Arnold L. Lippert, former Dean of the College of Graduate Studies; and Dr. Helen Gouldner, Dean of the College of Arts and Science.

A special word of gratitude is owed to my several colleagues, research assistants, and students in the Department of Sociology for their indispensable help in a variety of ways.

Thanks also go to the fine people at Greenwood Press, especially

James T. Sabin, Cynthia M. Harris, Betty Pessagno, and Sandra Soderberg, who attended to the publication of this volume in such a professional manner; and to my colleague, Professor Don Martindale, editor of the Contributions in Sociology series of which this volume is a part, for his kind endorsement and constructive suggestions.

Finally, and as always, none of my own efforts in this undertaking would have been possible without the intellectual and psychological support of the characters in my own little, and ever changing, America: Mary Kathleen, Maria Giulia, Chiara Vernonica, and Marco Santo.

G.J.D.

Little Baltimore Farms
Newark, Delaware
JULY 1976

WE,
THE PEOPLE

1

Introduction: Social Change and Social Character in America

GORDON J. DiRENZO

The phenomenon of social change has been a somewhat fashionable focus of study in the social and behavioral sciences during the past twenty-five years or so. This is not to say that this concern has been a mere expression of the social and intellectual fashions of the times. In fact, social change has been both very real and omnipresent. The novel aspects of social change in contemporary society are its extent, magnitude, and force. Indeed, these characteristics of social change have comprised one of the singular sets of pervasive attributes of contemporary Western society. Change, like the principle of life itself, has touched even the most remote corners of human societies.

One dramatic indicator of social change in the United States can be found in Alexis de Tocqueville's description of Americans (1840:621) as "the most unmilitary people in the world." At the time of his observation, the 1830s, our army numbered a mere 6,000. There has been a veritable explosion of changes since then, especially during the last twenty-five years. Affected have been all of our fundamental institutions: the family, law, religion, government, education, and economics. Alterations in these institutions that mold the human personality have had profound consequences for the American social character. Accordingly, this volume inquires into the extent to which the extensive social changes of the post-World War II period have altered the American social character. More importantly, it inquires into the significance of a new, or changing, pattern of social character in

America for the function and future development of our society as well as for other parts of the world. The fundamental questions, then, of the succeeding chapters are: What are the modal patterns and composition of social character in American society today? What prognostications can be made in terms of their societal consequences on both the collective and the individual level?

Overview of Substantive Issues

One pivotal dimension of social character is that comprised of the dominant values existing among a people. In this regard, many of today's scholars frequently focus on "core values"—the central conception and expression of desirability and/or preference from which the day-to-day decisions and choices that confront a society and its members are typically made. We begin our specific assessments of social change and social character in America with a consideration of core values, and the succeeding chapters continually return to this principal focus.

American Core Values

In the next chapter, Professor George Spindler provides an assessment of the changes, continuities, and paradoxes in the system of American values during the past quarter century. Within a comparative perspective, he offers value profiles of various segments of our society, especially of racial and ethnic minorities. Of central significance in his presentation is a set of core values (e.g., equality, honesty, work, action, and sociability) that he describes as not only constant but also classic and peculiarly American. Spindler argues, perhaps somewhat in the spirit of de Tocqueville, that these enduring hallmarks of the American value system "hold the nation together."

Spindler's analysis is based on data drawn from college students. Value data from youth populations naturally lend themselves to projections and predictions of future socioeconomic expectations. The core-value profile of today's young generation probably can tell us much about the kind of social character that can be expected to mark the next generation or two of Americans. More than any other segment of our society, American youth have been and continue to be the principal producers and products of social change. Here, therefore, are strong roots for characterological change in America. Moreover, characterological change in its political perspectives and experiences is nowhere more dramatic than among the young people of our society.

In Chapter 6, Professor Gabriel Almond expands these dimensions considerably by examining the characterological effects of the countercultural revolution of the late 1960s. Almond describes a new value trend among young people, especially the highly educated ones, which is in marked contrast to the dominant values (e.g., security and acquisition) of the older generations of Americans. The most significant aspect of the cultural innovations in values and ideology produced by the political radicalism of the 1960s is that they appear to be spreading to noncollege youth in American society. As such, they indicate the development of a strong basis for militating against the "end of ideology" (Bell, 1960) and strengthening the promise of "civic culture" (Almond and Verba, 1963). Yet, both Spindler and Almond perceive the development of a new kind of humanitarianism and altruism as distinctive features of the emerging social character in America—an expectation that frequently seems to be contradicted by other considerations of our basic values.

Morality

The concept of morality in American society has undergone tremendous change in recent years. Throughout most of the past decade, much was heard about the new morality, situational morality, personal morality, and the "hang-loose" ethic. Has there been a loss of common morality in the United States? Have we become immoral or amoral? Or, rather, has our morality merely shifted from a traditionally absolute one to a relative or situational set of norms? These questions, particularly in the light of recent political crises in the nation (e.g., Watergate), are most compelling and, in many respects, they have been at the heart of the so-called generation gap that so preoccupied most of Western society during the youth rebellion and cultural revolution of the 1960s. Attempts to confront this particular issue appear to have fragmented our society in a number of ways and to have generated much psychological conflict on the personal level.

While several of the subsequent chapters are concerned with the question of moral values, Professor Nevitt Sanford, in Chapter 4, addresses himself directly to "The Loss and Rediscovery of Moral Character" in America. His message, reinforced by Professors Francis Hsu (Chapter 5) and Michael Maccoby (Chapter 8), is that the common morality of the golden rule has been replaced by organizational expediency—the needs of competitive survival in today's society. Sanford and Hsu share this concern for the loss of morality and its implications for personal happiness and affectivity, which they feel have grossly disappeared from social relations in our society.

Happiness and the enjoyment of life are, of course, crucial considerations in any discussion of social change and social character. The roots of both continuity and change in social character, however, lie in the context in which it is formed rather than in the actual contents or outcomes. Affectivity, like values, comprises a basic foundation for the contents of the psychosocial developmental processes of socialization and enculturation which are the primary vehicles for the formation of personal and social character. Hence, one of the major concerns in the succeeding chapters relates to how the structure and function of sociocultural systems produce social character and characterological changes.

Psychosocial Development of Character

A nearly exclusive emphasis in the field of characterological development is placed on infant care and early childhood experiences, both of which are held to be the supremely deterministic factors in shaping human personality. This prevalent view is challenged in several of the chapters that follow. Recent years have witnessed an expansion of interest in "adult socialization" and "middle-life personality formation." Contrary to the common assumptions and beliefs that heretofore have dominated the social and behavioral sciences, strong arguments are now advanced for the occurrence of psychological and characterological development throughout the life cycle. The cardinal issue in this controversy concerns the question of malleability versus durability in the structure and content of human personality.

Today, the human individual is thought to be much more plastic in terms of psychological formation, and the "permanency" of personality development in infancy and childhood is being challenged more and more. Such theoretical innovations are reflected in the growing interest in behavior modification, sensitivity groups, new forms of psychotherapy, and the like. Yet, despite tremendously high interest and curiosity on the individual level, the study of psychosocial development in adulthood has been neglected, indeed often tabooed. The chapters that follow, particularly those by Professors Richard Suzman

(Chapter 3), Daniel Levinson (Chapter 7), and Kenneth Gergen (Chapter 11), offer some remedial efforts along these lines.

Suzman elaborates on the development of a new and modern type of social character, the individual modernity syndrome, which is based heavily on the assumption that the social experiences of adulthood are playing an increasingly stronger role in the formation and change of individual personality. Levinson focuses on the meaning of "adult development" and seeks to create a sociopsychological theory for it. He describes a relatively universal and age-linked set of genotypic segments of the life cycle that are thought to follow an invariant developmental sequence, and he argues that the character of life changes in crucial respects from one era to another. These changes involve extended processes of "developmental transition" (as distinct from role transition). The focal process of his consideration is what Levinson calls the "Midlife Transition." He provides some new and provocative thoughts on the various personality changes that adults encounter in moving from one stage to another during the middle years of life.

Gergen joins the case against early socialization most directly. His argument, which assumes a relatively infinite malleability in human psychological characteristics, is that highly significant shifts in values, motives, beliefs, sentiments, and other characterological attributes can occur at virtually any point in the life cycle. Professor Amitai Etzioni (Chapter 12) offers an antithetical position based on the contention of a fixed human nature, which, while not entirely rejecting the role of "adult socialization," is absolute and durable.

It is difficult, nonetheless, to deny that a host of other changes are occurring in the structure of socialization and in the content of human development. For one thing, socialization functions are more and more being assumed by secondary social institutions. In addition, the mass media and other techniques of socialization (e.g., nurseries and advanced curricula) have changed extensively, and their impact on human psychological and characterological development has had profound, and even greatly unknown, consequences. Almond, for example, in his discussion of the changing character of youth in America, talks about the sharply increased scale of the problems in the socialization of youth; the difficulties created by the decreasing effectiveness of the major socializing institutions and experiences (e.g., the changing structure and culture of higher education); and the overloading of these principal agencies (family, church, and school) at the very time when they are losing their socializing capacity. Gergen's argument against early socialization is built on a parallel proposition: in an expanding, pluralistic, and complex society, there is a lack of strong and consistent learning experiences (nonreinforcing and nonsupporting social environments) that enhance the basic plasticity of the individual.

Perhaps one of the most dramatic changes in characterological formation stems from modifications in sex roles. Given the "liberation" of women and the "feminization" of men, we can expect profound changes in socialization-enculturation processes and psychosexual development. These androgynous dimensions of social learning are likely to produce significant modifications in the American social character. Similarly, social changes among racial and ethnic minorities, such as the decrease of discrimination coupled with the resurgence of minority pride, could effect tremendous changes in the future profile of social character in America.

Modal Types of Social Character

As our society has become more complex and more differentiated through social change, so too American social character may have become more pluralistic. More modal types, it appears, have arisen in recent years, matched by a corresponding multiplication of life-styles in various sociocultural segments of our population—racial, ethnic, sex, age, and occupational categories, among others. Much of this characterological and sociological diversity has always existed in terms of ethnic composition, as has been reflected ideally in the motto of our country: *E Pluribus Unum.* But what has happened to the United States as the popularly recognized crucible of ethnic and racial assimilation?

In very recent years there have been new, increasingly stronger, indications that the concept of America as the ethnic melting pot is no longer valid. Steadily greater numbers of Americans are now turning to a new concern with their ethnic and social origins. The past decade in particular has witnessed a tremendous resurgence of ethnic pride and social cohesion on the part of millions of Americans—and a corresponding set of individual movements for the revitalization of the culturally pluralistic structures of our society. We are in the midst of what Professor George DeVos describes in Chapter 10 as the phenomenon of the "passing of passing" and the stabilizing effects of the "unmeltable melting pot."

DeVos contends that American society is characterized more by political than by social unification, and that we are becoming less and less concerned with blending biological, social, and even psychological ideals. Americans, he argues, are abdicating the desire and/or need to suppress their socially diverse origins and backgrounds in the interests of a monolithic American social character. These developments hold profound significance for the future patterns of characterological structure in America.

DeVos maintains that the cultural and characterological pluralism of Americans can be discerned in a complex range of values, attitudes, symbols, habits, and patterns of social interaction that are not limited to ethnic classifications. He speaks, too, of the growing diversity in other social segments of our population, particularly sex. These developments suggest the possibility of a somewhat more complex and differentiated range of characterological modalities in our future society. One can see here the social and personal implications of what Riesman (1950) has called the "characterological struggle"—the mixing and interaction of different types of personalities and social characters. This question is of central importance with respect to the rapid acceleration of physical mobility which has become a principal facet of social change in America.

The multiplicity of modal types of social character is enlarged not only by the cultural and psychological differences among the ethnic and racial segments of our population, but also by the plurality and diversity of psychological types within these categories. For example, in Chapter 9, Professor Milton Yinger describes the expanding number of types of social character among Black Americans, and he argues that there are both extensive and intensive characterological modifications among them. Perhaps the most conspicuous of these modifications is a growing trend toward aggression and the externalization of whatever hostility may be generated by their minority status and experience.

Such negative attributes have constituted one of the strong themes in the consideration of the social character of minority people. The developmental situation is changing quite dramatically, however, and we need to inquire about these modifications. What have been the lingering psychological effects, for example, of the experiences of discrimination, segregation, the "culture of poverty," and the other aspects of minority status in the formation of social character among racial and ethnic Americans? Numerous judicial decisions and legislative reforms during the past twenty years or so have sharply curtailed the forms and incidents of public discrimination. In addition, a host of other types of newly enacted social legislation has also had positive effects. These major changes in strengthening the civil and political liberties of minority people have created a very different context for social relations in America.

The political, occupational, educational, and economic attainments of American minorities, coupled with a more favorable attitude and increased sensitivity on the part of other Americans, have been consistently closing the socioeconomic gap between the dominant and minority segments of our society. These new modes of social interaction have dramatically and profoundly affected the formation of social character among minority Americans. Major changes in the personal self-image, as well as in many other aspects of the character of minority people, have paralleled the new legal and other social statuses rightly accorded to these segments of the population. An increasing number of studies, as Yinger points out, reveal that the courage, poise, pride, and self-confidence resulting from decreasing social adversity are eroding the negative psychological and characterological effects of minority status.

With the likely possibility that these sociological and psychological changes will affect over 25 million racial Americans, and a vastly greater number of ethnic Americans, these social changes could have far-reaching effects on the characterological profile of America and on the structure and dynamics of our society.

This emerging phenomenon of multiple modal types appears to be equally visible in other segments of society, such as those based on occupational classifications. What has happened, for example, to "the organizational man" (Whyte, 1956) in corporate-industrial America, and what kind of character is emerging in its place? Maccoby in Chapter 8 describes four major types of social character in today's corporate field: "the craftsman," "the company man," "the gamesman" (modal type), and "the jungle fighter." He argues that similar types of social character can also be found in the field of politics. Some would even argue that academia and other social institutions, to the extent that they have become increasingly more corporate and more political, are moving toward those kinds of organizational psychostructure that Maccoby describes as recruiting and producing the corresponding corporate characters.

Basic to this expansion and diversity of modal types of social character is the question of whether American national character has changed in any common or fundamental ways. The majority view in these chapters is that it has and that such characterological changes are likely to continue. Suzman, for example, speaks in Chapter 3 of a basically new type of social character in America, represented by the individual modernity syndrome, which is not society-bound but rather emerges from the dynamics of industrialization, urbanization, and attendant social processes, and as such cuts across national, social, and even cultural boundaries. The new "modernity syndrome" (see Inkeles, 1966) seems to be a synthesis of the "inner-directed" and the "other-directed" characterological structures (see Riesman, 1950), which Suzman argues is a characterological prototype of postindustrial society. This new kind of social character results in particular from the experiences of increasing levels of mass education. The pivotal dimension of this new genre of social character is a service-orientation, and its value-emphasis is placed on such elements as humanitarianism, altruism, civic-mindedness, political awareness, and political involvement. These new dimensions of social character are the dominant ones that reoccur in several of the presentations that follow.

In a somewhat parallel sense, Spindler contends that the set of characterological features desired in the modal American of today and the future has undergone a distinctive and somewhat drastic change. Yet, despite these allegedly new characteroloical ideals, he argues that we seem to be retaining the fundamental core of the traditional characterological type upon which our society seems to be dependent. In this regard, Almond maintains that because of the rapid diffusion of a new political culture among young people, the characterological expectation in America is for a more open, change-oriented, and complex personality, with a greater analytical and problem-solving capacity than the more closed, rigid, and parochial type prevalent during recent years. Maccoby, in his profile of "the gamesman" as the modal type of corporate character in America today, describes this individual as a socially conscious and socially responsible personality—personal motivations notwithstanding. This type of character is dramatically different from those that have dominated American corporations as well as from the images of them that are still popular.

In a similar vein, Gergen argues that a repertory culture has emerged in our society: the lack of consistent and strong experiences in childhood has produced a type of social character that is marked by a multiplicity of self-concepts. This type is in contrast to that of the unitary and well-integrated self-image which, in Gergen's view, may have characterized a bygone era of our society. Gergen contends that this new psychocultural development is a positive one since it will create a more flexible and more adaptive individual who thereby will be able to respond more efficiently to the problems of our society. DeVos shares the basic perspective of multiple self-identities and the repertory culture, but he is less sanguine about their societal consequences.

Individuality versus Conformity

Has the dominant expression of American character become one of greater individuality or of greater conformity? In answer to this central question, Spindler contends that the typical American today is more inner-directed, but not in the sense that was popular a few decades ago. The new form of character is one of self-actualization and self-knowledge that is complementary to, and indeed functionally necessary for, the emergence of the new variety of social altruism mentioned earlier. It is not a mere variety of "other-directedness" distinguished by the internalization of a new set of values that transcend the pressures of the immediate situation. Rather, this "other-directedness," as Spindler explains, is now an end instead of a means—not sheer external conformity, but one with profound internal commitment. Individualism, he argues, has been significantly reinterpreted, and it has given way in the traditional sense to a more socialistic or communal variety. Maccoby also describes the modal corporate character as inner-directed and socially oriented, but states that it primarily and essentially represents an egocentric cohort of men committed to nobody but themselves.

This new emphasis on individualism is deplored by Hsu, who views the contemporary society as one in which individuals are out "to beat the system" in any way they can. Hsu maintains that the implicit social competition of individualism constitutes one of the basic causes of the problems and evils of our society. Sanford also argues against individualism on the basis that, through our loss of morality, we are conforming more and more to the demands and expectations of social organizations that essentially are amoral. Social organizations in our society, he states, favor authoritarian modes of adjustment and therefore tend to capitalize on authoritarianism in personality. Hence, organizations are assuming more and more control over our lives and are molding us into their authoritarian and amoral modes. Sanford does not believe that this corporate or organizational dehumanization is on the decline, and in his view the student liberation movements of the late 1960s might not have been as successful in this regard as many people believe or had hoped.

The question then is whether there is a lesser or greater amount of authoritarianism in American character today than was the case in the early 1940s when the classic work (Adorno, 1950) on this subject was conducted. Few would doubt that *attitudes* toward authority have undergone radical change during the past twenty-five years; respect for authority is no longer a dominant value in our society. This is not to say that *authoritarianism*, either in personal or social organizations, has necessarily diminished. Sanford contends that there is as much authoritarianism today as thirty or forty years ago. Hence, about one-third of the American people would be characterized as strongly or partly authoritarian. Sanford argues that authoritarianism is a psychohistorical concept, and that the type of authoritarianism that he and his associates studied in the 1940s may not be the same type that can be observed today. On these bases, Sanford raises the question of the probable rise of fascism in America.

The conformist character as the modal expression of Americans would not be a novel development. For example, Riesman (1950) and Whyte (1956) in their classic works on social character have described Americans as essentially conformist. The alleged exacerbation of conformist tendencies as modally typical of the American character is quite significant, however. One of the traditional hallmarks of American social character, however ideal, has been that of individualism. Many would argue, as Hsu does, that this characterological attribute has been a central catalyst for our great social and cultural achievements. On the other hand, many others would contend, as again Hsu does, that the individualism central to American social character has also been the source of our collective failures and social ills. The dilemma involved here is resolved by a kind of paradoxical boomerang: conformity is only the result of an intensified and egocentric individualism. Hsu states that our conformity, which appears to be altruistic and nonegocentric, is merely the price of a typically American, perhaps more broadly Western, identity-crisis wherein the resulting insecurity leads to associational and competitive interactions that are rooted in conformity. In other words, the motivations of individualism manifest themselves in the search for self-identity which requires conformity. Hence, despite increasing personal and civic freedoms, Americans now are in reality more easily controllable by social forces and correspondingly have become even less individualistic.

Self-Identity

The concern with self-identity, said to be one of the major characterological problems of modern America, may not be the mere manifestation of a psychological fad. As mentioned earlier, some maintain that an identity-crisis has become a hallark of the American social character. Hsu, as we have seen, asserts that the intensified individualism that is characteristically American stems from an identity-crisis, the outcome of which makes us a nation of nonconformists. The insecurity resulting from the identity-crisis leads the individual to join status-giving groups and thereby to conform to the customs and fads of the peer groups as a means of obtaining social recognition and personal identity.

Even the "passing of passing," argues DeVos, is neither a purely sociological phenomenon based on a resurgence of ethnic pride nor a newly found and faddish curiosity about one's ancestral past. On the personal side, the affirmation of ethnicity also involves fundamentally a set of psychological needs that are associated with the psychodynamics of self-identity and attempts to resolve certain sociological dilemmas. The individual finds it necessary, DeVos states, to achieve some form of separation into social categories that are not hierarchical, insofar as he realizes that social equality has become the dominant social ethics of our society and that racial differences are not likely to disappear. Hence, the advantages of ethnic identity are that it provides many of the sociological and psychological benefits of social recognition without the negative implications of a hierarchical or inequitable stratification. The idea of ethnic differences does not conflict with that of inequality, which is implicit in the notion of class differences. DeVos argues further that such new sources of self-identity are not confined to ethnic differences. The "liberation movements" in other societal segments (e.g., age, sex, and socioeconomic) may be additional dimensions of this new phenomenon.

In his iconoclastic presentation on "the decline of character," Gergen directly addresses the question of self-identity. He challenges the traditional thesis of a unitary self and the assumption that it is normal to have a coherent and stable sense of identity. Self-consistency, he asserts, is an erroneous, cultural perspective. Gergen argues that multiple self-identities are normal in an increasingly complex and pluralistic society. The individual in the corresponding repertory culture must play an increasing number of roles each day, and most of these roles, he states, demand a performance that is convincing, both to our audience and to ourselves. Hence, in such perspectives, social life in the future may indeed come to be dominated by the standard query: "Will the real me please stand up?"

DeVos also discusses the demise of self-consistency in contemporary society and sees the modal character of modern Americans as becoming essentially chameleon-like, changing its social appearance at will and taking on the coloring of a variety of social atmospheres. But, unlike Gergen, who considers the development of multiple self-identities to be a positive change for both individual and society, DeVos takes a problematic view of this expanding phenomenon. On the assumption that there is a conscious need for a consistent self, he discusses such dysfunctional states as anomie and alienation as they pertain to the modes of operation—on both the personal and social levels—that are related to a complex sense of self.

Functional Interactions: Characterological and Social Systems

The ultimate consideration with regard to many issues presented in this volume has to do with their functional consequences for both characterological and sociocultural systems. What is the nature of the interaction of these two systems?

Maccoby, for example, speaks of the American corporation as a "psychostructure" in which particular characterological types must fulfill various roles. From the point of view of the organization, the corporate executive without the proper kind of characterological "equipment" will not perform properly because he will not *want* to do what *needs* to be done. Hence, technical competence and intelligence in themselves may be insufficient for optimal organizational performance. Correspondingly, a given character type who finds himself in a sociocultural system with which he is not psychologically congruent may experience dissatisfaction and dysfunction on the personal level. Maccoby, for example, describes how the "gamesman"—the new modal type of corporate character—might make socially valued contributions to society because the psychological structure of this character type is responsive to, and congruent with, the more democratic and more autonomous social structures that are emerging in our society. A congruent interaction of the characterological system and the social system is required for the harmonious function of both. It is in the chasm of noncongruence between social character and society that the springs of psychological and social change are found.

We can expect, as social theory has traditionally held, that society will attempt to mold that type of social character which it deems essential or, at least, desirable. The more neglected, but equally crucial, consideration concerns the extent to which individuals will attempt to build those kinds of social systems that can gratify their characterological needs. Hence, in building and modifying society, we need to come to grips with human nature. This is no simple task, for it may require an extensive revision of psychological and sociological theory. The basic dimensions of this dilemma are seen in the contrasting positions advocated by Gergen and Etzioni.

Gergen argues that there is no fixed human nature or basic psychological needs and that the human being is quite plastic and adaptable to social and psychological situations. The normal individual is thus capable of myriad kinds of, and often discrepant, behavior. Etzioni advocates the antithesis to this position. For him there is a limited and fixed human nature as opposed to a highly variable and malleable one. Etzioni presents the case for "basic characterological needs" and seeks thereby to correct the "over-socialized conception of man" (Wrong, 1961) which has been quite prevalent in the social and behavioral sciences. Etzioni's view is reinforced by Sanford, Hsu, and DeVos, and it seems to be the more common one in this volume.

Basic characterological or human needs refer to a set of motivations that are psychological, not biological, in nature. They are universal, have attributes of their own, and rest neither on physiological foundations nor on specific social structures, cultural contents, and enculturation-socialization processes. The fundamental argument is that the processes that transform biological infants into functional members of society have certain essential features which, in turn, instill the basic characterological needs that represent functional imperatives for the individual. Hence, these universal needs may be described as inherent rather than innate.

It follows that what is required are social systems capable of meeting human needs—psychological as well as biological. The central question here, then, is the extent to which our changing society is responsive to the characterological structure and needs of Americans today. The corresponding question is whether the individual characterological system is able to make the necessary adaptations required by societal and social change and thereby to be functionally responsive itself.

One prevalent concern in this regard is that of the sociopsychological dynamics of alienation, which refers to social situations that are beyond the control of the individual and therefore unresponsive to his needs. Large segments of Americans today feel increasingly excluded from, and powerless in the face of, the evolutionary and structural dynamics of contemporary society. The evidence seems to show that our society has become a more democratic one, but how does this situation relate to the characterological structure of the individual citizen? Extreme forms of democracy can result in extreme degrees of anomie, or normlessness, and therefore in a psychosocial situation that is so overwhelming that the person is unable to gratify basic psychological needs. Hence, one may wonder about the possibility of America eventually facing, in Fromm's (1941) terms, an "escape from freedom" and all of its personal and social consequences.

Questions of affect and happiness as discussed above are related to alienation and anomie. Happiness is a dominant value among people, and some would argue, as Sanford does, that it is an imperative for morality and hence for the function of society and its members. In this regard, Sanford advocates the creation of responsive social organizations and structural processes (e.g., "developmental education") that can be adapted to the basic needs of human beings in order to counteract authoritarianism. Of direct significance here is Hsu's perception that the basic psycho-socio-cultural trend in America is the shrinkage of affect from social relations and the externalization of all human relations, with an impersonal and mechanical form of social interaction that is dysfunctional for both the individual and the collectivity. However true this situation may be in terms of the dynamics involved, not all would agree on the loss of affect, or even morality, as a distinctive characterological change in America. Gergen, for example, contends that rather than becoming diminished, affect has taken on a new meaning and a new mode of expression in the American character. While the more complex and pluralistic nature of our society has caused human relationships to become less permanent and more transitory, they remain as real as ever. The new meanings and functions of human relationships in this view are accidental and external, not essential or absolute, changes.

Nevertheless, human beings cannot function without minimal or sufficient degrees of affect. Its separation from social roles that have increased in both number and proficiency with the industrialization and modernization of our society has resulted in a search for affective outlets elsewhere, in secondary and transitory relationships, such as those provided by a variety of voluntary organizations, and even in abstract causes. Another consequence of this phenomenon, according to Hsu, is the lavishing of affect on the totally uncontrollable, such as pets and/or inanimate objects. Some social scientists contend that the attempt to structure society on the basis of nonprimary associations is dysfunctional, if not totally fatalistic, for society; hence, it is just as detrimental for the individual. Hsu advocates this position. He stresses the importance of responding to the nature and needs of both the individual and society, if each is to function smoothly and to achieve progress.

Changes in social character are not simply the effects or products of changes in sociocultural systems but in part they are also the causes and producers. The relationship between social character and society is a mutually dependent one. Changes in one will bring about changes in the other. Accordingly, as Yinger so aptly points out, we need to understand the nature of the cybernetic processes that operate among society, culture, and personality, and how, once created, the consequences of each variable flow back into the systems from which they came, reinforcing and modifying them anew.

We shall examine these and other theoretical questions, along with a number of methodological issues, in the concluding chapter of this volume.

Prospects

What kind of social character can be expected in the future generations of Americans? As suggested earlier, there is no consensus among the contributors to this volume on the various substantive and concrete issues of social and characterological change. Indeed, on some of the more significant questions, there is even diametric opposition; yet, overall, disagreement is minimal, perhaps because the contributors are basically discussing different topics and issues. All in all, however, the several presentations provide for a provocative but timely discussion.

Not surprisingly, the reader will encounter some pessimism in the following pages as regards the current state of social behavior and characterological development in our society. The more general tone, however, is one of optimism for the future. The essential message is one of promise: the American characterological profile will become more healthy and more socially productive than it has been during the past two hundred years. Let us turn now to some of the concrete dimensions of this potenial evolution of social change and American character.

2

Change and Continuity in American Core Cultural Values: An Anthropological Perspective

GEORGE D. SPINDLER

Introduction[1]

In my search for a data base for this essay on so challenging a topic as American cultural values, two strategies seemed attractive: (1) to examine ethnographies describing American communities or other segments of our culture and draw from them some generalizations appropriate to the topic; or (2) to draw from data that I had collected over a span of two decades, though sporadically, from Stanford students. I was motivated by a strong need for a data base. As I reviewed the writings by fellow anthropologists on American culture and national character, I was impressed anew by their speculative quality. Most of what anthropologists write on these topics is interesting but infirmly based on specific data. The ethnographies describing segments of American life are based firmly on data, but they do not address the larger questions pertinent to American culture.[2]

Despite certain hazards that will become apparent, I have chosen to use the Stanford sample as a data base. The ethnographies have not been left out entirely, however, for I found it rewarding, in the last part of the essay, to consider certain implications arising from them. In the main body of this essay, I will discuss values that appear to have remained more or less constant for the respondents as a whole during the period of the sample, values that have changed, and the value profiles of minority students.[3]

In 1955 I hypothesized that American cultural values were undergoing a transformation from "traditional" to "emergent," and that this shift was reflected in conflicts within our society, particularly between educators and various elements of the public (Spindler, 1955). The traditional values were Puritan morality, the work-success ethic, individualism, achievement, and future-time orientation. The emergent values were sociability, relativistic rather than absolute moral attitudes, consideration for others, present-time orientation, and conformity to the group. The data used in the analysis were gathered through (1) an open-ended sentence technique containing twenty-four items arranged around values about which there was consensus in the anthropological and sociological literature; and (2) a request that the respondent describe in one paragraph his or her conception of the "ideal American boy" (see Appendix). The sample, beginning in 1952, consisted of students at Stanford who were taking my courses in education and in anthropology. The technique was administered as a pedagogical device: the results were analyzed with the students in these classes in an attempt to clarify the probable influence of expressed values upon their behavior, including classroom teaching. (It occurred to me only later that I was also collecting research data.) Responses to the values-projective technique were occasionally collected for the same purpose from 1952 through 1961, and in 1968 Louise Spindler and I resumed collecting this kind of material. A total of 445 protocols has been analyzed, representing a socioeconomic range from upper lower to upper class, with the majority in the middle ranges and about equally divided between males and females. My discussion is based largely on these responses and their analysis.

The open-ended sentence technique elicits verbal responses. Students are asked to write down what "first comes to mind," and in this sense their responses can be considered verbally expressed values. There are, of course, discrepancies between verbalization and behavior. Nor do I claim that the technique reaches deep into the core of idiosyncratic values characterizing each respondent. However, the responses do represent an aspect of the verbal culture of the sample. They are ready-made statements of beliefs available to the respondents. They are cultural recipes, mind-sets. The cultural recipes represented by these responses may be regarded as influences, either directly or as counterpoints, on behavior.

It may be objected here that too much is made of a sample of a few hundred young people attending what some consider an elitist institution. There are also ambiguities in the analysis that are not easily dismissed. Both criticisms are to a degree valid. However, in defense it may be stated that these students actually represent a rather broad range of the American middle class and, after all, many of their parents came from the heartland—the Middle West. In addition, there is evidence that the patterns of response described for this population are widely shared outside of it.

To clarify the type of technique and data used, some examples are given here. The responses to open-ended sentence number 3, "Artists are" (see Appendix), fell into three values categories: *negative* ("queers," "nuts," "effeminate," "long hairs," "eccentric"); *neutral* ("different," "nonconformist," "artistic"); and *positive* ("valuable," "fascinating," "talented"). In response to sentence 5, "Intellectuals should," the same categories emerged: *negative* ("drop dead," "keep it under cover," "be more humble," or get "with it," "be more involved," be more "reality-oriented"); *neutral* ("share knowledge," "study," "make use of their minds"); and *positive* ("be admired," "be influential," "govern"). For sentence 12, "The future is," the three categories of response were: *pessimistic* ("uncertain," "lost," "frightening"); *noncommittal* ("before us," "to come," "tomorrow"); and *optimistic* ("wide open," "challenging," "ours for the making"). For sentence 17, "Nudity is," the three categories were: *negative-moralistic* ("indecent," "obscene," "vulgar"); *relativistic* ("okay at times," "comfortable some places," "alright—it depends upon who is looking"); and *positive* ("beautiful," "exciting," "wonderful," "free," "warm," "fun," "sweet," "loving," "sexy").

These value categories were obtained inductively, first by grouping responses in small categories of most similar and then by widening the categories to their present scope. The analysis of the 445 protocols produced rather impressive arrays of numbers. Direct comparisons were made of the proportions of the various response categories in relationship to the total number of responses. Most of the shifts, trends, or differences were so substantial as to make inferential statistical analyses redundant; for a more refined analysis, however, they would be essential.

As mentioned earlier, in addition to the open-ended sentences, the study technique included a request that the respondent write a paragraph describing the "ideal American boy." The rationale for this rather sexist request was that the male, as the dominant instrumental type at the time the technique was first administered in 1952, would be the cynosure—everyone would have a concept of the ideal American boy. This was true in the 1950s and early 1960s; but when we resumed sampling in 1968, we began to get complaints, and after 1969 we changed the request to "ideal person." Clear-cut modal configurations of valued personality or character traits appeared for each sample, and the later period (1968-1974) was distinguished in a number of features from the earlier period (1952-1961). These differences could be ascribed to differences between elicitation techniques ("ideal American boy" versus "ideal person"). This does not appear to be the case since, for those two later years (1968-1969) when the original phrasing was still being used, the same configuration of traits was apparent as in 1974 when "ideal person" was substituted. Interestingly, whereas many of the personality features valued in the early period were those traditionally ascribed to males, such as ambition, daring, and athletic ability, these were represented only weakly or not at all in the later period. (More details are given later in this essay.)

The data produced by both techniques do not argue against the originally posited traditional-emergent dichotomy of values, or against a continuum of mixed values of varying intensities of commitment between these polarized value positions. I have hypothesized that the conflicts between the traditional and emergent value positions have been a source of conflict in our society both between groups and within individuals. This hypothesis has been supported in studies such as Bernice McAllister's study of 655 West Coast educators (1967). Much of the "paradox" of American values and of the American character, it seems, stems from pulls and pushes ingrained in our culture—from having to be sociable, friendly, sensitive to the opinions of others, and responsive to group norms, and at the same time egocentrically individualistic, driven by the need for achievement, and oriented by an absolute set of morals.

Rather than become enmeshed in the subject of the conflicts produced by different allegiances to traditional versus emergent values, I shall confine myself to questions of stability, change, and reformulation over this twenty-two-year period. The questions directly relevant to this period and answered through analysis of the values-projective data are: Is there a stable core of values for 1952-1974? If such values can be identified, what changes or reformulations of them have occurred? What deviations from this stable core of values can be identified? Are minority students who attend Stanford culturally different with respect to the posited core values?[4] Other questions that must be discussed, using information extending beyond the data produced by the values-projective technique, include: Has the countercultural revolution of the 1960s had a lasting effect on our young? Has Watergate affected the values expressed by college-age youth? Has alienation gone so far as to endanger the continuity of our culture?

There is indeed a profile of core values, and they are not only constant, but classic. Virtually every serious analyst of the American scene has included some or all of these values in his or her interpretation. They are supported more intensely in some sectors of our society than in others. The position of minority respondents vis-à-vis these values will be of particular interest.

First, I will discuss these core value constants. With this done, I shall turn to shifts and changes in these and other values, and then to the position of minorities.

Constant Values, 1952-1974

In discussing the constant values for 1952-1974, I shall present specific percentages in a given response category, but I shall couch my discussion, in the interest of communication, in fairly general terms. Each constant value, as indicated by categories of response in both the open-ended sentence elicitation technique and the ideal person paragraph, is mentioned, and it is stated whether the value has declined or increased in frequency of mention over the twenty-two years of the sample. The "earlier period" indicates 1952-1961 and the "later period," 1968-1974. When 1952 and 1974 are compared, it is correct to assume that these two years represent these two periods. These periods seem to constitute quite different clusters of value orientation, in some, though not all, respects.

Now for the constants. Fifty percent of the respondents in 1974 say that "all men are born equal" versus 75 percent in 1952. Responses in the later period are more scattered, with an increasing number of cynical, wry, or idiosyncratic sentence endings, such as "equal, it is said," "single," "unclothed," "free," "with little choice." Nevertheless, the response "equal" is strong and has remained so over the twenty-two-year period.

The value of honesty appears to be a strong constant but has declined somewhat in the later period. Honesty "is the best policy" (or equivalent phrasing) was indicated by 80 percent in 1952 and 68 percent in 1974. New response categories, such as "is rare among public officials," appear in 1974. Honesty and sincerity as personal traits have gained in strength, however.

The value of effort and work and of clear goals in an open system has retained strength. This is a surprising finding in view of the alienation that is so often said to pervade our youth. There is, however, evidence of a decline, or perhaps a reinterpretation, in this value complex. "Anyone can get to the top if they"/"try" or "work hard" has declined from 80 to 60 percent of all responses; ambition in the traditional sense of the term is no longer a declared ideal value for most respondents, and there is little agreement that "Everyone should want to achieve" (2 percent in 1974 in contrast to 59 percent in 1952).

The value placed upon doing rather than talking, pretending, or having ascribed status and reward appears to be high, with only a minor decline in the later period (from 75 percent in 1952 to 68 percent in 1974).

Time is still valuable (45 percent so indicate in 1974), though fewer respondents regard time as "of the essence," "most valuable," and the like, as did 84 percent in 1952.

The value of living within the present and not mourning past mistakes, or as a modal response goes, "over spilt milk," has gained strength slightly and is an area of high agreement (80 percent in 1952 and 87 percent in 1974). About one-third of the respondents continue to be optimistic about the future (24 percent in 1952 and 30 percent in 1974). This proportion remained constant over the entire twenty-two years spanned by the sample. A pessimistic response has grown in the latter period, however, and will be discussed under "value changes."

The value of being sociable and personable still holds for a minority, but has eroded significantly (from 40 percent in 1952 to 25 percent in 1974). A conversion to consideration for others and sensitivity to their needs appears to have occurred. This change is considered in the next section.

These are the constant values expressed by this predominantly dle-class, largely Anglo-Euro-American sample over a period of two decades. These are some of the values that bind the generations together. They are the values represented in two generations. To the extent that the middle class is the majority segment and has the representative life-style of the United States, it seems reasonable to infer that these values are part of what has held the nation together. Former President Eisenhower and candidate Adlai Stevenson, as evidenced in their campaign speeches in 1952 and 1956, apparently considered these to be the American core values. Edward Steele's very thorough study of their speeches, available in his Stanford Ph.D. dissertation (1957), demonstrates this fact convincingly. In terms of core values, reiterated and played upon in many contexts, these two men, who seemed so very different in ideology and person, were saying the same things to the American public. One has the impression that a similar content analysis of the recent Ford-Carter debates would record little change in either the values or degree of agreement.

Nearly all of these constant values show a decline in degree of agreement. There is growing divergence, disagreement, conflict and reinterpretation. While this statement will come as news to no one, there is at the same time a considerable degree of continuity, as indicated by the sample, and there is evidence, not included in this paper, that the rate of change has flattened out. That is, from 1968 to 1974 there was no progressive decline or change in these key values. According to our data, the greatest changes occurred after 1961 and before 1968. This finding correlates well with our commonsense observation that indeed the 1960s were turbulent and that the 1970s have so far been relatively calm.

Value Changes

We can now consider major changes, shifts, and reformulations in values, beyond those represented in the erosion of the value constants just discussed.

As mentioned earlier, a constant proportion viewed the future optimistically. It was also regarded pessimistically by an increasing proportion (from 16 percent in 1952 to 40 percent in 1974). Worries about the environment, war, pollution, population, and natural resources are all represented in this youthful population.

Nudity is accepted or valued positively by an increasingly larger proportion of respondents. The largest emerging portion of responses is in the neutral or relativistic category. Nudity does not appear to be an issue in 1974 as it was in 1952, when 45 percent of all respondents stated that it was "obscene, vulgar, or shocking," and only 15 percent acknowledged that it had any virtues. A sophisticated minority said it was "alright in its place," or "too cold in this climate" (northern California can be surprisingly cold and damp!). In 1974, there are no negative responses: 30 percent say it is "beautiful, fun, free, warm, tender and sweet," and a substantial 66 percent say it is "okay in its place" but, in effect, nothing to get excited about. Attitudes toward nudity appear to be associated with other values diagnostic of a relativistic versus absolute moral position. We do not know, from our sample, whether they are associated with standards concerning sexual permissiveness. It is reasonable to assume, however, that the increasing tolerance and approval of nudity and the decline of moral absolutism are part of a shift in a whole complex of values and norms, of which changes in patterns of sexual behavior are a part.

The value of success in the traditional, individualistic, material sense has almost disappeared for the Anglo sample. Success as a state of competence and personal satisfaction, and particularly of happiness and harmony, is highly valued, and effort, work, and having clear goals are regarded as part of this satisfaction for the majority. But success both in the older sense, as achievement for its own sake, and in the competitive sense, as striving for rewards against or at the cost of others, has low or negative value. Today "Everyone should want to"/"be in harmony with themselves," "help others," "contribute something to society," or "gain self-knowledge." In 1952, "Everyone should want to"/"get ahead" or "succeed." Nevertheless, in 1974, it is acknowledged that to succeed one has to work hard and have clear goals. It is the meaning of success that has changed.

The individual is not what he or she used to be either. In 1952, 55 percent said the "individual is sacred," "supreme," "all important." In 1974, only 20 percent say that, but 32 percent state that the individual is "important in relation to society," "as a unit of self-awareness," and another 30 percent say the individual is "a threat to society" or a "myth." This does not mean that individualism is dead; far from it. Being yourself, knowing yourself, doing your own thing if it does not hurt others, developing your abilities, being a character (though preferably a kind, considerate one) are valued positively. Egocentric, "I'm Number One," "watch me beat the others at their own game," "get ahead at any cost" individualism is not valued.

Attitudes toward artists and intellectuals, two forms of deviants from standard middle-class norms in their traditional form, show interesting changes. In 1952, 42 percent of the respondents regarded artists as "nuts, effeminate, or screwy." In 1974, only 15 percent so regard them, and the majority view artists positively, believing them to be "creative" and "free." Intellectuals do not fare as well. In 1952, 32 percent said that intellectuals should "drop dead," "shut up," or "keep it under cover." But another 30 percent said they should take responsibility for government policy, lead, and be supported by society. In 1974 very few respondents say crude things about intellectuals, but very few have positive opinions (only 8 percent), and the majority (60 percent) are critical, believing that intellectuals should "face reality," "get out of the ivory tower," "get to know people and their problems directly," and "work more for the betterment of society." It is interesting, and somewhat depressing, that they say almost exactly the same things about college professors.

Otherwise, positive value is placed on tolerance, acceptance of individual and group differences, and cultural and personal deviations. I suspect, however, on the basis of qualitative indications in the responses, that the tolerance does not extend to deviations in traditional beliefs and practices in such areas as achievement, success, sex, and racism.

During the period covered by the sample, all values changed. Even the constants eroded or were reinterpreted. Surprisingly, however, they continued to have considerable hold. Certain other values, not less central perhaps but certainly less constant, underwent radical shifts. In general, the shift was from egocentric achievement, success by the individual, and absolute morality to a more humanistic, tolerant, relativistic position. The shift conforms to the traditional-emergent dichotomy as it was originally formulated in some, but not all, respects.

The Ideal Person

Certain rather sweeping changes occurred between 1952 and 1974 in the concept of the ideal person. In the 1952-1961 period, the modal values for the ideal American boy were: well-rounded, able to do many things but none too well; ambitious—concerned with getting ahead; average or acceptable IQ and academic performance; clean-minded and moral and sexually repressed; considerate of others; and sociable, liking others and being well-liked. Of these attributes, only consideration for others and sociability survive in the later period (1968-1974), though the meaning of "sociable" has shifted. The others are mentioned rarely or not at all. The new idealized personality traits, in rank order, are kindness and sympathy, concern for others, honesty and sincerity, a positive self-image and self-understanding, a sense of humor in general and about one's self, ability to lead and follow as circumstances demand, generosity, humility, and unassertiveness.

The quality of these traits can best be conveyed by quoting some of the paragraphs from the 1974 samples.

Someone who is friendly; helps and cares about others; tries to think of himself or herself less and others more; is honest; works hard. With these qualities a good life comes.

The most important value is to care about other people. Success is not a matter necessarily of acquiring material things but of trying to create a world where each person can live as he or she sees fit without hurting others, though obviously sometimes this may happen. One should also try to be happy with oneself. It's no good to go around with a hair shirt on.

Someone who has altruistic values and acts upon them. He is content and happy with himself and others. He is marked by fulfillment of his commitments and values. He accomplishes this with a humble demeanor.

The most important feature is the degree to which a person is selfless and considers others as ends not means. In short, that he is guided in his life by moral considerations. But he must also be certain of himself—have self-esteem, regard himself as worthy, as capable of accomplishments, able to lead or follow.

The ideal person is one who has enough self-confidence to be able to be gentle, kind, and loving . . . is able to be open in dealing with others . . . is not ruled by material goods and thinks about and works for others.

A sense of self-importance, flexibility in ideas, seeing the good in others, honest with oneself and what one really feels, unself-conscious, friendly and able to make others feel at ease.

These are not new personality traits or ideals, but they have been brought into prominence by young people who perceive them as functional in the kind of world they think they live in. In their view, the ambitious, moral, repressed, and presumably sublimating, egocentric individual whose sociability was largely instrumental to achievement may indeed be dangerous to the commonweal. It is difficult to fault the personal traits projected in the new image. There is a new kind of inner-directedness—of self-actualization and self-knowledge—that is complementary, or even functionally necessary, to the emphasis on concern for others and their welfare. The new social values may be internalized so that they have moral implications peculiarly satisfying to Americans, and that transcend immediate situational pressures, so the character type is not merely "other-directed," to use David Riesman's (1950) phrase.

Minorities

The final analytic step we must take is to attempt to define the position of the minority respondents. The students attending Stanford, including Blacks, Chicanos, American Indians, and Asian Americans, are not necessarily representative of all minority persons. They are presumably achievement-motivated or they would not be attending Stanford, but it is also true they are likely to serve as influential models for others.

The pattern of responses among these students does not deviate radically from that among the Anglo sample of 1974, except that they tend to support the core values more frequently. They are, it can be said, more American, in the frame of reference we are using here. That is, they are less pessimistic about the future and the value of success, more goal and achievement-oriented, more work-oriented, and more concerned with mobility than the Anglo respondents. They are also more interested in helping others, particularly the disadvantaged, and they are not as concerned with self-knowledge. It should be clear, however, that the congruence in core values does not mean there are no differences between minority and Anglo students in other areas of belief, behavior, sentiment, and value. Nor does this congruence argue against the possibility of separate identities, for identities are supported by social interaction, associations, and symbols extending beyond our concerns in this discussion.

The patterns expressed by a small sample of Stanford minority students are paralleled in a study done by Peggy Warth (1972) on seventh and eighth graders in a Bay Area public school with a sample of forty-one Anglos and twenty-three Chicanos. These young Anglos and Chicanos expressed a profile of support and deviation for the values discussed here that is remarkably similar to the one described for Stanford students. The Chicano students place about the same emphasis on honesty, the value of time, the "doing," or activistic, orientation, and equality, as do the Anglos. They more frequently support the linkage between success and effort, the belief in the openness of the system, and the value of the individual.

Such findings run counter to common sense. Why should groups who have had less reward from the system, and who in fact have experienced deprivation and oppression, support traditional values? I hypothesize that they need to believe in these values, that these values are the best chance they have for advancement. Indeed, if it were true that "honesty is the best policy," that one can succeed if only he tries hard enough, that the system is open, that individuals are important, and that all men are born equal—these groups would have no serious problems. The fact that the system has not been these things for them does not mean that these values are not honored. It may be that these values will ultimately triumph over present reality. With the growing number of minorities achieving middle-class socioeconomic status, this may indeed be happening already—however far we may yet be from a total realization of justice.

Again, it should be stated that agreement in these value areas does not mean that there are no differences between groups. Cultural pluralism is expressed by a much more complex range of habits, attitudes, values, symbols, speech communities, and identities than can be elicited by a simple, short, open-ended values-projective technique. And yet, the suggestion that there may be some agreement on some central value-ideals is heartening in a context where it often seems that there are no agreements, no basis for communication, and little hope for a viable society.

Let me turn briefly to yet another minority, which is also part of the Stanford community (DuBois, 1972). The Jewish sample from Stanford consists of members of Hillel, all religiously conservative, and deviant within the Jewish community as a whole only with respect to this conservatism. These Jewish students represent a strongly traditional American pattern within the framework of values used in this study. They support the work-success-achievement ethic more strongly than do the non-Jewish students, give more materialistic answers to "I wish I had. . . ," value the individual in the old-fashioned sense of being "supreme," "most important," and are more optimistic about the future. They are strongly family-oriented. Only one in the sample of twenty-five expressed any rejection of parents, and nearly all of the women want to settle near their families, as do about half of the males. The Hillel Jewish sample is also conservative in the area of sexual behavior. Fifty percent of the women do not feel that intercourse before marriage is permissible. Another 10 percent feel it would be justified if there were a deep emotional commitment and a plan to marry. All males in the sample feel that exclusiveness and emotional commitment are necessary. This information supports the characterization of the group as conservative beyond the specific values evoked by the values-projective technique.

It is apparent there are, within the student body, deviations in the degree to which the values elicited by the values-projective technique are supported. These deviations are in degree, not kind. These two types of differences may easily be confused. The core values are supported by all groups, but the strength of support varies. The minority groups support the core values most strongly. Each group expresses some particular emphases, such as self-knowledge on the part of Anglos and helping others on the part of minorities, but these emphases do not override the areas of agreement.

Conclusion to Values Analyses, 1952-1974

Those questions pertaining to the Stanford sample posed at the beginning of this chapter for the 1952-1974 period have been answered. There is a relatively stable core of values, though none remained static during this twenty-two-year period. Some values that were once a part of the central core configuration, such as individualism and material success, have eroded, been reformulated, or been bypassed. Other values, such as nudity and concern for others, have moved from a peripheral to a central position during this period. The minorities in the sample support the core American values. In fact, compared to the Anglos, they are more supportive. Some value emphases, as mentioned above, are specific to each group.

Further Discussion

The more general questions posed earlier require that we go beyond the data provided by the values-projective technique for the period 1952-1974. Has the countercultural revolution of the 1960s had a lasting effect on our young? The answer is a tentative yes and requires further exploration. Many of the shifts described in this essay, such as the turn to consideration and concern for others, the questioning of the validity of success and achievement as traditionally defined in American culture, and the more intensive search for self-knowledge, are expressed in an exaggerated form in communes, hippie ghettos, and with various twists, in the proliferating religious sects. These values may be so exotically expressed in these contexts that they are difficult to recognize. I do not think, however, that they have merely diffused indirectly or that they have been transmitted directly from these contexts to the larger population of middle-class youth. There appears, rather, to have been a large-scale cultural ground-swell, of which these groups are exaggerated expressions. In whichever direction the flow has come, these groups and sects are not wholly removed from the mainstream of American culture, however much it may be their intention to so remove themselves. William Partridge (1973) convincingly argues that the hippie movement is an attempt by largely middle-class youth to return to peculiarly American "first principles," such as self-fulfillment and freedom from rules, conventions, and authority, and to egalitarianism and individual salvation through spiritual growth. Even the "children of Krsna" described by Francine Daner (1976) in her sympathetic but objective ethnography, appear, despite their exotic subculture of religious worship and belief, to emphasize certain old-line American values such as hard work, aestheticism, salvation through service, austerity, and self-knowledge (as defined by their belief system). They are "un-American," and also "unhippie," in their obeisance to their Eastern-derived religious authority and in their rigid adherence to ritual and rule. In any event, the hippies, the children of Krsna, and others who have tried to isolate themselves from the mainstream of American culture have done so because the mainstream appeared to them to be too affluent, too driven by superficial needs, too inhuman to accept. In their separation, however, they have sometimes rediscovered and reasserted—often explicitly, more often in various guises—the "original" America, the "first principles."

My ethnographic journey through American communities such as the Appalachian Valley described by Hicks (1976), the rural New York community described by Johnson (1973), the carpenters of Alaska described by Clinton (1973), the snake handlers described by LaBarre (1962), and the longshoremen described by Pilcher (1972), reveals that values such as egalitarianism, rejection of external authority, and emphasis on personal fulfillment, independence, and competence, appear consistently among these groups. I believe further ethnographic studies of communities and groups in the United States will reveal that there is a pattern of values that appears in various forms among hinterland and working-class Anglo-Saxon-European-Americans that is different from that of the success-driven urban middle and upper-middle class. The pattern will be seen to converge in some ways with the values created or rediscovered by largely middle-class youth striving to deviate from mainstream culture. These values include the rejection of authority, stress on egalitarianism, and tendencies toward austerity and piety. It would be erroneous to assert that hippies, cultists, and other youthful groups have been rediscovering these values in their traditional form and that they were there all along in hinterland and working-class America, but there appears to be some convergence.

Whatever the patterns of value for Anglo-Americans, whether hippies, cultists, or hinterlanders, we must keep in mind that there are millions of Americans who are not Anglos. An examination of ethnographies describing Black and Chicano groups (Aschenbrenner, 1974; Dougherty, n.d.; Kunkel and Kennard, 1971; Madsen, 1973; and Davidson, 1974) suggests that the Stanford students in our sample (both Anglo and minority) and these minority groups would agree on some values. Despite the substantial qualitative differences in cultural values between Blacks and Whites, Anglos and Chicanos, and Chicanos and Blacks, these groups agree on certain points: namely, that it is more important to recognize essential human characteristics, to have a sense of personal worth, to experience and express feelings, and to be concerned about others than it is to evaluate people and things in terms of their instrumental capabilities for success and achievement. Mainstream American culture in its twentieth-century form is seen as driven and inhuman by both the Blacks and the Chicanos described in the ethnographic literature and by the Stanford students in our sample, regardless of ethnicity. This generalization is not contradictory to the fact that Stanford students as a whole supported certain "old-line" values such as egalitarianism, honesty, and the value of work, and that minority students supported these and related values more frequently than Anglos. These are not the features of contemporary mainstream culture that are being rejected.

For many young people and minorities, the "old-line" values exhibited in Appalachian Valley and upper New York State appear to many to have been overlaid in mainstream culture by the mania for expansion, power, affluence, and personal achievement, as well as by the compulsive sadomasochism of the mass media. Hippies, radicals, members of communes, cultists, young and old intellectuals, and many cultural minorities have turned against success-drivenness, personal isolation, egocentric self-aggrandizement, meaningless affluence, and meaningless violence and have embraced a humanistic reorientation that is self-, other-, and life-valuing. This is an idealized statement of their values, but the pattern seems to be there, even if it is also overlaid with material needs, ego strivings, social competition, and surrealistic attempts to adapt to our socially and morally chaotic times.

Has Watergate affected the values of American youth? In at least a superficial sense, the answer is yes. Twenty-five percent of the Stanford respondents said that honesty was rare among politicians and public officials. They may well have been thinking of something like Watergate, but there is evidence from our sample and elsewhere that most Americans have been suspicious of politicians, public officials, and corporate representatives for some time. Watergate confirmed their suspicions. Furthermore, the prosecution's concern for a clean breast during the long continuing Watergate trials and more recent charges against public figures must convince some youth that honesty might be, sometimes at least, the best policy, and that some Americans are very concerned about it.

Has alienation gone so far as to endanger the continuity of our culture? The Stanford sample indicates continuity in the core values discussed in this essay. This sample also indicates that there is significant erosion in even the value constants and that there have been shifts and changes in the overall configuration of values. The massive survey conducted by the American Council of Education on entering freshmen in 1966, 1968, and 1970 in 350 colleges and universities gives substantial support to both conclusions.[5] Whether the erosion of core values and the changes in values constitute a danger to the continuity of our culture is a matter of judgment. The evidence suggests that continuity will outweigh change. There is more of a redefinition of values and goals than an abrupt break with them.

The danger to continuity and to creative, positive change comes not from the majority of the American people, or from any ethnic minority as such. Rather, the threat is posed by the growing "underclass" (Myrdal, 1963) of unemployed and unemployable who have no stake in our values; by a tiny but dangerous minority of sociopathic persons from all classes whose defective socialization separates them from constraining norms, and who, in times of conflict and turmoil, may remorselessly commit any crime; by that part of our leadership in government, industry, and education that is contemptuous of the values, needs, and rights of the majority; and by our mania for expansion, material progress, and mastery. Of course, these threatening elements and forces, as well as the crassness, destructiveness, violence, and racism endemic to the American scene, have basic causes that constitute threats not only to cultural continuity, but to our very survival. These basic causes lie beyond the scope of my discussion.

Paradoxically, American youth appear to have rejected not the core, long-term values of our culture, but their excesses and perversions—equality as conformity, individualism as self-aggrandizement and loneliness, success, and achievement in an atmosphere of cutthroat competition and materialism, optimism as boosterism, and as Jules Henry (1963) said, the substitution of a rising standard of living for an inner self. More than we realize, the young may represent the core values of our culture and those values that will survive.

APPENDIX

VALUES-PROJECTIVE TECHNIQUE

Complete the sentences with the first thing that comes to mind, no matter what it is.

1. I wish my parents had ______________________.
2. All men are born ______________________.
3. Artists are ______________________.
4. Honesty is ______________________.
5. Anyone can get to the top if they ______________________.
6. Intellectuals should ______________________.
7. If I had a son I would want him to ______________________.
8. College professors should ______________________.
9. The most successful people ______________________.
10. Wealthy people should ______________________.
11. Everyone should want to ______________________.
12. The future is ______________________.
13. I wish I had ______________________.
14. What counts is what a person ______________________.
15. It isn't a person's background that counts, it is what ____________.
16. The individual is ______________________.
17. Nudity is ______________________.
18. In order to be successful one has to ______________________.
19. French night clubs are ______________________.
20. The standard of living of the laboring classes should ____________.
21. It isn't what one says that counts, it is what one ____________.
22. Time is ______________________.
23. There's no use crying ______________________.
24. Popular people are ______________________.

[UNTIL 1974]
DESCRIBE IN ONE SHORT PARAGRAPH *YOUR* CONCEPTION OF THE IDEAL AMERICAN BOY.

[1974]
DESCRIBE IN ONE SHORT PARAGRAPH *YOUR* CONCEPTION OF THE IDEAL PERSON.

NOTES

1. It has come to my attention that my analysis is germane to certain recent publications on attitudes and values among college-age youth by other social scientists. Professor Gabriel Almond's presentation in Chapter 6 of this volume is especially relevant in this regard. Rather than take these interpretations into account, I have left mine as originally formulated, in order to enable the reader to see where similar results were obtained when independent procedures and data were used.

2. In my own earlier work I tried to resolve the search for a data base by using observations drawn from a specific context, the military, that served as a nonlocalized, nondated type of social structure to which civilians responded in various nonrandom ways (Spindler 1948a, 1948b, and 1951).

3. I am indebted to Dr. Louise Spindler for her suggestions as well as for the materials she made available to me. I am also indebted to numerous students at Stanford who have done relevant studies, particularly to Barbara Nay, who did her senior honors thesis on American values (Nay, 1974), and to Ted Geredes (1969), Robert Lennox (1969), Peggy Warth (1972), and Linda DuBois (1972), who graciously shared the results of their work with me.

4. "Anglo" is used as a convenience in this essay to stand for Anglo-European-American or Euro-American. It is a common usage in the West, particularly when Chicano and Anglo are contrasted, but has extended to contrasts between other minority groups and the mainstream as well.

5. Over 200,000 freshman in 350 colleges were surveyed each year in 1966, 1968, and 1970 by the American Council of Education. The data have been summarized by Helen S. Astin and Ann S. Bisconti, *Trends in Academic and Career Plans of College Freshmen*, Report No. 1, the CPC Foundation (for the College Placement Council), 1974. These data first came to my attention through the *Campus Report* (Stanford University), July 24, 1974, p. 4. I am indebted to Professor Franzia Cancian for making the fuller report available to me.

In this report the life goals are arranged under the following categories: self-fulfilling, entrepreneurial, materialistic, altruistic, and societal goals. The categories are not the same as the core values upon which my analysis centered, but they overlap. Achievement, success, working hard and acquiring skills, and helping others are directly represented. These values, and others, are supported by approximately the same proportion of respondents during the five years covered by the ACE survey. There has also been significant erosion of these goals. This finding supports my analysis of changes in values. Though there is continuity, decreasing enthusiasm is reported for leadership and success, materialistic goals, and societal achievements, and there is a rising interest in self-fulfilling goals." . . . more recent freshmen have become less ambitious, more doubtful, and, possibly, more pessimistic about future accomplishments. The apparent trend is inward; that is, recent freshmen have become more inner-directed in their life styles and goals" (Astin and Bisconti, p. 15). There is also evidence in this massive survey to support my finding that minority students espouse core American values more than do mainstream "Anglo" students. "The responses of men and women at traditionally Black colleges followed the general downward trend [in certainty]—but to a lesser degree—and, even in 1970, this group displayed much greater ambition for a wider variety of achievements than did the general freshmen population. In particular, they were more interested in entrepeneurial goals . . . materialistic goals . . . and business success. They also cared more about being an authority in a selected field, helping others in difficulty, and obtaining recognition from peers" (ibid., p. 16).

The Modernization of Personality

3

RICHARD M. SUZMAN

The convergence thesis argues that industrialization leads to common forms of organization in widely differing societies, and that these organizations have standard, powerful environments which then produce common values, perceptions, and ways of thinking. Put more generally, institutions with similar structures tend to induce common psychic structures or regularities in the personalities of their participants. This is especially true if, as in the case of schools and the workplace, the individual spends time in the institutions, and they control powerful rewards and punishments. This essay examines changes in the American psyche that may be related to industrialization both at the level of schooling and work. Thus, the analysis does not focus on personality character changes that are directly generated by changes in the parental family, which is traditionally seen as the major source of character. In a society such as the United States, which is complex and changing so rapidly, childhood cannot fully prepare its citizens for an adult life too difficult to predict twenty years in advance. Hence, there is a strong case for emphasizing late childhood and early adulthood socialization experiences as determinants of character.

Personality, itself an element of character, is a broad term. The focus here is on two very different levels or systems of personality. The first system, called the *individual modernity syndrome,* is a moderately cohesive organization of overt beliefs, attitudes, values, perceptions, and behaviors that are closely related to societal development. The content of the syndrome includes qualities such as efficacy, control over nature, planning ahead, aspirations, active citizenship, secularism, openness to new experience, women's rights, and tolerance for diversity. The second system of personality is a developmental concept called *ego development*. This system is close to, but much more complex than, the development of the self. The person, seen in terms of ego development, moves from an impulsive, narrow, self-centered being to a richly multifaceted, mature, autonomous, empathetic person. Although these new concepts are controversial, they have a high potential of increasing our understanding of the effects of societal change on individual functioning in modern industrial nations, in terms of the complex articulations between personality and the social system. This undertaking entails the difficult task of integrating disparate processes: social change and its effect on individual attitudes and values; and individual growth and maturation as seen from the perspective of ego psychology.

First, it will be necessary to outline a model for the relationship between industrialism or modernization, and changes in psychic functioning and development; to present the results of research on developing countries and the United States; and to argue that the model is relevant to understanding aspects of social change in America over the last several decades. In the middle of these findings, it will be necessary to digress and describe more fully the schema of ego development and its relationship to the social system. Finally, the results, which look at special populations in the United States in only one point in time—1969-1970—will be extended to more nationally representative samples in which some of the changes that have taken place since the early 1950s can be examined.

The point of departure for this argument is the ideas and research of one of my mentors, Alex Inkeles, who has had a considerable influence on my own intellectual development, starting with his 1960 paper, "Industrial Man." In "Industrial Man," Inkeles showed, albeit with skimpy evidence, that people holding the same position (e.g., manager, foreman, skilled technician) in the occupational hierarchies of a widely differing set of industrialized nations (including the United States, England, Germany, Austria, the U.S.S.R., Japan, Norway, and Sweden) shared many common behaviors, perceptions, values, and attitudes regarding themselves, their environment, and the upbringing of their children. Indeed, it was striking that in many instances a person's occupational status appeared to be a more powerful predictor determinant of his beliefs than did his nationality. Thus, foremen, unskilled laborers, or managers in the same country often had more in common with their respective occupational classification in differing countries than they did with each other in the same country.[1] The idea that institutions shape the character and views of the men who function in them is not a new idea. Marx and Engels (1967: 92), after writing of the conditions of the proletariat in *The Communist Manifesto*, noted that "modern industrial labor, modern subjection to capital the same in England as in France, in America as in Germany, has stripped him of every trace of national character." However, in the Marxian model, unlike the model used here, many of the effects of the immediate occupational environment are predicated upon the larger system, particularly the ownership of the means of production.

Inkeles (1960) argues that the cause of this process is that the work situation is an environment that controls powerful reinforcements and one in which people spend a considerable proportion of their lives, with the result that they tend to internalize aspects of the environment. Further, the industrial systems in the industrialized world tend to become similar in their structure and organization. His thesis is as follows: standard environments or institutions, such as factories or schools, tend to exert standard or uniform pressures on the individuals within them, and ultimately induce a set of quite uniform values and attitudes that cut across ethnic, religious, and national boundaries.[2] The thesis does not state that there are no ethnic and national differences, but rather that industrialization is a countervailing force which generally pushes toward uniformity in certain socioeconomic spheres.

Also in 1960, a group of social scientists, including Clark Kerr, John Dunlop, et al., argued in *Industrialism and Industrial Man* that there is a logic or imperative to industrial systems which produces a convergence or uniformity that tends to override national or cultural tendencies. Their argument is based on the supposition that the demands of efficiency and technology will necessitate the development of roughly similar forms of industrial organization.

Further work on the process of the modernization of societies shows that in most cases industrialization lies at the heart of the process. The work of economists such as Kuznets or Adelman, and of historians such as Landes, shows that while there is some lagging or leading of elements, the percentage of the population employed in the industrial system corresponds closely to such indices as per capita GNP, educational levels, degree of urbanization, and number of scientists per 10,000 of the population. Table 1 shows the correlations for about 130 countries (taken from Russett, et al., 1964) between per capita Gross National Product (GNP) and a number of indices of societal modernization. The convergence thesis is not accepted by a widely varying group of scholars who study the development process, including historians and anthropologists. Many of these scholars argue that each

TABLE 1.

Correlations Between Per Capita GNP and Indices of Modernity [1]

	PER CAPITA GNP
Births per 1,000	-.76
Deaths per 1,000	-.41
Natural increase in population	-.59
Percent of population in urban areas of 20,000 or more	.71
Percent employed by general government and public enterprises as a percent of working age population	.83
Daily newspaper circulation per 1,000 population	.80
Domestic mail per capita	.89
Foreign mail per capita	.61
Radios per 1,000	.85
Cinema attendance per 1,000	.65
Percent of labor force in agriculture	-.86
Percent employed in industry as a percent of labor force	.79
Life expectancy for females	.86
Percent literate 15 years and over	.80
Primary and secondary school pupils as a percent of the population age 15-64	.80
Percent of population Moslem	-.44
Percent of population Catholic	.31
Percent of population Christian	.68
Percent of population voting	.46

1. Correlations from Russett, et al. (1964); based on approximately 130 countries.

society is different and has its own singular pattern. Obviously, there is considerable substance in such a position; each country is a mixture of both unique characteristics and characteristics that are shared with many other societies, especially those at the same level of economic development. For countries that are at the same level of development, the uniformities in many areas often tend to outweigh the unique differences. It is probably a matter of taste as to whether one studies what is unique or what is universal. Clifford Geertz (1963:147) has expressed the problem well. After stressing the flexibility of tradition and of systems of economic production, he says:

> Nor must such a procedure necessarily lead to the sort of atheoretical, "every case is different" indeterminateness for which anthropologists are, unfortunately, so notorious. The range of sociocultural variation in the developmental process is as far from being infinite as it is from being non-existent. Not everything is possible: some interrelationships between economic and non-economic processes are more nearly invariant than others, and there are, we must suppose, genuine regularities of social and cultural change which are associated with economic rationalization generally.

For the past decade Alex Inkeles (1974) has worked on a massive project related to his earlier "Industrial Man" concept, in which he has investigated the effects of modernizing experiences, especially industrial experiences, on the individual.[3] He undertook a large survey in which over 6,000 men were sampled from regions of six countries: East Pakistan, India, Nigeria, Chile, Argentina, and Israel. The sample of each country included farm workers, factory workers, and men who lived in cities but did not work in factories.

Inkeles' purpose was to demonstrate that exposure to industrial environments does produce common sets of attitudes, values, perceptions, and behaviors in the individuals who work in them: attributes related to planning ahead, efficacy, active citizenship, openness to new ideas and change, and the like. In this regard, he wanted to show that all of these attitudes and values formed a syndrome that would be roughly similar in each of the very different countries. A second major concern was to show that experience during late adolescence and early adulthood could change the individual in very basic ways, and that experience in the family was not the end, but only the beginning, of character development.

Inkeles names the set of attributes comprising the syndrome the Individual Modernity Syndrome. Modernity is defined in terms of the characteristics a person needs in order to function in an industrialized society, and *not* in terms of mere contemporaneity. The choice of the term *modern* has its unfortunate aspects[4] since everyone has his own idea of what it is. Perhaps a more appropriate, though more unwieldy, term such as Educated-Industrialized-Man would have been better than Modern Man. However, individual modernity, like authoritarianism or need achievement, is a state of mind and an outlook that is not unequivocally tied to industrialism. In fact, it can be argued that the men of Elizabethan England, ancient Greece, and early America had this state of mind, or at least elements of it.[5]

Let us now briefly summarize the results of Inkeles' six-nation study on individual modernity. An extremely wide and diverse set of individual attitudes and values do hold together statistically in the form of a multidimensional syndrome in each of the countries; the core of the syndrome in each country is virtually similar. The elements or themes in the modernity syndrome include a high sense of personal efficacy and a belief that one can control one's own fate; an interest in keeping up with the news; and greater interest in national than in sports or purely local news. The modern individual is open to social change, to new experiences, such as travel and meeting new people, and to doing things differently *if* they prove to be better. The modern man believes in punctuality and in planning ahead. He wants to hold positions of high status and, in contrast to the traditional man, is active in civic affairs. Modern man is ambitious and places a high value on education. He believes in modern medicine and technology, and wants to control the size of his family. He shows increasing independence from traditional authorities and feels one can be good without religion (though he does not practice religion less—quite the contrary). He tends to approve of women's rights and to value the dignity of other people who are different from himself. On the basis of the startling fact that all these very different elements form a syndrome across six different societies, Inkeles concludes that the "same structural mechanisms" underlie the sociopsychic functioning of men everywhere, despite the tremendous differences in underlying culture.

The number of years of education a person has turned out to be the single most important determinant of a man's modernity or traditionalism.[6] Factory experience, measured in years, even when holding everything else constant, also was an important determinant of modernity. It was not quite as powerful a determinant as education, however, since it took two to five years of working in a factory to produce the same increment in modernity as did one year of schooling. Exposure to mass media was another powerful determinant, while urban experience was relatively weak.

My own research on individual modernity (which forms the substance of this essay) has three objectives. The first is to enlarge the scope of the syndrome by showing that it is interrelated with such central structures of personality as the level of ego development. The second is to find out the form and nature of the modernity syndrome in the United States (until recently it had been measured only in developing countries), and to understand its determinants and significance both at an individual and cultural level. The third is to assess the relative importance of early childhood socialization versus adolescence and adulthood experiences as determinants of both individual modernity and ego level.

Individual and Societal Modernity in the United States

Does the individual modernity syndrome have any relevance for the United States where everyone is "modern"? Indeed, can we not assume that America has been modern (as we defined the concept earlier) in its work ethic and in its acceptance of social innovation since its founding? Even if the set of attitudes we are talking about has changed within the United States during the last century toward an even greater degree of modernity, are we not now in the postindustrial or postmodern era? Would the tradition-modern dimension, derived as it was from the concept of industrialization, have any general relevance in the highly industrialized United States? What is the degree of comparability between a peasant who goes to work in a factory in Nigeria or India, an Appalachian farmer who moves to a Detroit factory, and a European who migrated to New York in 1900?

One can easily argue that some American values have changed little since the founding of the colonies and the Declaration of Independence, or, more certainly, since de Tocqueville's visit. Many observers of early America found the central values to include egalitarianism, the perfectibility of man (e.g., by education), unfounded optimism, tolerance of diversity, pragmatism, and all the Protestant Ethic qualities of achievement, instrumentalism, and accumulation of material goods.[7] As noted earlier, the theory of societal modernization does not preclude an essentially rural society having modern values.

There is a long debate as to whether these values arose during the Reformation or during the Industrial Revolution. Some social historians, such as Weber, see the values derived from the Reformation as leading to, or making possible, the Industrial Revolution. Others see the Reformation as a response to already existing pressures. Clearly, the early American values were either imported or were a response to the colonial situation and open frontiers. However, we do not know exactly how widely spread they were, or how they were communicated to the waves of immigrants who moved into this country. For many developing nations, their educational and industrial system "produced" many of these values, while in early America they already existed, at least in part, within its culture as ideology.[8] Thus, unlike many other developing countries, America already had a culture that facilitated the development of some of these ideas in the schools and workplaces.

There also seem to have been many reversals and accommodations in American values. The early post-Puritan tolerance for diversity and individualism encouraged by the expanding frontier[9] gave way, at least by 1900, to bouts of intolerance and strong pressure for comformity. In the 1960s, there was an apparent gain in tolerance and a decline in respect for the authority of the conventional.[10]

If there is a link, at least today, between schooling, the occupational structure, and individual modernity (and possibly ego level as well), then how might changes in the level and distribution of education and in the occupational structure have affected those psychological dimensions? To the extent that psychological modernity is a central and integral element of national character, can we argue that the changes in education and work have led to changes in the national character?

Between 1860 and the present, American society has undergone two major transformations: first, from a basically rural society into an industrial society in which the production of goods is the principal economic activity; and second, from an industrially dominated society into a service economy (finance, health, research, recreation, education, government, and the like). The first change occurred after 1850. Daniel Bell, who has written about *The Coming of the Post-Industrial Society* (1973), points to 1956 as the year in which the white collar workers first outnumbered the blue collar workers.

Some of the changes that have been taking place (in part gleaned from Bell, 1973; the Historical and Census reports; and the 1973 OMB Report on Social Indicators) have been quite remarkable.

In 1870, America was still a largely rural society. Fifty-eight percent of the labor force was in agriculture. A single doctorate and some 9,300 first degrees were awarded.

By 1900, the transformation toward an urban-dominated society was well under way, with about 39 percent of the population already living in urban areas (i.e., towns over 2,500). Only 37 percent of the labor force worked in agriculture. Blue collar manual workers comprised 36 percent and white collar workers 18 percent. The student population accounted for 6 percent of the eighteen to twenty-one age group, and 382 doctorates and 27,400 first degrees were awarded. The average life span was only forty-nine years.

By 1940 America had become an urban society with over 56 percent of the population living in urban areas. Agriculture retained only 17 percent of the jobs. The percentage of the blue collar workers was nearly the same (40 percent) as in 1900, but the white collar group had increased to 31 percent. Some 60 percent of those over age twenty-five had only been to elementary school. The student population was 16 percent of the eighteen to twenty-one age group, and 3,000 doctorates were awarded. After World War II, the GI bills led to the increased equalizing of educational opportunities.

By 1960, white collar workers predominated in the labor force (42 percent), with agriculture accounting for only 8 percent. The baby boom of 1955-1965 was well on the way. The student population was 35 percent of the eighteen to twenty-one age group, and 9,800 doctorates were awarded.

By 1970, America had become the only country in the world in which the service sector was preeminent: only 5 percent of the labor force was in agriculture, with 34 percent in industry, and 61 percent in services. Among the white collar jobs, the clerical, professional, and technical jobs have increased most rapidly since the 1950s. Only about 25 percent of those over twenty-five have just an elementary education. In 1970 750,000 first degrees and 29,000 doctorates were awarded. Nearly 74 percent of the population now lived in urban settings. There were also changes in a variety of other social "indexes": an increased divorce rate, increased governmental social services, the eighteen-year-old vote, the striking demographic changes in the distribution of young and old people, the nearly halving of the birth rate since 1910, and the changes in female participation in the labor force.[11]

It is difficult to imagine that these momentous changes have not had an effect on the national distribution of levels of individual modernity and ego level—if indeed the syndromes are responsive to changes in amount of schooling and type of job held.

In order to adequately answer the questions of what are the distributions of individual modernity and of ego development levels in the United States, and how (and why) they have changed over the past few decades, we would need a considerable bank of different types of data, ranging from nationally representative surveys to longitudinal and quasiexperimental studies. Alas, this sort of data is simply not available, though recent attention to social indicators has aroused considerable interest in the general problem of social change.[12]

In general, from the perspective of national character relevance, few nationally representative U.S. sample surveys have contained more than one or two short psychological measures that were not primarily political attitude scales.[13] With even more limited exceptions, very few surveys have used projective psychological tests (such as the Thematic Apperception Test or the Rorschach) from which inferences about less conscious layers and structures of the personality can be made. This type of inference cannot easily be made with multiple choice questions. In terms of actual U.S. national character studies, we seem barely removed from the state of the field as described more than twenty years ago by Inkeles and Levinson (1954). However, improvements in survey design and methodology, data analysis, psychometrics, and a growing body of theoretical concepts make national character studies seem more feasible than in 1954 (budget aside). Even if representative data showing changes over time in individual modernity and ego development were available, ascertaining the causes of the change would still be a problem of considerable magnitude.

Demonstrating and accounting for change over time is one of the more difficult problems in social science.[14] For example, if only a cross- sectional (one point in time) sample is available and personality and characterological differences are found between those in their twenties and those in their fifties, a variety of possible explanations could be cited, some of which would have little to do with a shift in national character. The difference might simply represent the physiological or existential part of being aged twenty or aged fifty. Or the difference might be a function of the economic reality that those in their fifties generally have greater economic resources than those in their twenties. The difference might also be the outcome of those aged fifty having had a very different early socialization experience, or less education. Those aged fifty might have undergone a special experience such as wartime service or the 1930 economic depression which left a permanent mark on their personality.[15] A difference between the age groups might also express the effect of a current and transient historical reality, such as the draft, which impinges differently on each age group. The problem here is that we are dealing with the combined effects of age, cohort (i.e., those aged fifty to sixty), and the historical period at the time of testing. Since each one is a direct combination of the other two, disentangling causality becomes very difficult.

Likewise, when we compare two nationally representative samples spaced thirty years apart, any differences that are not artifacts of the sampling design[16] or random error might be the result of a new generation with a different early life or adult socializaton joining the population tested. To sort all this out would require a rather grand design, which would compare the cohorts aged forty at 1970 with the cohorts aged forty in 1960, 1950, 1940, and so forth.

Unfortunately, such data are not available. Hence, we will have to make do with what few pieces of the jigsaw puzzle are available, keeping in mind the methodological hazards of assembling findings from several different studies into a cogent argument.

Individual Modernity and Ego Development in the United States—The Evidence

Not surprisingly, the full modernity scale has not yet been administered to a single national representative sample within the United States, let alone to a series of national samples.[17] Only a few small surveys within the United States have included a modernity scale that approximates the one used by Inkeles and Smith (1974). One such study of a Black population in Boston is used as the major data base of this chapter to show that schooling and work experience are more closely tied to the modernity syndrome than early life background factors, and that psychological modernity is connected to ego development. Part of the way through, a fuller description of a model of ego development is presented. By presenting findings from other surveys, the conclusions drawn from the black sample in Boston are extended to the national level. Using the results from both past surveys and formal surveys, an attempt is made to chart, despite the methodological hazards, possible changes in the modernity syndrome that may have accompanied some of the changes over the last few decades in the labor force and national educational levels.

The Black Survey in Boston

In 1969, I worked on a Boston survey of black migration and occupational achievement, directed by Marc Fried. The survey interviewed a random sample of over 500 black men and women, aged twenty-five to forty-five, from the core Boston ghetto in Roxbury and Dorchester, as well as from some of the surrounding suburbs. Since two-thirds of those interviewed had been born in the rural South to parents with little education, the sample was ideal for studying the modernization of a subgroup within an industrialized society.

Luckily, enough modernity-related questions were included to enable the construction of a modernity scale (cf. Suzman, 1973, 1974). While several items had to be discarded because almost everyone answered them in a modern direction, many did give a traditional response to the remaining items. Many did not plan ahead, were not open to new ways of doing things, did not believe that someone could be good without religion, and knew little about their political system (e.g., who the mayor of Boston was, or what the NAACP did). Those items that were not discarded did correlate well with each other, so that if a person answered an item on the openness to change in a modern direction, then he or she was likely to answer other items in a modern way. The items used covered a wide variety of themes, including planning, active citizenship, universalism, information, efficacy, new experiences, and aspirations. The fact that such a wide set of diverse items correlated together in the scale showed that these themes and issues did form a coherent and cohesive syndrome.[18] The scale was constructed so that a score of 100 equaled highly traditional, and 200 highly modern.

For the men and women combined, the strongest correlation (see Table 2) between a person's social characteristics and this scale of individual modernity was the number of years of education a person had completed (r = .413), followed closely by occupational status (r

= .400). Among those women who had an occupation (r = .45), occupational status was even more strongly related to modernity than was true for the men (r = .28). The longer a person had worked, the more modern he was, while conversely, the more often he had been laid off, the more traditional he was in his outlook.

Women were generally quite traditional if they were not currently

TABLE 2.
Zero Order Correlations Between Demographic or Background Variables and the Modernity Scale (OM13) for Full Sample, Males and Females: Boston Black Sample

VARIABLES	MODERNITY SCALE		
	Full Sample N=502	*Males* N = 136	*Females* N = 365
Early Childhood Background			
Area born (1 = South/2 = Border/3 = North)	.227	.187	.228
Urban-rural experience age 0-6 yrs.	.253	.217	.235
Boston born (vs. not born in Boston)	.144	.074	.162
Education of main parental breadwinner	.266	.111	.303
Education of mother	.261	.096	.300
Education of father	.248	.125	.271
Parental family social class	.247	.071	.285
Parental family intactness age 6-18 [1]	.140	-.064	.190
Middle Childhood Socialization			
Urban-rural experience age 6-12 yrs.	.257	.227	.233
Urban-rural experience age 12-18 yrs.	.273	.265	.251
Education (years)	.413	.358	.430
Quality of school age 6-12	.209	.204	.196
Quality of school age 12-18	.130	.045	.251
Adulthood Background			
Occupational status	.409	.280	.449
Military service (0 = no/1 = yes)	.238	.199	—
Employment (0 = not working/1 = working)	.263	.192	.189
Age when started first job [2]	-.011	-.072	.025
Current job duration [3]	.136	-.007	.172
Worked last five years (0 = no/1 = yes)	.174	.097	.138
Period since last job held [4]	-.123	-.248	—
Number of times laid off [5]	-.127	-.195	-.080
Marital status (0 = single/1 = married)	.243	.194	.185
Age	-.083	-.182	-.032
Sex (0 = male/1 = female)	-.261	—	—

1. 0 = nonintact/1 = semi-intact/2 = intact.
2. 1 = under 13/ . . . /8 = 35+.
3. 1 = less than 5 years/2 = 1-5 years/3 = 5 years+.
4. 0 = 3 months/ . . . /7 = 8 years+.
5. 0 = never/3 = many

Note: Significance levels not shown.

working, or if they had not worked in at least five years. Those who were born in the rural South were relatively traditional, though some Boston-born men with little education and low-status jobs turned out to be rather traditional. For the sample as a whole, those with high-status parents were somewhat more modern, though parental family status was not nearly as strongly correlated with modernity as was the respondent's own status.

These correlations, coming from cross-sectional data, do not easily allow causal interpretations. Thus, one cannot be sure whether it was the high occupational status that caused the more modern outlook, or the other way around. One means of making interpretations from cross-sectional data more sturdy (although one cannot prove them to be correct) is to control statistically (or hold constant) other factors that might be seen as alternative causes.

A prime concern in the study was to show that such adolescent and adult experiences as education and work increased individual modernity. Hence, variables such as urban-rural experience to age six and social class and degree of intactness of the parental family were held constant (Table 3) in multiple regressions. When this was done, the years of education variable was still strongly related to modernity. (Interestingly, the quality of the schooling seemed to make only minimal difference.) Next, in order to determine the effect of employment status, all of these early background variables, in addition to education, were held constant; current employment was found to remain moderately associated with being modern. Next, all the early childhood variables as well as education and employment status were held constant. While the magnitude of the association between occupational status and modernity was reduced, it still remained significantly positive, especially for women. Further, even when all of the other variables plus occupational status were taken into account, the length of time on the job remained associated with modernity. Finally, when all of these variables were held constant, the males were still slightly more modern than the women.

In order to investigate the seemingly great importance of occupational status as a possible cause of modernity among women, a different way of looking at the data, known as analysis of variance and covariance, was used. Table 4 shows that when education was held constant, men were more modern than the women in the low occupational level, but in the higher levels of occupational status, there

TABLE 3.
Cumulative Percentage of Variance Explained (R^2) in a Stepwise Regression of Selected Demographic and Psychological Variables on the Modernity Scale (OM13) for Full Sample, Males and Females: Boston Black Sample

VARIABLES	PERCENT OF VARIANCE OF MODERNITY EXPLAINED		
	Full Sample N = 502	*Males* N = 136	*Females* N = 365
Personal Background[1]			
Early Childhood			
Area born	5.6	3.5	5.2
Boston born	5.6	3.9	5.2
Parental family social class	8.5	3.9	9.8
Mother's education	9.6	4.2	1.5
Parental family intactness	10.8	4.7	13.7
Urban-rural experience age 0-6 yrs.	13.0	7.1	15.1
Middle Childhood			
Education	21.8	17.1	23.9
Quality of school age 6-12 yrs.	22.2	17.8	24.1
Urban-rural experience age 12-18 yrs.	23.6	21.0	25.4
Adulthood			
Employment (0 = not working/1 = working)	27.3	24.7	26.9
Health (0 = not working because sick/ 1 = other)	27.7	26.5	27.2
Occupation	30.4	27.2	31.2
Worked last 5 years	30.8	27.5	31.9
Number of times laid off	31.1	30.6	32.0
Duration of present job	31.1	31.4	32.4
Marital status (0 = single/1 = married)	32.5	33.5	33.2
Sex (0 = female/1 = male)	33.8	—	—
Military service	34.1	—	—
Age	34.1	34.6	33.4

1. Listed in order in which variables are forced into the regression equation, with the variables entered in rough chronological order.

were no sex differences.[19] This finding is an important one, for it seems to suggest that certain occupational experiences may result in a common set of attitudes and values in men and women who may have started out with very different psychic structures based on their early socialization.[20]

As a followup, whole sets of variables were grouped together. Thus, all of the early background variables (parental socioeconomic status [SES], parental intactness, place of birth, and urban-rural ex-

TABLE 4.
Percentage of Variance of Modernity (OM13) Explained by Subsets of Early Childhood Urban-Rural Experience, Middle Childhood, and Adulthood Background Variables for Full Sample, Males and Females: Boston Black Sample

VARIABLES	PERCENT OF VARIANCE OF OM13 EXPLAINED		
	Full Sample $N = 502$	*Males* $N = 136$	*Females* $N = 305$
Early Childhood Background Alone [2]	10.9	3.2	15.5
Urban-Rural and Geographic Alone [3]	9.2	7.6	7.8
Middle Childhood Background Alone	22.7	17.7	21.6
Adulthood Background and Socialization Alone [4]	23.3	19.3	25.1
All Demographic and Socialization [5]	34.1	34.6	33.4
All Demographic Plus IQ, Cognitive, and Selected Personality Variables [6]	51.0	50.5	53.7

1. Variables entered according to "best" criterion.
2. Early childhood variables: parental SES, mother's education, father's education, main breadwinner's education, parental family intactness, area born, Boston born, urban experience age 0-6 years.
3. Urban, geographic variables: area born, Boston born, urban experience age 0-6 years, urban experience 6-12 years, urban experience 12-18 years, urban experience 0-18 years.
4. Middle childhood variables: urban experience age 6-12 years, urban experience 12-18 years, education, quality of schools 6-12 years, quality of schools 12-18 years.
5. Adulthood variables: occupational status, employment status, marital status, military service (for males only), year last worked, length of time in present job, number of times laid off, health if not working, age.
6. IQ and personality variables: vocabulary information, comprehension, EFT (field independence), Ego-R (ego development), inventory measure of field dependence.

perience aged zero to six years) formed one set; the later childhood and adolescent-related variables (including education), another set; and the late adult-related variables (such as occupational status, time on the job, present health, and age), another.

When the different sets were correlated with individual modernity (Table 5), the early childhood-related variables explained only half as much of the variation in modernity as did the adult experiences. This finding suggested that adult experiences were particularly powerful determinants of the syndrome.

For the women, the variables relating to early life were over four times as strongly correlated with individual modernity as for the men.

TABLE 5.
Modernity (OM13) Means Within Parental SES by Occupational Status by Sex, Adjusted for the Covariates Education, Urban Experience Age 12-18, and Age (Only Subjects Presently Working Are Included): Boston Black Sample

PARENTAL FAMILY SOCIAL CLASS	OM MEANS ADJUSTED FOR COVARIATES EDUCATION, URBAN EXPERIENCE AGE 12-18, AND AGE — OCCUPATIONAL STATUS: *Low*		*High*	
	Male	*Female*	*Male*	*Female*
Low	163.5 (29)	147.1 (42)	166.1 (20)	161.9 (29)
High	158.4 (25)	151.2 (28)	165.6 (32)	164.8 (42)

Total N = 247
Harmonic Means of Cell Counts = 29.3

ANOVA[1] [*adjusted for covariates*]	*F*	*Significance*
Parental Family Social Class	0.08	p = NS
Occupation	12.5	p < .001
Sex	13.4	p < .001
P x O	0.0	p = NS
P x S	1.0	p = NS
O x S	2.8	p = NS
P x O x S	1.2	p = NS
Covariates	9.26	p < .001

Regression coefficients: E = 1.869; U = 0.598; A = .045

1. Using an unweighted means technique.

To test whether this correlation was a function of the women having had less contact with jobs that could take them out of the house, enable them to make use of their education,[21] and change the values they absorbed from their parents, housewives were compared with working women. Indeed, it was found that this powerful association between early family background and current attitudes and values was confined to the housewives.

Thus, within the limits of a cross-sectional analysis, it seemed certain that schooling and work experience strongly affected the modernity syndrome. No doubt, the relationship is reciprocal, with elements in the modernity syndrome influencing the impact of education and work, and, for some women, influencing the very decision to go to work.

Modernity and Ego Development

We are now ready to show that individual modernity is interrelated with some of the central structures of personality. This task will require a fairly lengthy digression into the nature and measurement of ego development.

Ego Development

Ego development, difficult as it is to explain in a short space, is nonetheless described here since it is an important key to understanding both character and how people may change as they become more educated. Piaget's stages of cognitive development from concrete to more abstract thought, Kohlberg's scheme of moral development, and Maslow's conception of the hierarchy of needs are all valid to the concept of ego development.

The ego is close to the concept of self (which is itself more complex than "self-concept") but is also much more than the self. It is an organized system that includes the superego (i.e., the conscience, which partly consists of internalized social values, goals, and restraints), unconscious ideals, orientations towards others, impulse controls, and a wide repertoire of defenses and adaptive mechanisms.

The very concept of ego development is still in the early stages of development as a psychological concept and scale—both in conceptualization and in measurement. The ancestry of the concept on the psychological side starts with Freud, and includes, among many others, Anna Freud, Heinz Hartmann, Erikson, Rapaport, Klein, Arlow, Havighurst, Robert White, and Piaget; and, on the sociological side, Talcott Parsons, Weinstein, and Platt. Perhaps the most salient contemporary researcher in the field is Jane Loevinger (1971), whose model includes six sequential stages: impulsive, self-protective, conformist, conscientious, autonomous, and integrated. Although the models advanced by some of the above theorists are very different, they share many common elements.

While ego development is intimately correlated with chronological, physical, psychosexual, and intellectual development, it is also conceptually distinct from these sequences. Like the Piagetian and Kohlbergian development sequences, each stage of ego development is sequential and hierarchical, with each successive stage dependent upon the successful completion of the last stage and at the same time more complex and differentiated than the preceding one. Thus, none of the stages can be skipped. The sequence and content of the stages, as given by the various authors, are quite similar, especially at the early levels. The six stages in Jane Loevinger's model are sketched briefly and then they are related to modernity and the study of national character.

The person in the *impulsive* stage is controlled by a fear of retaliation, and his or her interpersonal orientation is dependent and exploitative. Emotions are experienced mainly as bodily feelings, and cognition is stereotyped. The person is consciously concerned with sexual and aggressive feelings.

The person in the *self-protective* stage is controlled by the fear of being caught and works on the principle of expediency. The person tends to be opportunistic, wary, and exploitative, and is consciously preoccupied with acquiring material goods, advantage, and self-protection. When things go wrong, blame is usually externalized.

The individual in the *conformist* stage is dominated by conformity to external rules and shame and guilt for breaking the rules. Interpersonally, the person is preoccupied with being accepted by being nice, and with appearance and materialism. Cognition is simple, with great reliance on cliches, and the expression of feelings is banal.

The *conscientious* individual is basically self-guided, and his or her own self-evaluated standards are important. At this level, action is controlled by guilt for consequences and by long-term ideals. Interpersonally, the conscientious individual is oriented toward mutuality of responsibility in relationships and is capable of differentiated feelings and motives. Such a person often has a high need for achievement and appears to be the driven individual of our age. Indeed, individual modernity (as defined in this chapter) can be estimated to reach a peak at the conscientious level. Loevinger has probably underestimated the moralistic certainty and bureaucratic rigidity that such individuals can demonstrate in the right setting.

At the *autonomous* level, the person becomes more psychologically minded, is better able to cope with inner conflict, and develops a tolerance of his or her own ambivalences and contradictions, thus allowing a greater respect for the autonomy and vagaries of others.

At the *integrated* level, Loevinger adds to the autonomous stage the reconciling of inner conflict, the cherishing of individuality, and the seeking of identity.

A particularly noteworthy feature of Loevinger's scheme is that she has developed a highly reliable scoring method for ego level from a set of sentence completions. Thus, she has worked simultaneously at the conceptual and empirical levels.[22]

Since the ego level stages have considerable potential for synthesizing and organizing the myriads of traits traditionally included in national character studies,[23] the concept of ego development should perhaps become a central organizing and explanatory variable in delineating the relationship between personality and the social system.

By placing traits into the context of a developmental stage or configuration, the concept of ego development can increase the interpretability of a wide variety of personality dimensions. For example, authoritarianism might be considered to be closely related to the self-protective and conformist stages of development. Thus, authoritarianism is a stage that we all experience, in which some fixate, and to which some can regress given the right psychic or societal circumstances. Need achievement, many Protestant Ethic qualities, and Riesman's inner-directedness are probably found most frequently in conscientious individuals. A model of ego development can not only help integrate and synthesize such diverse psychological characteristics, but it can also help us make critical distinctions that have often been ignored. For example, we might then begin to differentiate different types of conformity in terms of ego level. While conformity occurs at all levels of ego development, it probably means something very different for conscientious and impulsive individuals.

Because they also embody a good deal of cultural content, the ego development stages seem helpful in articulating the interfaces between personality and social system. As noted earlier, Alex Inkeles (1960) advanced the thesis in his "Industrial Man" paper that there tends to be something of an isomorphic congruence between powerful and salient institutions and the psychic structure of the people within them. Analogously, one might consider the fit or articulation between ego level and the institutions of the social system. The relationship between ego level and the social system might be either isomorphic or reciprocal. Thus, those in the impulsive stage might need strong external controls and structures, while those at the autonomous level could function more effectively in relatively unstructured situations because of their well-developed inner controls. Those at the conscientious level might function best in middle levels of bureaucracies, while individuals at the autonomous stage would find the rigid environments of middle-level bureaucracies intolerable.

Because relationships between the ego levels of individuals in a society and the social structure are so complex, a few are delineated here. First, what is the preferred organizational, familial, cultural, and institutional environment for individuals at each stage of ego development? How do individuals at specific ego levels function within a particular type of environment? Second, what distributions of ego levels do societies require at each stage of their development in order to function adequately? Third, what would be the effect on a person who is operating within an institutional context that is one step above (or below) his preferred social environment? How would this affect the functioning of the institution? Fourth, which social environments facilitate ego development and which are likely to cause a premature arrest of development? Presumably, factors that are conducive to development will differ from stage to stage as well as for people of different ages who share the same stages of ego development.[24] Compared to education and work, how important is early family environment as a determinant of ego level? Fifth, what "determines" the "production" of the distribution of ego levels in a society? Is it the availability of education or the needs of industry? Might the society, as some Marxian theorists suggest, actually attempt to arrest ego development at a specific level to provide for the "efficient" functioning in the productive systems? Sixth, what is the relationship between ego level and a person's orientation toward society? It would seem necessary to develop a conceptualization of mediating attitudes or ideology between an individual's level of ego development and his orientation toward society.

This last point about the need to take into account a person's attitudes toward the legitimacy of his society and its institutions needs expanding. Individuals who share the same ego level may behave very differently in the same situation or institution, depending upon the degree to which they accept or reject the legitimacy of the institution. While the concept of ego development includes a conceptualization of the individual's orientation toward his environment (in terms of his experience and understanding of the world and himself), the item being measured is actually more a function of the generalized cognitive level at which he understands and relates to the social environment than of whether he approves or disapproves of the environment. Thus, at each ego level individuals can be alienated from aspects of their environment, with the nature of the alienation differing from level to level. The ego level essentially filters the alienation and sets up the framework for the "rules of the game." Although Loevinger's impulsive ego level is described in terms of impulsivity and passivity, the orientation should not be seen as a one-way dependent relationship. There is an implied pact that runs something like, "I will behave in such a way *and* the world will respond to me in given ways." If the bargain is broken and the authority system does not fulfill its reciprocal role (in terms of perception of the individual), then normally the passive or conformist individual may resort to protest or violence.

It would be expected that different nations, social classes, and institutions are composed of differing proportions of people at each of the ego levels. The conventional or conformist level, or perhaps the intermediate conformist/conscientious level, is probably modal in the United States. In a cross-cultural study of the level of moral reasoning in different countries, social classes, and rural and urban areas, Kohlberg (1971) found that some groups never reached some levels or reached them at a much later chronological age.[25]

Education appears to be a significant determinant of ego development.[26] It remains to be seen, however, whether certain types of work experience can affect ego level. If both educational and work experience facilitate ego development, which is certainly central to personality, then the implication is that change in personality is possible at least into early adulthood.

From this digression on the nature of ego development, we can finally return to the relationship between ego level and the modernity syndrome. Before the digression, it had been shown how the individual modernity syndrome seemed to be affected by adolescent and adult experiences such as schooling and work experiences. Now, if the attitudes, values, and behaviors of the individual modernity syndrome are indeed also linked to ego level, then the implications are that education and work experiences may lead to significant changes at both the level of overt attitudes and behavior, *and* of underlying personality or character. Methodologically, this can only be a suggestion; proof, of course, requires longitudinal data that are not yet available.[28]

Understanding the linkages between ego level and overt values and behaviors brings us into the contentious area of the interface between overt behavior and "deep" personality structure.[29] While it was hypothesized that a modern outlook would be correlated with relatively high levels of ego development, it was also assumed that the correlation would be only moderate and that there would be considerable play in the relationship, with the exceptions representing important subgroups.

The Empirical Relationship Between Ego Development and Modernity

Within the black survey in Boston, the individual modernity syndrome proved to be positively and significantly correlated with a sentence completion measure of ego development coded for the Loevinger stages (see Table 6).[30] Thus, it can be stated that those with a modern outlook (especially in the case of working women) had high levels of ego development.[31]

TABLE 6.
Means for Modernity (OM13) and Education Within Levels of Ego Development[1]: Boston Black Sample

EGO DEVELOPMENT LEVEL	OM MEAN[2]	YEARS EDUCATION MEAN	N
1-2 Impulsive	150.46	9.61	13
Δ Self-Protective	143.47	9.64	14
Δ/3 Transitional	148.7	10.8	80
1-3 Conformist	153.3	11.4	128
1-3/4 Transitional	164.1	12.06	33
1-4 Conscientious	172.0	12.00	4

1. Ego-R.
2. F-test for Ego and OM13: $p < .01$, percent explained variance = 7.9 percent.

Extension of the Findings

We now turn to the question of the generalizability of the findings from the Black sample in Boston.

ELECTION SURVEY

In 1970, in an election survey of the Massachusetts Third Congressional District, 300 registered voters from the towns of Acton, Marlboro, Newton, and Watertown were randomly sampled. In this sample, education and occupation showed a similar pattern of relationships with modernity.[32] Parental SES had only a low correlation with modernity. Not surprisingly, even when SES was held constant, the citizens of the small isolated, semi-industrial town of Marlboro were less modern than those in wealthy suburban Newton. Significantly, modernity was completely unrelated either to political party preference or to a measure of economic conservatism versus economic liberalism. In addition, no consistent relation was found to a crude measure of belief in the political efficacy of the social system.[33]

In the election survey, the relation between age and modernity was curvilinear, even when education was held constant. Thus, overt modernity was highest among the thirty-five to forty-five age group and lowest among the young and old. As these are cross-sectional data, it is difficult to say whether this is a generational or aging difference. Retirement was associated with high levels of traditionalism, especially for low educated females. Parental SES was again a particularly powerful modernity correlate among the nonworking low educated women.

NATIONAL SAMPLES

Results from probability surveys of the voting age population of the United States conducted between 1956 and 1960 by the Michigan Survey Research Center suggest considerable variation in the components of modernity within the country as a whole. The percentages giving traditional answers to questions about planning ahead, work commitment, scientific rationality, respect for tradition, and openness to change are informative:[34]

"Are you the kind of person who plans his life ahead all the time or do you more live from day to day?" Forty-seven percent answered, "I live from day to day."

"If you had your choice would you rather have a job where you gave the orders or a job where somebody else told you what to do?" Forty-five percent said that they would prefer being told what to do.

"It is highly unlikely that astrology will ever be able to explain anything." Forty-seven percent disagreed.

"We must respect the work of our forefathers and not think that we know better than they did." Fifty percent agreed with the question. (Some reference to the most efficient ways of doing things would have improved the question since modernity emphasizes efficiency rather than merely the new.)

"A man really doesn't get to have much wisdom unless he is well along in years." Forty-four percent agreed.

Of course, these questions tap only a few dimensions of modernity. The correlations between items are unavailable, and it is not known how they would correlate with each other. However, as a check, a set of items from the 1973 ICPR-NORC General Social Survey (a probability sample of the United States), which measured a variety of modernity themes (work commitment, growth of opinion, valuation of individuality, universalism, science valuation, active citizenship, and authoritarianism), was formed into a short, crude, and incomplete modernity scale that showed moderate reliability. The scale approximated many of the relationships found in the black sample in Boston between modernity and rural experience, education, and occupation.

Changes in the Modernity Syndrome in the United States

The collection of representative national data over time for American values and beliefs relevant to individual modernity is a thankless task. Substantial poll data have only existed since the 1930s, and until recently polls focused almost exclusively on specific political issues. Many tapped fleeting and evanescent opinions rather than more stable values. When only isolated items are available, one runs the hazard of tapping fluid, issue-oriented public opinions rather than a stable general dimension made up of a large number of questions on many themes. The methodological difficulties in measuring and understanding change, discussed earlier, should be kept in mind.

My general impression is that, since 1930, many elements of the modernity syndrome have moved in the direction of increased modernity. Thus, while in 1936 somewhat over 50 percent of Americans were in favor of legalizing the distribution of information on birth control (80 percent by 1956), a majority would not fly in an airplane to Europe even if the ticket was prepaid. In 1938, 78 percent of voters opposed married women working if their husbands could support them, and in 1939, only 17 percent favored reducing the voting age to eighteen (this percentage increased to 45 during World War II and to 60 during the Korean War).

If an analysis is made of responses to the acceptability of a Jew, Catholic, woman, or Negro as president of the United States, some dramatic and steady changes are seen. In 1937, only 31 percent would approve of a woman, 38 percent of a Negro, 60 percent of a Catholic, and 48 percent of a Jew becoming president. By 1967, 57 percent would accept a woman, 50 percent a Negro (70 percent by 1970), 82 percent a Jew, and 87 percent a Catholic.

Thus far, it can be assumed that on dimensions such as universalism, women's rights, and minority myths, the U.S. population has become more modern in the last three decades.[35]

However, other themes have shown little change, and some elements of individual modernity, such as attitudes toward capital punishment, sense of control over one's life, and belief in the return and reward for hard work, seemed to have reached a modern peak between 1930 and 1970 and have since tended to move toward the traditional pole.

Duncan, et al. (1973) asked the same questions in 1971 that had been first asked at least fifteen years previously (in some cases twenty-one years earlier) of a cross-section of Detroit residents. In 1956, 80 percent said that there were types of work a woman should not do, while in 1971, 13 percent fewer gave this response. Between 1958 and 1971, the percentage believing that someone who did not believe in God could be a good American rose from 57 to 77 percent.

The 1971 survey also found a decline in overt anti-Semitism and a greater acceptance of religious intermarriage (but people had fewer friends of a different religion). There was also an appreciable decline in prejudice towards Blacks.

Between 1953 and 1971, there was a trend among the under thirty-five year olds towards a belief that children should be taught to think for themselves rather than be taught by their elders what is right. The use of psychic rewards for good behavior increased, and people were more tolerant of allowing children to follow their own interests, even if it meant not being with other children. This finding suggests a change among the adults toward valuing autonomy rather than obedience or conformity, and, perhaps a move toward inner- rather than other-directedness.

The Detroit data ended with the year 1969. The years since 1969 have been filled with turmoil and change: the height of the Vietnam War, the radical student movement, the publication of the Pentagon Papers, the new sexual morality, the beginning of the women's movement, economic uncertainty and inflation, Watergate, and the relative decline in America's imperial power and centrality in the world. How have these extraordinary years affected the people?

Fortunately, a representative U.S. sample of youth aged sixteen to twenty-five, both college and noncollege, polled by Yankelovich in 1969, 1971, and 1973, has made it possible to compare people of the same age group but with very different education levels. Yankelovich

(1974) found many startling changes between 1969 and 1973. In 1969, there was a considerable gap between the attitudes and values of college and noncollege youth. In 1973, there were still many gaps, but the ideas held by college students in 1969 had spread to the noncollege students now. In 1973, the noncollege youth were close to college youth in what they wanted from work, as they ranked interesting work and a chance to use their minds well above salary and an undemanding job. In 1969, 72 percent of the noncollege youths, compared to 42 percent of college youth, believed homosexuality to be wrong, but by 1973 25 percent fewer of the noncollege youth believed it to be wrong. Respect for authority generally declined.

College students had also changed. By 1973, education, devalued in 1969, was once again highly valued. The work ethic (traditional in America but modern by our definition) was generally strengthened on campus but was attacked among working-class youth.

Some observers of the campus such as Kavolis (1970) have seen the development of a postmodern man, who is a hybrid of modern and traditional attributes. Tolerance and openness to change and new experience are part of the new personality, but achievement and technological control over the environment are replaced by the desire for self-fullfillment, together with the wish for harmony with nature. Although Yankelovich's data suggest that this hybrid might have been a fleeting phenomenon caused by a set of historical coincidences, rather than a universal of sociocultural evolution, the growing popularity of the ideas of critics of modern industrial societies such as Schumacher (1973) suggests a more permanent constellation.

By studying all the changes youths have experienced in the last ten years, it is possible to see a variety of ongoing processes—some cyclical, some dialectic, some linear, and many paradoxical. With regard to some elements of the modernity syndrome, notably efficacy, planning, the achievement ethic, and scientific rationality, college students were moving towards traditionalism in the late 1960s, followed by a resurgence after 1971 of a modern outlook. The noncollege youths are following, perhaps a cycle behind.

Other components of the syndrome, such as openness to new ideas and experience, tolerance and acceptance of different groups such as homosexuals, decline in authoritarianism, concern for the dignity of women, valuation of individual autonomy, increased amount of abstract thinking, and increased awareness of one's psychic processes, show a more linear and uniform shift toward the modern pole for both college and noncollege youth. Many of the changes may also be indicative of an increase in ego development.

Paradoxically, this development has often been accompanied by regressive acts and symptoms. Perhaps this situation is a reflection of the truism that, in order to go forward, we often have to go backward. Many of the changes are open to differing interpretations. A decrease in the acceptance of the authority of the "boss" in the workplace, and a general decline in the respect for authority, may be seen as a maladaptive regression into oppositional hostility and as a breakdown of inner controls. If accompanied by a degree of realistic constructivism, however, these changes may represent a healthy reduction in the idealization of authority, an increase in self-autonomy, and a decline in dependency.[36]

Certainly, greater desire for self-actualization, demand for interesting and mind-stimulating work, and desire for an integrated and whole self (by not splitting one's life into two by having to adhere to strict conventionalism on the job) can all be taken to be hints of an increasing level of ego development among college students and working youth.[37]

There is a danger, however, in making too much of the Yankelovich youth data, since the changes in modernity and ego development that interest us are central to personality and perhaps are likely to show only glacial change. The youth poll shows dramatic changes and reversals over a relatively short term. How does this square with our contention that education and occupation are major determinants of the syndrome, and the fact that the country showed no dramatic increase in education levels between 1969 and 1973? These changes came after the economic boom and opportunities of the 1960s had raised aspirations and corroded the ability of the workplace to impose traditional restraints. Vietnam also reduced the legitimacy of major institutions and, aided by the vastly increased proportion of the population who were youth and college students (resulting from the baby boom after 1945), created a mass phenomenon. Perhaps all this provided the opportunity both for psychic change and the expression of the pent-up and previously hidden effects of long-term increments in education. Brenner's findings (1973) on the massive effect of the economy on psychic health cautions us to respect the power of the economy to change people.

Most likely, we are seeing the effects of both a series of long-term secular changes in education and in the occupation structure, and a series of short-term economic cycles. Ego development, though correlated with the modernity syndrome, is more likely to be affected by the long-term changes in education, while modernity is likely to reflect both changes.

Considering the changes and trends found in the Gallup and Detroit surveys, it would seem safe to attribute them to such long-term changes in the social structure as urbanization, increasing education levels, and changes in the occupational structure, as well as to contact with the culture of the educated elite.[38]

Conclusion

The evidence presented here suggests that a constellation of attitudes, values, and behaviors defined as individual modernity partially reflects important qualities of the social structure such as the educational and occupational hierarchies. This modernity syndrome is related to ego development, a sequence of stage development partially independent of simple aging. The combination of the two represents a significant slice of what is called "national character." Cross-sectional data show that ego development and modernity are influenced more by education and work than by parental family social class. Finally, the evidence presented from a variety of sources shows that level of individual modernity (and possibly ego development) has increased perceptibly in the last few decades. Throughout the chapter, the focus is on the commonalities implied by the syndrome quality of individual modernity stressed here. However, there is some evidence that only some elements of the modernity syndrome have changed and that significant hybrid variants may be emerging. While the cohesion of the syndrome is a fact that cannot be argued away, concentration on the overall syndrome still leaves open the possibility of both a profile analysis of the changing elements, and an examination of subgroup (regional, age, ethnic, and the like) variants of the major syndrome.

While both modernity and ego development might seem to be couched in terms of positive (some would say middle-class, liberal, or Western) values, it is a mistake to think of them in these terms. The modernity syndrome and ego development are as applicable to the East as to the West, but are fused with other nonrelated cultural values and social systems. Such elements of modernity as technical competency and organization still can become fused with primitive and malevolent social forces.

Individual modernity and ego development are depicted as being "produced" by the social system rather than the reverse. While the relationship is undoubtedly reciprocal, societal action should not be reductionistically explained in terms of individual characteristics without recourse to social structure and culture.

What of the future? Some have suggested that "Postindustrial Man" is now upon us. The new emphasis on the service sector as opposed to production and the rise of the white collar professional and technical expert indicate a major transformation, which, according to the model, ought to affect personality.

At the level of the individual, there will probably be a continued move toward greater individual modernity, with such things as tolerance or psychological mindedness becoming more central to the syndrome, perhaps transforming it into a "postmodern character."

The conformist stage of ego development is probably modal for the country, perhaps with some of skewness toward the conscientious stage in which the salient internalized rules and achievement can easily be intertwined with bureaucratic rigidity or technological impersonality. While the proportions at the conscientious and autonomous stage have probably increased over the last few decades, the proportion of these character types is still small, though they are likely to be found more frequently among the influential, educational, and occupational elite.

However, there are many cross-pressures such as inflation and the loss of comparative economic advantage. If the opportunity structure contracts and if education, now mainly in surplus in many areas, becomes a luxury, then there may be a halt in the progression and perhaps a return to an earlier character. Such economic pressures might also redress the tensions between an unchanging production system and the developing individual with an increasing taste for psychological rather than material income.

If we accept that we are, and will be, in a period of rapid social change, "future shock" if you will, with the society becoming even more complex and differentiated and with up-do-date knowledge as one of its main products, then an important inference follows. Since one cannot know exactly what to socialize children for, then as Inkeles

(1968) suggested, adult socialization such as occurs on the job must become more important. Thus, to understand the course of future changes in the structure of a segment of the American modal personality (or personalities), one should probably concentrate more on work and schooling than on early family socialization.[39]

Appendix

Short Modernity Scale [1]

CHART II

Have you ever (thought over much) gotten so highly concerned (involved) regarding some public issue (such as . . .) that you really wanted to do something about it?

1. Frequently 2. Few times 3. Never

If schooling is freely available (if there were no kinds of obstacles) how much schooling (reading and writing) do you think children (the son) of people like yourself should have?

Two twelve-year-old boys took time out from their work in the corn (rice) fields. They were trying to figure out a way to grow the same amount of corn (rice) with fewer hours of work.

1. The father of one boy said: "That is a good thing to think about. Tell me your thoughts about how we should change our ways of growing corn (rice)."
2. The father of the other boy said: "The way to grow corn (rice) is the way we have always done it. Talk about change will waste time but not help!"

Which father said the wiser words?

What should most qualify a man to hold high office?

1. Coming from (right, distinguished, or high) family background
2. Devotion to the old and (revered) time-honored ways
3. Being the most popular among the people

---

1. From the six-nation study (Smith and Inkeles, 1966). Scales used in the analysis contained from 30 to well over 100 items. This scale, the short form, is presented as an example of items used in the six-nation study by Inkeles and Smith. It clearly needs substantial revision before it can be used in the United States.

4. High education and special knowledge

Which is most important for the future of (this country)?

1. The hard work of the people
2. Good planning on the part of the government
3. God's help
4. Good luck

Learned men (scholars, scientists) in the universities are studying such things as what determines whether a baby is a boy or girl and how it is that a seed turns into a plant.

Do you think that these investigations (studies) are:

1. all very good (beneficial) 2. all somewhat good (beneficial)
3. all somewhat harmful 4. all very harmful

1. Some people say that it is necessary for a man and his wife to limit the number of children to be born so they can take better care of those they do have (already have).
2. Others say that it is wrong for a man and wife purposely (voluntarily) to limit the number of children to be born.

Which of these opinions do you agree with more?

Which one of these (following) kinds of news interests you most?

1. World events (happenings in other countries)
2. The nation
3. Your home town (or village)
4. Sports
5. Religious (or tribal, cultural) events (ceremonies) or festivals

If you were to meet a person who lives in another counry a long way off (thousands of kilometers away), could you understand his way of thinking?

1. Yes 2. No

Do you think a man can be truly good without having any religion at all?

1. Yes 2. No

Do you belong to any organization (associations, clubs), such as, for example, social clubs, unions, church organizations, political groups, or other groups? If "Yes," what are the names of all the organizations you belong to? (Scored for number of organizations)

Would you tell me what are the biggest problems you see facing (your country)? (Scored for number of problems or words in answer)

Where is (in what country is the city of) Washington/Moscow? (Scored correct or incorrect)

How often do you (usually) get news and information from newspapers?

1. Everyday
2. Few times a week
3. Occasionally (rarely)
4. Never

NOTES

1. The occupational quality that most concerns Inkeles is occupational status, which is probably the single most important descriptive feature of a job. Other studies, by Melvin Kohn (1969) and George Stern (1970), have shown that facets of a job, such as the degree of autonomy, control over decisions and people, and working with ideas rather than things, also have an impact on personality, but the effect is small compared to status.

2. While Inkeles acknowleges the force of ideology, he perhaps underestimates its effect on values. However, Inkeles does stress that there will be variation caused by historical, national, and cultural differences. These differences tend to be outweighed in certain areas by the noncultural similarities. In my recent thinking, the rate of expansion and contraction of the opportunity structure has begun to assume great relevance as a determinant of such psychological traits as a sense of efficacy.

3. Recently published as *Becoming Modern* with David H. Smith.

4. The use of a dichotomous or unidimensional concept such as traditional-modern has many pitfalls, not the least of which are dangers of oversimplification and of becoming too easily equated with good-bad overtones. Some agree that the traditional pole of the concept is a residual category not as well defined as the modern pole. Others such as Geertz (1963) and Rudolph (1967) show how traditional values and institutions can also easily serve modern functions. Some critics suspiciously charge ethnocentrism and that the concept emerges from a simplistic line of unilinear evolution. Others argue that the modernity syndrome can even be antithetical to development (cf. Portes, 1973). Still others contend that the syndrome shows little cohesiveness and coherence as a single entity. See Suzman (1973) for a discussion of these issues.

5. There is also persuasive evidence that individual modernity is not just a figment of the Western mind, but that it is a real and relevant dimension in non-Western societies. Thus, the cross-cultural scale correlates very highly with more particularistic modernity scales that have a high degree of local content. Non-Western countries differ in their mean level of individual modernism along ways very difficult to explain in terms of differential Westernism. The syndrome is not technology or per capita GNP bound; it has been found in contemporary rural communes or collectives, and it is unlikely to be found in its complete nonhybrid form in countries such as Kuwait or White South Africa and Nazi Germany where relatively primitive social systems were joined with advanced technologies or wealth.

6. Almost all the comparisons were made within each country; thus, those who were relatively more modern were compared with those who were relatively more traditional. Recently, comparisons have been made between countries (Inkeles, 1974). While absolute differences do exist between countries, the differences decrease when education, factory experience, and mass media exposure levels are statistically controlled.

7. Portes (1973) has suggested that modernity is found in two hybrid forms: one in which consumption and individualism are emphasized, and one in which saving and the collectivity are stressed.

8. Portes (1973) argues, though with little data, that much of the modernism syndrome in developing countries is a Western import and is the result of culture contact.

9. There are many paradoxes to American values. Egalitarianism and the hierarchy induced by differential wealth seem incompatible unless each is confined to separate sectors of social life, such as egalitarianism in the law courts but not in the occupational hierarchy.

10. Of course, to understand a value fully one needs to understand what it is opposed to, its latent and unconscious connections, its use, and whether it is both a personally held value as well as a public or official value. Some people keep their values compartmentalized from each other, while others acknowledge the conflict among their values. For some, a value is a rote cliché, or a limited manifestation of self-interest; and for others the same value may be complex and differentiated, and understood in terms of a social contract. Such complexities are, alas, more the province of the novelist, the anthropologist, and the psychoanalyst than of the public opinion pollster.

11. Between 1950 and 1970, the percentage of married women in the labor force increased from just over 20 percent to just over 40 percent (the percentage of all nonfarm women between fifteen and sixty-nine increased about 10 percent). Still, by 1970, in no age group in the United States were more than about 55 percent of the women working. While the percentage of degrees awarded to women in the United States doubled between 1950 and 1970, there was no commensurate increase in their occupational status.

Between 1950 and 1970, the percentage of women in the nonfarm U.S. workforce increased about 12 percent, while the percentage of married women who worked rose from just over 20 percent to just over 40 percent.

12. Cf. Land and Spilerman (1975) and Glenn (1974).

13. Some notable exceptions are Gurin, et al. (1960), Kohn (1969), Bradburn (1969), and perhaps Hyman, et al. (1975). Although short forms of the Adorno F-Scale (authoritarianism) have been administered nationally, most of the psychodynamically oriented development was done on nonrepresentative samples. Many of the factorially oriented personality trait inventories administered to wide-scale samples have yielded little of interest for our purpose.

14. See Glenn (1974) and Land and Spilerman (1975) for extensive discussions of the problem. Inkeles (1974) was able to effectively demonstrate causal connections in cross-sectional data by using large samples and a quasiexperimental design.

15. The work of Glen Elder (1974), who studied a cohort of high school subjects from Oakland who were socialized during the depression and retested several times, and of Brenner (1974), who has studied the effect of economic cycles on mental health, demonstrates the profound and lasting effect of economic events. Brenner's work shows that over a 127-year period in New York State the economic cycle accounted for a staggering percentage of the variance in first admissions to mental hospitals, even when a number of other variables were controlled, with the effects of a downturn resulting in a peak in new admissions some six months to a year later. The results are so striking that, if they hold up, Brenner's work will become a classic in social science. In thinking of the economy as a major dynamo of social and psychological change, we should not forget the role of population dynamics, such as the baby boom of the 1950s moving through the system, the increased percentage of older people in the population, and the rise of the birth rate. (The decline of the birth rate from about 3.1 in 1965 to 2.1 in 1975 has reduced the projected GNP of the United States for year 2000 by some $80 billion.

16. For example, sampling designs changed after the mid-1950s to include more women, Blacks, poor, Southerners, and especially southern Blacks.

17. Apart from this study of Boston Blacks, there have been very few surveys of individual modernity in the United States. The studies that have been done have in most instances used somewhat inappropriate measures of modernity. Of course, many components of the syndrome (such as occupational aspirations, efficacy, and active citizenship) have been studied extensively.

18. Suzman (1973) also administered a short version of the scale in a survey of a Massachusetts congressional district; Armer and Schnaiberg (1972) administered the Inkeles short form, together with the modernity scales of Kahl, Armer, and Doob, to a nonprobability sample of about 150 white Chicago males. While Armer and Schnaiberg, who would ally themselves with those social scientists who are more interested in the unique than the universal, maintained that their data did not support the concept of an empirical modernity syndrome, their data seem to support the opposite conclusion (cf. Suzman, 1974). More recently, Gough (1976) administered a modernity scale that showed moderate reliability among a large sample of college students and a much higher reliability in a smaller sample of nonuniversity students. As part of an ongoing study of the psychosocial effects of education, I administered a modernity scale and a measure of ego level to a sample of 550 people (eighth through twelfth graders and college students) in the San Francisco Bay area in 1975. Preliminary results indicate a moderately cohesive modernity syndrome. An augmented scale was administered to about half of the sample one year later, but these results are not available yet.

19. This might be a function of the greater prejudice against male than female black clerical workers.

20. See Block (1969).

21. Initial impressions from my school survey on the modernity syndrome suggest that part of the effect of education on the syndrome is mediated through posteducation experiences and status.

22. There are a number of problems with her scheme and scoring system. There is good evidence that she portrays the ego as more unitary than it probably is. Apparently, there are many elements that might lag and lead in relation to intellectual and moral development. While Loevinger describes the ego as a holistic integratory process, others, such as Arlow and Brenner, view the ego as a compendium of functions, a view that would imply multiple lines of development. Ideally, the measure should also include some assessment of the degree of overall integration of the ego. The self-protective stage should probably include a sublevel in which distrust and rejection of authority are salient, and some of the higher stages may be found to embody too many cultural biases to become adequately generalized. A set of sentence completions from which Loevinger derives her measure is probably too meagre an instrument to assess the complexity and richness of the ego structure, and probably overrewards verbosity, articulateness, and complex sentence structure with inflated high ego levels. The measure was originally standardized on only women. While the measure seems to work well with men, some stages may need revision to take into account the different developmental paths of men and women.

23. See Inkeles and Levinson (1954).

24. Loevinger has not progressed to the point of providing a model of the process of ego development and the determinants of the process. We should also bear in mind that the model is not as intertwined with life events as is the Eriksonian model of development.

25. Given the great measurement problems with the Kohlberg scale, such findings must be treated with great caution.

26. However, the specific contributions of chronological maturation, early childhood experiences, and education have not yet been definitely untangled.

27. A close reading of some recent psychoanalytic literature on ego and superego development suggests that it is erroneous to accuse the whole classical psychoanalytic school of saying that no significant change takes place after childhood. While some early fantasies change very little and other characteristics change only with great difficulty, most contemporary analytic schools allow for considerable development well into adulthood (Suzman, 1973).

28. I have just completed a one-year retest of the ego level of a sample of school children. Even if an increment in ego level is found, it cannot be assumed that schooling rather than other maturational influences led to the increment.

29. This raised the important question of why both overt attitudes and the underlying ego structure should be studied. For a start, it was assumed that when the two were not in consonance there would be important behavioral consequences, and the "same" attitude held by people of differing ego levels would, in reality, function very differently. The important concept of personality integration comes into play here. Furthermore, since surface attitudes can be changed more easily than complex ego structures, there is the possibility that attitude changes could ultimately lead to ego level changes.

It should be clear that my position on the relationship or nonrelationship between behavior, situations, and enduring personality characteristics and structures is at variance with the positions of psychologists such as Mischel or Gergen. While there might seem to be a superficial similarity in the emphasis on the effect of situations, the situations considered here are not those of the social psychology experiment, but rather long-term, enduring contacts with powerful, significant, and culturally legitimate institutions such as the school or work.

30. With the modernity scale corrected for reliability, the correlation was R=.38, though for technical reasons this is probably an underestimate. Moreover, the relationship remained substantial even when one controlled the number of words and syntax quality a subject used in an answer, or measures of intellectual functioning such as vocabulary, or maze performance. In my unpublished school study, cited in footnote 18, an uncorrected correlation greater than r=.40 (N=541) was found between modernity and ego level.

31. Modernity was also positively correlated with the embedded figures test, a measure of field independence and psychological differentiation (Witkin, 1962), both of which are developmental concepts with some similarity to ego development. Field independence measures the degree to which one sees the social and material world in a sharp and differentiated way (field independence), or in very simple, vague, and global terms (field dependence). It also seems to tap the degree of inner psychological differentiation, and people who are field independent tend to use inner guides for action rather than rely on such external cues as authority. This finding in the Boston sample is substantiated by recent work by Gruenfeld and MacEachron (unpublished, no date) showing that field independence is correlated with high SES in the United States, and, for an international group of managers and technicians, with origin from a country with a high per capita GNP.

32. Because of methodological issues, including the use of a slightly different modernity scale, the white and black modernity levels are not compared. Yankelovich (1973), however, presents data suggesting that black youth may be more modern in some areas when education is held constant.

33. Traditionalism was also strongly correlated with authoritarianism. However, some individuals were both modern and authoritarian; this hybrid is most likely to be found in industrial totalitarian states. This is an important finding, since it helps to negate a tendency to think of individual modernity as being, in terms of liberal values, unmitigatingly good.

34. Some answer categories have been collapsed.

35. In reference to these themes, I am reminded of a speech in Capetown, South Africa, by Erik Erikson, in which he pointed out that in ancient Greece, women, children, and slaves were put into the same categories, and that such prejudice constituted a focal resistance to inner psychological insight and development.

36. Jeanne Block (1969), in a study of the inferred ego levels of the parents of groups of Berkeley students, found that the parents of those who were socially inactive fitted Loevinger's conformist stage, while the parents of those who were active in both protest and social service activities were distributed at the conscientious level and higher. Those who protested but had no service activities were similar to those who engaged in service activities but not protest

activities: both of these groups had parents who fitted Loevinger's opportunistic stage.

37. The signs of this are all about. In an ultramodern General Motors factory in Lordstown, Ohio, the young workforce sabotaged the assembly line and became highly frustrated. The well-articulated demands for more challenging, interesting, and integrated work, and the requests for greater control over one's work habits and working-pace all belie that this was just a function of a speeded-up assembly line.

38. As we noted, the average level of education has risen, and most of the values and attitudes in the surveys we have cited are correlated with education and occupational status. Unfortunately, the long-term poll data are not broken down by education so that we can see whether a person with a high school education in 1930 would have the same level of modernity as someone with comparable education in 1970. If we found comparability, then we might assume that it was actually education, and not the current culture or status conferred by education (very different in 1930 and 1970), which produced the syndrome.

There is considerable evidence from the studies by Sanford, Heath, Perry, and others, of personal growth in college to conclude that education can produce (or coincide with) something close to ego development. In comparison to seniors, Sanford (1962) portrays freshmen as perceiving only the surface characteristics of problems, as intolerant of ambiguity, as submissive to the powerful, and as hostile to people different from themselves. In contrast, seniors are more flexible, have accepted relativism, and are more unorthodox and less authoritarian; their values are more internalized, their perceptions of the world more complex and differentiated, and their conscience more integrated into their ego.

39. This does not negate the developmental importance of early, especially Oedipal, experiences in the formation of many aspects of personality. Differentiating the areas of personality most influenced by early or late socialization remains a task for the future.

The Loss and Rediscovery of Moral Character

4

NEVITT SANFORD

Today the university is much like other corporate structures, functioning in much the same way as banks, manufacturing companies, hospitals, government agencies, and the like. Work is increasingly differentiated and specialized, roles are rigidly defined, communication among various divisions and departments is difficult, responsibility is diffused, individuals are alienated from their work, themselves, and each other, and they feel powerless to change anything.

Interchangeability and Innocence

These processes are effective at the top as well as in the lower echelons of organizations. Corporation or university presidents may be replaced without a ripple of disturbance in the ranks. The incoming president simply does what the outgoing one did and life goes on. Organizations may break the law, commit immoral acts, and engage in racist and sexist practices without any individual being blamed or being made responsible for what happened. Even though most people in the organization are, as individuals, against these practices, they contribute to them merely by performing their assigned tasks.

Without doubt, this situation reflects an inexorable tendency of technology under capitalism or, perhaps, of technology under any other modern economic system. In any case, it is well to remember that corruption in high places, credibility gaps, and the domination of our lives by the military-industrial-educational complex did not begin with Watergate.

Erich Fromm and Michael Maccoby are correct in insisting that systems and patterns of social relations such as are considered here "shape the energies of people in such a way that their behavior is not left to conscious decisions whether or not to go along with social demands, but people want to act as they have to act to keep the system moving" (Maccoby, 1970:2). It also may be agreed, as Maccoby states, that the "social character" required by the modern organization includes such traits as punctuality, accuracy, orderliness, efficiency, detachment, competitiveness, cooperativeness, fairness, and playing by the rules. But the rules, as they really function, are rules of survival, not rules of morality.

Contractors, Codes, and Consternation

Let me offer some subjective examples from my own recent experience and from recent history. After a fire that half destroyed our home, we decided to rebuild from the remains. First, we consulted a contractor. One might suppose that approximately one-half of a unique house built in 1905 (that is old for California) ought to be preserved. Not a chance—we were told that the house had too many features that were not up to code. Well, as we are living in a time of dwindling natural resources, we not unreasonably requested that at least the old boards and timbers be preserved. We proposed to the contractor that we use the old boards for subflooring, so that we could enjoy looking at them from below, getting the effect achieved in the Monterey colonial houses. No, he said; that would not be economical. The only course was to have machines knock down and chew up the remains.

The contractor thus advised rebuilding from scratch. He tried to get us to build what would have been essentially a tract home. How about a nine-foot ceiling, I asked. Not unless you want to throw your money away, he answered. Two-by-fours come sawed in eight- or sixteen-foot lengths; any deviation from the standard would be costly both in material and in labor. And so it went.

I think I understand the situation of the contractor. He is a well-meaning man. He has a home in the Hills, a wife, and two children in college; he goes to church, performs other civic duties—and takes for granted that he will get a rake off on materials purchased at a lumberyard where he has been doing business for years. Not only is he bound in his aesthetics by the system, but his conduct of his affairs is on a low moral level as well. If you are to come out ahead in the contracting business, it is almost impossible to build anything that does not look like a tract home—and the social-economic pressures are such that you cannot afford to be overly honest.

Discouraged by our experience with that contractor, we decided to do our own contracting. If you want to build your own house in Berkeley, you apply for a permit in the category of "owner-built." "Owner-built" is a deviant status in the housing code, and it is meant for only the hardy and the curious. We became immersed in a "real world" of insurance adjusters, estimators, inspectors, building contractors, wreckers, haulers, carpenters, electricians, plumbers, day laborers, representatives of various public utilities, and occupants of various bureaus in City Hall.

Unhappiness and Skullduggery

Probably no one will be surprised to hear that few of the people I had to deal with were happy in their work, and that it was almost impossible to get anything done. Having spent almost a lifetime in the academic world, I believe I am familiar with most forms of rascality and skullduggery, but I was still not prepared for the low level of moral conduct commonly encountered in the "real world."

Few of the people we dealt with seemed to feel any obligation to do what they said they would do; we encountered few remnants of the old idea of honest work for honest pay; and it was necessary to remain constantly on the alert to avoid being cheated. Almost as distressing was the absence of the aesthetic, ecological, conservationist, or antiquarian values in all agencies, bureaus, and small businesses. So many people we encountered filled roles for which they had no passion and with which they were not truly integrated.

The situation is not much better within the university today. Knowledge of our building effort may be of some comfort, albeit of a somewhat chilly sort, to university students who enter their various schools or departments with high hopes but soon find that it is always extremely difficult and often impossible to do what really interests them. It happened that at about the same time that I got involved with building problems, my colleagues and I at the Wright Institute were considering the results of an essay contest for graduate students. We had offered $2,000 in prizes for the best autobiographical essays on the experience of graduate education. The dominant theme in the ninety-six essays submitted had to do with how a student could preserve something of his or her self, some integrity, something of the curiosity and inspiration that had led to graduate work in the first place, while meeting requirements that seemed arbitrary, senseless, and unfair. They had to spend a great deal of time either trying to figure out a way to "beat the system" or deciding whether they would remain within it.[1]

Many assumed that their difficulties stemmed from the whims or special needs of professors and thought that when they got their degrees and became professors themselves they could help to change things. Not likely. Departments and universities really are "systems" as many students say. They are corporate structures that go their way regardless of which individuals occupy their diverse roles. Since World War II, our universities have entered the marketplace and, while strengthening their ties with national academic guilds, have become integrated with our vast business, industrial, governmental, and philanthropic structures. While the traditional functions of advancing knowledge and training young people for useful roles in society remain, these have been distorted and downgraded by the need to adapt to the demands of the larger society. As David Breneman (1970) has shown, the behavior of university departments can best be explained on the assumption that their primary purpose is "prestige maximization"—to become the strongest department in the university and the most highly rated in the country. To this end they economically use all available resources, including students.

Being a team player is of enormous importance to high-level decision-making in our national life. For example, when Adlai Stevenson was our representative in the United Nations, he began going against his principles because, as he said, he had to go along with the team. His choice, in the words of Hampden-Turner (1974:3), was between "powerless conscience and conscienceless power." Irving Janis (1972) has shown the vital role of assumed consensus in the decision leading to the Bay of Pigs fiasco. The current trends in Washington require no comment. In my own experience, I have had a number of colleagues and friends who, once they became deans and accepted the obligation to go along with university policy, began lying to me, apparently without great discomfort.

People who work in large organizations generally accept the required values, at least enough so that work-related behavior is usually in accord with these values. Indeed, organizations reward conformity with their values and ways. Moreover, individuals who remain in organizations vest an interest in their roles, giving the appearance that in order to change an organization it would be necessary to change the personalities of the people who work there. Some student leaders of the protest movements of the 1960s used to say that the university, instead of educating its students, merely prepared them for taking the roles necessary to keep the industrial and governmental wheels turning. "Radical historians" of education tell us that this grooming process begins far earlier and that the chief function of the schools in our society is to develop the social character desired by the powers that be. Hence, the schools will not change until the whole society changes and, if this seems a remote possibility, we can at least go about "de-schooling."[2]

Constructive Optimism

Clearly, there is much to the notion that the social structure is an irresistible force dominating and directing human behavior. But, as a note of optimism, it may certainly be asked if there is not some alternative to this despairing analysis. Things are far more complicated than the student leaders, radical historians, and building contractors know. For one thing, individuals are not totally determined by the social structures in which they live or work. The graduate students who took part in our literary contest were, for the most part, aware of the psychological costs of the course they had taken, but they were strong enough to push on toward the promised future rewards. In addition, they had their life-styles and ample opportunities to find gratifications outside the academic structure. For that matter, the young bureaucrats at City Hall have their life-styles too. I observed what I took to be indications that they intended to preserve some independence and individuality, as in the wide variations in dress and grooming and in the relaxed slowness with which they went about their work. One young man was even tempted to give me a break in connection with a building permit but finally decided he had better stick to the rules.

It should be acknowledged that our organizations are not, on the whole, as bad as they might be. They induce conformity by their system of rewards and threats of loss of income or status; they operate mainly without inducing hate which would be directed to outgroups. But they are bad enough, and it is appropriate to ask what has been their impact, over the past thirty years, on the American national character. I offer no easy solution; yet I think there is a constructive approach to the problem.

Personality and Social Structure

A full analysis of our institutional and moral character must make use of the concept of personality—of individual character—as well as the concept of social structure. It is not only that individuals have their own inner functioning but also that, in the final analysis, they create social structures. No matter what the social or organizational pressures at any given time, personality will have some part in determining what the individual actually does. Personality formation is well along on its course before the individual enters school, and, whereas it may be shaped there, in college, or work situations, it will always retain something of its early nature, for each individual assimilates the experiences of these settings in his own way.

How does the individual personality interact with or adapt to organizational requirements? To answer this question, we may begin by noting individual differences. Some people take to their jobs as if the two were made for each other. They seem from the start to embody the competencies and the values required. Others come slowly to this kind of fit between person and work role, not realizing that they are defining themselves according to the organization's objectives. Still others remain fully aware of the differences between themselves and their role behavior, but do what is necessary, with varying degrees of unhappiness, cynicism, resignation, or demoralization. A very few—a particularly interesting group—try to change the organization, while many leave. (In recent years, business organizations have had to abandon various consciousness-raising activities for employees because as a result too many left the company.)

People who adapt themselves to the ways and values of organizations do so in accord with different psychological processes, and when these ways and values are assimilated, they are ordered to different parts of the personality. For example, some managers and administrators may be said to identify themselves with their roles. I have known academic men who, when they became deans, began by saying, "I don't like to do this but it is university policy," but they soon began to neglect the distinction between themselves and their role, in time becoming every inch an administrator. We may suppose that in such cases deeply based personality needs found expression in the role. Other deans insist on doing some teaching or some research, moving easily from one role to the other while maintaining a strong sense of self.

Again, some men in the business world, in adopting the traits of the social character, order those traits to that system of prohibitions, sanctions, and inspirations that were automatically or unconsciously assimilated when they were children. I know of a cotton planter who genuinely regretted that the mechanization of his business threw fifty men out of work, but having taken it upon himself to make a profit he felt morally bound to do what General Motors did. So with our contractor. I think he would feel guilt as well as shame if he did not do what he knows is required to be a success in his business. Both of these men, I think, have fundamentally sound personalities. They have come to terms with an internalized, though primitive, conscience, but they are not altogether dominated by it. They could adjust to another way of doing things without great difficulty. Men with less responsibility, such as those in middle management positions in organizations, are aware of the sacrifices they have to make; they are familiar with conflicts of conscience, but they have made rational decisions to accept the rewards and restraints of middle-class status. They are like the political liberal who, as they say, is a radical with a wife and two children.

Other people find in their work roles, particularly in business, opportunities to gratify primitive personality impulses, for example, a lust for power based on a more or less unconscious fear of weakness or the criminal impulses to get one's own no matter what the cost.

In sum, I am proposing that individual needs, fostered in infancy, become gratified through adaptation to a system, giving the *appearance* that social structure is the exclusive causal agency. Change can come only through radical social change. What may appear to be social causation can often be interpreted from the perspective of personality.

Although each personality is unique, there are many similarities among personalities, and certain patterns are common, or modal, in different national, regional, social class, or ethnic groups.

I would like to approach the question of change in the American character or modal personality by considering what we know, or suspect, about authoritarianism in personality. There is a special point in attending to this pattern of dispositions, for individuals in whom it is pronounced are likely to receive preferment in organizations.

Authoritarianism in personality is a deeply based structure, deriving from inner conflicts and personal strivings. It is expressed in such traits as uncritical acceptance of authority and the belief that one's chosen leader can do no wrong; rigid adherence to conventional values and readiness to punish any violation of them; preoccupation with the dominance submission aspect of human relationships and exaggerated display of strength and toughness; and insistence on the virtues of one's own group and the rightness of one's own course and a disposition to ascribe all manner of evil motives to other people—the enemy, who may or may not be "listed." In the middle 1940s, scores on a scale for measuring authoritarianism—the F scale—were found to be closely associated with anti-Semitism and generalized ethnocentrism (Adorno, Frenkel-Brunswik, Levinson, and Sanford, 1950). Gump (1951) showed that people who disapproved of President Truman's dismissal of General MacArthur were distinguished by their authoritarianism, and Milton (1952) found a correlation of .73 between scores of the F scale and the tendency to prefer "authoritarian" candidates for president (e.g., MacArthur versus Stevenson) in the election of 1952.

There is a very interesting study of psychological difference between supporters of Nixon and supporters of McGovern in the election of 1972. Shortly before that election, Comstock and Duckles (1972) administered the Fromm-Maccoby "love of life" scale to 589 Oakland residents, chosen at random, and found extremely significant differences between pro-Nixon and pro-McGovern respondents. I think this scale taps something deep in the personality that has much in common with authoritarianism. At the low end of the scale, as Comstock and Duckles say, "is the person who craves order, certainty, obedience, the past, and the mechanical rather than the organic, who avoids deep feelings, who is fascinated by sickness, dirt, troubles, and finally by death."

When scores on this scale were divided into high and low, 85 percent of the Nixon supporters and 51 percent of the McGovern supporters had low scores.

A set of thirteen items pertaining to authority and leadership showed the same kind of sharp differentiation.

Assuredly, there is plenty of authoritarianism around today. Is there more or less than in the middle 1940s when my colleagues and I collected data for our book *The Authoritarian Personality*? (Adorno, Frenkel-Brunswik, Levinson, and Sanford, 1950). Is there more or less than at various times since?

Psychohistorical Considerations

I have a strong impression that the number of "hard core" Nixon supporters is not larger, in proportion to the total population, than the number who revered General MacArthur and wanted him to be president. We were very much interested in this matter at the time (1951-1952), paid close attention to relevant public opinion polls, and concluded that about a third of our people were significantly authoritarian. I find little reason to believe that the proportion is higher today. It should be possible to get sound evidence on this matter, since the F scale has been used with various samples of people every year since 1945. There are great difficulties in the way, however. Different versions of the scale have been used from time to time, and rarely has the same version been used consistently over the years with adequate samples of people having the same social characteristics. Not even students. When Vassar College students took the F scale each year from 1952 to 1959, the mean score per item showed no significant trends during these years, nor did the Vassar students as a group differ significantly from the Berkeley students of 1945-1948 (Webster, Freedman, and Heist, 1962). Stanford and Berkeley students in the years 1962-1967 produced F scale responses that were not very different, in respect to the mean score per item, from those produced by Berkeley and Vassar students in the 1940s and 1950s, respectively (Katz, et al., 1968). In a recent publication, Gough and Lazzari (1974) report a mean item score, for over 200 Berkeley students in elementary psychology classes, that is remarkably similar to means my colleagues and I obtained from student groups in the middle 1940s. To be quite concrete, the mean response to the item "Obedience and respect for authority are the most important virtues children should learn" was almost exactly the same as that for student groups reported on in *The Authoritarian Personality:* it was approximately half-way between "uncertain" and "agree a little." (It may be noted that Gough and Lazzari were mainly concerned with examining authoritarianism in Italians and Americans. The mean scores overall were very similar, but there were interesting and expected differences on particular items. As a predictor of other specific attitudes, e.g., toward contraception, the scale performed pretty much as always.) As our critics have never tired of pointing out, Berkeley, Vassar, and Stanford students are not exactly typical of American students in general. Who knows what has happened at Central Michigan, Northern Illinois, and Middle Tennessee?

As suggested earlier, it might be possible by means of an enormous piece of library research, aiming at comparability of samples and scales or items used, to get a useful picture of trends in authoritarianism over the years. This effort would be a worthwhile one. What I have to say now is that those of us who thought that students in general were really being liberated during the 1960s probably have to take a more sober view. This is not to say that students who were indeed liberated, mainly at the great universities and first-rate liberal arts colleges, have not had some influence on our culture generally. At the same time, those of us who have been frightened by the dehumanizing tendencies of our large organizations may have to admit that things may not be as bad as we thought.

I have suggested elsewhere that authoritarianism in personality ought to be regarded as a psychohistorical concept, that it ought not to be assumed that the authoritarianism we studied in the 1940s is the same as the authoritarianism of today. I may have overstressed the point in my insistence that researchers stop relying on the F scale and do some real work, that is, study personality and ideology as we did in the 1940s: by means of intensive interviews and various projective techniques. They might come up with some important differences between then and now, if not in the basic structure of the syndrome, then in its content, in the way various attitudes relate to or are excluded from the authoritarian pattern. As a matter of fact, Fromm and Maccoby (1970) have already done the sort of thing I had in mind. From their intensive studies of individuals, they not only arrived at a somewhat different, and perhaps better, formulation of destructiveness than we did, but they also developed a new scale. The "biophilia-necrophilia" scale, according to M.B. Smith (1971), is from a psychometric point of view pretty bad. About the only thing in its favor is the fact that it works.

Actually, there are good reasons why we should not expect major changes in authoritarianism to have taken place during the past twenty-five years. The basic structure is laid down in childhood, in the setting of family life. Although it may be altered, for better or worse, in school, college, and the work setting, change, especially change for the better, comes hard. Family life, it seems to me, did not change all that much during the years in question, or if it did, not soon enough to affect in any important way the upbringing of people now old enough to take the F scale. But there can be little doubt that family life is changing, at least in the middle and lower middle classes, in consequence mainly of the liberation of women and other factors making for smaller and more democratic families. A few years hence it will not be at all surprising to find lower levels of authoritarianism in our society.

Antiauthoritarian Versus Antiauthority

If authoritarianism has changed but little, attitudes toward authority have changed a lot, mainly in the direction of increased dislike of authority. Many of the people I see every day in the academic world make a point of displaying their "antiauthoritarian" valor. (They say "antiauthoritarian," but I say antiauthority, for having found myself in a position of leadership I complain about their failure to see the distinction between authoritarian and other kinds of leadership.) In California, we have seen many young professors socialized in the Ivy League who, arriving at their new jobs during the student protests, promptly identified themselves with the students, revealing that their academic social character was not very deeply based. I, like many other observers, ascribe the change in attitudes toward authority mainly to the fact that we have been betrayed too many times by people in positions of authority, and to the fact that the leaders we need have long since disappeared into a tangle of occupational roles and social group memberships.

The new attitudes toward authority are not very helpful; they favor neither individual development nor the building of better institutions.

They make it more difficult for people in positions of leadership to exercise the authority necessary to maintain an organization and to insure the freedom of the people in it. They, of course, do less than nothing to serve the underlying need for structure and for leadership, which the true antiauthoritarian refuses to admit he or she has. During the past ten years, we have seen the starting up, and the early falling down, of many new, typically small-scale, educational institutions. Many were started by groups of people who had little in common except their opposition to the establishment. There was no shared vision, or, if there was, little knowledge of how it might be realized; nobody would lead and nobody would follow, so nothing happened. Almost always the new schools were to be totally democratic; decisions were to be made in "town meetings" and by consensus. Usually, it happened that what looked like decisions were made by the people who could demonstrate that they cared the most, with the result that power was centered in a small clique; other members of the group, effectively silenced, soon departed and the end of the experiment was at hand.

Psychology and Social Theory

To make sure that I am not considered a totally unreconstructed personality psychologist, I want to underline once again the determination of behavior by broad social forces and by social structure. Most people, as has often been pointed out, are middle on authoritarianism. They may move toward either extreme, depending on social circumstance. As Eugene McCarthy said during his 1968 campaign for the Democratic nomination for president, when someone protested that the majority of the American people favored the Vietnam War, "Yes, but if the President of the United States said he was against the Viet Nam war a majority of the American people would be against the war." Suppose we have a deep economic depression, or suppose we have to begin paying, in ways that involve real hardship, for our exploitation of the world's resources, and then a president of the United States says we must use totalitarian methods to keep order? Which way would those middle on authoritarianism go? Instead of congratulating ourselves on our surviving the Nixon administration, which was really not much of an achievement given Nixon's essential weakness and the incompetence of those around him, we have to consider the real possibility of a major swing toward fascism. The matter is serious enough to warrant our planning countermeasures right now.

In the same light, most people are neither charmed nor completely turned off by their organizational lives. This means that those middle on authoritarianism could tolerate a major rise in organizational rigidity, just as they would adapt readily to a change in the direction of organic management.

It is no more difficult to change an organization, in a way that benefits everybody in it, than it is to change in any fundamental way the personality of one of its denizens. For example, if all the assistant professors in a major university were given job security (not necessarily promises of increases in pay), the functioning of the whole institution would be improved; the level of communication would go up, the level of paranoia down; teaching would improve, to the satisfaction of professors as well as students, and so would research, in quality but not quantity. There would seem to be no question about where the social scientist bent on improving the quality of life might best direct his major efforts, namely, toward social rather than individual change.

On the other hand, the two problems are really inseparable. It seems clear that a redution of authoritarianism in the leaders of organizations can bring immense changes within those organizations, particularly among those large numbers of people who are middle on authoritarianism and take their cues from their leaders and the expectations of their environment.

Another way to emphasize the inseparability of the psychological and the social is to ask what is the purpose of social change if it is not to do something that is good for people. And what is good for people, after their survival needs have been taken care of? It seems to me that the great values of life can be brought under the general heading of development toward full humanity. As we say every day to our social activist students at the Wright Institute, students who are studying what we call social-clinical psychology: "Just as it is not too good to study and practice clinical psychology unless you prepare to use what you learn in the service of collectivities of people, so it is not too good to work at social change unless you know enough about personality so that you can anticipate the gains and losses to individuals that flow from what you do."

As I see it, the purpose of social science is to build a better society.

Accordingly, the purpose of the Wright Institute is to learn enough about how social settings of various kinds affect the people in them so that we can help bring about social changes that favor human development. This means starting with a conception of man as self-reflecting and, to some degree, self-determining; it means developing theory to explain how experiences in social settings work to favor or hamper his development, and how social settings may be changed or created so that they will be maximally developmental in their effects (Sanford, 1970; The Wright Institute, 1974).

This is the context for my concluding remarks about the loss and rediscovery of morality. I have assumed that organizations, like nations, are usually amoral, and as they achieve more control over our lives, they force more and more individuals to be less moral in their behavior than they would otherwise be. Organizations tend to favor authoritarian modes of adjustment and to capitalize on authoritarianism in personality. Authoritarianism in personality can be regarded as, at best, a middle level of moral development.

Depending on Well-Developed Character

To suggest how moral character develops and how it may be sustained, let me first note that in our house building episode we did encounter, and come to rely upon, some people who *could* be trusted—who showed up when they said they would, enjoyed their work, held to aesthetic and conservationist values, and kept honest timesheets. They were students of the university, who came through that institution's employment office, and college-educated young men who had either recently found their vocation in a building trade or had changed their vocations after having succeeded in a profession. We had some stunningly beautiful carpentry performed by a young man who graduated in social science from the university four years before, and fooled around for a couple of years before finding his true vocation, that of what he calls "an artist in wood." He works—accepts a contract— when he feels like it, or when he needs to, and he devotes most of his time to reading, studying music, and keeping abreast of the work of his wife, who is a journalist. The bulk of the work or rebuilding is being done by two young men who are building their own homes but must hire themselves out to get money for living and for buying materials. They do everything: draw plans, build forms, pull nails, pour concrete, buy and deliver lumber, do the wiring, plumbing, carpentry, and cabinet work, each of these things at the optimum time. They go about their work with enormous energy and enthusiasm, happily making do with used materials and changing plans when something being done begins to look not quite right.

These young men were in situations that favored moral behavior. They had freedom—of the sort enjoyed by students and people over sixty. But some did, in fact, have young children. They had circles of friends; were in intimate relationship with people who expected something worthy of them; and were spared the anonymity so common among people in the "real" world. They quickly developed personal relationships with me.

Intentional Alternative Structures

All this, I think, is an argument for the development of small social structures—productive and other—outside the major systems which provide the conditions that allow, reward, or even teach morality. If these small-scale structures, within areas such as science, education, or homebuilding, become numerous enough and if they then connect themselves one with another, they can become a significant force for good.

Reduction of scale, however, is not enough to solve the problem and, in the short run at least, is impractical for many American institutions. Therefore, those in charge of large organizations must work toward setting up within them means for realizing the values of smallness. What is most needed is an institutional ethic that would have the immediate effect of reducing authoritarianism and raising the level of moral behavior. This ethic can help to strengthen moral character, or personality, and to raise it to a level above authoritarianism. Leaders of corporations should address the task of developing and sustaining standards of organizational behavior that deserve the loyalty of the people they employ or recruit. Until this has been accomplished, people who work or study in large organizations can only be encouraged to heighten their consciousness of themselves and their situation and to find opportunities for self-expression in the interstices of the systems.

We must acknowledge, however, that moral character develops over time and that, whereas it may be deeply influenced by experiences in work roles, it is largely a product of upbringing and education. The young men who worked for us were able to choose and largely to create their situations because, in large part, they had had more or less favorable childhoods and good educational experiences, especially at the college level.

After the work of Selznick and Steinberg (1969) on anti-Semitism, no one can doubt that there is a strong relationship between level of education and freedom from authoritarianism. This is not just a matter of belonging to the enlightened culture. The right kind of education works to change authoritarianism in personality. I have been saying for some years that it can effect this change through giving individuals the competencies necessary to deal with external authority and the self-insight to enable them to avoid projecting their own forbidden impulses onto other people (Sanford, 1956, 1962, 1967, 1973). These arguments for a developmental education have not, as yet, swept the country. I want now, very briefly, to put the case for developmental education in a different way.[4]

Education for the Enjoyment of Life

In these rather grim times, we must insist that the central goal of education is the enjoyment of life. The basic argument is that if you don't enjoy life you can't be very moral. This point was brought home to me as I watched the Senate hearings on Watergate in 1973. A dominant feature of the conspirators was their humorlessness; the contrast with Senator Ervin and Senator Talmadge was sharp. I think there is enough evidence to permit our saying that the Watergate conspirators were men who had found no way to gratify basic emotional impulses; they had to suppress them, and to do so it was necessary to make sure that everybody else suppressed theirs also. This is the fundamental source of an insatiable need for power.

A major goal of education, then—a goal generally ignored by educators—is the liberation of impulses. This liberation is best accomplished through giving people the means to express impulses symbolically, imaginatively, and vicariously through the study of literature and the arts. The great asset of my moral "artist in wood" was his ability to enjoy reading and the study of music.

Moral behavior is largely a matter of being able to make choices. The wider the range of alternatives available to an individual and the greater his ability to see the various possibilities in situations, the greater the likelihood that he will find ways to act that are at once satisfying to himself and favorable to the well-being of others. Such alternatives and such perceived possibilities flow directly from the kind of education that enables people to be responsive to diverse aspects of culture and that offers them diverse avenues for self-expression. If they have these capabilities, then their openness to themselves and hence to other people is enhanced and the way is prepared for the development of still further capabilities.

In sum, morality and the enjoyment of life go together. Both are marks of the relatively well-developed personality. We would do well to remember Thomas Jefferson's advice to his nephew: "I repeat my advice, to take a great deal of exercise, and on foot. Health is the first requisite after morality." Jefferson, as we all know, was a man who knew how to enjoy life.

NOTES

1. Winning first prize was the essay by Richard Rodriguez of the Department of English, University of California, Berkeley. The essay is entitled "Memories and the Graduate Student Who Became a Chicano" (1975).

2. Examples of first-rate works by writers who call themselves, and each other, radical historians are Gold (1974), M. Katz (1968), and Spring (1972).

3. For a discussion of ways in which individuals may resist the actions of an organization of which they are members, see Howard and Somers (1971).

4. A fuller discussion of these ideas may be found in my recent papers (Morality and Education for the Enjoyment of Life," 1974, and "Notes Toward a General Theory of Personality Development—at 80 or Any Old Age," 1973).

Individual Fulfillment, Social Stability, and Cultural Progress

5

FRANCIS L. K. HSU

The other day I saw a TV ad about an aerosol spray with a child-protection top. Normally, the user of the spray can simply takes it in hand and uses his index finger to get the action. In this case, the "new" spray can is equipped with a special cover so that a child's finger cannot press it.

This seemingly minor illustration is most instructive of what is happening in American society and culture today and deserves our serious attention. It is not an isolated illustration; we can name thousands of others. For example, nowadays when I buy a bottle of medicine I cannot simply open it. I have to tinker with it o read the complicated and sometimes not so lucid instructions, and then I still have to use force before it will yield its contents. The number of reported cases of child-poisoning is so large year after year that we must child-proof medicine bottles. Our need for child-proofing is ever expanding in scope. We now have a commission (at the taxpayers' expense) to study ways and means of making book matches child-proof, because every year there are some 11,000 emergency calls to our hospitals for children who have burned themselves playing with matches.

The message is a simple one: instead of teaching our children what they should or should not do, we try to make it *impossible for them to do or not to do it* by external inducements or restraints. The implication is that our children are little monsters who will get into everything unless we plug up all the loopholes.

What we are doing with children is symptomatic of what is occurring in our larger society and culture. We are now striving for adult-proof automobiles so that motorists can drive in any way they like but cannot kill themselves even if they want to. We have seat belts that prevent the start of the car unless you are all tied up, and air bags that will automatically inflate when you are in a collision. We are busy developing ways and means to make houses burglar-proof, public transportation mugger-proof, schools vandal-proof, supermarkets shoplifter-proof and shopping cart snatcher-proof, all the way to ensuring that girls will be rapist-proof. (The University of Colorado's student government has just distributed 3,000 whistles free to coeds, and in an effort to catch a rapist, a midwestern university hired a female detective last summer to walk the campus at night staked by four male guards.) There is currently an effort to develop antidrug injections so that adolescents will, hopefully, be addiction-proof.

The ultimate expression of this pattern of relying solely on external restraints recently came to my attention. The city of New Orleans, Louisiana, is situated between a bay on one side and a big river on the other. Since only one bridge spans the river, the inhabitants have been calling for the building of another bridge, but the city has so far decided against it. Why? It has to do with racial integration. At the present time, 35 percent of New Orleans is black and 65 percent is white. New Orleans is one of the best integrated cities of the United States, and they want to keep it that way. If you build more bridges and make things convenient, so the city fathers reasoned, the Whites would escape across the river to the suburbs. In other words, you have to make it impossible for the Whites to move away in order that they will stay.

There is no psychological difference between using the absence of additional bridges over the Mississippi River to insure racial integration and designing aerosol caps so that children cannot hurt themselves. Both are reasonable and effective ways of manipulating the behavior of animals, but neither is a satisfactory way of making human beings do, or not do, certain things. In fact, this reliance on external restraints or inducements constitutes a fundamental flaw in our American thinking about man. In turn, it is at the root of most, if not all, of the major difficulties confronting our society today. We need some serious rethinking.

Role and Affect

There is a basic inconsistency in the minds of most Americans vis-à-vis our American way of life. We tend to attribute our achievements, including our great military, but especially economic, power and technological sophistication, to our basic value of individualism, but we regard our social ills as the result of foreign influences or the work of misfits and deviants. We do not realize that both the strengths and the weaknesses of our society come primarily from within ourselves and our individualistic way of life. External intrusions can take hold and lead some of us astray only if there is so much discontent that many of us become receptive to them. For example, drug importers and pushers can prosper only if a large number of Americans are attracted to what they wish to sell.

Instead of blaming outside influences or deviants, it is more realistic to view our problems as side effects of individualism and to deal with them forthwith. In medicine, drugs are used in very stringent dosages or not used at all if their side effects are worse than their intended benefits. Why should we not be as intelligent about our most cherished value—individualism with all its ramifications?

In all societies, and ours is no exception, human beings relate to each other by role (usefulness) and by affect (feeling). We know role in terms of skilled or unskilled labor, white collar or blue collar, dentists and diamond cutters, housekeepers and politicians, and so forth. As our society has grown in complexity, the number and variety of roles have grown with it. In fact, role differentiation is the major concomitant of the growth in societal complexity. For example, in today's conditions, each candidate for national office is supported by an army of experts, including speech writers, public relations men, technicians, and foot soldiers far beyond the imagination of yesteryear's small town politicians. Giant corporations often have more diversified personnel and more workers and specialists on their payrolls than many small member states of the United Nations.

This development is inevitable as a large society becomes more industrialized. The number and variety of laws have increased, as have bureaucratic departments, ways of crime and methods of fleecing the public, problems of production, and, of course, the size and complexity of machines. Each giant modern jet plane has about two million parts. That is why their handling requires computers, for the human mind and hand are no longer speedy enough for the task.

On the other hand, while our roles have evolved in number and proficiency with the complexity of the industrial society, our affect has not. We still have the same kinds of feelings as our ancestors who lived two or three thousand (and probably more) years ago: love, hate, rage, despair, endurance, hope, anxiety, forbearance, loyalty, betrayal, and so forth. The list is not long, and many of the terms used to describe them are similar to each other, or can be partially or wholly subsumed under each other. That is why great literature and great art, and even great philosophy and ethics, survive the ages, for we moderns encounter the same agony and joy and the same loyalty and duplicity as the ancients did. We can relive their lives through what they have written, and they, too, were they alive today, would be able to discuss with us our problems with our children, parents, friends and enemies, employers and employees, sweethearts and spouses. In contrast, old books of science and technology are useless to us except as curiosities or as material for histories of science and technology. Not only the ancients, but our fathers and even our older brothers would have found it impossible, or at the least extremely difficult, to catch up with our present generation's developments in science and technology.

How easily and well insights and concepts from literary works can be used to illuminate modern events and personalities is exemplified by the words of a writer who described President Nixon's frame of mind during the Watergate affair as follows:

> His loyal friends, a shrinking circle of the faithful, saw Richard Nixon as a modern-day King Lear who raged magnificently at the storm around him. But Mr. Nixon lacked Lear's grandeur. Mr. Nixon's enemies cast him as Richard III, the king long supposed crippled by his malevolence. But Mr. Nixon did not have the eloquence of that other Richard of Shakespearean notoriety or his purity of evil purpose. Mr. Nixon was confused. Like Macbeth, who listened to the witches' prophesies and found comfort in their riddles, he was both brave in facing his peril but doomed by his blindness to it.
>
> Shakespeare wrote the curse:
>
> He shall spurn fate, scorn death, and beat
> His hopes 'bove wisdom, grace and fear,
> And, you all know, security
> Is mortal's chiefest enemy.

Nixon's false security was that "mandate of '72" which he "carried . . . with him like a shield." Explaining how Nixon felt about this shield, the writer quoted the words of Lady Macbeth:

What need we fear who knows it when
Non can call our power to account? [1]

I know of no modern scientists and engineers who can make comparable analyses, and so pertinently, of the problems they face in their present-day research or technology.

Culture and Affect

The patterns of affect that operate in the West, especially the United States, are different from those that motivate other parts of the world, such as China and Japan. Westerners may experience love, hate, and despair much as Easterners, but their means of expressing love, hate, and despair, and especially their motivations for these emotions, are not universal.

Literature is one of the best evidences for this distinction between cultures. The spectacular differences between Western novels, drama, and art and their Chinese and Japanese counterparts will not be detailed here, as they have been discussed elsewhere (Hsu, 1970: 17-41; 1971b: 38-40; 1975: 16-23). Briefly, the two outstanding psychological characteristics of Western and American novels and drama are individualist ambitions and preoccupation with sex. Individualist ambitions express themselves as characters in search of identity, such as Holden Caulfield in *Catcher in the Rye*; as characters who go it alone to prove themselves by conquest, such as Captain Ahab in *Moby Dick* or "the Old Man" in *The Old Man and The Sea*; or as characters striving to be something they can never be, such as Herzog in *Herzog*. There are other even more purely individualist manifestations such as *Papillon* or *On the Road*, but they are not substantively different from the varieties already named.

Preoccupation with sex expresses itself either in romance as an end in itself under the veil of puritanical repression (overcoming all difficulties so that the lovers can come together without reference to their social propriety) or in proliferation of the sensuous and the pornographic in the name of sexual liberation (as is happening today). But puritanical repression and sexual liberation are two sides of the same coin. The simple psychological truth is that denial is one way of underlining a subject, as for example in the Christian myth of the Virgin Birth. Furthermore, the two characteristics of Western and American novels and drama—individualist ambitions and preoccupation with sex—are also part and parcel of each other. Of all emotions and experiences, the sexual is among the most privatized. Is it any wonder, then, that social researchers of recent trends tell us that today's youths are more interested in the intensity of relationships than in their durability?

Individualist ambitions and preoccupation with sex lead to contradictions and unexpected consequences. For example, conformity is anathema to the individualist. He considers it degrading; it makes him not true to himself. But Americans are among the most conforming in the world. All that "keep up with the Joneses" and what William H. Whyte, Jr., described in his *The Organization Man* (1956) and David Riesman in his *The Lonely Crowd* (1950:11-26) attest to the reality of this conformity. All sorts of tortuous devices have been offered to explain this contradiction, including "paradoxes" (Cuber and Harper, 1948:369), the "inherently dualistic nature of Americanism" (Laski, 1948:738), or the "changing American character" (Riesman, 1950). To the contrary, American conformity is nothing but a result of intensified individualism.

It is obvious that no one can stand alone. When individualist ambitions deny the basic importance of other human beings in one's life, one cannot be sure of where he is—whether in ascribed or achieved relationships. And that, we know, is insecurity. Such circumstances motivate the individual in a perpetual attempt not only to compete with his fellow human beings, but also to belong to status-giving groups. As a means of attaining these ends, the individual conforms to the customs and fads of the peer group that are vital to his climbing and/or status position at any given time and place.

In other words, intensified individualism leads to its exact opposite. Or as expressed in the jargon of science, there tends to be a direct relationship between individualism and conformity. The stronger the one, the stronger the other.

Another unexpected consequence is the link between preoccupation with sex and discrimination against women. Under our egalitarian ideals, the demand for woman's liberation is a foregone conclusion. But in spite of such ideals, American women have suffered from an extraordinary degree of discrimination by American males. Women doctors were once refused admission to the American Medical Association; women lawyers had great trouble in joining the American Bar

Association; and women had to fight for their fundamental right to the American ballot box. Wives of American political leaders are evaluated as to their beauty and their involvement in charity, but none has gained great power in her own right. Now and then a woman presides over a corporation, but there is not, at this writing, even a single female president of a bank (Hsu, 1970:53-57).

My prediction is that under intensified individualism there will not, in the foreseeable future, be a woman president or even vice-president of the United States, regardless of what people say in response to sociologists' surveys. (It has become fashionable to say or not to say certain things.) Most American women will remain "Uncle Toms" and they, too, will not vote for a female chief executive. The situation in the United States is in sharp contrast to that in far less industrially advanced societies where women have attained high public power—Madame Chiang in Taiwan, Madame Mao in the Peoples' Republic of China, Mrs. Indira Gandhi of India, Mrs. Bandaranaike of Sri Lanka, Madame Nhu in South Vietnam, and Madame Bing of North Vietnam. In the Western world Golda Meier is the only exception.

Obviously, this condition does not exist because American females lack ability. As long as our culture is preoccupied with sex, we are not easily going to eliminate the discrimination against women. American males will always feel, consciously or unconsciously, that female professionals and colleagues present unfair competition by virtue of traditionally being the sex objects.

The Shrinkage of Affect

The most widespread and unforeseen result of the drive for individualist ambitions and preoccupation with sex are first, the shrinkage of affect, and, second, the separation of affect from role altogether.

Shrinkage of affect takes a variety of forms: loyalty becomes scarce, friendship turns shallow, people refuse to consider each others' needs or to be involved in their affairs. It is also linked to the fact that American males have a strong aversion to physical contact with each other. In contrast to males in most of the world except the English, American males can only accept close bodily contact in emergencies (such as mouth-to-mouth resuscitation) or in certain sports (such as wrestling). The inability to make close bodily contact is only the external symptom of an inner inability to form deep friendships. American men simply cannot be sentimental toward each other. They will combine to conquer the external world, but they must shun lasting and undying attachment to each other.

Why? The answer, of course, lies in their conscious or unconscious fear of homosexuality. If sex is everywhere, then the only safe area for intimacy is between members of the opposite sex. This is why Holden Caulfield, the young hero in J. D. Salinger's *Catcher in the Rye*, bolted out of his favorite teacher's apartment with haste when he found the older man sitting on the edge of his couch and stroking his hair. This is also what the other itinerant farm laborers suspected when, in John Steinbeck's *Of Mice and Men*, they questioned Lenny and George as to how long they had been traveling together. The more our culture is preoccupied with sex, whether repressed or openly flaunted, the less Americans of the same sex will be able to develop and maintain *affective* relations with each other. At first this inability was confined to males, but American females have been catching up, so that American females also are afraid to walk hand in hand with each other.

A strong drive toward individualist ambitions must inevitably lead to an atomistic situation in which one man's gain is necessarily seen as another's loss. The individualist man may need others for his rise to power or fame or fortune, but he cannot afford to be loaded with a lot of affective baggage which will slow him down or become stumbling blocks to his status-seeking efforts. This is the basic reason for a phenomenon that Philip Slater (1970) speaks of as *The Pursuit of Loneliness*. Our news media and popular publications are full of stories of the struggles and successes and creative exploits of some single individuals. But what we must realize is that for every girl who is crowned Miss America there will be thousands of disappointed and heartbroken girls. Are we so naive as to think that a society of driving individualists bent on cut-throat competition provides a suitable psychological climate for the defeated or vanquished to love the victorious or for the latter to develop genuine and lasting friendships with the former?

The Defense Against Affectlessness

The distance from the reduction of affective links among human beings to their total elimination is a short one. After all, "business and sentiment don't mix" is a universally accepted American saying. And the emphasis on rationality is that part of the European heritage of which Americans are proud to claim ownership. If affective links are out of the question, the only avenue left is for human beings to externalize their relationships with each other by way of role. That is what constitutes the dehumanization of human relationships.

Human beings cannot live without affect. Many Americans have, therefore, devised a number of defenses. They play their myriad roles in offices, factories, and workshops. Some of them may be devoted to certain tools of their trades, but many think of blue collar crime, and even vandalism and sabotage, as part of the order of nature, and they feel they must avoid sentimentality toward their bosses, subordinates, colleagues, and coworkers. For affective outlets they must look elsewhere. Work for them is therefore only a means, not an end in itself. The work situation is where many Americans suffer so that they can get or maintain something they really love.

The resort to material Great Walls and formal church or other club affiliations is another and far more widespread method of defense against affectlessness. This is why profit has priority over questions of human misery or other social ills, and why church exclusiveness is more important than church spirit or the brotherhood of man. Since "business and sentiment don't mix," can we allow affective considerations to stand in the way of the size of our enterprises' profits or the national ratings of our churches?

Another mode of defense against affectlessness is the love of people and causes, preferably distant people such as jungle-people and abstract causes, including freedom of the Tibetans and democracy in Chile. There are still many Americans who want to better the lot of the Chinese, if not to Christianize them at least to worry about the seeming lack of romantic love among their young. I suspect Linus of Peanuts comic fame once stated this psychology with some honesty: "I love mankind but I hate human beings."

Yet another defense against the scarcity of affect is to lavish affect on the totally controllable: pets and/or inanimate objects such as curios, rare editions, bottle caps, duck decoys (I once went to a convention of duck decoy collectors in a Chicago hotel)—the list is endless. Even the casual viewer of TV cannot fail to note that dog and cat food ads outrank all others in frequency. In addition, we not only have animal hospitals and animal beauty parlors but also restaurants whose clientele is exclusively pets, and pet cemeteries that are segregated.

It was Mark Twain, I believe, who once said something like "The more I look at human beings, the more I like dogs." But I think Mark Twain said this after he found out how crafty, vicious and unpredictable his fellow human beings were. Those who profess a preference for pets over human beings, or think that they can get along fine sitting on their pile of material wealth, really prefer human company. Silas Marner in George Eliot's celebrated novel certainly felt he was more than well recompensed for the loss of his gold when the little girl appeared at his door.

Externalization of All Human Relations

The net result of all these systems of defense is the escalation of role and increasing externalized inducements or restraints. As an example, take our approach to crime and violence. In 1974, then Attorney General William Saxbe said in Chicago that the core of our crime problem was the "habitual offender," who should be rooted out. In an address to the International Association of Chiefs of Police in Washington a few weeks later, President Ford echoed the same line by announcing a "program to take 'career criminals' . . . out of circulation."[2]

Our leaders are merely mouthing the basic American psychocultural trend: shrinkage of affect and externalization of all human relations. A look across the country will reveal that the main approach held by those grappling with the crime and violence problem centers on increasing escalation and sophistication of external surveillance, detection, and control, but little or nothing else: more secure locks and fences, more hidden cameras, more guards, more electronic alarms and other devices, and so forth. Yet, the alarming increase in crime and violence in our society continues month after month and year after year. To quote statistics on the subject is an elaboration of the obvious. The creativeness of the externalized means for stopping crime and violence will surely be matched or outmatched by the creativeness of those bent on breaking the law.

Another example of externalized inducements is in the area of civil rights. Blacks have been emancipated since the Civil War. Some one hundred years later the Supreme Court handed down its decision on school integration. But twenty years after the Supreme Court decision, school integration is still a big problem in many areas of the United States, not to speak of biases in connection with jobs, residence, and membership in clubs. This state of affairs is not the result of a lack of educative and propagandistic efforts or of energetic and democratic-minded leaders and workers who labor in the desired direction. Turn on the TV set today and you are as likely to see black faces as white faces. The core of the problem is that role arrangements have been modified by the Court decisions on integration and busing, but our patterns of affect have lagged way behind. That is why we have racial riots in schools and the sorrowful mess in South Boston today.

Currently, a whole series of what one reporter dubbed "60-second brotherhood" TV commericals has been aired, financed by HEW and produced by the University of Chicago's Media Center. One of these commercials features three black basketball players and one lone white player in a school locker room after a game. The three Blacks joke about the game and the white boy laughs along. Suddenly one of the Blacks turns to him and says coldly, "What are you laughing at, honky?"

Bob Greene of the Chicago *Sun-Times* [3] described the tapes as "a last-ditch effort to try to bring some understanding and order into public school desegregation," by demonstrating "to students how badly they are capable of acting toward one another and perhaps help convince them to think twice about what is going on." I do not agree with Greene's statement that the tapes "are necessary; unfortunately, there doesn't seem to be much question about that." There is no question about the problem the tapes aim to eradicate, but I do not think they will be effective in decreasing the problems of school desegregation any more than films and lectures have been in decreasing drug addiction and the spead of VD.

Although I view such measures for reducing antisocial acts and for generating enthusiasm for socially desired ends as useless, I understand why our lawmen, educators, and public officials have such great faith in them. Shrinkage of affect, separation of affect from role, and the externalization of all human relations have led them to nowhere else. This is the social context in which public relations (PR) is all important, in which high officials of the Department of Agriculture could seriously propose a plan to send among the people a song-and-prayer tent show to convince them that food prices are not all that bad.[4]

Affectlessness and Social Unpredictability

In the normal course of events, every society is held together by two kinds of "glue." The "role glue" enables its members to do business with each other and to meet the society's necessary and usual functional requirements. The "affect glue" generates in its members devotion, loyalty, succorance, sympathy, love, and charity to each other and to ideals, institutions, and great men and women. The role glue is often discontinuous and is certainly subject to change without notice, but the affect glue is typically continuous and sudden alteration creates emotional upheaval. An utmost case of pure affect in action is that of Romeo and Juliet; the opposite case of pure role in action is that of the Midnight Cowboy and any of his clients.

The affect approach may invade an otherwise role domain, as in nepotism, or as when Admiral Nogi, the commander-in-chief of the Japanese naval forces which defeated Imperial Russia (1904-1905), committed hara-kari to follow his Emperor Meiji in death. In American society, the role approach has invaded and predominated over affect domains, so that nearly all human relations tend to take on business characteristics, to be handled by PR techniques, to be subject to change without notice and, therefore, freed from the ethical rules inherent in human relations but not inherent in man's dealings with objects.

To put it simply, a man who thinks of new ways of taking advantage of his friends used to be regarded as a skunk. Now that the role approach is predominant, however, the man who can get more out of his friends by trickery is doing good business. He, too, will be seen as clever and creative.

Social Stability and Cultural Progress

When we devise new ways of taking advantage of animals and objects, the most the animals and objects can do is to die or get exhausted. They cannot fight back. Even though animals have feelings, we can have them confined, control-bred, artificially increased or decreased, and conditioned in the manner of Skinner's pigeons or Harlow's monkeys. But humans develop resentment and hatred when they are outsmarted and they can and will take steps to outsmart the outsmarters or find their own victims for an emotional outlet. They will escalate the use of snooping devices because they need to know even what their close associates are up to, not merely their adversaries. They will escalate the employment of security, accounting, and detection equipment and personnel because they fear dirty tricks or open sources of bodily or other harm. They will form more and more interest and lobby groups to fight other interest and lobby groups. The result is a society in which all members have to be watchful of each other because most of them are, or are suspected to be, something of the proverbial used car dealer or worse.

It is often decried that America lacks discipline. This is not true; there is ample evidence of discipline in American life. Take a look at the Outer Drive of Chicago and its thousands of cars which ply at high speed twenty-four hours a day. This would be impossible without discipline. Our huge hotels, offices, government, waterworks, and mines cannot be run without discipline. In fact, no human endeavors can be accomplished without it.

What is wrong is that our discipline is more and more being externally imposed, and less and less out of respect or care for others—for their rights, their safety, and their happiness. Driving within a speed limit so that the police will not catch you is one thing, while doing so from a wish not to injure someone is quite another. Operating a machine strictly according to instructions for fear of its blowing up in your face in the manner of Alex Inkeles' "Industrial Man" is one thing, while doing so because you wish the factory well is quite another. We emphasize rules of survival, not rules of morality, as Dr. Sanford has done in his presentation.

In this context, our egalitarian ideal cannot but exacerbate the socially deleterious effects of shrinkage of affect and expansion of role. Given a society which feeds its young a steady diet of success stories and the notion that everyone can be president, the number of people who will raise their sights will be great. There will be more and more people who aspire to be more clever and more creative than others, and success includes the ability to commit crimes without being caught. That is precisely the kind of reason many gave for not wanting to condemn Nixon. "Why should I! I would have done the same thing." That is why we witness so many senseless "Bonnie and Clyde" type murders. Only the other day two young convicts were interviewed on a TV show. They robbed and then ran over their victims with a car. Asked whether they would do it again, they both answered yes without any remorse. Why should they do otherwise? Is shooting animals a crime or immoral?

In every society, the truly creative and daring who exercise their talents for socially desirable ends are the minority. This is the case whether we think of art and literature, or science and technology, or politics, business, religion, and philosophy. I do not mean to denigrate the majority and say they do not count. But the majority are usually too normal, too lacking in obsession with single objectives, and too enmeshed in the nitty-gritty of their daily lives to stick their necks out. They are too tied down by inertia to achieve something that will make large differences to the society as a whole.

In every society, the truly creative and daring who exercise their talents for antisocial ends are also the minority. The men who run the Mafia and other gangster organizations must be regarded as entrepreneurs. The various successful men and women who think of and execute schemes to defraud the government and their fellow citizens, such as successful kidnappers, embezzlers, and hijackers, are men and women of above average ingenuity and courage. But compared to the entire population they are still a minority.

Furthermore, even if all police and other external restraints are suddenly absent (as when the Batista forces withdrew from Havana before the coming of Castro's forces, or during any riot in the United States), the individuals who go out to rape and to loot are the minority. The majority will shun such opportunities for illegal acts or gains. Instead, they tend to shut themselves behind their closed doors and hope for the coming of some new leaders who will bring about law and order so that they can return to their former peaceful lives.

But it is the minorities who make the big difference to the majority. One Alexander Graham Bell, one Benjamin Franklin, or one Albert Einstein makes a tremendous difference to the lives of millions, as would one Adolf Hilter, one Richard Nixon, or one group of hard core members of the Mafia. In fact, even one gunman at large in Evanston, Illinois, can terrorize the whole town of 80,000.

What confronts us today as we complete our two-hundredth year as a nation is that individualism with its attending corollaries of driving initiative and cut-throat competition has gone beyond a point of no return.

These psychocultural characteristics have given Western men their singleness of purpose and their absolute zeal in pursuing many objectives of which they may be proud: conquest of space, exploration of the high seas, spreading social benefits through their missionizing spirit, elimination of poverty and disease via science and technology, and more. They have also given Western men the same singleness of purpose and the same zeal in pursuing other objectives from which they themselves and the rest of the world have suffered and are still suffering: the Inquisition and the witchhunts, the many Crusades, organized slavery on a scale mankind had not seen before, genocide in the name of maintaining racial purity, and the spread of democracy and freedom of which My Lai was but the tiniest known episode.

With shrinkage of the affect domain and escalation of the role approach to all human relations, the number of the beneficially creative and daring has greatly increased (and that feeds cultural progress). Unfortunately, the number of creative and daring bent on antisocial purposes has also increased greatly (and that undermines social stability). Since many antisocial acts of creativity and daring are easier to accomplish than socially beneficial ones (instant fame for Evel Knievel and for the assassins of Martin Luther King and President Kennedy, as contrasted to the usually many years of drudgery and work before an invention or discovery or even a Ph.D. in anthropology is possible), can we blame self-reliant men if they prefer to seek the greatest returns for the smallest investments rather than vice versa?

Individual Fulfillment or Individual Aggrandizement

In thinking about the meaning of individual fulfillment, I find an old formula by William James unsurpassed: Happiness equals Performance over Aspiration ($H = \frac{P}{A}$).[5] In the light of the above discussion, the aspirations of a majority of Americans have gone up dramatically, but performance often fails to match these heightened aspirations. The yield of happiness at the other end of the equation is therefore understandably unimpressive.

How heightened some of their aspirations have become is illustrated by a recent news report in *Time* under its "Education" section.[6] A professor was found to hold three "full-time" positions—one at California State College, sixty-five miles south of Pittsburgh; another at Bronx Community College in New York City; and a third at State University of New York at New Paltz, New York. He secretly commuted some 400 miles per week. Students noted he was sometimes late for classes or absent from them. The *Time* reporter compared his "accomplishments" with those of Alex Guiness in *The Captain's Paradise*. The most outlandish aspect of this episode was that when the professor was caught and forced to resign from two of the institutions, he "indignantly" asked, "What if a Picasso wanted to teach at Bronx College, New Paltz, and State College? Do you think he would be denied?"

My question is, what will happen to our society if all the professors (and all the janitors, carpenters, employees of all the corporations, and all mothers) think they are Picassos, and each takes special privileges and liberties unilaterally?

Industrialization and Mobility Not the Causes

From what has been written in this volume and written and taught by my fellow social scientists, I gather they believe there is a simple answer for the problems outlined here. They will see all of them, including depersonalization, as the results of industrialization with its corollaries of mobility and modernization.

All this enthusiasm for industrialization as a prime mover of social and cultural changes is misplaced. It is based on the same Western fallacy of another era, namely, that Christianization of the world was the road to free mankind from greed and violence and war. Western men took to both Christianity and industrialization because both were consonant with the requirements of their pattern of Psychosocial Homeostasis.[7] Most of the world has rejected Christianity, even when it has been forced on them by the West, and they have only begun seriously to consider industrialization because their only alternative to it is Western domination or extinction.

The germs of the so-called changes brought about by industrialization were inherent in the West's psychocultural orientation long before the appearance of Christianity or the Industrial Revolution. In fact, we can go straight to the myth of Noah and the flood.

To punish the wickedness of men, God decided to flood the earth and to kill all except the chosen man Noah and his immediate family. Noah made an ark into which he packed his wife, his three sons and their wives, together with seven pairs of all "clean" animals and one pair of all other animals. After they floated around for some forty days, the flood subsided and the ark landed on Ararat where Noah at once thanked the Lord by appropriate rituals. Next, Noah drank the wine he had made and, while under the influence of liquor, he did something sexual in his tent.[8] Ham laughed at his father's condition and called in his two brothers. They all expressed disgust toward Noah and covered him up. A quarrel between father and sons then ensued. Noah cursed Ham and condemned his son Canaan and future descendants to be eternal slaves, but he blessed Shem and Japheth and told them to disperse in their separate ways to people the earth.

This celebrated Western myth contains all the ingredients of what some social scientists claim to be the results of industrialization: the generation gap, brittleness of kinship bonds, sex, violence, and high mobility. Ham was not alone in not revering his father; earlier, when the flood came, Noah left his own parents to perish. Moreover, his son's lack of reverence for him was more than matched by Noah's vindictiveness toward his own flesh and blood. The evidence for mobility is equally strong. Not only did Noah and his family escape the disaster by boat, but also they never returned to their old home after the flood waters subsided. What is more, even though they were the last eight people left in the world, Noah and his kin could not stay together.

Finally, in this myth there is even clear indication of Western absolutism, in which role approach has erased all affect considerations: a God who decided on his own a final solution, a solution that some other notorious dictator was later to attempt on the Jews. Myth is not, of course, reality. But myths, like art, not only inform an audience of traditional values, but projectively reflect the fantasies of the people and, as such, represent a kind of waking-dream fulfillment (Mitchell and Schwartz, 1974:134). The myth of Noah and the flood has particular importance to Western society because it is still being taught in churches and schools, dramatized on the stage, thematized in literature, and serialized in comics. Such a myth is at least as reliable an index to how people feel about themselves, about each other, and about the rest of the world as the results of public opinion polls, or even some of our scholarly questionnaires.

There are two kinds of support for this contention. For three years, I performed a little experiment in three separate classes of mine at Northwestern University (1968 and 1971) and at the University of Hawaii (1969). A total of 114 students were involved. I asked my students to exercise their wildest imagination and rewrite the story of Noah and the flood with plots entirely different from the version they knew so well.

None of the 114 stories I received deviated seriously from the Old Testament model, not even those by my respondents at the University of Hawaii, about one-third of whom were of Asian extraction (Hsu, 1974:164-176).

The other kind of support for my contention becomes evident when we view this Western myth cross-culturally and realize how the contents of its Chinese counterpart point to a totally different pattern of affect, also under no influence of modern industrialization.

In the reign of Emperor Yao (c. 2357-2258 B.C.), a terrible flood devastated the country. Yao appointed a certain Kun to control the flood but Kun, after nine years of work, was unsuccessful. Yao took full responsibility, resigned from office, and offered the throne to Shun (said to have reigned between 2258 and 2206 B.C.). Emperor Shun executed Kun for his failure but appointed the executed man's son Yu in his place. Yu worked over all the country for thirteen years, during which he passed by his wife's door three times. Being absorbed in his official duties, Yu did not once go in to see his wife. After Yu's success, Emperor Shun gave Yu his throne. Yu became the next emperor, thus exonerating the name of his father, and the Chinese lived happily ever after.

The Chinese myth reveals a pattern of how the Chinese feel about themselves, about each other, and about the rest of the world, which is very different from that revealed by its Western counterpart. For one thing, the Chinese legend names no chosen man; instead, all Chinese suffer from the disaster together. It does not provide for escape by boat to a new world; instead, all Chinese stay where they were born and raised and do the best they can. There is no question of sons going in different directions from their parents; instead, the son works hard to succeed where his father failed. In his toils, Yu does not visit his wife even when convenient, for larger duty takes precedence over matters of his own heart. Finally, it is most significant that the supernatural has no place in this Chinese myth, and that there are no gods who would impose the final solution on all Chinese as punishment for their evil ways.

Industrialization did not shape the Western myth of Noah any more than it did the Chinese myth of Yu. In either case, the myths contained important psychocultural germs that were to unfold, spread, and proliferate in their respective societies and cultures independent of economic developments.

In the light of our analysis, the well-known concept of Economic Man which explicitly governed the thinking of Western political economists in another era has not really died. May we say that emerging today is an old Western wine contained in a new Western bottle?

Kinship and Affect

The real hothouse for patterns of affect in each society is the kinship system, at the core of which is the nuclear family. The kinship system is the first web of human relationships of the individual. It sets the basic feeling tone and establishes the affective foundation for all subsequent interpersonal patterns because it comes first, because it catches the individual *tabula rasa,* and because it conditions the individual when his or her cerebral development is faster than at any later time. The kinship system is the psychic cell of every society. It holds the key to social and cultural development in the same sense that the germ cell holds the key to the biological organism and provides us with some idea of what the growing animal is going to be like (Hsu, 1971a:3-29).

Regrettably, in spite of much scholarly attention to the kinship system, its real significance vis-à-vis varieties of human society and culture has yet to be understood. Sociologists tend to see American and Western developments as pan-human. Anthropologists concede more importance to cross-cultural variations, but most of them still hold the economic factor ("maintenance systems," "ecology," "poverty," "climate,") as the prime determinant of kinship practices and behavior (Harrington and Whiting, 1972:469-501; and Hsu, 1973a:1-19). Psychoanalysts not only fail to see that their supposedly universally applicable theoretical gyrations are based on Western individualism, but they also confuse individual behavior and problems with those of society and culture (Hsu, 1971b:23-44).

The pace at which the shrinkage of affect leads to more and more externalization of human relationships is likely to be quickened unless we become less obsessed with economic, technological, or other nonhuman solutions to human problems.

NOTES

1. William Greider, *Washington Post.* Reprinted in *Chicago Sun Times,* August 1, 1974.
2. Reported in *Chicago Sun-Times,* September 25, 1974.
3. October 6, 1974.
4. Reported in the news media on about September 26, 1974.
5. I use the term *Aspiration* to replace the word *Pretension* used by William James in his original.
6. September 1, 1974, p. 64.
7. For an exposition of the concept of Psychosocial Homeostasis (PSH) and how it operates to produce the major Western and American social and cultural characteristics, see Hsu (1971b:23-41 and 1973a:4-14).
8. Many interpretations exist concerning exactly what occurred when the

younger man first encountered his father in the tent. In the post-King James versions of the Bible or the Torah, Noah is described as being naked, after becoming intoxicated by the wine he made, and thus exposing himself to Ham. The many interpreters' works generally speak of drunkenness and nakedness as *the* sin that Noah committed, of how that sin was but a momentary weakness after the man had shouldered the burden of the great flood, and of how he should be forgiven. (See, e.g., the *Interpreter's Bible,* compiled with Exegesis and Exposition under an editorial board led by George Arthur Buttrick as Commentary Editor, 1952, pp. 554-555.) But if we accept the statement that Noah merely exposed himself in his drunken condition, as various modern versions of the Bible and Torah would have it, it becomes puzzling that Noah should be so angry with Ham and inflict such severe punishment on his own flesh and blood, his grandson Canaan, and future descendants.

Furthermore, even in the *Interpreter's Bible* referred to above, the author or authors of the "Exposition" portion speak about Noah's "own impulses and appetites" and then go on as follows: ". . . and the same man who has been magnificent in public affairs may fall into ignominy in his private life. Samson was invincible against the Philistines, but he had no defense against Delilah. Anthony had an empire in his grasp, but he lost it in the snares of Cleopatra" (ibid., p. 555). It is hard to imagine why a case of mere drunkenness and nakedness in the privacy of one's own tent should have elicited comparisons with cases in which men destroyed themselves because of seduction by women.

Finally, my observation that Noah "did something sexual" is also based on the following considerations. Many Dutch people over forty-five years of age with whom I have come into contact believe that Noah was masturbating. Note 22, on p. 47 of the Chumash Chumashi Torah (The Five Books of the Torah, also known as *The Foncino Chumash,* published by Jewish Publication Society, Philadelphia, 1950), contains these lines: "Some say that he castrated him; others that he indulged a perverted lust upon him." I realize that the Old Testament is a conglomeration of many pieces of tales of different ages and from different sources and that, therefore, it cannot be expected to be totally consistent and logical. But I also presume that the old Jewish teachers of the Torah would hardly have commented the way they did had such thoughts been totally absent from their minds.

Youth Character and Changing Political Culture in America

6

GABRIEL A. ALMOND

In the quiet of contemporary university life, it is difficult to believe that just a few short years ago our campuses were the scenes of bullhorn confrontations, bombings, police charges, window crashing, and even killings. The copious literature on the student rebellion and the counterculture was produced in the heat of the events themselves, and principally by participants or scholars directly affected by them. So great has been the relief over the subsidence of the rebellion that even curiosity about its causation and significance has now dwindled to almost nothing. A few years ago it was impossible to discuss anything else at academic dinner tables; today the student rebellion has practically become a nonsubject.

What caused it? And does it have any long-run significance?

Social scientists were poorly prepared to deal with the campus phenomena of the 1960s. The prevailing theories of political socialization and political culture had no place for such tidal waves of youth rebellion. These theories had arisen out of an interaction of three developments in the social sciences. The first of these developments was psychoanthropology, which brought the clinical insights of psychoanalysis to bear on the study of child-rearing practices and their relationship to cultural patterns and values. The second was Weberian sociological theory, which, elaborated in the work of Parsons, stressed the importance of the subjective side of culture for the processes of social change and introduced a theory of historical modernization in which secularization and rationalization were central themes. The third development was the invention of modern social science research methodology—sample surveys, sophisticated interviewing, rigorous data analysis, statistical techniques, and the like.

The psychoanthropological part of this heritage led to conceptual models stressing childhood and adolescent socialization as an explanation for the persistence of cultural patterns. The Weberian-Parsonian part of the heritage stressed the interrelationship of the modern social and political structural tendencies of industrialization, urbanization, bureaucratization, mass political organization, mass education and communications, with the cultural tendencies of secularization, achievement motivation, and participant propensities. These two intellectual traditions suggested the research designs that were employed in the empirical studies of political socialization and political culture that began to proliferate in the 1960s.

The socialization literature tended to view youth as an adaptive and assimilative phase in the life cycle in which the young acquire the skills, attitudes, and expectations appropriate to their roles in society. Associated with this process during the immediately preadult or adolescent years, there is a certain amount of experimental, resistant, and disruptive behavior, a conflict-filled period of "coming of age." To come of age implies giving things up, "settling down," taking on disciplines and responsibilities, all of which tend to produce uncertainty, anxiety, and rebellion. The political aspect of youth in this model of the socialization process is a tendency toward hypo- and hyperactivity. Studies of political participation (see Nie, 1974) show that the rates of voting and the like among young people tend to be low compared to those of the older generations. But youth is also a time of openness to political novelty. Young people tend to be more liberal and idealistic in their political views (see Milbrath, 1965; Lane, 1959).

Studies of political culture change did not attribute any particular innovative role to youth. Surveys of attitudes and statistical studies of social change emphasized broader trends of modernization contributing to the emergence of an increasingly secular, worldwide political culture based upon industrialization, urbanization, the spread of mass media, and modern education, and producing a more participant, pragmatic, and pluralistic political culture. The flower of this literature was the "end of ideology" hypothesis (Bell, 1960), which predicted a gradual trend toward incrementalism and peaceful bargaining processes in the solution of political conflicts.

The ink was hardly dry on this "end of ideology" hypothesis before events began to challenge it. The younger age groups throughout the advanced industrial world, particularly in the United States, pitted themselves against the dominant political culture and for a period of five years challenged the adult world and behaved in ways that confounded the social and political theorists. It seemed for a while that youth was creating the political culture and that the adult society was adapting to it.

Three different kinds of literature were produced in partial response to these events: (1) a romantic, prophetic current typified in the work of Theodore Roszak (1969) and Charles Reich (1970); (2) a revisionist social science critique attacking the prevailing notions of political culture and socialization as well as the model of a stable society, functionalism, pluralism, incrementalism, pragmatism, and the like, typified in the work of Gouldner (1970), Hymes (1972), Lowi (1969), and others; and (3) a speculative-historical-empirical polemic regarding the prospects of advanced industrial society and the significance of the "great disturbances" of the 1960s. The conflicting points of view engaged in this polemic sought to interpret these youth phenomena by varying combinations of three explanatory principles. Roszak, Reich, and others come close to a pure cultural revolution explanation, viewing the youth mobilization and counterculture as a dialectical rejection of the establishment culture, and as moving man to a higher cultural and spiritual level. Inglehart (1971) and Yankelovich (1972), reporting results from attitude surveys during the events of the late 1960s, offered some support for this generational-discontinuity, cultural revolution interpretation. We shall present and discuss their evidence at a later point.

The third explanatory principle stressed life-cycle phenomena as the major cause of the student rebellions of the 1960s. Lewis Feuer (1969) comes close to this opinion, though he does include some specific "period effects" that may impart explosiveness to these life-cycle phenomena. Feuer finds in an historical study of student movements, including the rebellions of the 1960s, a general tendency toward "elitism, suicidalism, populism, filiarchy and juvenocracy" which intermittently combined with a "de-authoritization" of the older generation to produce explosive and violent youth politicization. He rejects an out-and-out "Oedipal determinism," offering instead the hypothesis of an endemic generational conflict that may be mitigated, if not dispelled, by understanding. The student revolts of the 1960s are thus explained by reference to these inherent generational conflict impulses, multiplied and accentuated by the loss of confidence in adult authority resulting from the black rebellion and the Vietnam War.

Seymour M. Lipset offers a combination of life-cycle, period, and generational effects to illuminate the dimensions of the youth rebellion, particularly its impingement on university campuses in the 1960s. In Lipset's review of the history of student movements and youth politicization, historical events such as the Revolution of 1848, World War I, and the depression intermittently combine with life-cycle propensities to produce student movements of an explosive sort, though he argues that the scale, extent, and duration of the recent rebellion were greater than any of the earlier manifestations. In arguing the case for generational change, he points out that in the last decade the size of the youth cohort relative to the population as a whole has increased substantially, and that the proportion of that age cohort moving into higher education has similarly increased substantially. The historical experiences and memories of these student generations may affect their attitudes for a long time to come, but he points to evidence suggesting a tendency toward the attenuation of these liberal-activist impulses as these age cohorts mature (Lipset and Schaflander, 1971:236).

Now that we have the advantage of a time perspective and now that passions have cooled, perhaps we can assemble the pieces of the puzzle in a more orderly and satisfying way than the earlier interpreters could. An eclectic explanatory strategy is followed here. First, we examine demographic, sociological, and cultural trends affecting the life situations and contexts of choice of young people, and then we review the salient events and issues impinging on them. Taken together, these sociological trends and political experiences enable us to view value and attitude changes among young people as being constrained and conditioned by structural and cultural developments. We can also study the changes from a problem-solving perspective. The evidence on value and attitude change can be evaluated as transitory and responsive to immediate historical stimuli, or as having possible long-run implications based on enduring social changes or lasting political issues.

Demographic, Sociological, and Cultural Trends Affecting Youth

A demographic and sociological profile of those Americans fifteen to twenty-four years of age as of the 1970 census is given in Table 1. These 35 million young people were born during the years 1946-1955. The oldest cohort would have been of college age in 1964, at the beginning of the Berkeley rebellion. The median age groups born in 1950-1951 would have been of college age in 1968 and 1969 during the peak of the college disorders.

TABLE 1.
Size of the Youth Cohort in the American Population, 1950-1970

AGE COHORT	*1950*	*1960*	*1970*
Number of persons aged 15-24	23,000,000	24,000,000	35,500,000
Percentage of persons aged 15-24 in total population	15	13	17
Ratio of persons aged 15-24 to persons aged 25-64	1:3.5	1:3.5	1:2.6

SOURCE: Adapted from U.S. Department of Commerce, Bureau of Census, *General Population Characteristics, U.S. Summary*, January 1972, pp. 1-259, and U.S. Department of Commerce, Bureau of Census, *Statistical Abstracts of the United States, 1952*, p. 134.

One of the most important characteristics of this youth cohort in the late 1960s was its rapid growth, both absolutely and as a proportion of the population. In 1960, it constituted 13 percent of the total population, while in 1970, it had risen to 17 percent, an increase of almost one-third. The ratio of these youth cohorts to the older, active population (ages twenty-five to sixty-four) was sharply rising during this decade. While in 1950 for every individual between the ages of fifteen and twenty-four there were 3.5 individuals in the age cohorts twenty-five to sixty-four, and while this proportion remained constant in 1960, the ratio of youth to active adults had increased to 1:2.6 by 1970.

This demographic evidence suggests that for this generation there was a significant shortage of experienced older persons and an oversupply of peers. For this generation the objective opportunities for interaction and communication with older, more experienced persons had seriously declined, while the opportunities for peer group interaction and communication had sharply increased. Based on this evidence, it is safe to assume that peer group socialization would acquire greater importance and that adult-youth socialization would attenuate. Peer group socialization tends to accentuate the life-cycle propensites of the particular age cohort involved. For adolescents this would mean the accentuation and proliferation of rebellious tendencies, enthusiasm, idealism, and experimentalism.

TABLE 2.
Percentage of Arrests by Age Cohort Compared with Percentage of Age Cohort in Total Population

AGE COHORT	*1960*		*1970*	
	Population	*Arrests* [1]	*Population*	*Arrests*
Under 14	29	6	26	9
14-17	6	9	8	16
18-24	9	16	12	27
25-34	13	21	12	17
35 and over	43	48	42	31
Total	100	100	100	100

SOURCE: Adapted from U.S. Department of Commerce, Bureau of Census, *Statistical Abstracts of the United States, 1974* (Washington, D.C.: U.S. Government Printing Office, 1974); and from Department of Justice, FBI, *Uniform Crime Reports for the U.S., 1960, 1970* (Washington, D.C.: U.S. Government Printing Office, 1961, 1971).

1. Arrests for 1960 are reported for under 15 years of age.

The unusually rebellious nature of this generation is shown in Table 2, which reports statistics of arrests among various age groups in 1960 and 1970. The age cohort eighteen to twenty-four constituted 9 percent of the population in 1960 and contributed 16 percent of the arrests; in 1970, it had grown to 12 percent of the total population but was involved in 27 percent of the arrests. Its percentage of the population had increased by a third, while its percentage of arrests had increased by more than two-thirds. A similarly sharp disproportionate increase in arrests occurred among those between the ages of fourteen and seventeen. These increases are only partly attributable to changing patterns of law enforcement and the reporting of enforcement statistics.

These findings lend support to the view that the "baby bulge" of the 1950s, which became the youth bulge of the 1960s, had not only produced a higher proportionate incidence of adolescent clashes with authority, but had also accentuated these tendencies through peer group socialization, a kind of swarming effect.

This big, disorderly generation had grown to adolescence during a period of declining ethical and normative indoctrination and attenuating authority structures. By virtue of its size alone, it would have strained the socializing institutions of family, school, church, and community. But during these decades families, particularly middle-class families, were democratizing, schools were becoming more participant-oriented, and church influence was declining.

That families and schools are becoming less authoritarian and more participant is suggested in Table 3. These trends were reported for all five countries included in the Civic Culture study (Great Britain, Germany, Italy, Mexico, and the United States), but the highest percentages were reported among the young American respondents (see Almond and Verba, 1963). The younger respondents in this survey were recalling family and school atmospheres during the 1940s and 1950s. There is reason to believe that this trend continued for the age cohort that was adolescent and attending school during the 1960s.

Similarly, the impact of organized religion was attenuating. Thus, Gallup surveys show that, in 1954, 46 percent of a cross-section sam-

TABLE 3.

Percentage Reporting Participation in Family and School in the United States, by Selected Age Groups, 1959-1960

	18-25	*36-40*	*61 and over*
Participated in family decisions at age 16	85	72	48
Ever protested teacher treatment while in school	66	48	29

SOURCE: Adapted from Almond and Verba (1963: 339). See also Glen H. Elder, Jr., "Democratic Parent-Youth Relations in Cross-National Perspective," *Social Science Quarterly* (September 1968): 216ff.

TABLE 4.
Percentage Decline in Church Attendance in the United States, 1954-1970

	1954	*1963*	*1970*
Cross-section			
sample as a whole	46	46	42
By age			
21-29 years	42	41	32
30-49 years	48	47	45
50 and over	46	47	45

SOURCE: From George H. Gallup, *The Gallup Poll*, vols. 1, 2, 3 (New York: Random House, 1972). The question was worded: "Have you attended church within the last seven days?"

ple of Americans reported having attended church within the preceding week (Table 4). While this proportion had only declined to 42 percent in 1970, the drop was most marked among the younger age groups and those receiving higher education. While 45 percent of the respondents aged fifty and over reported attending church in the preceding week, this was true of only 32 percent of the twenty-one to twenty-nine year olds. A survey in 1972 showed a strong relationship between amount of higher education and rate of church attendance (Table 5). Thus, 45 percent of the freshmen respondents in 1972 reported having attended church within the preceding week, compared to only 27 percent of the seniors and 20 percent of the graduate students.

TABLE 5.
Church Attendance, by College Years, 1972, in Percentages

Freshman	45
Sophomore	37
Junior	36
Senior	27
Graduate	20

SOURCE: Gallup Opinion Index No. 80, February 1972.

Thus, the childhood and early adolescence of this bulging age cohort had been marked by a loosening up of the socializing agencies. While the scale and difficulty of the process of socialization of the young had sharply increased, the institutions normally performing these functions were losing some of their authority and indoctrinative capacity.

In addition, there was little disciplinary impact from the economy. From the perspective of this generation, as it entered the high schools, colleges, and graduate schools during the 1960s, their material futures were assured. Access to higher education was open. Per capita income (in constant 1958 dollars) in the United States rose from $1,810 in 1950 to $2,157 in 1960, to $3,043 in 1970 (Table 6). The discipline of the market was lacking; it was a job-hunter's economy. The childhood of these young people had been spent amidst rising affluence and consumerism. Nothing in their own experience suggested an adult day of reckoning.

TABLE 6.
Per Capita GNP and Personal Income in the United States, 1950-1970
(Constant 1958 Dollars)

	1950	*1960*	*1970*
Per capita GNP	2,342	2,699	3,524
Per capita income	1,810	2,157	3,043

SOURCE: U.S. Department of Commerce, Bureau of the Census, *Statistical Abstracts of the United States, 1973,* p. 322.

The Changing Structure and Culture of Higher Education

This raw aggregative account of the sharply increased difficulty and scale of the problem of socialization of youth into American culture, along with the suggested declining effectiveness of the major socializing institutions and experiences, applies to this age cohort as a whole. Of particular interest here is that part of the youth population that attended colleges and universities, since they have been the presumed bearers of cultural innovation. The number of undergraduate students registered for degree credit in institutions of higher education rose from a little over two and one half million in 1950 to over three million in 1960, to over seven million in 1970. The number of graduate students increased from 247,000 in 1950 to 381,000 in 1960, to 551,000 in 1970.

By 1970, more than 40 percent of those aged eighteen to twenty-one were enrolled for degree credit higher education. The absolute numbers tell the story more impressively than do the percentages. A more than doubling of student enrollment in a single decade could not be accommodated without a large increase in educational facilities and faculties. Thus, the number of colleges and universities increased from 1,851 in 1950 to 2,525 in 1970; college and university faculties jumped from a little over a quarter of a million in 1950 to over 550,000 in 1970 (Table 7).

TABLE 7.
Growth in Higher Education in the United States, 1950-1970

		Number	
	1950	*1960*	*1970*
Undergraduate degree credit students in institutions of higher education	2,659,000	3,216,000	7,136,000
Students per hundred persons aged 18-21	28.58	34.86	44.43
Graduate students	237,000	342,000	828,000
Colleges and universities	1,851	2,008	2,525
Faculty members	247,000	381,000	551,000

SOURCE: U.S. Department of Commerce, Bureau of Census, *Statistical Abstracts of the United States, 1973,* p. 131.

At the same time that the physical dimensions of higher education were rapidly increasing, the culture and social structure of these educational institutions were undergoing significant changes. The triumph of the scientific revolution brought with it a rapid increase in the research and graduate training activities of faculties, a rapid proliferation of specialized and technical courses, as well as a growth of para-faculties in the form of research and teaching assistants (Smelser, 1974). In this context, the exposure of a large proportion of students to senior and experienced faculty, and to ideal-setting, synthesizing, and evaluative educational experiences was declining.

Along with this shift in the curriculum in the direction of specialization and technical virtuosity, the social structure of student bodies was undergoing change. The dominance of fraternities and sororities in social life, and of athletics as an arena for the creation of campus heroes, became increasingly suspect as American campuses filled with returning GIs, first from World War II and then from the Korean War, and finally from disadvantaged ethnic groups as they were increasingly recruited into student bodies during this period. The ethos of campus life no longer tolerated the older forms of snobbery, and a new set of campus heroes emerged from the leaders of marches and the veterans of "Mississippi summers." The important point here is that there were no new primary structures to take the place of the discredited older ones, so that these new and more socially heterogeneous student bodies tended to become relatively unorganized masses, volatile and susceptible to sudden mobilization and politicization in response to the events of the period.

These social trends pointing to a substantial overloading of the agencies of socialization, at a time when the principal socializing agencies of family, church, and school were losing their socializing capacity, suggest a volatile generation, a value-searching generation, a generation less likely to comply with authority. They also suggest some themes of cultural innovation growing out of the conditions just described. But these "pronenesses" do not add up to the "counterculture" or to the great youth disorders of 1965-1970. The salient events of the period created the issues of the rebellion and triggered some of the cultural innovations.

The Youth Rebellion as Problem-Solving Behavior: Issues and Events of the Period

The campus disorders cannot simply be explained in these sociological and psychological terms. They also have to be examined as coping and problem-solving behavior, often primitive, but intended to attain ends and relieve stress. Alongside these sociological and cultural changes in the condition of youth in America is placed a chronology of salient events, beginning with the Eisenhower "silent generation" period (see First Chronology below). As we glance at the "big

First Chronology: The Eisenhower Years

1953	January	Eisenhower inaugurated
	March	Death of Stalin
	June	Rosenbergs executed for espionage
	July	Korean Armistice
	August	Russians explode H-bomb
1954	May	Brown vs. Board of Education School Desegregation Decision
	December	Senator McCarthy censured by the Senate
1955	December	Bus boycott in Montgomery, Alabama (Martin Luth King)
1956	February	Khrushchev's Secret Speech on the Crimes of the Stalin Era
	July	Polish revolt crushed
	November	Hungarian revolt crushed
1957	October	Soviets launch Sputnik
1958	January	U.S. launches earth satellite
1959	January	Castro takes power in Cuba
	September	Khrushchev visits United States
1960	May	U-2 incident—summit conference canceled

stories" of the Eisenhower era, it is evident that the Cold War set the issues of the times, even though Stalin died in March 1953, just two months after Eisenhower's inauguration. In June 1953, the Rosenbergs were executed for espionage. But the McCarthy period of security paranoia and domestic American communism was coming to an end, as the Senate censured Senator Joseph McCarthy in December 1954. Conflict with and anxiety over the Soviet Union during this period fluctuated. In August 1953, the Russians exploded their first H-bomb, not long after America's first successful H-bomb explosion.

De-Stalinization in the Soviet Union began in February 1956 with Khrushchev's "Secret Speech on the Crimes of the Stalin Era," but the thaw in the Communist orbit was arrested when the Polish and Hungarian revolts occurred in July and November 1956. Detente with the

Soviet Union had its ups and downs as Soviet and American competition in the development of satellites intensified in 1957 and 1958. Khrushchev visited the United States in September 1959, but in May 1960, the U-2 incident resulted in the cancellation of a summit conference intended to allay East-West tensions. The seizure of power by Castro in Cuba in January 1959 introduced a new element of potential contention between the Soviets and the United States.

Two other events in the 1950s suggest tendencies that were to surface in the 1960s and give that decade its style and character. In May 1954, the Supreme Court issued its school desegregation decision, and in December 1955 Martin Luther King, Jr., led his first boycott in Montgomery, Alabama. Nevertheless, this decade was dominated by foreign policy and Cold War issues; it was a period of bipartisan foreign policy and broad consensus on other issues.

The Kennedy years (see Second Chronology) were also dominated by security and Cold War issues. The year 1961 was marked by the Bay of Pigs, the Laotian crisis, and the building of the Berlin Wall by the East German regime; in 1962, the Cold War reached a high level of crisis in the Cuban missile confrontation. In the last years of the Kennedy administration, the black rebellion was acquiring momentum with riots at the University of Mississippi over the admission of James Meredith in September 1962, and in the 200,000-strong march on Washington led by Martin Luther King in July 1963.

Second Chronology: The Kennedy Years

1960	January	Kennedy inaugurated
1961	April	Bay of Pigs
	"	Laotian Crisis
	August	Berlin Wall
	October	Soviet 60 Megaton blast
1962	September	Riot at University of Mississippi over admission of James Meredith
	October	Cuban Missile Crisis
1963	July	Biggest demonstration ever in Washington led by Martin Luther King
	November	Assassination of President Kennedy

In the first year of the Johnson administration (see Third Chronology), the three themes of the great disturbances of the 1960s were struck. In June 1964, student volunteers streamed into Mississippi in the first stages of a major voter registration campaign. Three of these "freedom fighters" were murdered and their bodies were discovered in August. In July, the first of the "hot summers" occurred with race riots in Harlem, the Bedford-Stuyvesant section of Brooklyn, and Rochester. In August 1964, the destroyer *Maddox* incident and the Gulf of Tonkin resolution opened the overt phase of the Vietnam War. And in December 1964, the Berkeley campus of the University of California exploded with the free speech sit-in and demonstrations.

By 1965, the Black rebellion and the Vietnam War began to impinge directly on university campuses, just when the baby bulge was

Third Chronology: The Johnson Years

1964	June	Registration campaign in Mississippi
	July	First "hot summer"—Harlem-Brooklyn-Rochester
	August	Destroyer *Maddox* incident and Gulf of Tonkin Resolution
	December	Free speech sit-in at Berkeley
1965	July	U.S. troops in Vietnam exceed 100,000; draft doubl[e]
	August	Second hot summer: Watts riot
1966	May	Protests at University of Chicago and CCNY against use of class standing for draft deferment
	May	U.S. casualties in Vietnam reach 1,000 per week
	July	Third hot summer: Chicago West Side and Hough section of Cleveland
1967	August	Johnson announces Vietnam commitment to exceed 500,000
		Fourth hot summer: Newark
1968	January	Tet offensive
	March	New Hampshire primary and Johnson's withdrawal
	April	Martin Luther King assassination
	April	Columbia University sit-in
	May	Vietnam preliminary peace talks begin
	June	Robert Kennedy assassination

moving into the colleges. The Black rebellion had trained a generation of student activists who had participated in the nonviolent movement and in registration campaigns. The number of Blacks admitted to higher education also began to increase rapidly during this period, as many universities actively recruited in efforts to equalize opportunity. The Vietnam War touched university campuses through the increasing demands of the draft and through the granting of draft exemptions to students enrolled in higher education. Troop commitments rapidly increased during this period, with the total exceeding half a million men by the end of 1967.

The peak of student protest and activism was reached in early 1968 with the Tet offensive in January and Senator Eugene McCarthy's remarkable showing in the New Hampshire primary in March. In April, the Martin Luther King assassination mobilized American campuses and, as an aftermath, produced a major influx of Blacks and other ethnic groups into the university communities. In June, the assassination of Robert Kennedy, and in August, the riots at the Chicago Democratic convention, brought the student rebellion to a fever pitch. It was during 1968 and 1969 that strikes, sit-ins, violence, and "trashings" struck American campuses one after the other—Columbia, Cornell, Harvard, the University of Wisconsin, San Francisco State, Stanford, Boston University, and many others. War issues, ethnic issues, and student power issues all combined to produce these years of extraordinary mobilization and politicization.

The signing of the Vietnam Peace Agreement in January 1973 (see Fourth Chronology) and the withdrawal of the last remaining American troops in Vietnam eliminated the Vietnam issue as a cause of campus disorders. The racial issue declined in salience with the liberalization of admissions policies and the development of the "Black Power" movement.

The cessation of the rapid growth of higher education, declining support of fellowship and research programs, the declining rate of growth in the national economy, and the consequent increasing difficulties in finding suitable employment changed the campus mood. Finally, in 1973, the Yom Kippur war, the Arab oil embargo, and the energy crisis brought a new set of issues to the fore in America.

Only by combining an account of changing social trends affecting young people with an account of the salient issues affecting their lives and concerns can we begin to suggest some plausible explanations of

Fourth Chronology: The Nixon Years

1969	January	Nixon inaugurated
	April	Harvard University sit-in
	April	Cornell University sit-in
	July	First moonlanding
	October	Vietnam moratorium
	November	Total Vietnam casualty figure of over 300,000 announced
1970	April	U.S. attack on Cambodia
	April	Millions celebrate Earth Day
	April	Yale student strike over Bobby Seale trial
	May	Kent and Jackson State killings
	August	Fatal bombing at University of Wisconsin
1971	May	12,000 arrested in Washington demonstration
	July	26th Amendment (18-year-old vote) ratified
	September	Riot and occupation at Attica prison
1972	February	Nixon visit to China
	March	Watergate break-in
	May	Nixon visit to Russia
	August	Nomination of McGovern
	November	Nixon reelected
1973	January	Signing of Vietnam Peace agreement
	April	Beginning of Watergate hearings
	July	Double-digit inflation begins
	October	Arab oil embargo and energy crisis begins
1974	July	Impeachment hearings begin
	July	Supreme Court decision on subpoena of tapes
	August	Nixon resigns

both the level of protest and its content. The demographic youth bulge, the declining effectiveness of socializing agencies, the increasing concentration of this numerous generation in university campuses, which themselves were undergoing significant changes, tell us something about the overloading of institutions of higher education, the fragility of their authority, and the declining vitality of their solidaristic institutions and norms. As the sparks of the ethnic rebellion and the Vietnam War were thrown into these volatile populations, it is not surprising that they went up in flames. The challenge to university authority and the issue of "student power" can be explained by this generation's earlier experience in participatory families and schools, by a general decline in its faith in the legitimacy of a social order which produced Vietnam and segregation, and also by the changing culture and structure of the institutions of higher education themselves.

Evidence of Value and Attitude Change

It almost seems that we have more explanations for the violence in the 1960s than we need, that the explosion was "overdetermined." But the youth rebellion and the counterculture were complex and multidimensional. Hence, all of the explanatory components reviewed here are needed to illuminate its various dimensions and to separate the lasting from the transitory trends.

Before turning to these problems, the evidence on value and attitude trends during the periods that concern us will be reviewed. Two major surveys of youth attitudes were carried out during the 1960s: one covering European countries and the United States by Ronald Inglehart, a political scientist at the University of Michigan; and the second by the Yankelovich Survey organization which was limited to American data. Both studies have the advantage of time perspective, since the same questions have been asked several times in recent years. Thus, they report data gathered during the heat of the rebellion, as well as during calmer times.

Inglehart's first findings were reported in a striking article published in 1971. The article aroused great interest and has produced at least two polemical-empirical responses (see Ike, 1973; Marsh, 1975). Since his first report, Inglehart has administered two other surveys which include a number of additional European countries and the United States. The results of all these investigations are reported in a recent book (Inglehart, 1976).

In his first study based on surveys in France, Germany, Great Britain, Italy, Belgium, and Holland, Inglehart concluded:

> A transformation may be taking place in the political cultures of advanced industrial societies. This transformation seems to be altering the basic value

priorities of given generations, as a result of changing conditions influencing their basic socialization. The changes seem to affect the stand one takes on current political issues and may have a long-term tendency to alter existing patterns of political partisanship.

Inglehart links his hypotheses to Maslow's "need hierarchy" concept and the theory of socialization. Maslow (1954) argues that there are five basic need areas: (1) physiological-subsistence; (2) safety and security; (3) affection and belonging; (4) esteem; and (5) self-actualization. The needs are sequential or occur in a hierarchy, the basic level being physiological, the second level safety, the third level affection and belongingness, and so on. As you satisfy the one, you go on to the next.

Inglehart argues that the generation born after 1945 in Western Europe had experienced a period of peace, uninterrupted economic growth, and rising living standards. Hence, for this post-1945 generation physiological and safety needs have been met, and their value priorities *ex hypothesi* should be of the affection-belongingness, esteem, and self-actualization order. From socialization theory, which argues that value orientations formed in childhood persist into adulthood, Inglehart predicts that the newer values would be more frequently encountered among the young, while the older generation would continue to give greater weight to scarcity and security values that were salient in their childhood and youth.

In testing his hypothesis in Western Europe, Inglehart used a forced choice question in which respondents were required to pick two out of

TABLE 8.
"Postbourgeois" and "Acquisitive" Value Choices by Age Cohorts in Four European Countries

Ages	*Germany*		*France*		*Italy*		*Great Britain*	
	P.B.	*Acq.*	*P.B.*	*Acq.*	*P.B.*	*Acq.*	*P.B.*	*Acq.*
16-24	23	21	20	21	28	18	14	25
25-34	15	35	11	35	15	30	9	29
55-64	4	60	6	48	7	42	8	41
Total spread across cohorts	56		47		60		34	

SOURCE: Adapted from Inglehart (1971: 1000).

four sociopolitical goals. Two of these four were security and economic goals, and two were libertarian and participatory.[1] His findings were substantial. Table 8 shows a clear pattern from country to country of greater preference for what he calls "postbourgeois" value patterns among the younger age cohort born after 1945, and a declining preference for these values as we go to the older age groups.

Table 9, controlling age by socioeconomic status, shows an even more striking pattern of difference. Thus, the more educated, affluent stratum of the post-1945 generation opts for Inglehart's postbourgeois values to an even more striking degree and in sharp contrast to the older, less educated stratum, the percentages being 49 to 3 for Germany, 31 to 5 for France, 40 to 7 for Italy, and 16 to 8 for Britain. The fact that Britain, though manifesting the same trends, had a smaller postbourgeois sector and smaller differences according to age and socioeconomic status, Inglehart attributes to the relatively low rate of economic growth in Britain in the postwar period. Indeed, a separate analysis shows a strong and symmetrical relationship between rate of growth in postwar years and postbourgeois attitudes in the six countries surveyed.

One of the main difficulties with Inglehart's first study was the discrepancy between his theoretical variables and his operational indicators. He identifies participationism and libertarianism as postbourgeois, and concern with economic stability and security as bourgeois or acquisitive values. Since liberty and participation were central be-

TABLE 9.

"Postbourgeois" Value Preference by Age and Socioeconomic Status, in Percentages [1]

Ages	*Germany*		*France*		*Italy*		*Great Britain*	
	Upper	*Lower*	*Upper*	*Lower*	*Upper*	*Lower*	*Upper*	*Lower*
16-24	49	15	31	8	40	23	16	10
25-34	35	10	23	2	37	11	8	10
55-64	16	3	8	5	5	7	14	8

SOURCE: Adapted from Inglehart (1971: 1002ff., Table 7).

1. Inglehart bases SES status on a combination of educational and occupational criteria. The "upper SES" category would include those respondents who have had secondary education or higher and are employed in nonmanual occupations in the modern sector of the economy; the "lower SES" category would include persons with primary school education or less, and employed in manual work.

liefs of the bourgeois revolution of the eighteenth and nineteenth centuries, his first formulation left many students intrigued by the magnitude of the generational differences he uncovered, but unconvinced by his interpretation of their significance.

In his second report, Inglehart confronts this and other problems. Not wanting to lose the advantage of comparison over time, he repeats his four-item forced choice question, but calls the libertarian-participatory pair "postmaterialistic." He adds additional items, tapping other issue areas such as the environment, economic democracy, and the impersonality of modern society. Although he offers interesting evidence from his data to support Maslow's "need hierarchy" hypothesis, he does not insist on it. He offers a less complicated hypothesis—the marginal utility notion that "people tend to place a high priority on whatever needs are in short supply" (Inglehart, 1976:3, p. 2). Thus, in an age of affluence and peace with material and safety needs satisfied, people turn to nonmaterial attitudes and values.

The data from the later surveys as they relate to age, and now including the United States, confirm the earlier finding of a higher incidence of postmaterial options among the youth cohort and materialist options among the older groups (Table 10). Inglehart attributes the smaller spread in youth and older age attitudes in the United States and Britain to the fact that, while experiencing an age of affluence in the postwar period, these two countries did not experience the remarkable rates of growth enjoyed by France, Germany, Italy, and

TABLE 10

Value Types by Age Cohorts in Advanced Industrial Societies, 1972-1973

	U.S.		*Great Britain*		*France*		*Germany*		*Italy*	
Ages	*PM*[1]	*M*[2]	*PM*	*M*	*PM*	*M*	*PM*	*M*	*PM*	*M*
19-28	17	24	11	27	20	22	19	24	16	26
59-68	6	37	5	36	3	50	7	52	4	49
Total spread across cohorts	26		17		51		56		42	

Source: Adapted from Inglehart (1976: Chapter 3, Table 4).
1. PM="postmaterialist."
2. M="materialist."

other continental European countries. His findings on changes in the distribution of value types from the first survey in 1970 to the second series in 1973 show some slight tendency to decline in postmaterialist orientations (Inglehart, 1976: Table 14). But by and large the pattern persists. He also demonstrates that the postmaterialist-materialist scoring device genuinely taps these dimensions. Thus, those picking the postmaterialist pair are much more likely to prefer the human interaction and creativity aspects of their work than the security and moneymaking aspects, to favor helping the developing nations, to be internationalist and cosmopolitan rather than nationalist and parochial in their orientations, to favor women's rights, to be open to new things, to prefer a less impersonal society, and to view themselves as "liberal" or "left" in their political inclinations.

The percentage differences in all these respects among the materialists and postmaterialists are quite large. They do indeed suggest that Inglehart has identified a significant new value trend among the young, particularly the educated young, in advanced industrial societies. However, he leaves unresolved the question of whether these changes are of the "period-bound" sort, or whether they are the harbingers of genuine, persistent culture change. The explanatory workhorses upon which Inglehart relies are economic growth and associated affluence and peace.

Inglehart acknowledges that, in contrast to the 1960s, the decade of the 1970s is one of actual and impending scarcities as population and technology press on limited resources and as rising levels of demand produce inflation. Unanswered is the question as to whether this postmaterialist cluster of new cultural values is likely to be generalized over time as advanced industrial societies move into a "no-growth" or "slow growth" phase and encounter the uncertainties of inflation and of critical shortages. Inglehart's work was primarily focused on Europe. He only included the United States in one of his most recent surveys and did not administer his full instrument to the American sample. It is still of interest that the generation gap in the United States, according to his findings, was not as large as it was among the continental European countries. A more recent survey exploring these hypotheses is still unreported.

Daniel Yankelovich's work is solely concerned with the United States and centers on the university and college student population, though general and working class youth samples are included as well.

Overall, Yankelovich has carried out five surveys of American youth attitudes—in 1968, 1969, 1970, 1971, and 1973. Two of the studies (1969 and 1973) include a noncollege youth sample.

In his first major report on the culture of the American college student population based on his surveys through 1971, Yankelovich claimed to have discovered a new "culture" among college youth in America, which he called "The New Naturalism." Among its principal features were a turning off on the achievement ethic, competition, science, technology, and bureaucracy, and a turning on toward direct sensory experience, adapting to nature rather than seeking to master it, cultivating deep and honest relationships in small groups, and seeking self-knowledge through introspection. In his analysis of trends during the four years covered in his first report, Yankelovich (1972) argued that, while political radicalism was beginning to subside by 1971, the specifically cultural value innovations were persisting. In his 1974 report, he pointed out that much of this cultural innovation was surviving, and even spreading to noncollege youth in America.

In the second report, he dropped the concept of a "New Naturalism" culture in favor of the "New Values" (Yankelovich, 1974). He divides them into three categories: (1) new moral norms, (2) new social values, and (3) a self-fulfillment ethic. The new moral norms include the adoption of a liberal attitude toward sexuality; a skepticism toward the legitimacy of such institutions as the legal system, government, political parties, business corporations, and religious institutions; and a dilution of national feeling and patriotism. The new social values include changing attitudes toward work and success and toward marriage and the family—a kind of general reevaluation of adult roles and expectations. The new ethic of self-fulfillment is closely related to the first two categories of value change. It implies establishing a place for self-gratification and creativity beyond "making a living" and fulfilling role obligations to others.

Yankelovich's evidence is reported in Tables 11 and 12. Table 11 shows that in the period 1969-1973 the proportion of college students favoring more sexual freedom, more privacy, and less emphasis on money increased, while the proportion stressing the importance of religion and patriotism decreased, despite the dramatic subsidence of student radicalism and activism in this period.

Table 12, on the other hand, demonstrates a return to the work and achievement ethic, with stress on the advancement, security, and

TABLE 11.
Trends in College Student Values, Yankelovich Surveys, 1969-1973, in Percentages

Values	*1969*	*1973*
More sexual freedom	43	61
Importance of religion	38	28
Importance of patriotism	35	19
Importance of privacy	61	71
Less emphasis on money	65	80

SOURCE: Adapted from Yankelovich (1974: 12ff.).

TABLE 12.
What College Students Want on the Job, Yankelovich Surveys, 1969-1973, in Percentages

Job Goals	*1969-1971*	*1973*
Self-expression	56	68
Challenge	64	77
Opportunities for advancement	35	51
Security	33	58
Money	36	61
Prestige	15	28

SOURCE: Adapted from Yankelovich (1974: 17ff.).

money aspects of jobs increasing among college students; but at the same time, the preference for self-expressive values on the job also increased.

A particularly interesting finding of the Yankelovich surveys is that noncollege youth seem to have assimilated these new values in recent years and that there has been diffusion of "new" cultural values from higher to lower SES youth. Table 13 shows that the new morality has been adopted by almost half of the noncollege youth, that the authority of church and nation has attenuated among these groups, and that

TABLE 13.
Noncollege Student Values and Attitudes,
Yankelovich Surveys, 1969-1973, in Percentages

Values and Attitudes	*1969*	*1973*
More sexual freedom	22	47
Importance of religion	64	42
Importance of clean moral life	77	57
Importance of patriotism	60	40
Less emphasis on money	54	74
Belief that hard work pays off	79	56

SOURCE: Adapted from Yankelovich (1974: 24ff.).

work and money motives have lost some of their glamor.

Inglehart and Yankelovich are emphasized here because they have been directly concerned with the problem confronted in this essay. Inglehart's work, having already involved three surveys, is now in its fourth and major phase. Since this current phase includes the United States, trend data for America will soon be available. Two studies—one of Japan and one of Britain—challenge some of Inglehart's conclusions. Nobutake Ike, in a secondary analysis of Japanese survey data for the period 1953-1968, finds some evidence supportive of the Inglehart thesis. "Japanese youth, when compared to their elders, appear to be less acquisitive, more democratic, and somewhat more inclined to value freedom; in short, they show signs of prefering the kind of values defined by Inglehart as Post-Bourgeois" (Ike, 1973: 1200). Ike argues, however, that the pattern of political culture change in Japan is more complex than that presented by Inglehart for Europe. Thus, the older age groups over time have been moving toward democratic and participant values, and the trend has been toward a convergence in attitude among the young and old rather than a divergence as in Europe. He also points to a marked tendency among Japanese young people toward privatization and individuation rather than in the direction of "belongingness," consistent with the Maslowian "need hierarchy" hypothesis. Inglehart's more recent work seems to be more concerned with differences in historical experience and cultural characteristics as they may explain differences in the political attitudes and values of generations.

Alan Marsh's analysis of a survey administered to a British sample in 1971, which included the Inglehart items as well as measures of satisfaction with various aspects of life, produced mixed findings. On the one hand, he found that the postbourgeois respondents were younger, better off, and better educated than the "acquisitives." On the other hand, he discovered that the postbourgeois respondents, while dissatisfied with their social surroundings and the political and qualitative aspects of their lives, were also "more prone to material dissatisfactions and security anxieties than are the acquisitive group" (Marsh, 1975:9). Marsh's findings for Britain would appear to be more consistent with those of the most recent Yankelovich survey, which noted a return to "materialistic" job values and concerns among American college students.

Other studies tend to confirm Inglehart's and Yankelovich's findings, particularly those that suggest a decline in the legitimacy and stability of the political and social institutions of advanced industrial society. Arthur H. Miller (1974), in a study of "trust in government" in America based on five University of Michigan Survey Research Center election studies over the period 1964-1970, found a strong trend toward decline in trust in government and political alienation among American respondents, particularly among the younger age groups. The younger, educated respondents tended to manifest a left-oriented distrust in government that was associated with support of student demonstrations, dealing constructively with problems of poverty and discrimination, and bringing the Vietnam War to an end. Gallup surveys in the last decade have shown a similar decline in confidence in American governmental, economic, and social institutions; this decline was most marked among the young and the more educated.

The literature pointing to increased volatility in partisan voting in advanced industrial society, and particularly the decline of class as a predictor of party affiliation, is so substantial as not to merit citation here. This tendency is most evident among the educated young. Some evidence already cited shows that the attenuation of party commitment, confidence in government, church, and other social institutions among the educated young seems to be associated with support for unorthodox and relatively violent political practices. Inglehart's work showed this to be the case for support of student demonstrations in his European studies. Alan Marsh (1974), in a more focused study in England involving fifty each of university students, young workers (ages sixteen to twenty-four), older working-class people (forty-eight to fifty-four), and older middle-class people (forty-five to fifty-four), found a strikingly unorthodox "protest potential" among the university students and an almost equal protest potential among young workers. In sharp contrast, the older middle- and working-class respondents tended to prefer more moderate and orthodox methods.

Further evidence suggesting greater alienation from American institutions and greater liberalism and unorthodoxy among the younger generation is reported in the University of California (Berkeley) Survey Research Center study of political alienation.[2] Although the study is limited to the San Francisco Bay area, it has the great virtue of depth and discrimination in testing satisfaction-dissatisfaction with a variety of American institutions and values. Its preliminary findings support the view that Americans in the younger age groups (eighteen to twenty-six) are somewhat less trustful of their national government, less confident of its honesty, responsiveness, efficiency, and the like, than the older age groups. They also support the view that young Americans tend to be more liberal in welfare, environmental, racial, and foreign policy attitudes than older groups, more distrustful of the business community and of organized religion, and somewhat more turned off by materialism and the work and achievement ethic. The differences in satisfaction-dissatisfaction and trust-distrust in this study are reported on a five-point scale; the distance between the younger and older age groups tends to be of the order of one scalar point, which is not a very large contrast but tends to be consistent. The findings also suggest that the educated young manifest these tendencies of alienation, liberalism, and antimaterialism to a larger extent than the youth cohort as a whole.

Conclusions

Any satisfying interpretation of the late 1960s requires an explanation of the remarkable combination of large-scale political rebellion and cultural experimentalism among young people, particularly among college students. An extraordinary set of causes is needed to convert the normal pattern of political apathy, liberal impulses, and experimental behavior characteristic of young people into the massive and violent political mobilizations and cultural explosions of the period.

Table 14 cites a series of mental experiments showing how different combinations of causes might have affected youth behavior during this period. This step-by-step analysis may help us speculate about the future directions of culture change. The table suggests that a life-cycle interpretation has no explanatory power at all. Even Lewis Feuer's combination of life-cycle tendencies with political period effects producing a loss of legitimacy on the part of adult authority cannot explain the explosiveness of the youth rebellion and the lush cultural innovations of the period. Item 2 in the table suggests that the Feuer combination would have produced politicization on the campuses, but there is no logic to suggest that the Vietnam War and the black rebellion would have produced the counterculture with its rejection of the work and achievement ethic, its communalism, its primitive and "instant ideologism," and the like.

Similarly, the socioeconomic period effects—the youth bulge, the

TABLE 14.

Explanation of the Great Disturbances of the 1960s

1. Life-Cycle Effects Only	→	Political Apathy-Liberalism-Wild Oats Behavior
2. Political *Period* Effects But No Socioeconomic Period Effects	→	Politicization on Smaller Scale; Less Cultural Experimentalism
3. Socioeconomic *Period* Effects but No Political *Period* Effects	→	Private Rebelliousness Plus Cultural Experimentalism
4. Political *Period* Effects Plus Socioeconomic Period Effects	→	Political Rebellion Plus Cultural Experimentalism

quantum jump in higher education, the increasing technicization of the curriculum, and the rising trend of economic growth and material affluence—can be seen to have a causal connection to the various cultural innovations and to the crisis of university authority. However, they cannot account for the political mobilizations of the period. Rising affluence and opportunity made the rejection of materialism and the work ethic possible. The rapid growth of student bodies and the decay of the traditional social structure of university life may have contributed to the commune movement and to the emphasis in the youth culture on "meaningful" personal relationships. The size of the youth cohort and the consequent enhancement of the role of peer-group socialization at the expense of cultural transmission through adults and authority figures help explain the "generation gap," the lack of a sense of history in the "now generation," and the primitive quality of its ideological, political, and aesthetic formulations. These socioeconomic period effects can help us understand Woodstock, the commune movements, and the "countercurriculum," but not the massive political demonstrations and confrontations of the period.

When we combine these socioeconomic and political period effects, we begin to get a set of independent variables capable of explaining the complex set of dependent variables that made up the great disturbances of the late 1960s. They suggest that the political and cultural rebellions were essentially period bound, being tied to the political issues, the state of the economy, the age distribution of the population, and the educational developments of the time. Both the socioeconomic and political sets of period-bound developments had a distinctive relation to each of the two components of the disturbances—the socioeconomic ones with the cultural manifestations, and the political issues with the political rebellion. In addition, the two sets of period-related causes interacted one with the other and fed upon one another, making the political rebellion more explosive and the cultural rebellion more bizarre. The loss of legitimacy of political and social authority resulting from the ethnic rebellion and the Vietnam War weakened the moral and cultural order and made it fair game, justifying the experimentation with new values and social arrangements. On the other hand, the youth bulge, the rapid growth of higher education, and the boom economy created volatile masses, responding quickly and on a large scale to political stimuli.

The political rebellion began to subside after the turn of the decade. As the ethnic mobilization lost its intensity and as the American role in the Vietnam War drew to a close, the political stimuli lost their force. What seems to have persisted in the population as a whole, but particularly among young people, is an increased skepticism of the distrust in nation and government, an increased partisan volatility, and, among the younger generations particularly, an increased acceptance of "unconventional" forms of political participation and protest.

The fate of the counterculture is intriguing and offers an interesting case history for the ruminations of social theorists. A sharp change in the age structure of the population and an accentuation of peer group socialization seem to have conspired with a sudden increase in investment in higher education to turn the educated young into a cultural-innovating generation. The hedonism, the sexual libertarianism, and, in some respects, the communitarianism of the counterculture have been co-opted by the dominant culture, affecting legislation, sex roles and behavior, clothing styles and fashions, residential patterns, and the like. These innovations were consistent with, but sharply discontinuous in degree from, the longer run processes of cultural secularization affecting these patterns.

In the 1970s, a new set of political issues and problems has begun to dominate our politics. These issues have arisen from the slow-down of economic growth and actual or impending scarcities resulting from population growth and increasing pressure on resources. While the more pessimistic forecasts of the future are undoubtedly exaggerated, the basic assumption of limitless material progress and an ever-improving standard of living that has dominated the political ideologies (both left and right) of the West for the past two centuries can no longer be seriously entertained. If our basic economic realities and expectations undergo this fundamental shift, our politics and culture cannot help being transformed in similarly important ways.

The difficulty in projecting these tendencies into the future is that we have no sure way of predicting the rate and pattern of this slowdown, or of forecasting the technological inventions that might mitigate and postpone its consequences. It seems clear, however, that the material optimism that lies at the basis of Western culture and politics will begin to abate. A slowdown in the rate of growth is bound to produce a domestic and foreign politics dominated by the issues of conservation and redistribution. These are conflictual policies, and they suggest an increasing power in governmental agencies, and an increasing creation of supranational authority and institutions.

The kind of political culture that fits this set of emerging problems, issues, and institutions is one that is less rigidly committed to the enhancement and defense of material interests, and to the full sovereignty of the nation-state. Table 15 suggests a kind of race between the politicoeconomic issues and problems growing out of the slowdown of economic growth on the one hand, and political-cultural adaptations on the other. The slowdown of economic growth brings with it sharpened political antagonisms over the distribution of the material product both within and between countries, particularly the rich and the poor ones. Increased political tension and antagonism contribute to governmental instability and are particularly threatening to liberal democratic systems. If we press the known relationship between economic stagnation and decline and intensity of partisan antagonism and group conflict into the future, it is realistic to expect political culture change in the direction of ideological confrontation and a domestic and international politics of protest.

As the remaining natural space contracts and precious materials begin to reach the point of exhaustion, we may expect an increasing spread of a conservation and recycling ethic and a reverence for nature, particularly in the advanced industrial countries and among the materially advantaged strata in these countries. But the

TABLE 15.
Long-Term Developments in National Problem Solving

1. Slowdown of Economic Growth	→	Domestic and International Politics of Redistribution
2. Intermittent Scarcity Crises	→	Development of Conservation Ethic
3. Continued Secularization	→	Increased Openness to Value Change and Rational Problem-Solving Propensities
4. Increased Higher Education	→	Governmental Legitimacy Increasingly Based on Performance
5. Continued Spread of Electronic Media	→	Rapid Diffusion of Information and Values Across Classes and Nations

development of this conservation ethic and reverence for nature among the privileged will sharpen the politics of redistribution, for if benefits for the poor are not to come from a high rate of growth, then they have to come from the benefits going to the privileged.

The long-run tendencies toward more rational problem-solving propensities listed in Table 15 conceivably may mitigate the sharpness of this class antagonism and rich nation poor nation confrontation. We have already referred to the waning indoctrinative powers of the modern family and church. This process of secularization, decreasing dogmatism, and greater ecumenism and cultivation of individual responsibility in the making of choices contribute to a greater openness to value change. While these tendencies are already far advanced in the area of sexual morality, they have yet to be tested in the area of political ideology.

Contributing to this openness to value change and rational problem-solving capacity is the increase in the proportion of the population in advanced industrial societies experiencing higher education. As the indoctrinative power of family and church has declined in the last decades, the impact of formal education and the mass media has increased. During the 1960s, this growth was a special period effect. Students in higher education in the United States doubled from around 20 percent to 40 percent, and in Western Europe and Japan, they increased from roughly 10 percent to 20 percent. Whereas the elite members of advanced societies have for some time been predominately college- or university-educated, the middle echelons of society are increasingly obtaining a higher educational experience. However one may fault it, higher education creates a more cosmopolitan world-view, an increased capacity to assimilate information, and the development of cognitive analytic skills.

The generations that matured in the 1960s were the first television generations. Surely television contributed to the "great disturbances" of the 1960s. It brought the Vietnam War, the ethnic rebellion, the campus demonstrations, and the counterculture to the attention of practically the entire population of the advanced industrial societies. It helps explain the swift spread of values and styles from college youth to noncollege youth, noted in the recent Yankelovich studies. In the future, the electronic media will continue to facilitate the diffusion of information and values across classes and nations. It seems to be playing a role similar to that of higher education, widening horizons and facilitating the flow of information.

The decline of dogmatism and the spread of rational analytic skills and information attributable to these long-run social changes will not only increase the human problem-solving capacity, but will also transform the bases of political and governmental legitimacy. The evidence for this trend is already impressive. Class position and party identification have been losing their capacity to predict voting behavior during this period, and implicit trust and faith in governmental institutions have been declining. The test for governmental support is increasingly based on performance; political elites are held on a shorter tether than was true in the past.

In these continued processes of culture change, young people are unlikely to play the special role characteristic of the 1960s. The accidental concatenation of demographic, educational, and economic trends, and political issues especially impinging on them, is unlikely to be repeated. The youth cohorts who made and supported the rebellion are now passing into full adulthood, carrying with them the special memories of those extraordinary days. Similarly, the political and social elites who sought to cope with the problems they posed carry memories that continue to affect the structure of social authority.

Each passing year in the advanced societies will see an influx of new members carrying with them this greater value openness and analytical capacity, and replacing older cohorts who are more parochial and more rigid in orientation. We can therefore say of the politics and political culture of the future that on the one hand the problems are more threatening and more divisive, while on the other hand our problem-solving capacity is being enhanced. To say more would be yielding to wishful thinking or to despair.

NOTES

1. The actual question was worded as follows: "If you had to choose among the following things, which are the *two* that seem most desirable to you? Maintaining order in the nation; Giving the people more say in important political decisions; Fighting rising prices; Protesting freedom of speech." In our adapted version of some of Inglehart's findings, we report the data only for the four larger European countries, selected age groups, and selected socioeconomic categories.

2. The principal investigators for this study are Merrill Shanks, Herbert McClosky, Jack Citrin, and Paul Sniderman. Reported here are my interpretations of raw tables showing attitude differences by age.

The Changing Character of Middle Adulthood in American Society [1]

DANIEL J. LEVINSON

7

Since the mid-1960s there has been a growing interest in the problems and possibilities of life in middle age. This interest is evident in the research world of psychology, psychiatry, and social science as well as in the public domain. The study of aging, formerly limited chiefly to the years beyond sixty or so, now includes the latter part of middle age. A number of agencies and committees are involved in this study. The American Psychological Association has a section called "Adult Development and Aging," although its emphasis continues to be much more on aging than on development. In 1972, the Social Science Research Council established a Committee on Work and Personality in the Middle Years (roughly ages forty to sixty). The basic tasks of this committee were to define and legitimize "the middle years" as a field of study and to stimulate theory and research in the relevant disciplines. In applauding this new enterprise, we must also note why it is needed: it is needed because of the tremendous resistance, individual and institutional, to the study of middle age.

Outside the halls of academe, there is a growing recognition that middle age can be a tough time of life and that something needs to be done about it. Industry, for example, is beginning to try to face the fact that large numbers of its middle-aged employees, workers as well as middle and top managers, are alienated from their work and their employing organizations. From the point of view of the business firm, there are serious problems of underachievement, staff obsolescence, alcoholism, and faulty management. From the point of view of the disaffected individual worker or manager, work is dreary, organizational life oppressive, and the possibilities for personal fulfillment nil. Again, despite the increasing acknowledgment of this problem, industry has thus far made only limited efforts at understanding and change. It is easier to focus on accident prevention and physical fitness than on alienation, corruption, and meaninglessness. Similar problems are to be found in schools and colleges, the church, government, and other organizations. They are truly societal problems with roots in our culture and our basic institutional forms. They affect individuals of all ages. However, the effects vary somewhat by age, and our main focus here is on the middle adult years.

The growing desire to improve the quality of adult life is also expressed in the "human potential" movement, with its emphasis on personal growth and self-actualization. While it has had a strong appeal to youth, in fact most of its leadership, practitioners, and clientele are middle aged. Its appeal is especially great for persons who, as they approach or first enter middle age, are reappraising their past lives and seeking a way to live more in accord with their own values.

Finally, contemporary literature and the mass media are showing an increasing interest in the midlife period. It seems that the number of novels and plays in which the central characters are in the age range of roughly forty to sixty has gone up sharply in the last ten years. One of these, Joseph Heller's *Something Happened* (1975), is perhaps the most harrowing novel ever written about midlife stagnation in the suburban middle class. There has also been a marked increase in the number of popular books offering insights and helpful hints about marital woes, heart trouble, sexual dysfunction, and other afflictions especially common in middle age.

Given the widespread awareness that we need to examine and improve the character of life in middle age, one is struck by the remarkable reluctance to proceed—to talk about it, study it, attempt various kinds of social change. We are still engaged in a virtual conspiracy of silence about middle age. What it is like to live through the middle years is one of the best kept secrets in our society, and perhaps in human history generally. Most persons who are at that age or beyond have trouble talking about it with their peers or with youth. When people learn that I am studying midlife development, they frequently exhibit a kind of fascination, an awesome feeling that I am trying to penetrate an impenetrable mystery. There is both a hope that research will shed some light on it and a fear of what may be revealed. My colleagues and I have come to know both of these feelings in ourselves; dealing with our own feelings is an essential part of our methodology and a source of understanding.

The primary issue here is the *anxiety* about middle age. People would like to believe that life begins at forty, but the great fear is that it ends there—that there is no life after youth, that the middle years will bring triviality and meaningless comfort at best, stagnation and despair at worst. Middle age is often regarded as a vague interim period between youth and old age. It is defined largely in negative terms: one is no longer young and yet not quite old, but what *is* one in a more positive sense? The usual connotations of "youth" are vitality, energy, beginnings, possibilities, aspirations, illusions, the heroic. In contrast, "age" connotes death, vulnerability, endings, stasis, the brink of nothingness. It is terrifying to live one's middle age in the shadow of death, and it is a self-defeating illusion to live it in the shadow of youth, as though one were still simply young. The key developmental task of middle age is to discover and utilize its own inherent possibilities as a season of life, a time when one can outgrow some of the immaturities and illusions of youth and build a fuller, more balanced life.

Eras and Periods in the Life Cycle

Terms such as *middle age* and *the middle years* are used in the vernacular, without precise definition, to refer to a part of the human life cycle. If we turn to psychology and the social sciences for a clearer definition of this phase of life, we get little help. At this point in history, there is no standard terminology for identifying the various seasons in the life cycle. It is generally agreed that roughly the first twenty years constitute a formative, preadult phase and that it evolves through an orderly sequence of stages: infancy, early childhood, middle childhood, pubescence, and adolescence. This view of preadulthood provides a useful framework within which to study a wide variety of developmental processes—biological, psychological, and social. At the other end of the life course, starting at, say, sixty or sixty-five, is a season usually referred to as "old age" or, more vaguely, "aging," about which we now have considerable information and little understanding. What about the interval between twenty and sixty? Does development occur in the main adult years? What are the phases or seasons in this part of the life cycle?

The usual assumption is that development ends with the end of adolescence. It is believed that individuals do not develop during adulthood, or that they develop in such idiosyncratic ways that it makes no sense to speak of developmental periods or to look for general principles of adult development. I question this conventional wisdom. There are fabulous variations in the forms of individual development at all ages, and these need to be examined and appreciated, but they occur within a more universal developmental sequence. Creating a social psychology of adult development is a crucially important task in our present historical situation.

If we are to talk about middle age from a developmental point of view, we must conceive of it as one phase within the sequence comprising the life cycle. We shall begin, then, with a framework for the analysis of the life cycle in which five eras, each of roughly twenty years' duration, are identified. The eras form the scaffolding or macrostructure for the life cycle as a whole. A series of developmental periods within each era, and at the boundaries between eras, shape the process of change. For present purposes, only the eras and the transitional periods linking the eras are considered.

This framework is based primarily on evidence regarding men. Our major study to date (Levinson, et al., 1974) deals solely with a male sample, and most of the research in our own and other societies has focused heavily or exclusively on men. The general shape of the life cycle, including the nature and timing of eras, can be assumed to be similar for men and women, though there are massive gender differences in the actualities of the life course. Research on the development of women is urgently needed, not only to understand women but also to sharpen and deepen our understanding of men. For an initial study of women, see Stewart (1977).

Our view of the life cycle is a product of our research. It is not an armchair speculation or assumption we made beforehand. We believe that the life cycle evolves through a sequence of five eras, each lasting roughly twenty-five years. The eras are partially overlapping, so that a new one is getting underway as the previous one is being terminated. The sequence goes as follows:

1. Preadulthood: age 0-22
2. Early adulthood: age 17-45
3. Middle adulthood: age 40-65
4. Late adulthood: age 60-85
5. Late Late adulthood: 80+

An era is a "time of life" in the broadest sense. Although important changes occur within the eras, each era has it own distinctive and unifying qualities, which have to do with the *character of living.* In studying the character of living, we consider its biological, psychological, and social aspects, but we do not focus on any one of these to the exclusion of the others. An era is thus not a stage in biological development, personality development, or career development. It is much broader and more inclusive than a developmental stage or period. The sequence of eras constitutes, as it were, the macro-structure of the life cycle. It provides a framework within which developmental periods and concrete processes of everyday living take place. The eras are analogous to the acts of a play, the major divisions of a novel, or the gross segments into which a biographer divides the life of his subject. The smaller units give a finer picture of the dramatic events and the details of living; the eras give an overview of the life cycle as a whole.

In order to provide a view of the entire cycle, I shall describe all of the eras, although the main focus of this study is on the years from the late teens to the middle forties. We identify early and middle adulthood as separate eras in the life cycle. Early adulthood comes to an end in the forties, when the character of living once more undergoes a fundamental change and middle adulthood begins to emerge. One of the most important—and most controversial—contributions of this study is the demarcation of early and middle adulthood as clearly defined eras. I shall give the reasons shortly.

I have given a single age at which each era begins and another at which it ends. This is not to say, however, that the eras are as demarcated as though they were rounds in a boxing match or classes in a highly regulated school, with a bell ringing at precisely the same age for everyone. Life is never that unitary or standardized. There is an average or most frequent age for the onset and completion of every era. There is also a range of variation around the average, although the variation is contained within fairly narrow limits—probably not more than five or six years. The discovery of age-linked eras is an unconventional finding, for it goes against the conventional assumption that either development does not occur in adulthood or, if it does, its pace varies tremendously and has almost no connection to age.

The move from one era to the next is neither simple nor brief. It requires a basic change in the fabric of one's life, and this change takes more than a day, a month, or even a year. The transition from one era to another consistently takes around four or five years—never less than three and rarely more than six. This transition is a developmental period that links the eras and provides some continuity between them. A developmental transition creates a boundary zone in which one terminates the outgoing era and initiates the incoming one.

Preadulthood ends at roughly age twenty-two, and early adulthood begins at seventeen. The span from seventeen to twenty-two is thus a "zone of overlap," a period in which the old era is being completed and the new one is starting. This period is the Early Adult Transition. It bridges the two eras and is part of both. Likewise, the Mid-life Transition extends from roughly forty to forty-five. It serves to terminate early adulthood and to initiate middle adulthood. There is a subsequent transition in the early sixties, and perhaps another in the early eighties.

The eras and the cross-era transitions are pictured in Figure 1. Let us now briefly review the eras in turn.

Early Adulthood

At about twenty years of age, the youth is beginning to take his place as a man in the society of adults. By this age, most of the mental and bodily characteristics that have been evolving so dramatically in the preadult years are at or near their peak levels. His body has ordinarily reached its full height, though it will fill out and become more coordinated over the next few years. He is close to his maximal level of strength, sexual capability, visual acuity, energy, cardiac and respiratory capacity, and general biological vigor. He is at near peak in intelligence and in those qualities of intellect that have grown so measurably until this time: memory, abstract thought, ability to learn specific skills and to solve well-defined problems, and other faculties measured by intelligence tests appropriate to the preadult years. The personality, which has been changing considerably during the periods of child and adolescent development, tends to become more stabilized

Figure 1
Eras in the Male Life Cycle

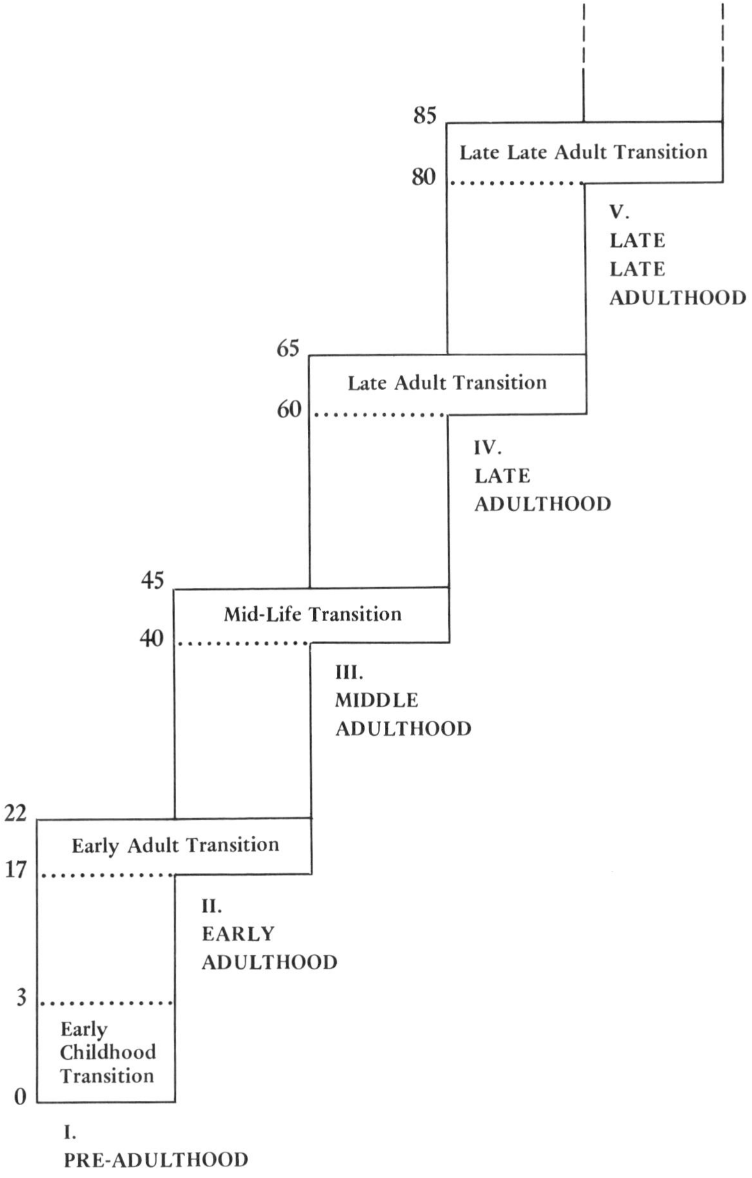

and integrated as adolescence ends. Indeed, the stabilization of personality is often assumed to be a criterion for the start of adulthood, despite evidence of continuing change at least through the twenties (White, 1952; Heath, 1975; Neugarten, 1965). The young man is in the process of giving up his protected status within the family (or equivalent nurturing-controlling context), of leaving his wider preadult world (school, adolescent peer group, community), and of starting a more independent life as an adult. The current controversy about defining the legal age for adulthood as eighteen or twenty-one stems in part from the fact that this age span falls within the Early Adult Transition. During this time, the youth is *both* adolescent and adult; to see him solely as either leads to serious misunderstanding.

Early adulthood extends from roughly age twenty to forty. During this era, the biological, psychological, and social characteristics formed in preadulthood remain relatively stable and near their peak levels. Biologists have found it useful to adopt age thirty as a reference point in studying age changes during adulthood. Most biological functions are close to their highest levels at thirty; from this point they decline gradually through middle and old age. Apart from problems of illness or accident, men at forty are only slightly below their maximal level of bodily functioning. The decline is often great enough to contribute to the man's *experience* of bodily decline at around forty, especially if other psychosocial changes are being experienced.

The span from twenty to forty is the era of greatest psychobiological abundance, as well as of greatest contradiction and stress, within the adult years. It is the time of fullest intensity, energy, strength, agility, endurance, ambition, initiative, passion, output, impulsive spontaneity or formal discipline. The instinctual drives such as sex, aggression, narcissism, and dependence are at their height. The young adult is tremendously involved in the search for personal gratification and at the same time is burdened by the residues of childhood conflicts regarding such gratification. He is also tremendously involved in establishing his place in society. His own needs and capabilities as well as tribal demands lead to his active engagement in collective life. This is true even for the revolutionary, the artist, and the solitary scholar who overtly oppose or withdraw from the established institutions. While rejecting conventional standards, they nonetheless struggle to change society or to create artistic-intellectual products that will in time be valued by society.

Although early adulthood has a certain overall character as a season of life, we can also discern a sequence of change. Over its course, the man normally moves from "novice adult" through a series of intermediate steps to a more "senior" position in work, family, and community. He goes through the process of forming an occupation (often making more than one provisional choice), establishing himself at a relatively junior level, and gradually advancing along some formal or informal ladder until, at around forty, he reaches a point that represents the culmination of his youthful strivings. He is now at the end of his early adulthood and at the beginning of a new era.

In marriage and family, too, the young man begins as novice lover, husband, and father, only gradually (and often painfully) becoming more understanding, skillful, responsible—more able to gain the satisfactions and to bear the burdens of being "senior" in the fullest sense. The first several years in the growth of the family are especially stressful: small children add to the complexity of married life and increase the financial demands on the young man, but his earning power and capacity for meeting responsibilities are still rather limited. Wilensky (1961) has referred to these multiple and conflicting pressures as the "life cycle crunch." He is correct in calling attention to the phenomenon but it deserves a more specific name, since it is just one of many crunches stemming from contradictions in the phasing of the life cycle.

A long-term developmental process is found not only in occupation and immediate family, but also in the man's relationships with parents and extended family. At twenty, he tries desperately to get them to regard him as an equal and a man, "not a kid." By forty, he is taking on parental responsibilities for his parents and the generation of the elderly who look to him for care and leadership. The youth now regard him as senior, as a full generation removed.

Middle Adulthood

At around forty, a basic developmental change occurs. Early adulthood as a season in the life cycle is coming to an end. A new season, middle adulthood, starts to make itself felt. A period of some four to six years is devoted to the termination of one era and the initiation of the next. This period is the Midlife Transition. On what grounds, one may ask, is so sharp a distinction made between early and middle adulthood? Compelling reasons must be given for positing a major developmental change at this time—a change so profound that a transitional period of several years is required to make the shift from one era to the next.

One compelling reason that many have looked for, and failed to discover, is a single, widely occurring event powerful enough to shake the foundations of a man's adult life. The prime example of such an event is puberty, which universally instigates the shift from childhood to adolescence. However, no single event, be it biological, psychological, or social, universally heralds the end of early adulthood. Specific events (such as divorce, depression, empty nest, illness, attainment of maximal income or job level) occur at different ages and for different reasons. The lack of a single criterion, or a simple set of criteria, for demarcating phases within adulthood has supported the cultural assumption that phases do not exist.

The picture is quite different, however, if we begin not by searching for single, specific criteria but by *examining the lived life as it evolves*. This approach yields compelling reasons for proposing that: (1) early adulthood comes to an end in the early forties; (2) the Midlife Transition is a developmentally given period that serves both to terminate early adulthood and to initiate middle adulthood; and (3) middle adulthood extends to age sixty to sixty-five when the Late Adult Transition begins. The following perspectives on the years from forty to sixty-five provide evidence bearing on these propositions.

The Reality and the Experience of Bodily Decline

In the context of the total life cycle, the peak years of biological functioning, as we have seen, are roughly from twenty to forty. By age forty, there is a moderate but noticeable drop in various capacities and skills, and there are "cosmetic" changes such as balding, skin wrinkles, paunch, and weight gain. The decline is normally not great enough to cause severe impairment of bodily function, but it does have a heavy psychosocial impact. It is experienced as a loss of youth and a reminder of one's mortality, and it requires an alteration in work, life style, and relation to self.

From a purely biological point of view, there is normally no sharp, dramatic change at around forty to signal the start of a new era. The bodily and mental powers that peaked in youth are somewhat diminished after forty, but they are ordinarily still ample for an active, full life throughout middle adulthood. A specific illness, accident, or defect may force a man to restrict himself in certain respects; he may have to give up skiing or decrease his sexual activity or reduce the time and energy he devotes to work. But if he is not severely ill or impaired, that is, if his normal development has not been grossly hampered, he can maintain most of his earlier interests, he can form new interests, and, through further psychosocial development after forty, he can experience and contribute much more in a qualitative sense.

The instinctual energies, too, pass their maximal level and are somewhat reduced in middle adulthood. Though a man is by no means lacking in the youthful drives—in lustful passions, in the capacity for anger and moral indignation, in self-assertiveness and ambition, in the wish to be cared for and supported—he suffers less from the tyranny of these drives. The modest decline in the elemental drives can, with midlife development, enable a man to enrich his life. He can be more free of the petty vanities, animosities, envies, and moralisms of early adulthood. His normal sexual capacity in middle age is more than enough for a gratifying sex life. Moreover, the quality of his love relationships improves as he develops a greater capacity for intimacy and integrates more fully the tender, "feminine" aspects of his self. He has the possibility of becoming a more mutual friend to men as well as women, a more facilitating parent to his adolescent and young adult offspring (as he recognizes that they are no longer children and that he is no longer the youthful controlling father), a more caring son to his aging parents (for whom he assumes increasing responsibility), and a more generative mentor, authority, and friend to young adults.

The potential for psychosocial change of this kind is developmentally given in the shift from early to middle adulthood. Its actualization is by no means assured, however, and it occurs only under reasonably favorable conditions. For large numbers of men, life in the middle years is a process of gradual or rapid decline and alienation from the world and from the self. Severe decline is common enough so that it is often seen as part of normal middle age. In many populations, a good deal of decline is *statistically* normal in the sense that it occurs frequently or "in the average case." It is not, however, *developmentally* normal. Drastic decline occurs when development has been impaired as a result of adverse psychological, social, and biological circumstances.

If the conditions for development in middle adulthood are reasonably favorable, and if impairments from the past are not too severe, this era can be one of great satisfaction, personal fulfillment, and social contribution. This requires, however, that the person come to terms with his own aging, with the end of youth and the actuality of death, and with the developmental tasks of the Midlife Transition.

Although the bodily decline ordinarily involves gradual, small decrements in each measured aspect, it often brings about a major, qualitative change in overall biological functioning in the late thirties and early forties. This change may require considerable accommodation in the man's style of living and social roles, especially with regard to work. The effect is most marked in occupations that depend on specialized bodily skills; for example, hunting, farming, athletics, singing, highly precise or strenuous labor. There is an approximate upper age limit (usually somewhere in the thirties) after which a man must either leave this occupation altogether or shift within it to a managerial, consultative, or physically less demanding role. The youthful John Henry and his hammer might temporarily win the struggle against age; before forty he would have to modify his occupation or be consigned to the dumping grounds of obsolete equipment. The professional football player, George Blanda, stayed in the game past forty by narrowing his scope to place kicking; other athletes become coaches, managers, broadcasters, or promoters, or they attempt a new life in a new occupational world (cf. Kahn, 1973; Robinson, 1972). The athlete who gives up playing at thirty has another ten years of early adulthood in which to establish himself. The one who leaves in his late thirties, especially someone like Jackie Robinson, who sought a new occupation and a new place as a leader in society, must go through difficult occupational change even as he is entering the stressful period of the Midlife Transition. Those who, for a variety of internal and external reasons, cannot alter their mode of work or find a new occupation get burned out or live a highly marginal existence. This is probably the case with countless farmers, miners, construction workers, athletes, and workers in all occupations that make heavy bodily demands.

Even occupations that depend less directly on bodily capacity or prowess require a midlife change in style of work and living. The psychobiological abundance of early adulthood produces qualities of intensity, strength, quickness, agility, endurance, output, impulsive spontaneity, or formal discipline. Middle adulthood is a season in which other qualities can ripen—qualities of wisdom, judiciousness, magnanimity, unsentimental compassion, breadth of perspective, and the tragic sense (Unamuno, 1954; Sewall, 1959). Jaques (1965) has shown that great artists who continue their creative endeavors after forty tend to produce more profound, more universal, more "sculpted" works than before. Examples are Bach, Michelangelo, Dante, Goya, Frank Lloyd Wright, and Eugene O'Neill. Gifted musical performers such as pianists, violinists, and conductors give less lyrical or less technically virtuoso performances after forty but show greater depth of interpretation and individuality in style. Middle adulthood is the time for the most effective contributions in politics, diplomacy, organizational leadership, philosophy, and the "human services" professions.

Even in science, where the most brilliant specific discoveries are frequently made in early adulthood, the more profound, integrative theoretical work and the setting of new directions for the upcoming generation are more characteristic of middle adulthood. Many Nobel laureates win the prize for discoveries made in early adulthood. Some of these go on to do more creative work outside the laboratory. As they enter middle adulthood, many talented scientists turn increasingly to management, consultative, and teaching activities. At their best, the new roles provide satisfaction and fulfillment; at their worst, they are a means of saving face and keeping busy, but have little value for self or society and are a tragic waste of human life.

This development occurs in every walk of life, whenever a man's work aims change. Rather than seeking technical skill or sheer quantity of output, he tries to achieve more long-range goals and to facilitate the work and growth of others who are "on the production line" in his workworld. Alternatively, he may decide that he lacks the interest or talent to continue in his current occupation, or that it provides no challenging possibilities for him. He then seeks a new way to live in accord with his personal values, either by entering a more satisfying occupation or by minimizing the importance of work in his life and giving a more central place to other interests such as family or leisure.

The crucial biological issue at midlife is *not* that a man is literally on the verge of death or undergoing marked senescent decline. True, he is suffering some loss of his youthful vitality and, often, some insult to his youthful narcissistic pride. For various reasons, however, the modest bodily change is typically experienced as a fundamental threat, as evidence that one is on the threshold of old age, senility, death.

Jaques (1965) has posited the "midlife crisis" as a normal, developmentally given period in adult development, ordinarily starting in the late thirties and continuing for several years. He suggests that experience of one's mortality is at the core of the midlife crisis. His conception of the midlife crisis has much in common with my own, though I prefer the term *transition* to represent the broad process of structural change. The Midlife Transition may be rather mild or it may involve considerable turmoil, stress and disruption; in the latter case it is, truly, a midlife crisis.

Having a crisis at this time is not in itself pathological. Indeed, the person who goes through this period with minimal discomfort may be denying the actuality of changes in his life and losing an opportunity for personal development. To experience the dangers and the possibilities of this period, however, is to open a Pandora's box of unconscious fantasies, conflicts, and anxieties. Dealing with one's mortality means that a man must engage in grief-work for the dying self of youth, so that the self can be made more whole. He must undergo the experience of chaos and despair. The process begins in the Midlife Transition, but it extends through middle adulthood and takes a new form in the next era. It is never completed.

Generations in the Individual Life and in Society

Another vantage point from which to explore the differences among eras in adulthood is that of the changing generations. The concept of "generation" is of great importance, though rarely used in the study of the adult life course. With the passing years, the young adult has the sense of moving from one generation to the next and of forming new relationships with the other generations in his world. Our anxiety about age, and the ambiguity of our language regarding age, is nowhere more evident than in the lack of a standard terminology for talking about the generations. The terminology used here is commonly employed in an indirect or implicit way; but to reduce the ambiguity that so often obscures discussion of age, let me make my meanings more explicit.

The following age categories are widely experienced during adulthood. We generally regard other persons as being roughly the same age as ourselves (age peers or coevals) if they are within seven years above or below our age. In the sense, "my generation" covers a span of some twelve to fifteen years. Where the age difference is somewhat greater, say eight to fifteen years in either direction, the distance between us is symbolically a half-generation; the older one is rather in the position of an elder sibling. We can be equal in many respects, but he has greater experience and an implicit claim to greater authority in the relationship. As the age difference increases to twenty years and beyond, we are a full generation apart and the older one tends to be symbolized more as a parent than as a sibling. When the age difference is greater than forty years, there is a distance of two generations, and the older one assumes the symbolic properties of grandparent—as for the five-year-old child with grandparents in their forties or fifties, or the young adult of twenty in relation to his actual grandparents or to other adults of sixty-five to seventy and beyond. These ages are suggested as rough guidelines. The age-linkages of the categories undoubtedly vary somewhat (though not, I suspect, a great deal) among individuals and cultures. The categories themselves are relatively universal. They exist not only in societies such as India and Japan where age-grading is heavily built into the language and customs, but also more informally in societies such as our own that have a special interest in ambiguizing age.

These age categories are widely experienced by individuals and are recognized in various ways within every culture. They are symbolized in the imagery of generations and of generational ties and conflicts. The symbolization often carries familial connotations such as sibling, parent, child, young adult offspring, uncle-aunt, cousin, or grandparent. The familial meanings are formed partly in childhood but also in the course of adulthood; the basic meanings are archetypal and are not unique to, or solely rooted within, family life.

The symbolization of generations, and the social patterning of relationships within and between generations, contribute to the social order and to the elemental meanings that persons and groups have for each other. At the same time, age-grades may operate too rigidly. They may create impassable barriers to spontaneous relationships across age levels, and they may hamper the individual's development as he moves from one generation to the next. How best to utilize the reality of generational levels, without either denying their existence or defining them too rigidly, is a major issue in modern society. While acknowledging the importance of generational levels, we must try also to maximize the transactions between them. At every age, all of us carry within ourselves aspects of every generation. Coming to know and use these aspects of the self is a relevant task in every era. It is difficult in childhood, and even in early adulthood, to become more aware of the "older" aspects of the self and to have much empathy for persons who are more than ten years older than oneself. One of the special tasks of middle adulthood is to get more in touch with both the child and the elder in the self and in others. Work on this task allows us to transcend in some measure the generational barriers and to relate in a more fully human way to persons of all ages.

A man of thirty-five is likely to be regarded as an older sibling (that is, as a half-generation removed) by persons in their twenties. This is usually his own preferred view as well. He regards himself as "young" and very much part of the youthful generation. In their twenties people often fear that reaching thirty means getting "old"; they are relieved to discover in their thirties that they still have their youthful powers, though they may be more settled and more ready to assume a variety of older sibling relationships to those in full youth.

A change in generational status ordinarily begins in the late thirties and is well established by the mid-forties. A man of forty is regarded by persons in their twenties as a full generation removed, as much more established and part of the establishment. He tends to be symbolized more as a parent than an older sibling—as "dad" rather than "buddy." This message, conveyed with increasing frequency and force, often comes as a surprise to the man entering midlife. Responding initially with feelings of puzzlement, irritation, and depression, he wants to say: "This is ridiculous! I haven't really changed—I am still with *you*, not with *them*!" The "you" in this statement is the youth: the youthful generation in society and the youthful parts of the self. The "them" is less clearly defined and experienced. It may refer to the "old," and to the generation that has lost its place in society and its capacity for youthful pursuits. At a more conscious level, it refers to that vaguest and most ambiguously disturbing of generational levels in modern society, "the middle aged."

Thus, another source of the distinction between early and middle adulthood is the sequence of generations. Generational levels are "givens" of individual and collective experience. They are institutionalized by culturally defined age-grades, by the phasing of familial, occupational, and other careers, and by the historical rise and fall of successive generations. Their meaning is shaped by biology, history, culture, and social institutions and is given its most developed, unique form by the individual personality as he struggles to make sense of his experience of membership in the changing generations.

My conception of generations in the individual life cycle owes much to Ortega y Gasset's (1958) conception of generations in the history of society. He identifies five generations in the life cycle:

Childhood: age 0-15
Youth: age 15-30
Initiation: age 30-45
Dominance: age 45-60
Old Age: age 60+

Youth and initiation generations (age fifteen to forty-five) occupy the era of early adulthood. Youth starts with the Early Adult Transition and extends through the "novice" portion of early adulthood; this generation is engaged in entering the adult world and making an initial place for itself there. The initiation generation (age thirty to forty-five) includes the culmination of early adulthood and the Midlife Transition. It is intermediate between the Youth, who are not yet fully responsible participants in adult society, and the Dominant generation, which has the main burdens and satisfactions of senior leadership, management, and authority. The Dominant generation (forty-five to sixty) makes its ideas and aims the governing ones in every sector of society (such as politics, religion, art, and science) and devotes itself to implementing and perpetuating those aims. The upcoming, Initiation generation receives the wisdom of its elders, discovers their faults and limitations, and creates moderately or radically new ideas and aims. It will have occasion to implement its aims after the succession, when it comes to power.

At any given moment in history, says Ortega y Gasset, the crucial generations are the Initiation and Dominant; the relations between them are fateful for the future of society. Even in a period when a youthful "protest" generation plays a dramatic part on the social scene (as it did in the 1960s), the immediate historic effect of the protest is carried by the two older generations; the Youth generation will have a more direct impact as it enters positions of increasing power and enacts its successive generational roles from thirty to sixty. The youth who were around twenty in 1965 will pass forty in 1985 and begin their entry into the Dominant generation. What serious aims will they have formed by then, and what direction will they give our national life?

Erikson (1950, 1969), too, has been interested in the generation as an aspect of both collective history and individual biography. In his theory of the life cycle as a sequence of eight ego stages, he gives great attention to the meaning of membership in successive generations. Erikson does not emphasize the age-linkages of his stages. Indeed, he is often rather ambiguous on this score, so that many of his readers assume that the adult stages vary capriciously in their age of onset and their duration. A closer reading indicates, however, that Erikson does posit age-linkages. His first four stages cover early and middle childhood. The fifth stage, *Identity versus Identity Confusion*, occupies adolescence and the Early Adult Transition. The sixth, *Intimacy versus Isolation*, becomes focal in the early twenties, the seventh, *Generativity versus Stagnation*, at about forty, and the eighth and final stage, *Integrity versus Despair*, at around sixty. His last four ego stages thus unfold with and characterize the successive eras of early, middle, and late adulthood.

Erikson's seventh stage, Generativity versus Stagnation, is of special relevance here. Its onset coincides with the start of the Midlife Transition, and it remains a predominant concern through middle adulthood. A central issue for a man in this stage is to come to terms with the shift from early to middle adulthood. Erikson's term *generativity* is often erroneously thought to mean the creation of new generations, that is, begetting and raising children. Being a father to young children is, however, a task of early adulthood. As a man passes forty, the key issue is to assume responsibility for new generations of adults—the generations of Youth and of Initiation, in Ortega y Gasset's sense. He has the developmental task of becoming paternal in new ways to his own offspring and others. He cannot treat younger adults as if they were children under his benign control. He must find new ways to combine authority and mutuality, taking responsibility and offering leadership. Yet, he must also take them seriously as adults, inviting their participation, fostering their growth toward greater independence and authority, and engaging collaboratively with them wherever possible. Even as he himself becomes a "senior" member of the adult world, he must relate to persons in their thirties as junior but fully adult members who will soon succeed him, and to persons in their twenties as "novices" going through their initial formative period within the adult world.

This stage is defined as a *polarity* of Generativity versus Stagnation. The polarity, the coexistence of opposites that must somehow be integrated, is essential to Erikson's conception. In all the stages, development is a dialectical process in which antithetical extremes are to some degree reconciled, synthesized, and transcended. Characteristically, most American readers have focused on the "positive" pole, generativity, and have ignored its antithesis. Yet, stagnation is a critical element in this stage. To become generative a man must know how it feels to stagnate—to have the sense of not growing, of being static, stuck, drying up, withering away, bogged down in a life full of obligation and devoid of self-fulfillment—in short, to be dying, to live in the shadow of death.

The capacity to experience, endure, and fight against stagnation is an intrinsic aspect of the struggle toward generativity and of development in middle adulthood. Although stagnation is, in a sense, the "negative" pole in the dialectic, it is not a purely negative matter, something to be expunged or eliminated. The experience of personal stagnation plays a necessary and continuing part in the further development of one's own vitality. The recognition of this vulnerability in oneself becomes a source of wisdom, empathy, and compassion for others. We can truly understand the suffering of others only if we can identify with them through an awareness of our own weakness, defects, and destructiveness. Without this self-awareness we are capable only of the kind of sympathy, pity, and altruism that reduces the other's hardship but leaves him still a victim.

Evolving Careers and Enterprises

Turning to a final perspective on the adult life course, we examine the evolution of a man's careers (in work, family, and other spheres), his involvement in solitary and social pursuits, his broader life plans and goals—in short, the changing fabric of his life over the adult years. During his twenties, a young man ordinarily forms a preliminary adult identity, makes the first major choices (such as marriage, occupation, residence, and style of living) that define his place in the adult world, transforms his initial hopes into more specific aspirations and goals, and sets a path for the future. In a developmental transition at around thirty, he modifies the initial life structure and starts building a new structure for the last phase of early adulthood.

By about forty, a man has had a chance to build a life, to pursue his goals, and to realize the fruits of his youthful labors. It is now developmentally necessary to review his progress and to ask: "From whence have I come? Where am I now? Of what value is my life to society, to other persons, and especially to myself?" He must deal with the disparity between what he is and what he had dreamed to become.

These questions present themselves regardless of the outcome of his youthful efforts. A man who at forty has failed to realize his most cherished dreams might begin to come to terms with the failure and to arrive at a new set of choices around which he will try to rebuild his life. A man who has succeeded brilliantly must consider the meaning and value of his success. He may decide (not as a rationally thought out conclusion, but as a growing awareness of a state of being that he at first only dimly grasps) that his present life gives him considerable satisfaction and provides the basis for a good life in the future. Even in the fortunate but rare case, however, it is evident that a turning point has been reached: his new life, though it emerges directly out of the past, will nonetheless be different in certain crucial respects. On the other hand, a man who has accomplished his goals may come to feel that he is trapped—that the rewards he has gained are meaningless and that he is now caught within a stultifying situation. Other men find their lives relatively satisfactory in some respects and disappointing or destructive in others. It is important now to sort things out, come to terms with the limitations, and consider the next steps in the journey.

If a man starts a family in his twenties, his offspring are in or near adolescence as he completes his thirties. During his forties, however, the offspring are entering adulthood and his relationships with them are changing drastically. The nest is emptying as the nuclear family divides into separate households. There are often emotional losses and stresses for the parents in this process. At the same time, the emotional, financial, and social burdens of raising a family are greatly decreased. Grandparenthood usually begins in the forties or fifties. This is an important generational experience in its own right, and it changes the character of parenthood as well. If the man's parents (and those of his wife) are still alive, they are ordinarily in their sixties or seventies as he enters middle adulthood, and he becomes more parental, caring, and responsible toward them. If the parents have died, he becomes part of the oldest, senior generation in the extended family;

his sense of paternity becomes more complex and includes more than his own biological offspring.

At around forty a specific event often serves as a "marker" indicating where a man now stands and how far he can go. This culminating event has an objective significance in the external world. It represents some form of success or failure, of movement forward or backward on one's projected path. In the late thirties and early forties, there are usually several such events—promotions or failures at work, major difficulties or satisfactions in family life, personal illness, the illness or death of loved ones, recognitions or devaluations in the community or the wider society—that have great significance in a man's life. The culminating event has a special internal meaning for him: subjectively, it symbolizes the outcome of his youthful strivings; it represents the highest affirmation he will receive in this phase of his life, and he uses it to estimate his chances for realizing his aims in the future.

An example is given by a biologist in our study. He had made continuing and brilliant progress in his work during his thirties, becoming a full professor and department chairman, and gaining national recognition for his research discoveries. His second marriage, in his early thirties, was much more satisfactory than his first. He completed his most ambitious research project at forty-one, solving an important problem in his field—but two weeks after another researcher made the same discovery. This last was the culminating event. The meaning he constructed from it was that he could be an excellent biologist but not a researcher of the "first rank" or a Nobel laureate. During his Midlife Transition (age forty-one to forty-six), he worked on a reappraisal and modification of his life as a whole.

A culminating event frequently plays an important part in instigating the Midlife Transition. A man may regard it as the primary cause of the changes that follow, especially if he has great difficulties. However, the same event would have different meaning and consequences if it occurred at another time. It must be understood from a developmental perspective, within the context of the man's evolving life in early adulthood and, more indirectly, in relation to his preadult life. Coming as it does at the end of an era, this event has the meaning of culmination: first, because it is in actuality part of the outcome of that era; and second, because the man endows it (for both rational and irrational reasons) with added significance as a sign of his personal worth and his potential for the future.

A man at around forty is not simply reacting to a culminating event or any other external situation. He is reappraising his life, making an effort to reconsider the direction he has taken, the fate of his youthful dreams, the future possibilities for a better (or worse) life. He interprets the culminating event and others within this context. We must do the same. We must take account of a man's initial adult aspirations and the evolution of his occupational career, his career in marriage and family, his involvement in politics, religion, community activities, leisure, friendship—all segments of life that have significance for him.

It is not enough to examine his occupational career or his marriage or his inner conflicts or any other single segment in isolation. We must consider the life structure as it is organized at a given time and as it evolves over time. This structure is an integration of self-in-world. To apprehend it, we have to consider both the external aspects (the institutions, groups, roles, activities in which a man is involved) and the internal aspects (the ways in which the self is lived out, giving personal meaning to the external situations and activities and integrating the diverse elements into a single, relatively unified life). At the beginning of every developmental transition, it is the life structure that comes into question. At the end of every transition, a man must make the crucial choices that form the basis for the next structure in which he will for a time live.

In most theories of human development, as already noted, adolescence is assumed to be the last developmentally given transition. It is recognized that significant change may occur during adulthood, but such change is usually attributed to remarkable external events (e.g., dramatic success or failure, severe trauma or illness) and major societal change such as war or depression. Carl Gustav Jung, who lived from 1875 to 1961, was the first modern depth psychologist to make adult development a central concern (1968; cf. Campbell, 1971). Jung distinguishes the first half from the second half of life, and he places the dividing zone at around forty.

Jung was the first to propose that, with the culmination of youthful strivings, a new process of individuation begins at midlife and continues through middle and late adulthood. Individuation involves a greater freeing of the self from the tyranny of both the tribal demands and the repressed (instinctual) unconscious. Under favorable developmental conditions, it is possible at midlife to begin giving more attention to the archetypal unconscious, the inner source of self-definition, wisdom, and satisfaction. In this process, a man can start to deal with, and partially overcome, the great polarities that so often produce a splitting in his self and his life during early adulthood. He can now come to terms in a new way with the *anima*, the archetypal figure of the loving-transforming feminine, and thereby transcend the polarity of masculine and feminine that had so divided him. He can become more aware of the *shadow*, the archetypal figure containing those personal qualities that were repressed under the influence of his consciously held, tribal values. He can confront more directly the twin archetypes of *puer* and *senex* (Hillman, 1968). In its pure form, the puer represents birth, youthful potential, energy, unlimited possibility without weight, structure, or constraint. At the other extreme, the senex represents aging, dying, stasis, structure without energy, reason without joy, deliberation without action. In the successive eras, there must be a changing balance and integration of this two-sided archetype. At midlife, a man needs to maintain an active tie with the youthfulness in himself and others, and to use his energies toward self-determined ends; but he must also create a firmer yet more flexible structure, finding new freedom and creativity within the constraints of existentially given necessities. In time, he may become a wise old man (a senex still connected to puer) rather than a dirty old man or a withered old man without vitality.

The archetypes are, so to say, multiple seeds within the self. Most of them remain dormant through early adulthood. Through the process of individuation in midlife and beyond, as a man nourishes the archetypal figures and gives them a more valued place in his life, they will evolve and enrich his life in ways hardly dreamed of in youth. Jung's view of adult development is more dialectical, and more tragic, than the recent popular versions of instant self-actualization through workshops, mutual exhortations, and do-it-yourself techniques. He portrays an individuation process that contains painful transitions and recurrent setbacks. Yet, his view holds out the possibility of continuing self-renewal and creative involvement in one's own and others' lives.

In summary, biology, psychology, and the social sciences offer various perspectives for studying the individual life course and the changes that occur with age. None of these perspectives is sufficient in itself, however, to generate a conception of the human life cycle and of adult development. An adequate basis for the study of adult development cannot be found, for the present at least, in any one of the following: a genetically determined program of biological development; a pre-programmed sequence of stages in personality development; a culturally defined sequence of generations or age-grades; a series of institutionally defined careers and timetables and socializing arrangements. A multidisciplinary approach to adult development is thus not a luxury but a prime necessity. This field will require a basic change in orientation and in the division of intellectual labor among the sciences of man.

By standing back and taking a more complex, bio-psycho-social view, we get a more encompassing and more useful image of the life cycle. We need to look with three (or more) eyes, as it were, and thereby gain a multidimensional picture unavailable to the single eye. The eras constitute an underlying order in the life cycle while allowing for the infinite manifest variety of individual lives. This order is grounded in the nature of humanity as a species and in the nature of human society as a complex, multigenerational, historically evolving system. This sequence of age-linked eras has probably characterized the male life cycle in human societies for the past several thousand years. To what extent it holds for women is an open question and one that needs urgently to be studied.

This view of the life cycle represents a middle ground between total cultural relativism and immutable universalism. Although the life cycle has certain underlying universal qualities during the present epoch in human evolution, myriad variations on the universal themes are produced by differences in culture and institutions, as well as in individual heredity and circumstances. In time, the universals themselves will change. The further evolution of individual and society will no doubt modify the nature and timing of the eras.

Late Adulthood

In the early sixties, middle adulthood normally comes to an end and late adulthood begins (see Figure 1). The Late Adult Transition, extending from roughly sixty to sixty-five, is part of both eras and provides a bridge between them. Again, the two eras are not demarcated by a single universal event, though various marker events (such as illness or retirement) may highlight the end of middle adulthood and shape the transitional process. The Late Adult Transition exists for the same kinds of reasons as the Midlife Transition, though the specific content is different. Through a multiplicity of biological, psychological, and social changes, the character of living is altered in fundamental ways at around sixty. A transitional period of several years is needed to terminate one era and to initiate the next.

At this time, there is a new reality and experience of bodily decline. As indicated earlier, statistical data on normal bodily changes with age show a gradual decline starting at about thirty and continuing its inexorable course over the remaining years. A man does not suddenly become "old" at fifty or sixty or eighty. In the fifties and sixties, however, many things happen to intensify a man's experience of his own aging and mortality. They remind him that he is moving from "middle age" to a later generation identified by the terrifying term "old age."

No one of these signs of decline happens to all or even most men, but every man is likely to experience several and to be greatly affected by them. There is the increasing frequency of death and serious illness among his loved ones, friends, and colleagues. Even if he is in good health and physically active, he has many reminders of his decreasing vigor and capacity, and of his increasing susceptibility to aches and pains. He is likely to have at least one major illness or impairment (such as heart disease, cancer, defective vision or hearing, endocrinal-hormonal dysfunction, and depression or other emotional distress). He will receive medical warnings that he must follow certain precautions or run the risk of more serious illness. The internal messages from his own body, too, tell him to make accommodations or major changes in his mode of living. Of course, men at around sixty differ widely in these respects. Some men face a late adulthood of serious illness or impairment, while others lead more active, energetic lives. However, every man in the Late Adult Transition must deal with the decline or loss of some of his middle adult powers.

Beyond the bodily decline as such, there is a culturally defined change of generation in the sixties. If the term *middle aged* is vague and frightening, what about our terminology (and imagery) for the subsequent years? The commonly used words such as "old," "elderly," "golden age," and "senior citizen" take on negative connotations that reflect the basic cultural and personal anxiety about aging. In the twenties, it appears that passing thirty is getting "over the hill." In the thirties, turning forty is a threat as grave as death. At every point in life, the passing of the next age-threshold is anticipated as a total loss of youth, of vitality, of life itself.

What can it mean, then, to approach sixty and to feel that all forms of youth, even those last vestiges remaining in middle age, are about to disappear, so that only the ultimate nemesis, "old age," remains? The developmental task, in Jungian terms, is to overcome the archetypal splitting of youth and age, of puer and senex, and to find in each season of life an appropriate balance of the two. In late adulthood, the senex aspect predominates, but it can take various forms of the creative, wise elder as long as a man retains his connectedness to youthful vitality and to the forces of growth in self and world. During the Late Adult Transition, a man fears that the puer within himself is dying and that only the senex—an empty, isolated, dry structure devoid of energy, interests, or creative supplies—will survive for a brief and foolish old age. The task is to sustain his youthfulness in a new form and to actualize the new potentialities of late adulthood rather than cling to the now-inappropriate life structure of middle adulthood.

Again, we can see the end of an era as the culmination of the aspirations and strivings that were important within it. During the Late Adult Transition, a man concludes the enterprises of middle adulthood. It is time now to move out of the center stage of his world. He is called upon (and increasingly calls upon himself) to reduce the heavy responsibilities he carried in middle adulthood and to live in a changed relationship with society and with the self.

Moving out of center stage means not only that a man receives less recognition but also that he has less authority and power. As Ortega y Gasset has put it, his is no longer the Dominant generation. In the family, he reaches a point in grandfatherhood where he can at best be modestly helpful to his grown offspring and a source of indulgence and moral support to his grandchildren. But his middle adult offspring must bear the major responsibility and exercise the primary authority in the family. If he does not give up his authority, he is likely to become a tyrannical ruler—a despotic, unwise, unloved, and unloving senex figure—and his adult offspring become puerile adults unable to love him or themselves.

In his occupational and community life, too, a man must find a way to engage in meaningful work or play, but he can no longer hold a position of hierarchical authority. If he holds such a position beyond a certain age, say sixty-five or seventy, he is "out of phase" with his own generation and with the upcoming generation in middle adulthood who need to assume their proper place in the establishment. It sometimes happens that a man in his seventies or older retains a preeminent position in government, religion, business, or another institutional domain. One thinks of political leaders such as Mao Tse Tung, Chou-en Lai, Churchill, Ben Gurion, Gandhi, DeGaulle, and Adenauer; of religious leaders such as Pope John XXIII; of businessmen such as J.D. Rockefeller and Henry Ford. Even when a man has a relatively high level of energy and skill at this age, it is, I believe, a failure in his development and very costly to his society if he retains power well into late adulthood. He tends to be an isolated leader, in poor touch personally and intellectually with his immediate staff and his followers, and overly idealized or hated by them. What is worse, the continuity of the generations is disrupted: the generation in middle adulthood suffers from powerlessness and conformism; and the generation in early adulthood suffers from the lack of innovation, moral support, and tutelage they need from their immediate seniors.

I am *not* proposing that there be a universal, constant retirement age at which everyone stops work altogether. Indeed, we need a flexible arrangement permitting retirement with dignity and security as early, say, as fifty and as late as seventy. The age at which a man retires from formal employment, and especially from a position of direct authority over others, ought to reflect his own needs, capabilities, and life circumstances. Moreover, "retirement" in this specific sense should not mean that a man no longer engages in some form of work that is satisfying for him and of some value to others. In late adulthood, however, his worklife should stem more from his own interests and creative energies than from external pressure and financial need. By this age, a man has paid his dues to society; he has earned the right to be and do what is most important to himself. He should be, in his own view and that of society, beyond the distinction between work and play, so that he can devote himself in a serious-playful way to the interests that flow most directly from the depths of the self.

Society should offer its citizens in late adulthood the financial and social security that are the external conditions for this freedom of choice. We must also learn to create facilitating environments for development, to use Winnicott's (1965) apt phrase, in early and middle adulthood so that more men will have the internal resources for meaningful work-play in their later years.

If a man creates a new life structure, a new form of self-in-world, late adulthood can be a season as full and rich in its own way as the others are in theirs. Some of the greatest works of art and philosophy have been produced by men in their sixties, seventies, and even eighties; and their creators have had vital, self-fulfilling lives. One thinks of celebrated figures such as Picasso, Yeats, Verdi, Frank Lloyd Wright, Freud, Jung, Sophocles, Michelangelo, and Tolstoy. In other fields of endeavor, there are Benjamin Franklin, Lawrence Olivier, Buckminster Fuller, and numerous Supreme Court Justices. A less known example is Nate Shaw, the black man whose remarkable life story was evoked and recorded by Rosengarten (1974). Countless other men have contributed their wisdom as elders in a variety of counseling, educative, and supporting roles in family and community.

An Evolutionary Perspective on Middle Adulthood

The human species has existed for at least half a million years and probably more than three million years. Until some 10,000 years ago, man led a precarious, unsettled life in small societies that lived primarily by hunting, fishing, and gathering food. The character of human life was transformed by the development of agriculture, the formation of more stable societies, the invention of more effective technologies, and the emergence of writing and other means of generating and transmitting culture over multiple generations.

In primitive hunting-gathering societies, only half the population reached age twenty (chiefly because of infant mortality), and not more than 10 percent survived beyond forty (Weiner, 1971:162-163). The high mortality rate in early adulthood was attributable not to earlier senescence—seventy to eighty years has probably been the normal life span for many thousands of years—but to the ravages of illness, accident, warfare, and inadequate food supply.

United Nations data on the age composition of contemporary nations provide some interesting comparisons. In Pakistan, where fertility is high and living conditions among the worst, only 17 percent of the population is over forty, and this figure is somewhat lower in Nigeria and Bangladesh. At the other extreme, 35 percent are over forty in Japan, 36 percent in the United States, and 42 percent in West Germany. Life after forty—the eras of middle adulthood and beyond—has been a significant part of man's collective experience for but a moment in our history. Small wonder that we are still anxious about turning forty and that we lack cultural wisdom about living in middle adulthood.

Primitive man had, as it were, little biological or tribal reason to continue living after forty. By that age the children were grown, the best years of productive labor ended, and the contribution to the tribe fulfilled. By forty the individual was obsolete. The tribe needed only a small cohort in middle adulthood to contribute their ripening wisdom in positions of leadership and responsibility. To have a large cohort would have put too great a strain on societal resources and created intolerable problems for individuals who had no viable social role.

The last 10,000 years have seen the emergence of more stable, complex societies that have been better able to sustain individual life through the full human life span. Society can now generate larger cohorts of middle-aged (and older) adults. It provides greater environmental support (protection from the elements, better medical care, improved living conditions) for survival beyond forty. It provides greater psychosocial support for continued individual development beyond the level possible by forty.

In addition, society increasingly *requires* larger cohorts as its social organization increases in size and complexity. More elaborate structures have been developed in every aspect of social life—agriculture, industry, government, religion, education, health care, science, art, even recreation—and occupational roles have become more differentiated and specialized. With these cultural and institutional changes, society must foster the development of larger numbers of persons in middle adulthood, persons who can contribute as leaders, managers, mentors, and sources of traditional wisdom as well as of vision, imagination, and innovation.

The required work of middle adulthood is different in crucial respects from that of youth. It involves greater responsibility, perspective, dispassionate interest, and judgment. To do it well, one must be able to care for younger (and older) adults, to exercise authority creatively, and to transcend the youthful extremes of shallow conformity and impulsive rebelliousness. The moderate midlife decrease in biological capacity must be counterbalanced by an increased psychosocial capacity to contribute—in countless intellectual, emotional, moral, aesthetic, managerial, and reparative ways—to the maintenance and growth of the culture.

To the extent that the person in middle adulthood does not develop in these ways and does not have viable social roles appropriate to his age, his life is of little value to society or to himself. Society does much better in maintaining bodily health after forty than in fostering psychological well-being and providing the conditions for a personally satisfying, socially productive life in middle adulthood. The problem exists in all societies, large or small, capitalist or socialist, agricultural or industrial or postindustrial. It is universal because its basic roots are in human evolution rather than in the nature of a particular society.

A few thousand years is not enough to learn what to do with middle adulthood and with the institutions that shape its course. The rapid development of powerful technology and of cumbersome institutional structures has created a need for greater numbers of productive middle-aged individuals. But the need has far outstripped our cumulative understanding of middle adulthood. For example, the family is above all an institution for early adulthood, for youthful parents striving to rear their preadult offspring and to establish their own place in adult society. What are the functions of the family, and what should be its form and its guiding values, under the new living conditions of middle adulthood and beyond? Again, most occupations are defined in terms of the work done during the individual's initial fifteen to twenty years in them, that is, during early adulthood. How should occupations, jobs, and careers change during middle adulthood? What new kinds of work are possible and desirable from the point of view of the individual and of society? These and countless other questions are so new, and run so counter to traditional ways of thinking and feeling, that we can hardly think about them at all, let alone find rational solutions. The paradox is that we must devote ourselves to thinking and testing out possible solutions, even though we know that we are not up to the task and that it will take generations more of "muddling through" before anything very constructive can be done with our institutions and our individual lives.

It was man's experience for several million years that he was not likely to survive beyond forty, and even now the possibilities for a good life in middle adulthood are obscure. Many persons at around forty experience an acute recognition of their mortality, a feeling that time is running out and that they may soon die or, worse, have a life without meaning for self or others. This profound anxiety reflects the ancient experience of the species. The move from early to middle adulthood represents a grave threat, which is based on the equating of youth with strength and vitality, and of age—even middle age—with weakness, vulnerability, and death. It is difficult to deal with the threat partly because it is symbolic, its meaning colored by the evolutionary experience of the species. It is difficult also because the tribe offers so little by way of cultural wisdom, instruction, or support. It is clear to a man that a new season is about to be born, that his life will be crucially changed in middle adulthood. But what are the options, what fates await him? He gets many explicit messages and vague vibrations about the likelihood of decline, loss, and restriction, but there are few positive cultural symbols of the middle-aged hero, the lover, friend or mentor, the person of dignity, wisdom, authority, creativeness.

The large-scale extension of the actual life span beyond forty is one of the great, though problematic, achievements in human evolution. It is one of the steps in the "ascent of man" that Bronowski neglected. We may need another million years—if indeed we have that much time left—to learn how to make pretty good use of middle adulthood. It is too much to expect that the Midlife Transition will be managed easily or well by most persons in any society within the immediate future. Still, given the importance of the problem and our limited individual and cultural resources for dealing with it, we are well advised to regard it as a major issue on our agenda for social change.

NOTE

1. This chapter is an outgrowth of a study of adult development; my collaborators in this study are Charlotte M. Darrow, Edward B. Klein, Maria H. Levinson, and Braxton McKee. We are now completing a book on adult development (Levinson et al.). The research has been supported in part by research grant number MH-15982 and by a Career Development Award, number MH-13032, both from the National Institute of Mental Health.

The Changing Corporate Character

8

MICHAEL MACCOBY

The whole life of an American is passed like a game of chance, a revolutionary crisis, or a battle. As the same causes are continually in operation throughout the country, they ultimately impart an irresistable impulse to the national character.

Alexis de Tocqueville
Democracy in America

The corporation has become the cutting edge of society. In both capitalist and socialist industrial societies, the center of society is production and progress is measured by the Gross National Product. Production comes first, and then people organize other services and institutions in order to do something about the production. We produce as much as we can and then worry about how to take care of the smog, pollution, or the bad effects on the health of the worker. We build as many cars as we can and then worry about how to route them in traffic.

The large corporation is the most dynamic institution of this society. (1) It controls and transforms wealth. (2) It creates the very nature of both work and leisure. (3) It organizes more human energy than any other institution. It appears exciting and rewarding to many of the most talented college graduates. Work with the corporation motivates and eventually changes them, bringing out and reinforcing some human potentials and not others. (4) The corporation is in constant touch with the rest of society. It is responsive to changes in people's attitudes, and it must *adapt* to these changes in order to sell products and to make them appealing, and in order to attract the young workers and managers.

The corporations, especially the most dynamic ones, also interact with and adapt to the other dominant forces or power centers in the society, such as the Congress, the Executive, the military, labor unions, and the international market. Indeed, our findings suggest that the emerging leaders of corporation and government are similar character types.

Thus, the large corporation operating in many states and many countries is at the heart of both the economic and the social system. It must be adaptable, but its ability to adapt and to influence the desires and goals of the society allows it to dominate the productive sector and increasingly to command the resources of the society. While the largest corporations are becoming more and more economically powerful, they are also laying the psychological bases for continued power. They are acting on people all the time both in the developed and underdeveloped nations, forming their view of reality and their desires. Corporate managers effect character formation particularly through their influence on television, movies, and advertising. They play on our appetites and fears in order to mold our needs, and they emphasize models of virtue. This is not to say that they create these needs and desires; rather, they are sensitive to what most people want and nudge these needs and desires in directions that they can satisfy and profit from.

In the 1950s, when the hegemony of American business seemed unchallenged in the world, sociologists predicted that after decades of domination, the old-style authoritarian and competitive entrepreneur would disappear from the management of large corporations, since he would lose his function. Cooperation would be maximized in a frictionless bureaucracy run by committees at the top and greased by new human relations techniques such as sensitivity groups. Observers like David Riesman (1950) and William H. Whyte (1956) saw the benign, conformist, "other-directed" "organization man" replacing the rugged individualist of the past. Whyte, seeing the corporation as the wave of the future, worried that the transformation of national character would produce a bland and mediocre society in which everyone sacrificed self for security. Others such as the psychologist Abraham Maslow (1968) were more hopeful; Maslow believed that the noncompetitive corporation would be the ground for a new flowering of the human spirit. Once the corporate manager achieved security and status, Maslow thought he would concern himself with "self-actualization."

The bases for these fears and hopes about the organization man of the 1950s were swept away in the 1960s with the rapid growth of international competition and the establishment of new national goals. With Presidents Kennedy and Johnson stimulating the competitive spirit in corporations by supporting the missile and space races and demanding that the United States be "number one," electronics, aerospace, and chemicals became the fastest growing industries and contributed most to the U.S. balance of payments. Companies like General Electric, RCA, Lockheed, Dow Chemical, Xerox, and IBM rushed to beat the competition. Their view was that they could not develop new products and market them against tough opponents if they were manned solely by benign organization men who never took any risks.

These large organizations also would have functioned poorly if their highly interdependent and delicate development and marketing teams had been staffed by traditional entrepreneurs, either rigid authoritarian bosses or primitive jungle fighters who might rip each other to shreds to gain power. In a not uncommon example in one corporation, a brilliant young entrepreneur soared to a key executive position in his early thirties, only to be relegated to an unimportant staff position a short while later. He was reportedly demoted because he had so used people and then betrayed them that he had "left a trail of corpses behind him and a deep desire for revenge which finally caught up with him." The ideal new corporate manager had to be competitive but not destructive.

Do such managers exist? If so, what kind of people are they?

For the past five years, members of the Project on Technology, Work and Character[1] have been interviewing over 250 corporate managers and executives and, in some cases, their wives and secretaries, about their work, emotional attitudes, and goals in order to understand how the corporation selects leaders and molds their charcter. Over 75 have also taken Rorschach tests. In the course of these interviews, most of which range from three to twenty hours, managers have spoken freely about their interests and anxieties, their beliefs, hopes, and dreams.[2]

Before the interviews began, we described the purpose of the study and emphasized our concern with understanding how the demands of their work affected the development of their character. Only two people refused to be interviewed. Most of the corporate managers cooperated with the study because they felt it could help them to understand themselves better and to improve their work. Some were conscious of connections between their feelings of anxiety and the highly competitive work they were engaged in; they hoped that the findings of the study would help both to improve the organization and to minimize anxiety. Some managers also stated that corporate life had been responsible for their failures as husbands and fathers. By talking to the psychoanalyst-interviewer, they hoped to learn why. In contrast, other managers saw the study solely as an opportunity to gain greater knowledge about themselves which they could use either in becoming more effective managers or bettering their position in the competition. This group agreed to cooperate only if the sociopsychoanalytic investigator promised to point out character "flaws" that were hampering their work and chances for advancement. Finally, in a few other cases, the motivation for participation was more narcissistic: these managers were flattered by the psychoanalyst's interest in them, and they used the opportunity to describe themselves fully.

Whatever the motive, the interview questions stimulated most interviewees to think critically about experiences. They welcomed the chance to talk with a sympathetic and nonjudgmental listener about matters many had never before articulated. Quite a few said they had never before considered what the concept of love meant to them. For some, the interview experience led to a reexamination of life decisions. On the whole, their responses to this experience were more open and sincere than expected.

There were three major findings. The first was the discovery of four major social character types in the corporation: the craftsman, the company man, the gamesman, and the jungle fighter. These are, of course, ideal types, for most people are mixtures. However, the managers themselves recognized these types, and their self-descriptions usually matched our judgment about type. While all four types spoke in similar terms, each had a different interpretation of a number of key concepts. For example, all four described themselves as competitive, but for the craftsman, this meant competing against one's own performance or the materials to build a better product. For the company man, competition was defined as moving ahead to protect one's security, in order not to fall behind. For the jungle fighter, competition meant destroying one's rivals or being destroyed by them. For the gamesman, competition was the thrill of the game, the goal of being the winner and avoiding becoming a loser.

The second main finding was that the corporation can be conceived in terms of a "psychostructure" in which roles must be filled by particular character types. Conversely, the wrong character type cannot function in a role where his emotional attitudes do not fit the work. This finding solves the theoretical problem of whether character determines role or role determines character. As we shall see in the discussion of the gamesman, role and character interact, but the psychostructure *selects* individuals for roles in terms of character.

This process of social selection was part of the third finding: that the character of managers changes over the years in order to adapt to the demands of the corporation. This might be called the process of internal selection; character traits adaptive to work are reinforced and strengthened, while unadaptive attitudes tend to wither away through disuse or suppression.

Of the major types, the gamesman seemed to be the most dynamic, since he (or she) fitted the leadership needs of both corporations and political teams based on:

(1) Innovation—continual creation of new products or plans
(2) Interdependent teams of experts
(3) Fast-moving flexibility—the need to meet
lines
(4) Competition—internal, national, and international

The gamesman is best defined as a person who loves change and wants to influence it. He likes to take calculated risks and is fascinated by technique and new methods. He sees a developing project, human relations, and his own career in terms of options and possibilities, as in a game. His character is a collection of near paradoxes understood only in terms of its adaptation to game-like organizational requirements. He is cooperative but competitive; detached and playful but compulsively driven to succeed; a team player but a would-be superstar; a team leader but often a rebel against the bureaucratic hierarchy; fair and unprejudiced but unsympathetic and contemptuous of weakness. Unlike other business types, he is energized to compete not because he wants to build an empire or accumulate riches, but rather to attain fame and glory and to experience the exhilaration of running his team. His goal is to be known as a winner, and his deepest fear is to be labeled a loser.

Many observers have pointed out that business has become more and more like a system of interrelated games—the money game, the marketing game, and R&D game—all requiring specialized players. Indeed, many businessmen will ask a new acquaintance, "What's your game?" rather than "What do you do?". In the most dynamic corporations, managerial meetings have a locker-room atmosphere where discussion of game strategy is punctuated with detached, mildly sadistic humor, employed by the superior to keep the inferior in his place. These little putdowns can be called "homeopathic doses of humiliation" necessary to maintain a minimum of hierarchy without having to humiliate a person definitively by, for example, having him eat in another dining room or calling his boss "Mister Jones" rather than "Jack." Interestingly, some women who reach top corporate positions remark that getting used to such joking is one of their most difficult hurdles. Those who respond best are those who have played team sports seriously. Learning to accept ego punctures without being deflated permanently may be something acquired in team sports. One female executive on the way up told us how she fought back. Kidded about her short skirts, she put a shapely leg up on the table and asked her challenger whether he saw anything wrong with it. Although such a comeback to a superior is unusual, her gamey spirit gained her high marks.

The gamesman's emotional attitude has meshed perfectly with the corporation's need for managers who can be turned on by the new competitive challenges of the post-Sputnik era. Charles L. Hughes, the industrial relations manager of Texas Instruments, wrote a book in the mid-1960s called *Goal Setting*. He pointed out that extensive research showed that the kind of people who were most successful in the high technology corporation were those who were "compulsively and habitually seeking to win." Speaking to older style bosses and organization men who might be put off by the gamesman, Hughes pointed out that the man who always wants to win and avoids jobs that have little chance of success is not a liability to the organization if he is put to work in the right places. Hughes also astutely observed another advantage to the corporation in that the compulsive winner's main goal was not to become rich but to win. For the gamesman, a high salary is important mainly because this is the way the game is scored, and he does not want to fall behind the others. He sees his salary not in absolute terms of becoming rich, but in comparative terms of staying ahead of others in his peer group.

The gamesman aspires to be a kind of quarterback or football coach. His view of the corporate game comes closest to professional football, increasingly the favorite spectator sport in the United States, replacing the slower, less aggressive, less innovative, and more individualistic game of baseball. His function is to integrate specialists into a unified team and to inspire them to work faster and more competitively. According to Gallup polls, football overtook baseball as the most popular spectator sport in America in the mid-1960s, exactly at the point where the advanced technology corporations were becoming the models for industry and government, the glamour companies that led the way in maintaining a favorable U.S. balance of payments as international competition intensified. The gamesman often uses the metaphors of football and its technology in his work. He will speak of the "game plan," of making "the big play"; he will say, "We're going to have to punt now," or "Let's try an end around and see if we can corner a few more yards of the market"; he will test out a new man by "giving him the ball and letting him run with it." This language is increasingly the vocabulary of corporate business.

The gamesman is not easily evaluated by traditional moral categories. In contrast to the authoritarian boss of the past, he tends to be unbigoted and nonideological. He believes that everybody who is good should be allowed to play, and that neither race, sex, nor religion nor anything else matters besides contributing to the team. Nor is he hostile. ("Nastiness and vindictiveness mean that person has already shown himself a loser," one gamesman told us.) Unlike the jungle fighter, he takes no pleasure in another person's defeat. But this does not imply that he is sensitive to their feelings or sympathetic about their special needs. He is not compassionate, but he is fair. Since he is so concerned about winning, he tends to evaluate people almost exclusively in terms of what they can do for the team. Unlike the more loyal organization man, he is ready to replace a player as soon as he feels that person weakens the team. ("The word loyalty is too emotional," said one gamesman, "and empathy or generosity gets in the way of work.") Although he may try to spark the "dead wood," the gamesman believes he fulfills his responsibility to others by giving them a "fair" chance to play the game. He ignores the fact that some people, because of their background or temperament, never have a fair chance to compete against those like himself who are quicker and more driven. He tends to classify people as winners or losers and to be contemptuous of the losers.

Gamesmen profess to be democratic but here the ideal does not always fit reality. While their dislike of both autocratic bosses and the trappings of position is genuine, their behavior with subordinates is often manipulative, even when they consider themselves to be democratic. Take the case of W, a high-powered thirty-six-year-old general manager of a large development laboratory. W is informal, enthusiastic, pragmatic, and antimoralistic. Our analysis of his interview and Rorschach shows he has a sadistic streak and is a gamesman with strong traces of jungle fighter which he controls by humor, putdowns, and putons. We asked him to name three people, either alive or historical figures, whom he admired. His tongue-in-cheek answer: Jesus Christ, Vince Lombardi, and Harry Truman. We asked why he chose these three. "Jesus, because he was so good at motivating people; Lombardi for his high ideals, and I've always admired Harry Truman's guts."

W saw himself as antiauthoritarian. "I hate righteousness," he said. "No one person has the answer. Everyone should have his own style and stick to it. Let everyone do his thing." W believes that decision-making from the top down is a thing of the past. He wants decisions to emerge from participatory democracy. We accompanied him to a meeting where, he had told us earlier, everyone was to have a chance to present a view of a new project. As the meeting proceeded, W cut off those who disagreed with him and called on those whom he knew shared his view. When the meeting began to go against him, as the cautious types questioned his plans, he warned the group that they were "cutting their own throats." Artfully, he spread fear that their decision would lead to business failure. Thus, he silenced his opponents, then quickly he dispelled the fear by promising great rewards if the group followed his way. It was a virtuoso performance, emotionally draining yet creating a spirit of excitement and adventure for the new project. But was it democracy?

We asked W, who dodged the question. "I like to win, and I don't like to spend too much effort if I'm going to lose. I don't like people who whine. I like people to be forward with me; a person should be man enough to say what he thinks." W considers the democratic meeting to be an arena in which each person has an equal chance to prevail, and he, like other gamesmen, believes he can come out on top in such a verbal trial by combat. (Another gamesman put it simply, "I have the knack of convincing people.") This definition of democracy does not include respect for each individual, and it is not for the shy, timid, or inarticulate.

Despite the democratic ideals, most gamesmen—even those who are not sadistic—will say that to do their jobs, they must be "tough." In the large corporation, this toughness does not necessarily mean using abusive language or firing incompetents. It does mean not letting any emotional or sentimental considerations stand in the way of reaching a goal, in contrast to the person who can be sweet-talked or threatened into abandoning a position. As one vice-president said, "Around a real tough guy, there is an aura of power, being right—a winning attitude."

W worries when some of the younger engineers leave, despite all the freedom he gives them. "Since I last saw you, one of my best guys turned in his resignation to go to Canada to farm. Can you believe it? We had a big investment in the guy. I wouldn't care if he was going to another company, at least he would still be contributing to the industry. But this guy is throwing it all up. That's scary. Guys don't want to play on the team anymore. They're not motivated. How can I do my job if they won't play?" What he does not realize is that one reason why some of the quiet young craftsmen leave the company is that they feel pushed around and manipulated by him.

Like other character types defined in terms of a dominant orientation, the gamesman classification includes a number of subtypes. Some subtypes operate well while they are young managers, but fail to resolve middle-aged and middle-management crises. One subtype focused on later in this chapter was more successful because he was able to renounce his adolescent rebelliousness and become a believer in the organization.

The typical gamesman's midcareer crisis exposes the weaknesses in his character. His strengths are those of adolescence: he is playful, industrious, fair, enthusiastic, and open to new ideas. But like many adolescents, gamesmen confuse games with life. More dependent than they realize, they fear both personal intimacy and social commitment because they fear feeling trapped. They want to maintain an illusion of limitless options.

At his most neurotic, the gamesman is unrealistic, manipulative, and a compulsive workaholic. His hyped-up activity masks his doubts about who he is and where he is going. When he lets down, he is faced with feelings of powerlessness. The reason he is a compulsive player is that he must be turned on, energized by competitive pressures. He is a compulsive consumer of crises. (Some tell us that as teenagers they were "hell raisers.") Deprived of challenge at work, he is bored and slightly depressed; he tends to sit around watching TV, playing games, or drinking too much, but once the game is on, once he can feel he is in the Superbowl, or one-to-one against another star, he comes to life, thinks hard, and is cool. While other character types found in the corporation, such as the traditional craftsman or the security-seeking organization man, find such high-pressure competition enervating and counterproductive, for the gamesman it is the elixir of life.

In effect, the gamesman finds normal everyday reality too humdrum and slow. He craves a more romantic, fast-paced, semifantasy life, and this need puts him in danger of losing touch with reality. The most successful gamesmen keep it under control and are able to distinguish between the game and reality. Even so, in boring meetings, they sometimes imagine that they are really somewhere else—at a briefing for an air-bombing mission, or in a hideout where the detested manager who is speaking is really a Mafia chieftain whom the gamesman will someday rub out.

The gamesman's yearnings for autonomy and his fear of being controlled contribute to a common midcareer uneasiness. Even the most successful gamesmen feel a kind of self-contempt that they are giving in, that they are performing for others rather than developing their own goals. A number of gamesmen respond ingeniously. Impatient with red tape and unwilling to be boxed-in, some try to skirt around authority to create their own organizations within the larger company.

G is thirty-six years old and manages 4,000 people in a division of a multinational corporation. His goal is to have power. "I experience power," he said, "as not being pushed around by the company; it's a kind of freedom. Also, I can tell others what to do and set the direction and the strategy and the tone." As a young marketing manager, G figured out the way to the top was "to get a relationship with a powerful customer to use against the company. You need a very big customer who is always in trouble and demands changes from the company. That way you automatically have power in the company, and with the customer too. I like to keep my options open."

In trying to win, gamesmen may gain power, but they can threaten the whole organization. One such gamesman, Q, has succeeded in forming his own "semiautonomous" team, but his superiors complain that he is trying to set up his own barony and making it more difficult to develop a more rational companywide policy.

Such gamesmen are unable to resolve the contradiction between their wish for independence and their desire to run the team. They may create a good project organization and may even energize a whole company for a while, but in the long run, they lack the patience and commitment to people and principles necessary to build a healthy organization.

The fatal danger of such gamesmen is that they will be trapped into perpetual adolescence, never outgrowing their self-centered compulsion to win, never confronting their deep boredom with life when it is not a game.

Bedazzled by the perpetually adolescent charm of the gamesman and sympathetic to his struggle against less attractive bureaucrats, our society romanticizes him. One might say that, although we have no heroes, the gamesman is our favorite antihero. In the popular motion picture "The Sting," two playful gamesmen, Johnny Hooker and Henry Gondorff (played by Robert Redford and Paul Newman) confuse and conquer Doyle Lonnegan (played by Robert Shaw), the hated boss of a large gangster organization, dazzling him with a fake reality created by the fast-moving teamwork of many specialists using advanced technology. In this modern morality play, the boyish, cooperative, informal gamesmen have the audience's full support because they are fighting killers. Although the master con artist, Gondorff, is shown as bored and hungover when there is no action, one tends to forget that these "heroes" are amoral, manipulative confidence men, lonely hustlers who drift apart after the game is over.

An old and tiring gamesman is a pathetic figure, especially after he has lost a few contests and, with them, his confidence. Once his youth, vigor, and even the thrill in winning are lost, he becomes depressed and loses his goals, questioning the purpose of his life. No longer energized by the team struggle and unable to dedicate himself to something he believes in beyond himself, which might be the corporation or alternatively the larger society, he finds himself starkly alone. His attitude has kept him from deep friendship and intimacy. Nor has he sufficiently developed abilities that would strengthen the self, so that he might gain satisfaction from understanding (science) or creating (invention, art). In contrast to the aging gamesman, there are seventy-year-old craftsmen whose goal in life is not winning, but making something better; when such men retire from the corporation, they are still energetic and interested in new ideas.

N is now forty-six. Seven years ago, he was on top, the manager of a project that gained great profits for his corporation. He was a winner. Speaking of the past, he said, "I never wanted security; I felt we were all good race horses and we'd be allowed to run. I wanted to be part of the winning team. The corporation had begun to take off. It was wide open." Now, two of his projects have failed, and he has been given a staff position with vague responsibilities. His superiors worry about what to do with him. He has become an alcoholic, and he is depressed. "I don't fear death now," he tells us, "but I fear discomfort. Hard knocks grind your ego down. There is a lot of pain there too. We sure had an ego then, partly because we were young."

Q is still at the top at age forty, but is starting to worry about the future. Despite his success, he feels he is a failure. "I am considering whether all this is worth it. I started thinking about this four or five years ago. Before, I never thought about it. I feel a lack of joy. I don't see where all this is leading to." I asked Q whether he felt his life lacked meaning. "Yes, it is running full tilt without direction. I'd like to do something that would make me *happy*. But I'm too lazy to do anything about it. I'd like to go fishing, but I'd probably go crazy in retirement. This environment is continually in a crisis mode. It's all high speed. You can't talk about trivia. It turns me off when my wife wants to chatter. It's stupid when you think about it; what else can you do but listen."

To avoid middle-aged disintegration, some gamesmen try to commit themselves to something beyond winning. They try to confront themselves and grow up. J is a thirty-eight-year-old divisional vice-president, one of the most brilliant and creative gamesmen we have interviewed. While he relishes the challenge and excitement of the work, he does not like his position in middle management. "The top guys feel free to do things and also the project managers, but here you are just a conduit from top management." J does not see how he can develop a sense of being his own man in the corporation, and he is not sure the company really benefits society. He feels he is sacrificing self and family for an organization he does not fully believe in. "At this pace," he told us, "you burn out quickly." Now, he is seriously considering leaving the company to become involved in work related to ecology, to realize his social values. But will he leave? He has a family to support, and he is not sure he will be able to give up his salary and stock options. He could go to another company, but he considers the one he works in now better than most.

In the largest corporations, the gamesmen who reach the very top have committed themselves to the organization. They have resolved the crisis by renouncing adolescent dreams and illusions to become a new type of hybrid gamesman/company man—more flexible and innovative, less moralistic and ideological, than the old-style executive. The gamesman attitudes are held in check by identifying the self with the total organization. The gamesman qualities contribute to success as an executive who must be open to constant changes in markets, technology, and the attitudes of the workforce. Furthermore, since he is stimulated by the give-and-take of argument, the gamesman-executive is less likely than more authoritarian types to surround himself with yes-men.

The executive gamesman must still maintain his constant activity, and he even does so in his dreams. Typically, he is on the move, being chased, or competing in a game. Or he may dream that he comes to an examination and suddenly realizes he is unprepared. The underlying fear in such a dream is that he may fail and be a loser, and the nightmare serves the function of making sure he does his homework. A more profound recurring dream of one highly placed gamesman is of a spinning top. He asked me what it meant and I suggested that he was the top which has to stay in constant motion: if he let up and relaxed, he would fall over. "Yes," he said, "I can't even take a vacation."

The dream symbolizes both the gamesman's psychic need for action and the corporation's demand that he keep moving to stay "on top." The gamesman correctly sees the large corporation as a place where you either move ahead or fall behind, but you cannot stay in one place.

Of course, the same is true in politics, where a new breed of gamesman leaders speak the same language as do gamesman executives. If John F. Kennedy exhibited the gamesman's positive tendencies—enthusiasm, openness to ideas, and playfulness—Richard M. Nixon, who was essentially a jungle fighter, seemed to embody the negative ones, including the need for perpetual motion, as he moved from the White House, to San Clemente, to Key Biscayne, to Camp David. Also involved, of course, were the need to win at any cost and the constant hunger for competitive excitement. After the 1972 election, Nixon remarked on the letdown he felt after the challenge of the campaign. "In speeches or press conferences or interviews," he has said, "you have to be up and sharp. You can't be relaxed. The Redskins were relaxed in their last game of the regular season and they were flat and they got clobbered. You must be up for the great events. Up but not uptight."

Although he still talks in the gamesman's language, the executive gamesman is less playful and enthusiastic and more cautious than the adolescent type. Ward Quaal, the corporate president interviewed by Studs Terkel in *Working*, sounds like an executive gamesman who transcends purely egocentric goals when he describes himself as "the captain calling the signals and every once in a while I call the right play and we're pretty lucky. . . . The company is doing well. My people are functioning as a team. The success story is not Ward Quaal. It's the great team of people."

Perhaps the crucial difference between the typical gamesmen who rises no higher than middle management and those who are able to reach the top is belief. While the personal need to be a winner may be enough to motivate a project team by offering others a chance to be winners with him, it does not serve to direct a giant corporation, much less to inspire thousands of employees. The executive of a large corporation must sincerely believe that the corporation represents something greater than himself and is worth dedicating his energies to. He must want to make it not only successful, but the embodiment of excellence. There can be no conflict between his goals and those of the company. Many presidents or vice-presidents of major corporations come to feel deeply sentimental about the company, and when they speak about it, their eyes water and they reach for poetry. These are men who normally are unsentimental, detached, and rather inarticulate when they speak about social issues. As the chief executive officer of a major corporation stated, "There is a religious fervor here. It is the belief in what we are doing. We are at the cutting edge of society."

The top executive increasingly merges himself with the company. Even his family life must contribute; he and his wife must appear to be models for others. A corporate president told me, "It is very unusual for someone to get ahead in the corporate world if his wife does not support him. They seldom get to the very top. People at the top generally have very attractive wives who are respected. They are the kind of people others want to emulate." Outside of work, the executive must be willing to spend time on committees and to perform civic duties so as to enhance both his own image and that of the corporation as socially responsible. He must be flexible, liberal, open to a constantly changing society, and not hung up on the prejudices of the past.

As a result of this effort at adaptation, such individuals tend to be extremely courteous, and there is an air of modesty about them compared to those gamesmen who have not resolved their internal conflicts. They listen carefully, evaluating, holding their own needs in check. They feel that they are servants to the corporation. One chairman of the board describes the company as "a growing child which needs to find its own way."

The gamesman who renounces his adolescence must pay a price. The executive has sacrificed his fantasies, which may be no great loss to him, but in doing so, he may also have betrayed his yearnings for independence, and he may repress his critical perceptions of the organization in order to maintain his belief. In many cases the sense of guilt and self-betrayal that results is not conscious, but it comes out in dreams and projective tests—particularly on the Rorschach where executives report self-images of humiliation and castration, or see themselves as insects or worms. This negative self-image tends to be related to suppressed anger that occurs when one gives up a part of himself or betrays his convictions in order to get ahead. At his own center, where there should be a sense of integrity and creative strivings, such a person experiences gnawing insecurity and self-contempt that are never quite overcome, no matter how many times he wins or how high he goes.

It is possible to redefine the well-known Peter Principle to say that in a corporation a person tends to rise to the level where his character fits the work. That is to say that no matter how smart he is, if his emotional attitudes clash with the requirements of the role, he will not do the job well because he will not *want* to do what *needs* to be done in order to keep the organization running smoothly. In this regard, it is instructive to consider cases of brilliant managers who came near the top and could go no further. Some of those we interviewed were gamesmen who could not master their egocentrism. Others were more mature individuals who began to question whether the goals of the corporation fitted their spiritual needs. Some felt increasingly trapped, and in their dreams or Rorschach responses, the corporation was symbolized as a lonely, empty place, where both creative talents and passions become rusty from disuse. Thus, the overly immodest, aggressive, flamboyant, and the exceptionally creative or humane tend to falter near the very top.

What can society expect from the top executive with the flexible qualities of the gamesman rather than the old-style autocratic attitude? He will, of course, be less stuffy than executives of the past. Employees will call him by his first name. But beyond superficialities, the best ones may make a contribution to society by supporting programs for improving the quality of work both for managers and for production workers, provided that social pressure for this continues to grow. Because of the importance of interesting work to their own feelings of self-fulfillment, and their own struggle for dignity in the organization, the most creative gamesman-like executives are particularly responsive to ideas for increasing autonomy and learning at work. They recognize that the new generation of more educated and self-affirmative workers is less productive in a hierarchical and mechanistic work organization than in one that minimizes status differentials and allows some participation in decision-making. (The more creative gamesman-managers are generally more concerned with issues of individuation and dignity than the social scientists they ask to help them improve the organization.)

One creative gamesman-president of a growing company has instituted new programs to give the workers more say in running the plant and organizing their work. Criticized by a student for not going further in giving up his own power, he answered: "I play the game which our society plays which is capital. The game of capital as I see it is how you deal with risk. Within this game, I try to make work as exciting and fulfilling as possible for all my employees."

As long as the corporation's relative standing is not threatened, the modern corporate executive will favor social programs that make the corporation more attractive to young people. However, he will not initiate social programs that will place his company in an unfavorable competitive position. Nor will he forgo a chance for a big win in the market.

His sense of responsibility is to his company and stockholders, not to the larger society or to humanity. He will trade anywhere he can, regardless of whether he approves of the regime. He will pollute the environment, unless the law dictates that each corporation must clean up its mess. He will produce and advertise anything he can sell, unless food and drug laws or other legislation stop him. But he is willing to play by the rules. As one top corporate executive phased it, "Our main ability is that we know how to win at this game of business. Society can make whatever rules it wants, as long as they are clear-cut, the same for everyone. We can win at any game society can invent."[3]

This attitude lacks the moral concern and social responsibility that some people hope for in business leaders, but it is also less rigid and self-righteous than many people expect of corporate executives. In fact, the gamesman may be the best character we can expect in both corporate and governmental leadership roles, as long as our society is dominated goals of profit, growth, and continual technological innovation.

NOTES

1. This project was sponsored by the Harvard Seminar on Science, Technology and Public Policy. The other interviewers included Douglass Carmichael, Rolando Weissmann, Dennis Greene, Cynthia Elliott, and Katherine Terzi. The full report is presented by Maccoby (1977).

2. This methodology is a development of social psychoanalytic methods first used by Erich Fromm (1936) in a study of German workers and employees, and later by Fromm and Maccoby (1970) with Mexican villagers.

3. Note the testimony of Dr. C. Lester Hogan, vice-chairman of the board of Fairchild Camera and Instrument Corporation before the Subcommittee on Multinational Corporations of the Senate Foreign Relations Committee, July 22, 1974:3.

But Fairchild has found it difficult to obtain a clear understanding of the government's position on the transfer of technology—particularly semiconductor technology—to Eastern Europe. This absence of a clear definition of policy has been especially disappointing to Fairchild in the light of its 15-month effort aimed at working with the government on a particular export license application, which was recently denied, involving a proposed transfer of semiconductor technology to Poland for use in consumer products.

In matters of East-West trade, Fairchild has been and remains willing and eager to play by the "rules of the game" as determined by this country's policy makers. But it would certainly like to find out what those rules are.

9

Characterological Change Among Black Americans: A Contextual Interpretation

J. MILTON YINGER

It would be foolhardy to undertake a discussion of such a large and complex topic without first offering a number of cautions as regards the concept of social character. There are clear limits to the concept when applied to members of heterogeneous societies, even to segments of such societies.

The term *character* means the repertoire of tendencies and capabilities of an individual, the total complex of possibilities for action that one brings into any situation. It is not behavior; nor can one infer behavior directly from knowledge of character. The cues and stimuli, the costs and rewards, in interaction with characterological tendencies of varying strengths, must be taken into account in any attempt to understand behavior.

Social character refers to tendencies that are widely shared by the members of some designated group, tendencies that make them somewhat distinctive from members of other groups. For the concept to have any value, there must have been a sufficiently large number of common and shared experiences among the members of a group that they are more like one another, in significant ways, than they are like persons in other groups. Being more alike, of course, does not mean being identical, even in a few characteristics. It means that the modal tendency, and the standard deviation around that tendency, are somewhat different from one group to another (see Inkeles, 1959; Inkeles and Levinson, 1969; Yinger, 1965:86-91). Social character, thus defined, can be based on the shared experience of socialization to a traditional culture and subculture, or it can express similar adaptations to significant aspects of the current situation. Commonly, both sources are involved in an intertwined set of influences; but the distinction is important. Failure to make it clear can seriously hamper the analysis of social character, particularly under conditions of rapid change.

We need to take other precautions in our use of the concept of social character. Intuitively, we believe that we know something about a person—not very much, perhaps, but something—when we know that he or she was raised in China or the Soviet Union or Quebec or in a barrio of Los Angeles. In that belief we run the danger of stereotyping. A stereotype is a highly exaggerated picture of the members of a group that leaves little room for individual variation or for change. It is not the product of careful study but of a conflict situation. Stereotypes may help to justify a group's actions and to deal with ambivalences of feeling and moral ambiguities. They frequently survive as tradition, affecting the interaction of groups generations removed from the conflict situation in which they arose (see Simpson and Yinger, 1972: Chapter 5).

Most educated and liberal-minded persons today abhor stereotyping—appropriately so in my judgment. In a day of emphasis on individualism, privacy, and personal dignity, gross pictures of shared characteristics not only contradict our perceptions of variety but also offend our moral sensibilities. This does not mean that we escape the use of stereotypes. We continue to employ them to simplify our complicated social world and to justify our positions in conflict situations. Even staunch opponents—and victims—of stereotypes find them useful. Some black writers, for example, think of all Whites as alike and assert a great unity of view and feeling among Blacks.*

In the face of these difficulties, the concept of social character should be used with great care. The existence of shared tendencies is not to be assumed, but to be explored by research. If they do exist, they make up only one "layer" of character and perhaps not a very

*I will capitalize *Black* and *White* when they are used as nouns and lower case them when they are used as adjectives. As nouns, *Black* and *Negro* will be used as synonyms.

significant one, compared with individual tendencies on one hand and common human tendencies on the other. We must not overlook latent and often unintended effects of social structural conditions. These effects may be quite different from those produced by cultural norms and values or by proclaimed ideologies. We must also be wary of our ethnocentrism and provincialism.

This last difficulty raises the "insider-outsider" problem. It is impossible, some persons are asserting today, to study any group but one's own. Too many perceptions, feelings, and experiences are unavailable to the outsider to make his observations cogent. Quite to the contrary, others argue. The outsider can attain a perspective, an objectivity, a comparative view that the insider lacks.

It would take us too far afield to discuss this important issue in detail. Yet, it requires some comment. Robert Merton (1972; see also Goldstein, 1971; Washington, 1971; Metzger, 1971) describes the weakness of the insider doctrine, when pressed to an extreme. At the same time he notes that the drive toward objectivity has undoubtedly blocked critical facts from view and has left important questions unasked. An unqualified insider view leads to the balkanization of social science, "with separate baronies kept exclusively in the hands of insiders bearing their credentials in the shape of one or another ascribed status. . . . If only black scholars can understand blacks, then only white scholars can understand whites . . . , only French scholars can understand French society and, of course, . . . only Americans, not their external critics, can truly understand American society" (Merton, 1972:13). The insider, we can add, and not only the outside interpreter or critic, has his own problem of ethnocentrism. If each can contribute to the understanding only of his own group, no comparative perspective is possible. Goethe's observation is as true of groups and societies as it is of languages: *"Wer fremde Sprachen nicht kennt, weiss nichts von seiner eigenen."* (He who speaks no foreign tongue understands not his own.)

Yet, there is more truth to the insider claims of spokesmen for racial minorities (and doubtless other groups) than most of us have been trained to realize. As Merton puts it, dominant group members may overlook the pain, humiliation, suffering, and frustration of minority group members by seeing in their place the rather bland concepts of social stratification, social exchange, dysfunction, and the like. These are analytically useful concepts, but they are blinders also. In Kenneth Clark's words (1965:75):

More privileged individuals may understandably need to shield themselves from the inevitable conflict and pain which would result from acceptance of the fact that they *are* accessories to profound injustice. The tendency to discuss disturbing social issues such as racial discrimination, segregation, and economic exploitation in detached, legal, political, socio-economic, or psychological terms as if these persistent problems did not involve the suffering of actual human beings is so contrary to empirical evidence that it must be interpreted as a protective device.

Clearly, the need is to try by some dialectic process to achieve a synthesis of insider and outsider views. To quote Merton again (1972:40): "When a transition from social conflict to intellectual controversy is achieved, when the perspectives of each group are taken seriously enough to be carefully examined rather than rejected out of hand, there can develop trade offs between the distinctive strengths and weaknesses of Insider and Outsider perspectives that enlarge the chances for a sound and relevant understanding of social life."

Two Examples of Social Character Studies

Keeping in mind the risks of stereotyping, ethnocentrism, and—in the present situation—outsiderism, perhaps we can reduce the hazards of studying social character by examining some of the literature on two themes dealing with racial minorities, notably, slavery and the "culture of poverty." By analyzing the changing, and often contradictory, interpretations, we may be able to formulate a theoretical perspective that will allow us to incorporate the concept of social character into a larger system of explanation when we turn to the contemporary scene.

Social Character Under Slavery

The study of slavery continues at a lively pace because of its great human importance, because it can tell us a great deal about other circumstances, and because its complexity and the ambiguity of the evidence have prevented anyone from making a definitive interpretation. This chapter is concerned only with American slavery, and with that only for the light its study may throw on the possibilities and difficulties involved in applying the concept of social character to America's black population. We need answers to these questions: Were there a sufficiently large number of important shared and common experiences so that persons who were enslaved developed, in some measure, similar characters? If so, what were the critical social and cultural aspects of those experiences? And what were their characterological outcomes?

Interpretations of slavery vary enormously. For example, in his influential work, U. B. Phillips (1918; 1929) described the slave plantation as an essentially humane environment, governed by paternalistic principles. He saw Blacks as childlike, submissive, lighthearted—inborn characteristics that made the plantation a congenial environment. This simple summation does not do justice to the richness of the descriptions in Phillips' work, but essentially the social character he pictured was a product of a widely shared social environment and set of experiences interacting with an inherited inferiority.

Modifications of this description have occurred through several stages. If one disputes the notion of inherited racial inferiority but continues to picture a slave population that is almost uniformly docile, ignorant, easygoing, and irresponsible, then one must look for another explanation. Serious criticism of the Phillips interpretation was scarce until after World War II. We now have an abundance of such criticism, but from widely differing perspectives. Rejecting the belief in racial inferiority, Stanley Elkins (1959) and Kenneth Stampp (1965) offer a different explanation for the social character they describe. They find it, in somewhat different ways, in the cruelty of the plantation. Elkins argues that the power of the plantation owner was so complete, so unrestrained by community or national institutions, customs, or laws that the slave's situation was scarcely different from that of a person in a concentration camp. Some of those who survived in the camps took on many of the values of the guards, who had the power of life or death over them. A similar response was common on the American plantation, according to Elkins. In his words (1959:129): "In a system as tightly closed as the plantation or the concentration camp, the slave's or prisoner's position of absolute dependency virtually compels him to see the authority-figure as somehow really 'good.' " In this view, slaves tended to become irresponsible children in an effort to deal with an absolutely crushing situation.

Stampp's interpretation is somewhat different. He also emphasizes the frequency of childish behavior, the feigning of illness, and the irresponsibility. In his view, however, these were not deeply structured elements of social character, but behavioral adjustments that in part disguised resentment and resistance. The resistance was usually quite subtle, probably of more value in maintaining one's sense of personhood than in changing the oppressive situation. One is reminded of Charles Johnson's phrase (1943) "pseudo-ignorant malingering," by which he described the subtle aggressions of the field hand trying to balance the scales of justice. Something of the same point is made by Hortense Powdermaker (1943), who sees self-effacing humility as a way of attempting to rescue victory from defeat. This humility is associated with a religious view that one gains power from suffering, a belief that suffering is only a prelude to ultimate victory and reward.

More recently, Genovese (1970; 1974) has developed this same point regarding the presence of resistance and effective adaptation hidden beneath a facade of capitulation. He emphasizes the group aspects of resistance:

> Although any individual at any given moment may be defenseless, a whole people rarely if ever is. A people may be on the defensive and dangerously exposed, but it often finds its own ways to survive and fight back. The trouble is that we keep looking for overt rebellious actions—a strike, a revolt, a murder, arson, tool-breaking—and often fail to realize that in given conditions and at particular times the wisdom of a people and their experience in struggle may dictate a different course, one of keeping together. From this point of view, the most ignorant of the field slaves who follow the conjurer on the plantation was saying no to the boss and seeking a form of cultural autonomy.

There is undoubtedly a heavy admixture of ideology in much of this work, ideology that is given rather free play on an ambiguous issue where the full range of facts is difficult to see. Fifteen years ago, Elkins was expressing his sympathy for American Negroes as follows: interpretations of the social character of slaves based on the notion of racial inferiority are false, and we must look to the crushing impact of the slave system. A few years later (and, for a few acute observers, earlier), Stampp, Genovese, and others were expressing their sympathy on another basis: despite the crushing impact of the slave system, America's black population found ways to express their resistance, to adjust to enormous burdens, and to make creative responses. Despite the range of interpretations, the scholars generally agree that slavery was an overwhelmingly important force in shaping the social character of Blacks.

These differing interpretations make clear the need for the distinction, noted earlier, between what we can call "traditional social character" and "adaptive social character." Both are modal tendencies based on shared or common experiences. The traditional, however, is a product of a set of traditional or cultural experiences; the adaptive reflects efforts to deal with changes or openings in the traditional arrangements—envisaged threats or opportunities that are shared among the members of a group.

In studies of slavery, a new line of argument has recently been developed: suppose that it is not only the assumption of racial inferiority that is false, but also that the description of most slaves as docile, irresponsible, and childlike is false. Then one no longer needs Elkins' sharply etched picture of the plantation as a closed system, a system that is not only cruel, but also utterly destructive of the lives of the slaves. Studying slavery from the perspective of economic history, Fogel and Engerman (1974) emphasize facts that have been overlooked or treated lightly by most earlier observers. In their judgment, slavery persisted not because plantation owners, filled with nostalgia, were clinging to a traditional way of life, but mainly because it was economically profitable. It could not be profitable, however, unless the slaves, the great bulk of the workers, were trained to do the wide range of necessary jobs and were reasonably well motivated.

Their argument is subtle and complex. By a series of calculations (see Haskell, 1974), they assert that, on the average, antebellum southern agriculture was efficient by the standards of the time and economically profitable. Slaves made up a higher proportion of skilled workers than has generally been noted (see Fogel and Engerman, 1974:38-39): 7 percent of the men were managers; 12 percent were skilled craftsmen; and 7 percent were engaged in semiskilled or domestic work. There were fewer skilled workers among the women, although about 20 percent worked at household tasks. Fogel and Engerman note (1974:84) that "planters promoted family formation both through exhortation and through economic inducements." Husbands were recognized as heads of families. By a range of rewards, planters sought to increase the morale of their workers. In the last analysis, of course, force was available and force was used.

Although Fogel and Engerman do not disregard the psychological burdens of slavery, they may tend to pay them insufficient attention as they try to correct what they see as an inaccurate picture of its influence on standard of living and jobs. They also may tend to overlook the fact that such tendencies as slow, inefficient work and an easygoing pace may be quite reasonable adaptations to an abhorrent life situation that one cannot escape. Scholars who see these as consequences of slavery, therefore, are not necessarily accepting a racist stereotype, as Fogel and Engerman believe, but are describing what they see as characterological consequences of racist institutions.

Despite the tendency to overstate their case, Fogel and Engerman have added a valuable new dimension to the study of slavery and, by extension, to the study of other repressive situations. This brief reference to some of the literature on slavery, however, is not meant to be a review and criticism of the various theories, implicit and explicit, dealing with social character. Rather, these comments are used here to

TABLE 1.

Changing Interpretations of the Effects of Slavery

Premises	*Available Descriptions and Traditions, Influencing What One Is Likely to See*	*Conclusions*
Inferiority of Blacks	Irresponsible, lazy, child-like behavior of slaves	Slavery a reasonably benign institution
Essential native equality of races	Irresponsible, lazy, child-like behavior of slaves	Slavery an utterly cruel institution
Essential native equality of races	Stimulated by civil rights movement, some change in picture of slave. Earlier picture seen as superficial, covering over patterns of resistance and of creative adaptation	Slavery cruel but unable to crush
System of production persists only if efficient. Essential equality of races	Skill, diligent work, quite good morale among slaves. Some autonomy for slave community and creative adaptations	System doubtless psychologically burdensome; but economic self-interest of owner plus capabilities of slaves lead to efficient work, reasonable adaptation

underscore a point: that studies of social character are peculiarly subject to the influence of ideological premises and to the fund of traditional descriptions available at a given time. In dealing with a problem where measurement is difficult, and where a large and heterogeneous population is involved, even the most diligent scholars are powerfully affected by the premises from which they start and by the traditional "information" on which they draw. Thus, studies of slavery, through the abbreviated period commented on here, might be described as shown on Table 1.

We have certainly not seen the end of the evolution of interpretations of the effects of slavery, of the pictures of social character that are believed to be its outcome. That there should be sharp disagreements among astute observers should remind us forcefully of the problems, even the hazards, of such analysis, not only with reference to slavery, but with reference to the contemporary scene as well. Indeed, our premises are often unrecognized, our measurements imprecise, and the groups with which we are concerned are heterogeneous.

Social Character and the "Culture of Poverty"

Another body of literature concerned with the concept of social character, although not always under the label, discusses the "culture of poverty." This literature does not necessarily deal with racial minorities, which are the subject of our interest; yet, racial and ethnic factors are often involved in the analyses. There is widespread agreement, if not unanimity, among recent students of social stratification that any differences in values and behavior among members of different classes are not to be accounted for simply by reference to individual character. That the poor are poor because they are lazy and irresponsible and lacking in talent is no more acceptable than similar explanations of the status of racial minorities. That does not mean that those in poverty are not characterized to a significantly greater degree by low motivation and low skill. But these are seen as dependent variables requiring explanation, not as the explanation itself.

Once this level of agreement is reached, however, a rather sharp divergence of interpretation emerges. Two distinct lines of argument are found among those who stress the importance of the class structure in creating significantly different learning environments for children in different classes. One group of authors stresses isolation and lack of opportunity among those in poverty; another emphasizes a traditional subculture of poverty that is believed to validate and reinforce the poor in their status, even if opportunities to change status are present. The former point to what is lacking in the experience of a child (stimulation and opportunity); the latter refer to what is present in that experience (norms and values that support a poverty subculture). Careful study of this divergence of interpretation is necessary if we are to use the concept of social character skillfully with reference to racial minorities, who make up a large proportion of those in poverty in the United States. Exclusive attention to either traditional social character or to adaptive social character is unlikely to be adequate to account for the range of facts (see Simpson and Yinger, 1972:172-177).

The work of Oscar Lewis has been crucial in setting the terms of this "debate." The phrase "culture of poverty," he writes (1966a:19),

> is the label for a specific conceptual model that describes in positive terms a subculture of Western society with its own structure and rationale, a way of life handed on from generation to generation along family lines. The culture of poverty is not just a matter of deprivation or disorganization, a term signifying the absence of something. It is a culture in the traditional anthropological sense in that it provides human beings with a design for living, with a ready-made set of solutions for human problems, and so serves a significant adaptive function (see also Lewis, 1959; 1961; 1966b).

A similar point of view is expressed by Edward Banfield in his well-known book *The Moral Basis of a Backward Society* (1958). He describes the life-style of villagers in southern Italy as a product of an ethos of "amoral familism," with a matching social character typified by suspicion, inability to cooperate, and failure to plan ahead. Banfield developed the same theme, not without various qualifications and inconsistencies, with reference to the American lower class in his book *The Unheavenly City* (1968). There are some references to opportunity in Banfield's work, as there are in Lewis's; but the emphasis is on a traditional subculture and the social character that is its product. This perspective can be summarized by a comment from Walter Miller (1958:18): "Lower class culture is a distinctive tradition many centuries old with an integrity of its own." This kind of statement is offered sympathetically by some (by Lewis and Miller, for example), indicating the hope that the culture of poverty can be accepted as a dignified life-style, or at least regarded with anthropological objectivity. Others, Banfield in particular, offer such descriptions more critically. Whatever the value orientation, however, these authors agree that culture is the main explanatory variable for understanding the social character of the poor, with character then stabilizing and reinforcing the culture.

A different line of argument is taken by those who see the culture of poverty itself as a dependent variable, as an often desperate effort at adaptation to a crushingly difficult situation caused by limited opportunity, discrimination, and isolation. The social character of the poor, then, insofar as they share tendencies as a result of the deprivation that they experience in common, is not the result of normal socialization to a subculture of poverty, but is a tentative adaptive system developed in an environment of severely limited opportunities. Elliot Liebow describes the subculture of the ghetto street-corner, not as an independent and traditional way of life, but as a "shadow system," "the cultural model of the larger society as seen through the prism of repeated failure" (Liebow, 1967:221). It is, in Hyman Rodman's phrase (1963), the result of a "value stretch," by which those in poverty seek to reconcile their belief in the values of the general society with the sharply contradictory facts of their own experience.

This structural interpretation of the culture of poverty and the social character presumably associated with it has been developed by many writers in recent years (in addition to Liebow, 1967, see Rodman, 1963; Rainwater, 1970; Valentine, 1968; Parker and Kleiner, 1970; Roach and Gursslin, 1967; Graves, 1974; Silverman, 1968; Muraskin, 1974; Coser, 1969; Han, 1969). Most of them recognize class differences in values, but they see them largely as the product of differences in opportunity. Whereas Banfield views members of the lower class as "radically improvident"—for example, without any sense of the future and entirely oriented to present enjoyments (here the line between social character and stereotype has worn dangerously thin)—Liebow sees them dealing with their actual situations in a way not drastically different, so far as their values are concerned, from the future-oriented middle class. In his words (1967:64-65):

> from the inside looking out, what appears as a "present-time" orientation to the outside observer is, to the man experiencing it, as much a future orientation as that of his middle-class counterpart. The difference between the two men lies not so much in their different orientations to time as in their different orientations to future time or, more specifically, to their different futures . . . . The future orientation of the middle-class person presumes, among other things, a surplus of resources to be invested in the future and a belief

that the future will be sufficiently stable both to justify his investment (money in a bank, time and effort in a job, investment of himself in marriage and family, etc.) and to permit the consumption of his investment at a time, place and manner of his own choosing and to his greater satisfaction. But the street-corner man lives in a sea of want. He does not, as a rule, have a surplus of resources, either economic or psychological. Gratification of hunger and the desire for simple creature comforts cannot be long deferred. Neither can support for one's flagging self-esteem.

If the structural interpretation is pressed far enough, the so-called culture of poverty is seen as simply a reflex of the level of opportunities, the extent of discrimination, and other external forces. The modal character that seems to express that culture—with tendencies toward apathy and feelings of powerlessness, focus on the present, low self-respect, poor job performance, and other such qualities—is seen as a series of adaptations to difficult conditions. It would follow that if the structural barriers and inequities were removed, the culture of poverty would shrivel and a different set of individual tendencies, inhibited under restrictive conditions but present in the repertoire, would come to the fore.

The structural approach is closer to the truth than the cultural, in the sense that analysis of the cycle of causes can most profitably begin with the opportunity structure, from which flow various cultural and characterological consequences. Once created, however, these consequences flow back into the system from which they came and reinforce it. These cybernetic processes are among the most important qualities of human systems. They require that we not draw too sharp a distinction between independent and dependent variables. Once developed, the culture of poverty and the social character that expresses it reinforce the conditions from which they came. This is true both in the sense that they influence perception of opportunities and in the sense that they affect the level of opportunities. The latter occurs because those outside the culture of poverty may respond negatively to its values and its related behavior, thus being led to restrict opportunities even further.

Changes in the Context for Social Character Formation Among Black Americans

It is hoped that the discussion of some of the difficulties associated with the concept of social character and the comments on various interpretations of slavery and the culture of poverty can guide us in our study of the contemporary situation. We need to keep continually before us the subtle interplay of structure, culture, and character. We need especially to be aware of the great variety of experiences and of tendencies among America's black population, which is the primary subject of our attention. They may be bound together in what may be called a community of suffering, but that cannot obscure the range of differences among them. We must not only think of social character as modal character, with wide dispersion around the mode; we must also think of multimodal distributions, with variations influenced by class, region, occupation, level of education, sex, age, and other factors. We cannot hope to cover the range, but will seek to sketch some of the dominant factors affecting the range and the change of social characteristics among Blacks.

Social character must always be studied in connection with the structural and cultural factors that shape it. Have these factors been significantly changed for America's racial minorities in the last several years? Attitudes among the dominant group, the legal and judicial situation, and occupational and educational opportunities are among the most important of these factors. In each instance, the evidences of change are ambiguous, or at least can be read quite differently, depending upon ideological starting points. It is easy to find interpretations ranging from optimism to cynicism. I shall try to keep ideological factors at a minimum here by being quite factual about sociocultural changes in recent years. Then some of the characterological changes that have occurred in the new context will be noted.

Beginning in 1944, to take a somewhat arbitrary date, the Supreme Court has pulled down most of the constitutional supports for racial discrimination in the United States. From the 1944 "white primary" decision, which began the great upsurge of voting among Blacks, to the school desegregation cases in 1954, and to the bans against segregation in public accommodations in 1956, against poll taxes in 1966, and against laws forbidding intermarriage in 1967, to mention only a few of the decisions, the Supreme Court has greatly strengthened the Thirteenth, Fourteenth, and Fifteenth amendments. In the Civil Rights Acts of 1957, 1960, 1964, and 1968, as well as in much other legislation, the United States Congress, often following after statutes passed by state legislatures, has sharply delimited the possibilities for discrimination in public accommodations, education, political rights, housing, and jobs.

No one is so naive to suppose that such judicial and legal changes have eliminated discrimination. They have, however, created a very different context for race relations and—with regard to the topic of our interest—for the shaping of social character. Officially, doors have been opened, new opportunities envisaged. One cannot understand changes in the attitudes, values, and actions of American Blacks without recognizing that fact.

Related facts are the changes in political, occupational, and educational attainments that have occurred. I can only briefly illustrate them, to suggest further the current context within which character is being shaped. In 1944, there were approximately 250,000 black persons registered to vote in the South and a total of perhaps two million in the nation. By 1972, the figures were four-and-a-half million in the South and over eight million in the nation. In 1950, there were three black congressmen; in 1974, there were seventeen. Median black family income, which was about 30 percent of white family income in 1930, climbed to 61 percent in 1971, but it has fallen since, to 59 percent in 1972 and probably to 58 percent in 1974. Among racial minorities, the percentage in white collar jobs increased from 16 to 30 between 1960 and 1972, while it increased from 47 to 50 among Whites. One can remark either that the gap was closed from 31 percent to 20 percent or that only about one-third the differential was eliminated during those twelve years. Both statements are true.

Educational changes are also critical. Disregarding the vital and complex matter of desegregation of schools, and possible qualitative differences, we must at least note the comparative amounts of education for the races. Here the evidence is clear: the gap between Black and White has been closing rapidly. The median number of years of schooling for Whites born between 1895 and 1904 was 8.9 years; for those born between 1940 and 1944 it was 12.6 years. Using the same age cohorts for Blacks, the gain was from 5.1 to 12.2 years (Jencks, 1972:21). Looking at a younger group and at higher education only, between 1967 and 1972 the proportion of Blacks aged eighteen to twenty-four who were attending colleges and universities increased from 13 to 18 percent; the proportion of Whites decreased from 27 to 26 percent (U.S. Department of Commerce, 1972:60, 62).

The structural situation within which Blacks develop has changed, perhaps one ought to say sharply, since World War II. What about the attitudes of Whites, which are also an important part of the environment for racial minorities? Here again we will have to be content with illustrative material, running the risk of not surveying an adequate range. I believe, however, that there is a clear trend toward less prejudice, greater willingness to accept interaction, and more support for equality of treatment. To be sure, actions sometimes contradict expressed attitudes, and such actions receive more public attention. A generalized attitude that one would not object to having one's children attend integrated schools may be accompanied by vigorous opposition to busing, which, in part, expresses a different set of attitudes. Conversely, persons holding strong prejudices may not discriminate because of the costs, the lack of social support, or the activation of other views in particular settings. Nevertheless, attitudes and opinions are part of the total environment within which social character is shaped; and we need to know something about the trends.

For several years in public opinion polls, national samples have been asked to respond to statements dealing with interracial neighborhoods. Table 2 records the percentages stating that "it would make no difference if a Negro with the same income and education moved into my block" (Hermalin and Farley, 1973:598).

TABLE 2.

Percentage of Whites Not Objecting to Interracial Neighborhoods

1942	35
1956	51
1963	64
1972	84

Some of the opinions, of course, have remained more stable and are less favorable to the idea of interracial equality and contact. Such opinions need also to be noted. We can draw on three national samples, taken in 1964, 1968, and 1970, to report further on the views of Whites. Table 3 records the proportion who agree with various statements.

In this six-year period, support for civil rights was strengthened, but substantial opposition remained—and is still visible. Stereotypes are also less commonly held, but have by no means been eliminated. The Harris survey has compared national samples of the white population for 1963 and 1971 on their responses to a number of stereotyped statements. In every instance, the percentage agreeing fell during the eight-

TABLE 3.

White Attitudes Toward Civil Rights for Blacks, in Percentages

Attitudes	*1964*	*1968*	*1970*
Negroes should have the right to go to any hotel or restaurant they can afford	41	48	56
White people have a right to keep Negroes out of their neighborhoods	29	24	21
The civil rights leaders are trying to push too fast	68	68	57

SOURCE: Adapted from Campbell (1971: 131, 133, 138).

year interval; yet, it is a bit startling to see, in Table 4, how high those percentages remain.

Perhaps we have cited enough evidence to suggest that the opinions of Whites regarding Blacks have become less harsh in recent years while still containing strong negative elements. One other set of opin-

TABLE 4.

White Stereotypes of Blacks in the United States, in Percentages

Percentage of a sample of whites who agree that—	*1963*	*1971*
Blacks have less ambition than Whites	66	52
Blacks have lower morals than Whites	55	40
Blacks have less native intelligence	39	37
Blacks breed crime	35	27
Blacks are inferior to white people	31	22

SOURCE: Adapted from Harris Survey (1971:5-B).

ions, dealing with perceived discrimination, will show some evidence of increased sensitivity on the part of Whites and less pessimism among Blacks. These data, summarized in Table 5, can serve as a useful bridge to our discussion of changing social character among Blacks. Having sketched some of the context within which those changes are taking place, we need to turn to their direct examination.

TABLE 5.

Perceived Discrimination Among Blacks and Whites in the United States, in Percentages

Percentage of samples who believe that Blacks are discriminated against in:	*1969*	*1972*
Getting decent housing		
Whites	46	51
Blacks	83	66
Getting white collar jobs		
Whites	38	40
Blacks	82	68
Getting skilled labor jobs		
Whites	35	40
Blacks	83	66
Way treated as human beings		
Whites	35	38
Blacks	77	64
Way treated by police		
Whites	19	25
Blacks	76	66

SOURCE: Adapted from Harris Survey (1973:9-A).

One might summarize Table 5 by noting that the average level of perceived discrimination against Blacks on the part of Whites was 35 percent in 1969, but that it had grown to 39 percent in 1972—an indication of slightly greater sensitivity. Conversely, the average level of perceived discrimination by Blacks fell from 80 percent in 1969 to 66 percent in 1972, a rather remarkable rate of decline. Nevertheless, two-thirds of the responses were still indications of belief that discrimination persisted. Put another way, the perceptual gap between Whites and Blacks was narrowed from 45 percent in 1969 to 27 percent in 1972. They still see significantly different worlds, but not quite the sharply contrasting worlds of just a few years ago.

Changing Social Character Among Black Americans

Against this background of changes in the political, economic, and educational situations and modifications of opinions, what changes can be observed in the social character of America's black population? (These changes are not simply effects of the contextual changes, but in part their causes.) Perhaps the most obvious change is the greater willingness to express resentment or anger or more focused protests against discrimination. On the surface, it appears paradoxical that protests should become more common at the very time when there has been fairly rapid progress, by objective standards. Such a development is not surprising, however, because, in a time of expanding opportunities, hopes and aspirations often expand even more rapidly, producing a "revolutionary gap." That gap between reality and hope grows particularly rapidly when a period of improvement is followed by a time of retrenchment, consolidation, and recession, for hopes are not turned off during such a period. They have acquired an energy of their own, which presses against the system if it cannot be expressed within it. Both of these things have been occurring in the United States, with one mode of expression being sharp protest, and the other a lively activism—political, religious, and educational. There is, of course, no sharp line between protest and activism.

It has been demonstrated in the laboratory that persons assigned a low-status position feel free to express hostility toward those in high-status positions until the situation is manipulated in such a way that they see themselves destined to remain low status. Protests and activism turn this relationship around: perceiving themselves as no longer destined to remain low status, some black Americans feel freer to express their hostility. This broad generalization, of course, requires qualification. There are many modes to this aspect of social character, reflecting different conditions, perceptions, and tendencies. Moreover, inhibition of anger or its displacement onto relatives and friends is still more common than protest (see Crain and Weisman, 1972: Chapter 4). But the trend is toward more outward aggression.

One way to express hostility and to protest one's status is to use violence. The American interracial experience has been filled with violence, of course. Until recently, however, it has been used much more commonly by Whites than by Blacks (and this form continues, although we shall not be discussing it). There were riotous protests by Blacks during and after World War I and World War II. Since 1964, however, the number of cities and the number of persons involved has been much larger. This does not mean that most Blacks have participated in or are even ready to condone violence to protest discrimination. Rather, the evidence shows that a small minority has become a somewhat larger minority. Thus, one of the modes, expressing a changed quality of social character among Blacks, is the greater readiness to use or consider violence.

In a summary of several studies carried out during the late 1960s, Nathan Caplan reports that between 11 and 20 percent of the black residents of cities torn by riots had participated in those riots. Other data show that one-third to one-half of the black residents of those cities expressed sympathy for rioters or believed that the riots were helpful (Caplan, 1970). Most evidence supports the view that it was not the alienated and powerless who participated in riots so much as it was those who had some confidence in their ability to control events and to influence their own futures, even though they were also the most aware of racial discrimination (see Forward and Williams, 1970; Gary Marx, 1967). I believe it is correct to say that recent trends have increased such characteristics among Blacks and are likely to increase them further.

The studies cited here do not directly take account of a time dimension. It is difficult to get comparisons through time among equivalent populations, but this is approximated in a study that uses data from fifteen American cities in 1968, prepared for the National Advisory Commission on Civil Disorders, and from the Detroit Area Studies carried out in 1968 and 1971 (Table 6). These studies show some increased readiness to use violence, but is should be emphasized that the findings are based on opinion measures, not on actions.

In the two Detroit Area Studies, those who did not answer "Use violence" to the first question were asked a second queston. They were asked if they thought Negroes should be ready to use violence if laws and persuasion and nonviolent protests did not work. The percentage answering yes went up from 24 to 44 between 1968 and 1971 (Schuman and Hatchett, 1974:8). Once again this was *opinion* about readi-

TABLE 6.

Negro Readiness to Use Violence, in Percentages

As you see it, what's the best way for Negroes to try to gain their rights — use laws and persuasion, use nonviolent protest, or be ready to use violence?		NATIONAL ADVISORY COMMISSION (1968)	DETROIT AREA STUDY (1968)	DETRIOT AREA STUDY (1971)
	Use laws and persuasion	44.7	33.6	41.0
	Use nonviolent protest	48.8	60.0	47.4
	Use violence	6.6	6.4	11.4
	N	140	430	210

SOURCE: Adapted from Schuman and Hatchett (1974:8).

ness, and thus in a sense is two steps removed from violence itself. Yet, it is further evidence of a growing restlessness and impatience in one metropolitan area.

This impatience is further documented by answers to a question put to national samples in 1964, 1968, and 1970. "Some say the civil rights people have been trying to move too fast. Others feel they haven't pushed fast enough. How about you, do you think that the civil rights leaders are trying to push too fast, are going too slowly, or are they moving at about the right speed? Among the black respondents, the percentage saying "too fast" fell from 10 to 7, while the percentage saying "too slowly" went up from 23 to 39 between 1964 and 1970 (Campbell, 1971:138). When the white sample was asked this same question, the percentage saying "too fast" fell from 68 to 57, and the percentage saying "too slowly" increased from 3 to 6. Thus, we have another sign of slight convergence, although the differences remain large. We need to remark the increase in the number of Blacks who believe that civil rights progress is slow. Yet it is scarcely a sign of extreme restlessness that 39 percent should say "too slowly" to such a question. Impatience is a growing part of the Blacks' social character, being modal in particular among the younger and better educated, but it is still somewhat restrained. Even in 1970, 52 percent of this sample of black Americans thought civil rights leaders were moving at about the right speed.

Against this background of reference to impatience and protest, we can profitably examine two other aspects of social character. Among some American Blacks, there are increasing feelings of hope and of rising aspiration; in this case protest expresses their desire to fulfill those hopes. Among others, there are increasing feelings of alienation and pessimism; for this group, protest expresses their desire to win some freedom and autonomy, to get out of the system, and to develop their own communities, businesses, religious groups, and schools. Here is a parallel with ancient as well as modern sectarian movements, some of which are prophetic efforts to remake society, and others ascetic movements to withdraw from a society considered to be evil past any hope of recovery.

This division into two distinct styles is, of course, too neat and precise. Most movements contain elements of both tendencies, as do most individuals who are striving to achieve a new life. Nor do we know very much about the different sets of experiences and characteristics that incline some Blacks toward prophetic reform or revolution and others toward "nationalist" separation and ascetic withdrawal. Moreover, there are many variations within each style. Yet the evidence is clear that two modal sets of protest tendencies are developing within the social character of America's black population, alongside the more conservative and probably more common set of integrationist tendencies. Once again it is difficult to get time-series data that allow us to speak confidently of changing character. For the most part, we shall have to be content with a description of the bimodal quality of the protest movement, while relying on our previous evidence for change to suggest that both sets of tendencies are more common.

Gary Marx has divided black respondents from several American cities into black nationalist sympathizers, militants, and conservatives, on the basis of their answers to a number of questions. The opinions of the first two groups can be compared to examine the variation in hope, alienation, optimism about the future, and other qualities differentiating the separatists from the militant reformers. In most cases, the opinions of the conservatives are in between those of the other two groups.

In each instance, the opinions reported in Table 7 show that the black nationalist sympathizers are more pessimistic and more anti-White than the militants. Belief in the possibilities of radical reform, as contrasted with belief in the desirability of withdrawal into racially

TABLE 7.
Optimism Among Black Nationalists and Militants, in Percentages

PERCENT AGREEING OR HOLDING STATED OPINIONS	BLACK NATIONALIST SYMPATHIZERS	MILITANTS
Civil rights demonstrations helped a great deal	40	67
Things getting worse for Negroes in this country	40	6
The day will come when Whites will accept Negroes	63	75
High in anti-White attitudes	44	22

SOURCE: Adapted from Gary Marx (1967:114, 199).

homogeneous communities, implies a hopeful view of the world and at least some measure of confidence in the white population. These qualities are more likely to be found among the militants.

One of the most difficult problems in this almost uniformly difficult area involves the question of personality damage. Many observers have stated that if discrimination is as widespread and as destructive as most of us believe, it must have devastating consequences for the persons experiencing it. Although extensive differences have been noted between lower and middle-class Blacks, between men and women, between those in the North and those in the South, along with other comparisons, some form of injury has been seen as a modal—not, of course, universal—consequence of minority status. Frazier (1957), for example, described what he saw as an identity crisis for the black middle class. Rejected by white society, feeling frustration, anger, and bitterness, lacking a strong sense of identity with the black masses, the black bourgeoisie—despite their relative economic success—lack a sense of purpose. They get caught up in a round of partying and conspicuous consumption. The lower class male faces a different set of problems. As described by Rohrer and Edmonson, he has little self-confidence, an insecure sexual identity, and a searing anger. These are expressed in the activity of the gang, a defensive and protective male "culture." "The psychic economy of the gang," they write, "demands aggressive independence, a touchy and exaggerated virility, and a deep protective secrecy" (Rohrer and Edmonson, 1960:160).

Whatever the range of responses, which I have merely suggested here, there has been a strong emphasis on low self-esteem or even self-hatred, repressed anger, faulty identities, and lack of ambition and ego strength. From studies of black children selecting white dolls to psychiatric interpretations of the injuries that flow from discrimination, one of the strong themes in discussions of the social character of American Blacks has been that of inadequacy and personality damage (see Crain and Weisman, 1972).

In recent years, a different point of view has become more prevalent. Blacks have shown a remarkable ability to deal with crushing circumstances. Their cultural inventions have been skillful adaptations to situations they were powerless to change. Descriptions of injury have been overly generalized to whole groups, when in fact most persons deal with a continuing series of discriminations in a mature and self-supportive way. This shift of emphasis toward creative and adaptive social character is referred to in the discussion above of slavery and of recent interpretations of the "culture of poverty." The injury thesis, developed by Frazier (1957), Kardiner and Ovesey (1951), Grier and Cobbs (1968), and many others, is also being sharply criticized.

How can one account for the change, or, more accurately, for the opening up of a sharper debate on this subject? Are contemporary observers seeing things more clearly, profiting from the errors of their predecessors? Is a shift in ideology bringing out new sets of observations while obscuring others, thus reversing an earlier situation? Or has there been significant change in the social character of America's black population, so that the new accounts are simply following the evidence? Or are all three of these things true? In my judgment, the answer to the last question is yes, and we should therefore also give a qualified yes to the other three questions.

Since accounts of personality damage are frequent and well known, we can profitably look at the increasing number of studies that show the emergence of courage, poise, and self-confidence among the Blacks in the face of adversity. Sidney Kronus, for example (1971), argues that the black middle class has not only become much larger, but more diverse as well. This group is now much less prone to emulate the white middle class rather blindly, to cut themselves off from the black working class, or to downgrade themselves. Most of the leaders and a large proportion of the supporters of the civil rights movement have been middle class.

Robert Coles (1967) gives a vivid illustration of the growing sense of confidence and control among Blacks. He describes an occasion at which he sat with a black student at a high school basketball game. The student attended a recently desegregated school, but the opposing school was still segregated. As the only Negro in the audience, he attracted a great deal of attention, which turned to serious heckling, cursing, and threatening behavior after the game. Without a quick call to the police there might have been a riot. Coles felt alarmed, sad, and angry, while the black student maintained his composure. Having known the student for several months by that time, Coles felt free to talk to him about the incident (1967:117):

> "I don't know how you can take that sort of treatment; I really don't." He smiled, and looked at me as if he understood my problems and would try to help me as best he could. In a moment he did. He started with a gentle criticism of me: "You don't know how I can take it because you haven't ever had to take it." He paused, "You see, when I grew up I had to learn to expect that kind of treatment; and I got it, so many times I hate to remember to count them. Well, now I'm getting it again, but it's sweet pain this time, because whatever they may say to me or however they try to hurt me, I know that just by sticking it out I'm going to help end the whole system of segregation; and that can make you go through anything."

"Sweet pain"—a keenly diagnostic phrase. In a context of "Black is beautiful," of confident assertion of rights with some support from the dominant society, of a declining sense of powerlessness and a growing sense of internal control, discrimination has a less crushing impact. There have always been such creative responses, but they are more likely to prosper in an environment where hope has been expanded.

Conclusion

We have examined only a few of the topics relevant to the study of changing social character among Blacks. The emphasis has been less on the characterological outcomes than on the context within which character is shaped, for therein lie the roots of both continuity and change. Few persons doubt that the experience of being a Negro in American society has changed dramatically since World War II, mainly, but not entirely, in favorable directions. There is still a great deal of discrimination; prejudice is widespread; and the ambiguity of social situations has increased, for the changes that have occurred are not found equally among all situations and all persons. But it is also true that opportunities have expanded, that the legal situation has been sharply redefined, that the world context within which American activities are carried out has been altered, and that substantial changes have occurred in the opinions of white persons. Modifications in modal tendencies among American Blacks have been extensive and intensive, although not, of course, universal. In the decades ahead, these modifications will become more significant because they have affected younger persons more. We are likely to see the truth of Karl Mannheim's thesis that social character is shaped, in vital ways, by the decisive experiences shared by a group during their early adult years—what he called the "generation effect." The world looks different in manifold ways to those who come of age during a depression or a world war or a civil rights movement than it did to their predecessors. To be Black is a different experience for those who have arrived at adulthood since, let us say, the Montgomery bus boycott in 1955, than it was for earlier generations. The new elements in the social character produced by this new environment now flow back into the system from which they came, modifying it further. We now see and will continue to see more action and less reaction. The actions will sometimes be harsh, sometimes moderate; new expressions will sometimes be negative and hostile, sometimes creative. Whatever the balance, the nation will be strongly influenced by the fact that the "shared modal tendencies" of the black population have been more significantly changed in the last generation than during any other period in our history.

The Passing of Passing: Ethnic Pluralism and the New Ideal in the American Society

10

GEORGE A. DeVOS

The Long Voyage Home: The Myth of the *Mayflower*

Every culture has its origin myth embedded in what becomes official history. Origin myths are of two varieties: the autochthonous myth of a sacred place where humanity originated; and tales of journey and the founding of a new society. The Japanese Isles were the result of a sacred pair—Izanagi and Izanami; the age of gods which they ushered in was followed by the appearance of men. The sacred texts, the Kojiki and the Nihongi, record Japan's transition from its mythical origin to the formation of the imperial line and the legitimacy of imperial power and social hierarchy.

In effect, everywhere in literate cultures, sacred scriptures are partially genealogies confirming the political community as it was constituted at the time of writing. Scriptures were sometimes commissioned by a court as was the case in ancient Japan. Today, in most countries, history is commissioned by educational agencies to serve the purpose of national allegiance. Whether through oral genealogy, mythology, or what is now presumed to be scientific history, the past serves the present society.

The writing of American history is now changing. It is becoming less a political tale of revolution and governmental succession in a supposedly unitary American culture. It is becoming more an ethnological, anthropological documentary of the origins and progression of an American pluralistic society. History, freed somewhat from patriotic mythology, is now documenting the continuing force of ethnicity in American social life.

Remnants of the ancient myths of Western man start far back. The Greek bards of the Homeric tradition sang the *Iliad*, which, in its preamble, lists the genealogy of ships and men assembled for the Trojan War. The gods from their sacred place, Olympus, intervened in the affairs of man. Greek mythology traced the origins of man in a retrospective mythology sung by bards that also legitimatized the power of the sociopolitical elite who listened to the paeans of praise to their ancestors.

The elite in Rome who listened to tales of their sacred past were informed of how their empire was founded by traveling twins. In origin, imperial Rome was actually a colony founded by those who had journeyed there from elsewhere. Christianity, when it inherited the empire and its religions, replaced Greek and Roman mythologies of origin with a Judaic myth of Eden and a Descent of Man from his unitary creation by a solitary, jealous, separate god. Diversity followed from the Tower of Babel. Man broke into racial and cultural traditions, only to seek reunion through a universal church.

The secular, legendary history of Europe as represented on the ceilings of Versailles ending with Louis XIV starts as a litany of power in images of imperial unification under Alexander the Great followed by Julius Caesar and then by Charlemagne. In the Dark Ages, Europe became a hopelessly fractured political and ethnic mass. Later, the most powerful kings, kaisers, and tzars aspired to redo the first Caesar's work and reunite the peoples of Europe. Despite all such efforts, the ethnic diversity of Europe was to prevail and to mock any attempts at amalgamation.

The ethnic quarrels of a divided Europe were to be transplanted to the New World—a simpler Tower of Babel rebuilt with four dominant voices: English, Spanish, Portuguese and French. Today the plebeian, technologically skilled American-English serves as the lingua franca.

American society today is not only composed of individual states, but in a sense is a confederation of ethnic minorities, drawn from all the land masses of the earth.

In anthropological perspective, America started as an empty continent and was first peopled from Asia. No myths are preserved, however, of man's entry by foot. Millennia later, European legends began recording ocean voyages, starting traditions of colonization and conquest. In the most recent past, waves of individual immigrants came supposedly to assimilate into a new unified identity as Americans.

American society, however, has achieved a more political than social unification. We have become a curious form of unified citizenry, but we are no longer melting together into some single image of biological or social ideals. In effect, a passing of passing is taking place. The official origin myth taught in schools for decades was that we were all sons and daughters of European colonists who came to an almost empty continent peopled only by savage red men. This myth is now being replaced by a direct avowal of our continuing multiplicity. The legend of the *Mayflower* and its Puritan fathers is being replaced by visions of multitudinous journeys, voluntary and otherwise. American Indians as well as the gold-besotted Spaniards and their ladened galleons are again more visible in their mestizo offspring. Dutch and British ships with chained Africans no longer slip silently into port to spew out chattel for the slave marts of New Orleans. We now hear the sound of self-assertion from those escaping the bonds of the past. We now know more of Hawaiian canoes and New England clippers with cargoes of Asian workers from China, Japan, and the Philippines. Unsettled Swedes are still settling in Minnesota on TV.

The myth of the *Mayflower* maintained by the Daughters of the American Revolution states affirmatively that anyone who mattered came over early. Not all early white settlers, however, kept alive the legends of their journey. It is not popular history in the South that the future elite of Georgia were an overflow from the English prisons. Some of these former inmates carried with them prideful images of becoming yeoman landowners or country squires on large estates in the New World. The slave ships that followed them were to expand the possibilities of such dreams into more atavistic ones of a landed aristocracy of manorial lords wih serfs. Out of English offal evolved Southern gentlemen riding the hounds. Such lowly origins have been suppressed. For their legitimacy, they sought no cataloging of ancestral passage as in the *Iliad* or the *Mayflower.*

Most of the settlers who became Americans were not concerned with their origins or past genealogy. Instead, they sought to establish lineages into the future, cutting themselves off from an unsatisfactory past. A Jewish rabbi from Europe, when visiting the United States several decades ago, once remarked: "How blessed you are. You have no heritage of the Middle Ages." Indeed, it is very true that the generally shared vision of American society has been future-oriented. Most Americans do not have a prideful past on which to draw. America was to be a land of promise for those who had the good fortune to come.

Today, however, we are more and more becoming preoccupied with our ethnic origins. What has happened to the United States as a crucible of assimilation? Why is it that past parentage persists as a determining force of our present identity? As part of our focal American preoccupation with identity, Margaret Mead (DeVos, 1975) has described the problem of whom to include or exclude, whom to accept and whom to reject. This is an abiding American dilemma. Ethically, if not ethically, we are founded on a premise of equality before God and law—an equality of citizenship and opportunity. In actuality, we have a history of ethnic dissension and conflict related to relative acceptability or absolute rejection. Yet, the fortunate trust of our history, while so unhappy and frustrating for many, has nevertheless been toward expanding concentric circles of inclusion. The myth of the melting pot brought promise for those who saw an opportunity for acceptance. At the same time, our history of racial bigotry is a hideous spectrum that ranges from shocking extremes of genocide, through various forms of exploitation, toward blander and more subtle forms of polite exclusion practiced quietly without display. Robert Heizer (1971), an archaeologist on the faculty at Berkeley, has unearthed public documents depicting the overtness of racial bigotry in the state of California. The examples are legion. California Indians were almost shot as game to remove their bothersome presence. Some of the Spanish-speaking minority in California were overrun without compunction, and others, from Mexico, were exploited as stoop labor on the land. Asians from China and Japan, brought in as temporary exploitative labor, were soon resented for their industry and excluded for their oriental faces when they dared embrace the image of the American dream and attempted to better themselves. The Yellow Peril hysteria even deprived them of the hope of eventual citizenship. The Chinese were driven back out of California. The relocation of Japanese-Americans during World War II under the pretext of wartime necessity was simply a continuation of a long-standing bigotry that allowed individuals to be stripped of hard-earned possessions. The rural migrants from the South—the white Oakies and Arkies—could somehow melt in easier, but only after awkward exclusion. More recently, black Southerners who came north for employment did so with the resigned knowledge that northern bigotry, though more subtle, was no less operative with regard to jobs and housing. The American dilemma, as Gunnar Myrdal has termed it, remains whereby the ethics and inherent moral trust of equality in acceptance is pitted against the problems of status related to the class, occupational, racial, and ethnic distinctions that separate us.

We have been curiously unsuccessful in the last stages of assimilation. Resistance to racial differences have, in effect, reawakened a latent, still smoldering, ethnicity in those already seemingly assimilated. I have watched at Berkeley, among some of our students, a reemergence of a sense of self-seeking for ethnic distinctiveness. Many of the young people are escaping the passing of their socially mobile parents who have been hiding precariously in white ghettos, seeking acceptability in that twilight zone between working class and middle class, and striving desperately for upward inclusion.

The typical American prefers to think of himself as "middle class." Social scientists such as Lloyd Warner and Geoffrey Gorer have noted that if you ask people to rate their class status in Britain, they are much more apt to call themselves working class than are individuals in the United States occupied in similar skilled activities. The American, whatever his occupation, attempts to pass not only ethnically but also in terms of class status.

The confusion of class and ethnicity in the United States is considerable among the young. For some of them, to affirm their ethnicity is often to resolve conflicts about hierarchy in status or occupation. Some consider it an act of peculiar honesty to identify the white Anglo-Saxon Protestant simply as another variety of ethnic rather than as a model for all. Since racial differences will not disappear and since a multiplicity of life-styles will become acceptable, they believe we must prepare for such differences by finding some form of separation into groups that is not necessarily hierarchical. If we as a society affirm class differences, then we cannot at the same time believe in our potential equality as Americans. If we are, however, to accept ethnic differences, we can still relate to one another without necessarily having to stand higher or lower than one another. Black Americans and Orientals or Mexicans or even Jews, Poles, and Irish can continue to distinguish among themselves, granting others the right to join in group competition to seek whatever benefits or political advantage can be gained by controlling the decaying cities into which they have migrated.

There are numerous personal and social incentives to rediscover or reaffirm ethnicity. Whatever the motives, one is witnessing, to some degree and for our society as a whole, the passing of passing—the passing of Catholics, Mexicans, Blacks, Poles, and other middle Europeans; the passing of the need to hide, to pretend to be among those WASP elite, all of whom descended from passengers on the *Mayflower*.

Ethnic groups other than ourselves may be seen to have potentials for free expression that our own heritage precludes. Thus, Americans can shop among the patterns present and even borrow from another group by emulation, if not by inner absorption. If we once again accept the illusion of unitary values, whether they be attributed to some preferred physical appearance or model of moral comportment, we exclude for everyone, including ourselves, alternatives of behavior that a pluralistic society should be rich enough to afford.

Vicissitudes in the Experience of Ethnic Identity

Just as ethnicity in a pluralistic society cannot be seen apart from the history of particular groups, so the origins of any particular American's sense of identity are part of his own personal history and his knowledge of ordeals suffered by his parents. How does one maintain or return to a particular ethnic identity in a composite society such as ours, made up of so many nationalities and points of view? How does one, in cities with mass populations, survive ethnically by using emblems that in some way continue to distinguish self from those of different origin? These questions, of course, are more easily answered in situations of rigid segregation where individuals are separated from childhood by economic barriers or by living patterns in which ethnic enclaves become territorially separate in segments of the many-faced American city.

A characteristic pattern of urban growth has indeed occurred in Chicago, New York, and most major American metropolises. American urbanization in the major metropolises is unique in that the symptoms of social disorganization, such as crime, delinquency, and mental breakdown, are greater there than in urban areas in other countries (see DeVos, 1976).

The combination of urbanization and the tensions of facing or fleeing from an ethnic minority status has created the stresses found in the American inner city. Urbanizing people in other lands, settling into cities with the same cultural traditions as found in their hinterlands, do not suffer by moving into a city. Indeed, on measurements of mental health, those who urbanize score better, in effect, than those who remain in a rural environment (Inkeles, 1976). Simply stated, the social ills found among our urban populations have resulted from the peculiarities of our American pluralism. At the turn of the century, New York was regarded by all the world as a place to visit, if not to live. Chicago, in competitive pride, sought to compete with New York in growth, as did other urban centers. Today our cities are corroding and in some respects unmanageable. Thus, we face another form of the American dilemma: our inability to translate our collective wealth into a satisfactory life-style which would allow the city to satisfy rather than to frustrate, harass, and even become an object of fear, a place to flee when possible.

To return to our specific topic, many Americans now consider themselves to be members of an ethnic minority. This sense of ethnicity has arisen not only from the outside, by those who tell us that we are different, but also from group and family experiences.

In many cultures, individuals are not mobile. From birth to death they identify themselves with place and group and they remain part of stable relationships. They know who they are because they know that they relate to others through characteristic, unchanging definitions of kinship and community. In contrast, in our mobile culture places of residence are not fixed. We move about frequently. Few die in their community of birth. Therefore, many of us—if we are not black or brown, that is—are relatively free to change our background as we wish. If we work at it, we can manage to change our gestures and comportment to suit the prevailing styles of acceptance. Such change in social participation only exists where others too are in flux.

One's pedigree is not defined by common knowledge of ancestry. The more we become a mass society, the easier it is for passing to occur. But now this process seems to be reversing. Many of the children of passing parents want to know more about some shreds of past heritage left behind by parents traveling light, by parents who have jettisoned much of their inherited peculiarities of language, food, dress and aesthetic values somewhere in the process of becoming "successful."

Maintenance of a Fixed Identity

From a psychocultural perspective, the presence of social discrimination does not adequately explain the maintenance of ethnic boundaries in the United States. The more subtle levels of identity maintenance that link self with social persona must also be examined. An ethnic self derives from a sense of integrity that comes only from the knowledge that we are true to those who have given us birth and life. Such integrity draws on some continuity with a community of peers who have tempered our childhood experiences. This sense of integrity is strengthened when one or both parents are members of a depreciated ethnic minority. Thus, an ethnic identity may be maintained out of a sense of responsibility felt toward stigmatized parents. We accept and assume the stigmas of the past as marks of acceptance and love. To assume stigma is to accept parents.

American society promises mobility. It is a society that assumes ideally that no one needs to be stigmatized. The American Revolution was to be a cleansing, a rebirth of identity dedicated to the future. This simple ideal, however, goes counter to psychological truth. Our emotional lives cannot be uprooted from past pain in the promised pursuit of happiness. Social mobility has its own price. How is one to measure the costs of bearing the heavy burden of a socially shameful minority or low-status inheritance on the one hand, versus the loss one suffers by casting off our intimate heritage, good and bad?

Each member of a forsaken group hides some aspects of ethnic life in shame. Of course, there is cost in living with an unflinching eye—to be willing to perceive those close to us as they are. Human acceptance demands an awareness of the fallibility in any culturally inherited way of life. Those with too sensitized nostrils turn from the odors of ineptness or vulgarity they witness in their own background and the corruption and contamination of contact.

The stigma of birth is not removed, it simply is hidden. The pain remains for most; few find it possible to live in the new environment without exterior defenses.

The sense of stigmatized identity and the use of ethnic stereotypes as weapons in social conflict are interrelated. Stigmas are subjectively experienced as a vulnerability because of group membership. The individual within the group becomes aware that he has problems in human experience because his group creates given difficulties for its members. Outsiders portray some perceived problems in hostile caricature to demean, degrade, and dehumanize. When this process of stereotype assault combines with an inner sense of vulnerability, the individual can become subject to self-hate. When the caricatures are false, the individual is genuinely affirmed in his group belonging, and these attacks do not wound or hurt in the same way. It is the inner vulnerability that a person feels as a member of a group that makes it difficult to maintain an identity. Social groups use one another in order to deny what they know exists within themselves. In this way, stereotypes become means of avoiding what we fear to know about ourselves. On the other hand, the individual who hides his identity is afraid of his own vulnerability. He knows that he is too ready a victim because he himself believes on one level of his being that he *is* the caricature created by others.

Those who obtain some level of objectivity manage to transcend, to some degree, problems of self-hatred in identity. One must see through caricatures that we paint on each other's faces and see that indeed the colors we paint are drawn from ourselves. The distorted images we hold of others are mirrored projections of our own disavowed selves. We know what we dislike because we ourselves contain what we dislike to see in others. We force our own inner fears and hates, or deceitful impassivity, or hostile inadequacy on the faces of others. The somber face of tragedy we keep for ourselves, only in gentler moments granting it to those of other origins in a sense of common brotherhood.

The Persona in Modern Society

In the complex mass societies of today, behavioral alternatives are increasingly possible. One can vary behavior with changes in the reference group. As used in social science, a reference group is one that is deemed worthy of emulation, either overtly or as a model for the inner construction of the self. Such models can be followed either consciously or unconsciously. Reference group models may be found in the social group in which one participates. In some instances parental models predominate, while in others, peer and contemporary models supersede. Reference group models may be drawn from those admired at a distance with whom one had no direct personal contact, or from various mass media that excite the imagination from childhood. With so many alternatives in sight, today's child can find a multiplicity of models for behavior. Robert Lifton (1970) has described modern man as turning into what he terms "Protean Man." Just as Proteus changed his appearance at will, so modern man can change form with social context and take on the coloring of a variety of social atmospheres. Unattached and undefined by permanent face-to-face community relationships, he learns patterns that allow for surface emulation. Socially mobile individuals become good actors in their social roles. To some degree, they enjoy alternately assuming and shedding roles at will.

Nevertheless, the question of identity remains: in these circumstances to what degree can an individual maintain his sense of identity? What remains of core commitment when there are so many opportunities to act in diverse contexts? Indeed, it is difficult to relate to an individual who is always "on stage." Today we are struggling to find some means of identifying the self as a vital experience. What kind of a living organism is the social self? Some have begun to fear that we may be onionlike, that the process of socialization is a layered growth.

Many of today's youth are socially radical. They deny, for example, that any special innate characteristics define the roles of men and women. Some would even like to peel off most of what they perceive to be the onionlike layers of their social learning. But what would be left? The ultimate dilemma, then, would be that the human being would relate to others socially through some form of mutually understandable expectations. Can we set up satisfactory social expectations related to what is genuine personality rather than to social persona? Does genuine personality have nothing to do with sex, age, ethnicity, or any other form of social demarcation? Can man live truly naked, or, conversely, can he so clothe himself so that no two of us are distinguishable, one from the other?

To have some concept of themselves, individuals have to say to others, and to themselves as well, that "I am a woman" or "I am a man," "I am young" or "I am old," "I am an American" or "I am a Swede." Without such self-defining markers, or, if you will, social vestments or emblems as points of reference, a sense of confused alienation that ultimately incapacitates must result.

Conversely, to say to oneself, for example, "I am a woman" is simply taking a conventional role. To mask oneself in a conventional pose sometimes does violence to one's inner nature. Acting out the expected is contrary to one's genuine inclinations and smothers spontaneity.

A hidden deviant identity that is not socially acceptable to others sometimes demands some form of symbolic outer expression. An individual who has homosexual inclinations, for example, may experience psychological, if not social, relief when he says openly, "I am a homosexual." But this is a deviant group identity and, ironically, the individual may feel compelled to deny other spontaneous inclinations so that he can gain and maintain acceptance within the deviant group with which he identifies. The maintenance of any group identity, however deviant, requires that the individual impose certain regulations and constraints upon his own individual inclinations. In the same way, the individual, for his own self-acceptance, if not the acceptance of some others, finds it necessary to give avowal to that which is socially disavowed. Hence he may choose to side with a minority identity as a mark of integrity even though that act may prevent him from realizing and actualizing other aspects of his personality that are just as integral to his true nature.

In our interviews (DeVos, 1966), Hiroshi Wagatsuma and I have found that some Japanese outcasts, or "Burakumin," who hide their backgrounds and pass at the university are sometimes part of social groups where discussion of the plight of the former "Eta" has come up. On such occasions, some feel a strong need to reveal their hidden identity as a means of shocking and giving the lie to their friends' supposed readiness to accept the "Eta." They know full well that once their identity is revealed, they will no longer be accepted for themselves. The Japanese Burakumin knows full well that a continuous social tension will be aroused by such overt affirmation. The seemingly enlightened Japanese intellectual from a majority background is still victimized by his own deeply emotionally felt repugnance to social pollution from which he cannot free himself.

In our work on the effects of outcaste status in Japan, we have translated poems by Tadao Maruoka (1966), who has affirmed his identity in his art by depicting the outcaste's plight:

Let Come the Day to Say "Once It Was So"

I heard whispering
Like the flow of wind from mouth to mouth
That under each armpit I am marked,
The size of an open hand.

Was it inherited from an ancient time?
My parents, too, or so I've heard
Were bruised by nature's brand.

Yet of them no memory affords
Sight or feel of such a spot.

But in childhood I learned,
Through cruel heavy winks, how instinctively to hide.

What was it I so naively wrapped with rags,
And hidden, dragged, through dark months and years?

In these concealing rags, I had hid my heart,
When refound, it was sorely bruised
Shriveled red from stigma I sought to lose.

Without some fresh exposure, my songs would end in lies;
Tightly bound but increase with inner plight.

Who marked my sides? For what unknown cause?
Why such a brand upon my very self and soul?
Even today, my ebbing thoughts,
So pale and cold, transparent as glass,
Hold me awake.

Why Flee?

At one time
Alone, in a land of strangers,
I denied my childhood home.

Peter denied his Lord thrice.
How many more times did I deny
My humble place of birth?

Constantly threatened by an unknown lurking shadow,
Like an oppressive weight cutting off my breath,

I dwell alone, in a strange land,
Fearing to meet my kind, like a crab,
Ready to scurry away in dread of contact.

Although Japan's emancipation edict declared all to be citizens over 100 years ago, the irrational, emotional problem of caste still plagues Japan's effort at true democracy. There is as yet only the beginning of the passing of passing there.

In the United States, the passing of passing is evident not only among ethnic minorities but also among women. It is appearing in the attempts of women to express themselves as complex, capable, and equal to men not only in the intellectual arena but also in the full defensive panoply of human aggressiveness and even destructiveness.

Human sexual behavior is being redefined beyond the strictures set by family concerns. Many of those who are deviant dare to assert their sexual proclivities, even those society generally condemns as signs of infirmity or incapacity. People now question the right of the state to punish those with private inclinations that cannot possibily harm others. If we learn to live with ethnic differences, surely we can also learn to live with differences in sexual behavior and life-style. In the present social atmosphere individuals are urged to reject pretense and to affirm their nature, as long as they do not harm other members of society.

The Passing of Self-Consistency

Everyone enjoys getting out of himself at times. From playing charades at parties to the taking part in a play, to the use of ecstatic experiences of possession in religions, to the more serious maladaptive patterns of individual psychopathology in which altered states of consciousness periodically reveal the repressed, the human psyche finds ways for a person to overcome the limitations imposed by the conscious need for a consistent self. Individuals in trance are able to act out roles that they would not tolerate in their normal conscious state. In his documentary film on Ghana, "Les Maitres Fous," made before independence, Jean Rouche gives dramatic evidence of this fact. In his film, factory workers participating in a new religion are put in a trance. A live dog is dismembered, individuals in trance eat and share this "communion." Mystically they assume power. They turn into white officials, posturing in prestigious roles as generals or administrators. In trance they can emulate members of the dominant white culture. Although the inner structuring of these assumed roles remains a mystery, nevertheless, for a brief moment, they can feel the enhanced state of power their play-acting and trance bring on.

When we are officially ordained to assume a given social role or occupation by society, similar mechanisms are at work. At some given point, society acknowledges our supposed competence and we are henceforth expected to change our behavior, to give up the inconsistencies and playfulness of childhood, and to assume the more sustained responsibilities of marriage and occupation that come with adult status.

We all know individuals who are passing as adults. Their inner nature remains childlike, sometimes engagingly so. But they are forced by social expectations to take on a demeanor of adulthood that their inner nature cannot, for various reasons, assume. Speaking of what we anthropologists call age grading, we see in American society the opposite phenomenon—the aging person who cannot give up his adolescent glory or the alumni harkening back to college and the peak experiences of a yet uncommitted adolescence. Such individuals love to pretend to others and to themselves that they are still young.

One might ask, what is age? Is it too not an assumed role? By custom Greek widows dress in black and quite early must live under the social constraints appropriate to those in mourning and the aged. It was not too long ago that sexual activity was supposed to cease at an "age-appropriate" time. Many still callously read with amusement the fact that a serious love triangle has caused conflict among the members of an old people's home. Youth can be cruel to the aging, demanding of them that they assume the roles "proper" to members of a grandparental generation.

For some, individual crises of self occur at fixed points of social transition, e.g., graduation from school, marriage, or parenthood. For others, the crises come on only gradually. These points of social transition or of inner reevaluation of self may be imperceptible or highly dramatic, or they can occur unexpectedly. One sees periodically a breakthrough of something hidden about oneself that the individual has been at great pains to disguise both publicly and privately.

In the realm of ethnicity, unexpected occurrences can abruptly cause a realization of ethnic identity. I once talked to a Welshman who only realized that he was Welsh at age thirty after living for many years in London as an Englishman. The realization came almost as a religious experience. After the discovery of his Welshness, it became incumbent upon him morally to affirm his ethnic origin symbolically and to act in accordance with a sense of integrity that his occupation as a journalist required.

The people of Eastern Europe have experienced tragic problems relating to ethnic loyalty. After World War II when many regions were divided arbitrarily, cousins and sometimes even brothers would take on different ethnic loyalties and come in conflict with one another. Sometimes ethnicity in Europe is layered expediently as one relates to different social groups. One evening in Germany I spoke with an individual whom I initially took to be a Frenchman. After several drinks he became a Pole and by the early hours of the morning, he had become a nationalist Puthenian, an ethnic identity whose meaning to me is still uncertain.

One difficult problem that arises with regard to social identity, and hence to the problem of passing, has to do with the levels and modes of operation related to a complex sense of self. One can, for certain strategic purposes, at a given time, define oneself in one's broadest sense as human, and for many, humanity stops at being an American. In some situations, one defines oneself more narrowly as a New Yorker, or a New York Italian, or a Jew, or an Italian from the Bronx, or a Reformed Jew from Manhattan. The specificities or complexities become even greater for the offspring from a mixed marriage, which in turn was entered into by individuals of mixed parentage. The greater the number of disparate ancestors, the more difficult it is for the individual to specify. Perhaps he is then left with a more residual identification. In psychiatric parlance he would probably be labeled a schizophrenic American, undifferentiated type.

In Mexico or in America, the condition of being mestizo in culture and in personality is complex. Physical appearance is important but not conclusive. Mexicans rank themselves not only culturally but also according to skin color and physical types. At the pinnacle of potential status definition are the more Caucasoid, the more "Spanish looking." At the bottom are the most "Indian" or "Indio." In between are the various degrees of Indianness in skin coloring and in comportment. Racial and behavioral cultural traits are almost always correlated in such instances with socioeconomic status. In Mexico, as elsewhere, there is a correlation between being darker and being poorer. The present situation in the United States is more confused. There are so many standards and such flux in regard to ethnic pluralism that individuals can transmit and receive many false signals. Passing is indeed widespread. Many foreign names have been changed. Modern plastic surgery even allows one to pick out a new physiognomy in an attempt to change one's "social acceptability."

Ethnicity and the Direction of Change in American Culture: Kin, Class, Caste, or Ethnicity?

American society as a social system is attempting to resolve the incongruities created by its special history. By examining societies very generally in social structural terms, a number of different forms of social organization and social hierarchy can be seen. Japan, India, China, and the various nations of Europe, each have distinguishing characteristics that tend to define how people relate to one another and how society changes from within.

Japan, as defined by Chie Nakane (1970), is a vertical society in its organization, but it is not a class society as we understand the term. People are organized in companies and organizations on a hierarchical basis, and these within-group organizations form strong ties of participation and interpersonal relationship. There is less direct concern in Japan than in most nations about social class or special ethnic backgrounds.

In contrast, India remains essentially a caste society of jatties that are ranked roughly by occupation. Ultimately, the society is stratified by concepts of ritual purity (Berreman, 1966). European societies display various forms of social class stratification, although they also are plagued by internal ethnic differences that extend far back into the past.

Anthropologists are aware of how simpler societies tend to be structured by networks of kinship and family ties. The remnants of kinship organization are still important in modern-day China, although the Communist Revolution all but obliterated the Confucianist family (see Fried, 1976).

The United States, with its mixed origins, has experienced elements of all these systems. The United States has a class structure, but Americans do not like to be told, for example, that social class considerations in the educational system prevent easy mobility (see Warner, 1944). Even more apparent in American society is the caste segmentation in the form of racial discrimination that has operated to create occupational stratification (see Warner, 1963). This caste structure has been slowly giving way in the United States to a structure that emphasizes the continuing viability of ethnic affiliation in the social world, if not in the occupational world.

Shifting Patterns of Loyalty

A great deal of American conformist and loyalty, which is particularly visible in lower middle-class individuals and strikes the European visiting the United States as frantic emphasis on nationality, is a reflection of second-generation ethnic immigrants, uneasiness over the legitimacy of a claim to be American. Many ethnics have "passed" by moving to the suburbs. Those moving into a "good" neighborhood particularly tended to be conformists since they were new to, and often insecure about, their claim to an "encompassing" middle-class status. The white suburbs of second-generation European ethnics have become encircled bastions, warding off other groups that might endanger their social status. This selective exclusion has been specially directed against racially visible groups. Individuals of Jewish origin, a more difficult group to exclude racially, are "visible" if one notes patterns of church participation, and so forth.

In such areas there is continued fear that hard-earned real estate would diminish in value if any minority members were to move in. These hotbeds of passing are particularly sensitive to individuals who are unwilling or not able to pass as easily due to their maintaining past group membership or revealing their racial difference.

Nevertheless, class and racial segmentation in the United States is slowly giving way to ethnic cohesiveness in political and social forms of group participation. This is particularly true of the cities. Ethnic groups themselves may manifest certain levels of segmentation according to class levels, but loyalty to the ethnic group is now stronger than loyalty to occupational specialization.

One general way of looking at a segmented social system is to observe the patterns of priority in group loyalty. The patterning of such priorities in any complex society contrasts present-oriented, future-oriented, and past-oriented forms of loyalty. On a social structural level, American society is shifting from an emphasis on present-oriented forms of loyalty, related to occupational specialization, to a more broad concept of citizenship. Forms of ethnic loyalty defined in terms of past heritage are being reemphasized.

Societies emphasizing present orientation in loyalty can be united by an overall concept of citizenship that disregards origin. In European societies, the French emphasize citizenship more than the Germans or Italians. An Armenian, for example, can become French, or at least his children can be totally accepted as French, regardless of whether he is an immigrant or not. This pattern is less frequent in Germany or in Italy. In France, newcomers are more readily absorbed in metropolitan than in rural areas. This pattern has also been characteristic in the United States and is part of the American ideology—that is, anyone can acquire citizenship, regardless of place of origin.

A second specific form of present-oriented loyalty relates very broadly to social class and more narrowly to particular professions or skills, so that individuals in some segmented societies develop occupational loyalties. This is true, whether it takes the form of labor unions or professional organizations. Although occupational loyalties are present in the United States, Europe tends to segment occupations more stringently according to broad class definitions.

Present-oriented forms of loyalty can come into conflict with a future-oriented universalist allegiance, which may take the form of a religious movement or a revolutionary ideology. That is, one's identity and loyalty can be directed toward a type of organization envisioned in future terms. The present system can be seen as bad, and one can give allegiance to forms of belonging that are to supplant those of the present. Revolutionary movements, however, may depend on certain present occupational allegiances that can be employed to change status levels, such as in the Marxian doctrine of the dictatorship of the proletariat. The Christian doctrine is another form of universalism that transcends the specifics of a given country or radical group in its ideal form.

In contrast to present- or future-oriented loyalties are past forms of loyalty that can be considered ethnic in nature: that is, loyalty to a tradition based on ancestry and continuity through parentage. The emblems of identity used may be religious, linguistic, or aesthetic; they may even be territorial or economic; and in some instances, racial or biological.

Religious differences in America often tend also to be ethnic when examined closely. In New York, the Italians and Irish, despite their common Catholic faith, do not share strongly in any formal social way. Granted, among the Protestant northern Europeans, there is some form of amalgamation, and in the cities at least, Scandinavians, Germans, and those of English ancestry have tended to forget their ethnic backgrounds. Intermarriage among these groups has been considerable, and, of course, there are many individuals of very mixed parentage among them.

In American cities that have had continuous large-scale migrations of particular ethnic entities, social participation largely remains ethnic. The Italians of New York remain a group as do, to a lesser extent, the Irish. The Irish in Boston are a very recognizable social force. In Chicago, Czechs, Poles, Italians, and Jews are conscious of one another and are very much aware that the black and Mexican-American populations have grown to much greater proportions in the last decade. In appointments for some political offices, locally and nationally, ethnicity is a more important variable than religion or, perhaps, social class background. Ethnicity, therefore, is a force in American life that ranks at least as strongly as socioeconomic class as a determinant of individual and collective behavior, whether of an economic, political, or social nature.

In effect, this ethnic vitality makes America less a class-segregated society than the European nations that have provided its majority population. It is certainly less of a caste society than India, although conceptions of racial purity have distinguished American social organization from its inception. Racism has been especially directed against the American Indians, Chinese, Japanese, and, even before the American Revolution, the Africans brought in as slaves. The United States is therefore a mixed system, but gradually becoming a pluralistic society, openly acknowledging pluralism as an acceptable form of organization. This open acknowledgment is both social and psychological. Hence it is that American society is witnessing the passing of passing in order to allow for social and geographic mobility, or for the admission of minority group members to the higher ranges of social participation. The singular advantage of ethnic segmentation is that it does not of necessity stratify an individual in a given, fixed position as does loyalty to a class or occupational position on the one hand or a caste designation on the other. The inequities that American democracy in its ethical opposition to hierarchy disavows can be more readily resolved by shifting caste or class definitions toward ethnic ones. The United States, then, becomes a society horizontally segmented by ethnicity in which ethnic loyalties remain binding for a good percentage of its people, despite vertical shifts in socioeconomic status.

Increasingly through television or personal conversation, it is becoming apparent that the overriding issue of the Black-White split in American society is gradually shifting toward a perception of the black population as another ethnic minority, albeit a large one. One begins, then, to think in national terms: of social blocks of over twenty million Blacks, five million Jews, and perhaps close to a million Orientals as part of the ethnic composition. Locally, in San Francisco, one thinks of the political and social force of the local Chinese community or the Mexican community. In New York, one considers Puerto Rican, West Indian, Irish, Italian, and Jewish populations. In Chicago, there are the Czechs, Poles, Italians, Jews, and the black majority. Each of these groups has its own local political clout.

At this point in American history, a past-oriented ethnicity seems to have more appeal to American Blacks as a means of reordering and enhancing their relative status in American society than membership in a religious group or in a self-consciously defined, exploited proletarian group. Black workers are aware that working-class people have more rigid caste attitudes than the middle-class or upper middle-class professionals. Generally, the professionals are more accepting of some Blacks in their professional communities. Blacks have greater difficulties with lower middle-class or working-class Irishmen and Poles than they do with the upper middle-class levels of management in various companies. Therefore, they find it difficult to see themselves as brothers being exploited on a class basis rather than on a racial basis. Hence, despite Marxist militancy and recruitment, Blacks have not been basically amenable to leftist definitions of their plight. This fact enhances the idea that, in the pluralistic America of today, primary-group participation is becoming increasingly defined as ethnic-oriented, even while occupational discrimination is becoming diminished.

My overall approach to this problem is more from a psychocultural than a sociological point of view. Therefore, my primary interest is in the subjective experience of ethnicity in the United States and how it too is changing with the passing of passing. The idea of passing is, of course, a psychological one. This concept cannot be understood without looking at the individual's experience in a situation of changing status. We do not speak of "passing" when an individual is totally and innocently part of a group; it is only when some form of instrumental maneuvering related to social comportment exists that the concept of passing is relevant.

Originally, the term *passing* applied to racially mixed Blacks who, for purposes of social and even psychological expediency, would deny their subordinate black caste identity and assume more acceptable and materially rewarding white identity. But this term has a much broader meaning. It applies to Poles who change their names and to Jews who change their Eastern European-derived names to Scottish or Anglo-Saxon names. At one time, it also applied to the Irish Catholic in Boston who assumed high-status Protestantism by joining the Episcopalian church.

In effect, passing occurs in any act of social mobility in which the individual fabricates a past that will enhance his legitimacy to a higher form of social participation. It is a process inherent to social mobility wherever it is practiced. It occurs between social classes, culturally distinct minorities, or racial groups in which mixture allows for inclusion across lines that distinguish individuals physiologically, one from another. As noted above, collective acts of passing can be observed in the white suburbs where socially mobile individuals are attempting to impress their equally socially mobile neighbors of the legitimacy of their status.

American society is undergoing a social revolution throughout its various class levels. In the upper middle class, students are attempting to rediscover their lost past origins. Working-class groups, whose ethnicity has remained more continuous, now more readily acknowledge a heritage that was less acceptable in the past. Blond hair and light skin and a thin nose are still highly desirable physical characteristics, but the appearance on television of members of different minorities with "foreign" names such as Columbo and Kojak marks a significant departure with the past, when Scottish, Irish, or English surnames dominated. The heroes more often than not are now Italian, vaguely middle European, and, of course, black. Even our image of beauty has become more diversified, and many comedies and serious dramas now utilize ethnicity as their underlying theme.

Finally, the processes combatting the historical force of caste as a social institution in America are far different from those operative in India or Japan. In those countries, an ethnic or religious definition is less readily available as a social force for change, although in India many former outcastes are converting to Buddhism as an anticaste religion as opposed to Hinduism. In Japan, many of the former pariahs attempt to give a Marxian interpretation to the discrimination they suffer. Given the nature of Japanese social organizational loyalties, however, belief in class solidarity is not sufficient to effect change in their continuing definition as social pariahs. They cannot readily be assimilated because of the patterns of intense familial-like participation that are operative in the vertical organizations comprising the Japanese social structure.

Psychocultural Motives for Identity Maintenance or Passing

We will now examine the more specific motivational patterns related to the maintenance of group belonging and the manifestation of loyalty in situations of conflict.

Some features of individual experiences of ethnic identity are examined elsewhere (see DeVos and Romanucci-Ross, *Ethnic Identity*, 1975). In our conclusions, we point out that both instrumental and expressive needs are involved in maintaining one's identity throughout life. There are various reasons at given times to attempt to pass or to become identified strongly with other groups. Ethnicity, or ethnic identity, can become a problem or a handicap for many. Not everyone is able to transcend a personal or social past without denying self-awareness or without resorting to excessive dissimulation or fabrication. Yet, a fuller maturity requires a degree of transcendence of family identity or social past. Ethnic background, while present and part of the self, is not the essential constituent of the individual as a human being. Transcendence of narrow ethnicity is desirable if we are to live together in some degree of harmony with others different from ourselves. Such transcendence is to be distinguished from passing. Passing is a more frequent and pervasive social phenomenon, one that will be considered in terms of the instrumental and expressive motives involved.

For this motivational level of psychocultural analysis, I shall use a scheme developed in the analysis of interview and psychological test materials which I have developed over a period of years in my research in Japan and elsewhere. This scheme broadly divides motivation into (1) basically instrumental, goal-oriented motivations referring to behavior governed by goals, and (2) expressive behavior in which behavior is an end in itself. This dichotomy has been used by sociologists such as Talcott Parsons in their analyses of social behavior. These instrumental and expressive categories are further differentiated into more specific forms of motivation.

Instrumental Goal-Oriented Motivations

The first form of instrumental motivation is that concerned with achievement and accomplishment. This type of motivation has been studied by psychologists such as David McClelland (1961) who have attempted to do cross-cultural analyses of the relative presence in a population of achievement motivation.

The second form of instrumental behavior is concerned with *competence*; that is, the individual's concern is with his own capacity to master given tasks. The contrary fear is over incompetence or inadequacy in performing the tasks.

The third form of instrumental behavior is related to self-control and to meeting standards internalized within the individual as social obligation or patterns of *responsibility*. Behavior is motivated toward the accomplishment of expected social standards. Lack of accomplishment or the violation of standards may lead to a sense of guilt in some individuals.

The fourth form of instrumental behavior is related to the use of *control* or power in dominant and subordinate forms of relationships. A person in a dominant position can induce expected behavior in subordinates. The subordinate can sense that he must behave in accordance with the instrumental ends of the person(s) in dominant social positions.

The final form is that of *cooperation* in which individuals unite their efforts to accomplish a goal, or, conversely, enter into *competition* with one another to attain the goals, so that there is relative success or failure measured between or among individuals. Such concerns are again instrumental as opposed to expressive, since the focus is on the goal rather than on the process itself.

Expressive Behavior

There are also five subpatterns of expressive behavior. The first concerns itself with *harmony or discord*. (This is the expressive counterpart to the instrumental concern with *cooperation and competition*, wherein the emphasis is on the emotional relationships of people in interaction.) Every culture or social group is concerned with peace and harmony or with discord, contention, and even violence as expressive components of behavior.

The second form of expressive behavior is what is considered *affiliation*—a human need for contact, closeness, and intimacy. The opposite are negative states of rejection, isolation, separation, and a sense of loss in human interaction.

Another major expressive concern which is a counterpart to dominant-subordinate instrumental behavior is that of *nurturance* and dependency. The meaning of behavior, according to this subpattern, is in the gratification of dependent feeling, on the one hand, or the gratification felt by individuals who are in a succorant position and thus are able to provide care for those needing it. A sense of deprivation is the negative contrastive concern.

The fourth subcategory focuses on a universal concern for social *appreciation* and recognition, or a fear of *degradation* and depreciation.

Finally, all expressive behavior is somehow related to sensations of *pleasure* and satisfaction, and to concern with *suffering* and displeasure. Intermediate to these is apathetic behavior, which contrasts to behavior characterized by enthusiasm and vitality.

ACHIEVEMENT

Depending upon group of origin, seeking success in a given pursuit may induce the individual to emphasize his ethnic belonging or to disguise it. Numerous examples in American society come to mind. The phenomenon often perceived of as class mobility might be better thought of in ethnic terms. Ethnic behavioral characteristics cause the individual to sense discrimination rather than simple identification with class origins. When a Jew finds it expedient to change his name in order to enhance his opportunities for social participation, it is not his class background which causes his need for passing as much as the anti-Semitic attitudes of our society. In the previous pre-Kennedy world of Boston society, regardless of wealth or refinement, Irish ancestry restricted and sometimes barred full participation in Boston society. The conditions that have made passing necessary are complex and varied, they have been treated in sensitive novels, not only in works written by Jews and Blacks, but also in works by members of other European ethnic minorities. In the United States, name changing is one of the most common practices employed to facilitate passing.

Knowledge that one belongs to a minority group may induce the individual to strive harder to overcome discriminatory experiences while asserting one's ethnicity. Parental striving may be passed on to the children who are taught that they must work harder as a member of an ethnic minority. This is especially apparent in the Japanese immigrants who internalized within their children the belief that the school could be an avenue to advancement if they worked harder than children of the majority.

A crisis in identity maintenance can occur when a choice must be made between conflicting group loyalties. For example, a tension may develop between one's professional commitment to treat individuals equally and the insistence by those of one's own group that they receive special privileges or special consideration in hiring or treatment. The ethnic composition of various professions and trades in the United States has been selective for years. Such situations are the result of a tendency for a particular ethnic group, either dominant or otherwise, to recruit or hire selectively, once established in a given profession.

COMPETENCE

The exclusion-inclusion process in trades and professions begins with an admittance or nonadmittance in training programs. Therefore, patterns of ethnic selectivity govern accessibility to competence. Advancement related to the quality in professional performance can be, and often is, ethnically controlled.

Differential socialization from childhood can, of course, determine whether given groups predispose individuals to become more adequate in the pursuit of particular occupations. Strictly speaking, opportunity will be better used by those whose childhood experience has been so organized that they can better understand and exploit the opportunities afforded them.

A particular ethnic identity may also determine a person's confidence in his own capacity to take on socially acceptable goal-oriented activities. Expectations of self are shaped by the capacities or incapacities attributed by others to one's group. As part of one's ethnic identity, one may be faced with a prevalence of situations that demonstrate personal inadequacy rather than increasing confidence. In other instances, an inherited high social status is at the same time an avowal of one's potential capacity.

It is therefore psychologically easier for members of certain ethnic groups to move up to expectations of group competence if they share in the collective confidence of their group. The social self in such a group is developed around supportive attitudes. Conversely, it is more difficult for an individual to manifest competence when he is a member of a group that has no supportive tradition. Such an individual may attempt to change his own self-percept by passing out of his group so as not to take the expectations of incompetence directed toward him. Many social psychologists recognize that American Blacks have had to overcome majority attitudes about so-called Negro inferiority by developing a supportive group identity within their own communities. Less obvious is how groups such as the Poles have tended to inhibit social mobility by maintaining ambivalent attitudes about themselves which have been brought with them from the Old World. In both groups members have passed as a means of avoiding a stereotype emphasizing incompetence.

RESPONSIBILITY

Loyalty to a group is partially defined by feeling compelled to obey its moral codes. One feels constrained to assume social obligations defined in traditional terms which can conflict with those stressed in the majority culture.

In addition to responsibilities, traditions of irresponsible or reprehensible behavior have also sometimes been defined ethnically. An individual may wish to escape the deception or disappointment related to maintaining his membership within a given group. A dilemma of identity occurs within groups who share an awareness of internal betrayals, disappointments, and moral lapses.

Some hold to the romantic notion that joining another group will free a person from such problems. In American society, the Puritan work ethic may appeal to a minority child who may be motivated to change his reference group through an identification with a white Protestant teacher. The child sees self-motivated achievement in idealized terms and he becomes progressively alienated from his own group. A sense of moral imperative and of achievement may lead him to become a member of a more highly evaluated group.

The group may resent individuals leaving. This is particularly true of leaders who are preempted by the majority once they become successful. For example the general fear among Mexican-Americans about leadership is that successful leaders may become "Falsos" and sell out to the dominant Anglos. They fear that their leaders, for their own aggrandizement, will give up their responsibilities to their group and pass into the dominant group when they are found acceptable by it. They have no doubts about Cesar Chavez, however. Chavez is considered a saintlike leader in the Mexican-American community because he demonstrates, by personal self-denial, a type of ideal assumption of responsibilities for enhancing his ethnic minority vis-à-vis those who seek to exploit them. Thus, there is an internalized moral dimension to ethnic maintenance.

Some seek to escape ethnic identity because they decide that the negative social and personal features of their inheritance outweigh the positive ones. If such people fail in times of crises, they may come to define their own moral failings as culturally inherited traits.

Unlikely as it may sound, some pass from a high-status to a low-status ethnic group. An individual may wish to take on a minority identity with a lower status group to take advantage of the seemingly freer patterns enjoyed by members of this group. Frequently, individuals find that high status implies not freer patterns of behavior but the converse; to maintain their high status, individuals often feel compelled to become circumspect in their behavior and find themselves inhibited by their status. There is, therefore, inducement in many situations to pass downward in order to find freedom of personal expression. The individual who passes downward may do so at the cost of self-degradation.

In short, embracing an ethnic identity invariably involves some assumption or avoidance of responsibility and guilt. The minority group member who acquires a negative self-image may become confused about ethical standards. Therefore, some seek to avoid ethnicity altogether as morally distasteful or burdensome, or as too demanding. Such individuals may give up striving for goals that are defined as the responsibility of their group.

CONTROL

Ethnic maintenance or passing is inextricably involved with patterns of relative power in a pluralistic society. In such a society, the individual as well as his group is accorded a superordinate or subordinate position with respect to other individuals and groups. The individual can view as legitimate the authority he wields in assuming dominance over members of other groups. However, this authority is very often assumed at the price of arousing hostility in members placed in inferior positions. An additional consideration is that members of the dominant group can use group ascendancy to hide problems of individual incapacity or impotence. Thus, our concern with patterns of control by being a member of a powerful group is intertwined with concerns about individual powerlessness.

When the authority of the dominant group is threatened, the leaders may pressure their subordinates into giving symbolic signals of deference. Members of the subordinate group may then seek to escape their ethnic membership so as to avoid deferring to the leaders. Dominance behavior may be destructive to members of a subordinate group. In this respect, dominance and patterns of violence may be intertwined.

Many of these features can be illustrated in the development of Nazism in Germany. The lower middle class, made impotent by the economic chaos of the late Weimar Republic, found an expressive outlet in doctrines of racial superiority directed externally toward their Slavic neighbors and internally toward their Jewish minority. German ethnicity imparted a feeling of power and dominance and thereby relieved the individual of his own sense of weakness. Belonging to a superior group helped resolve questions of individual incapacity and inadequacy. Many Jews were tempted to pass into the German majority to avoid the necessity of assuming deferential behavior when the Nazis came to power. German Jews themselves very often took a superior stance toward Jews from Slavic countries.

A member of a subordinate group can also feel an obligation to espouse liberation and autonomy as a moral imperative. This impulse brings up the questions of power and control in society as they are related to responsibility. In the negative sense, there may be ambivalence over the necessity to rebel when the attempt at autonomy is counter to an individual's sense of the rightness of authority. That is, an individual may want to rebel, but at the same time, he senses that rebellion may be an illegitimate act of infantile origin. The psychodynamics of submission, rebellion, or autonomy in ethnic identity is very complex. In fact, the same behavioral acts may spring from different levels of maturation. Submission, for example, may simply be the minority member's instrumental, mature decision to survive, or it may be an infantile form of dependency, unwarranted by social circumstances. In social movements, group pressures incline the individual either toward submission or toward a revolutionary assertion of a more acceptable status in society.

As part of his subordinate tradition, an individual may inherit modes of social trickery employed in maintaining himself vis-à-vis his superiors. An example is the "laughing barrel" tradition among American Blacks who outwardly gave the dominant White his expected deference, but inwardly preserved their self-esteem by mockery. The relationship of ethnic identity to power in society and to problems of exploitation is a very large topic that could be discussed at great length.

COMPETITION-COOPERATION

Patterns of competition-cooperation vary greatly within and between groups. Some problems of ethnic maintenance stem from the necessity of the group member's support of his kin and supplying to them whatever material possessions have been obtained. Some groups ill-equip an individual to operate competitively within well-defined social relationships. In a social system demanding individual competition, members of such a group are at a disadvantage. Other groups have patterns of mutual cooperation that sustain members of the group and support them in their competition with the outside.

Standards of ethical competition within a group may be quite different from those permitted in dealing with people outside the group. The same behavior that is considered unethical within a group may be condoned if expressed toward an outsider. In-group activities of an instrumental nature frequently emphasize the need for concerted behavior and mutual trust in acting together toward the realization of goals. At the same time, groups who fear they may be betrayed by another member or leader may find it difficult to unite themselves to attain political or social goals. In other words, mutual distrust vitiates cooperative behavior. The possibilities of passing for individual advantage may come into conflict with ethnic maintenance and cooperative behavior with members of the group.

With respect to each of these instrumental modes or their combination, individuals may face the problem of identity maintenance. Maintaining an identity within one's own group may be a severe instrumental disadvantage to the individual who seeks to realize his own goals. He then is faced with a crucial decision: whether to give up his group identity, or whether to maintain it and try to realize his goals, despite the inconvenience of minority ethnic status. In some cases, maintaining an allegiance to a group is reinforced when group membership affords support in cooperative or competitive realization of goals.

Expressive Behavior and the Maintenance of Ethnicity

In contrast to the instrumental problems of ethnicity maintenance are the very strong expressive needs that can be realized only by maintaining participation within an ethnic group. The psychological rewards of group participation may far outweigh the instrumental advantages of leaving or changing behavior to gain occupational or social advantage on an individual basis. Such decisions are very complex. In each instance, the relative strength of a variety of expressive vectors must be assessed in order to understand behavior related to group affiliation.

HARMONY

Human beings generally are motivated by a need to achieve peacefulness or harmony in their within-group relationships. On the whole, feelings of conflict and contention are muted, and, whenever possible, hostilities are displaced onto individuals who do not belong to the intimate group. Many groups, however, also embody in their traditions of membership, forms of discord, hostility, and resentment that are more internally than externally directed. There may be some dynamic tension between externalizing aggression or diffusing it within the group.

Social movements, such as religious revivalism, may arise from within a minority group as an attempt to unite the group to achieve internal harmony. Considerable emotional benefits can be gained by certain forms of church membership, as witnessed in the Black Muslims or in the Peyote cult practiced among American Indians. Symbolic participation in religious activities may permit a new self-conceptualization in a positive way. An emphasis on internal brotherhood can reinforce the individual's sense of adequacy, and group ritual can help the individual to overcome a sense of insecurity. Most groups use mechanisms of this type to maintain their existence. While they may thereby attain a greater sense of internal peacefulness, the consequence may be increased wariness, suspicion, and hostility toward outsiders who are then cast in the role of enemy. Scapegoating, a very well-established mechanism, is characteristic of both majority and minority groups in pluralistic societies. The member of a group used as scapegoat has a very strong motivation to pass to escape the consequences of continual destructive behavior directed toward him by a dominant majority.

AFFILIATION

Another basic human need is for some form of intimacy, companionship, and affiliation that can be afforded only by those with common emotional experiences. An outsider cannot provide the same kind of understanding. An ethnic group can provide a mutual sense of intimacy and communication for those sharing past common experiences. In this regard, a generalized ethnic identity may sometimes supplant more directly personal and intimate one-to-one relationships. Group belonging can compensate for individual difficulties in achieving intimacy.

The threat of separation from the group is one of the most stringent of human sanctions. Ostracism for behavior against the group is a far more potent social sanction than the more personal punishment or legal restrictions imposed on an individual from the outside. In order to maintain a sense of belonging with his group, the individual will strictly monitor his behavior. Such mechanisms are very visible in Japanese-American groups, especially among peers, and as such have kept the delinquency rate very low among them. Curiously, in some groups peer group sanctions may make it difficult for a school system to discipline an individual. Conformity to the demands of the school against the resistance of the peer group may result in severe sanctions of the member. An anthropologist studying an Indian group in the Southwest, for example, reported that when an Indian youth received a scholarship to college, his peer group killed his dog and then beat him up unmercifully. What was being expressed by the collectivity was the fact that he was not to undertake individual development at the expense of his group belonging and that his individual action was an implicit threat to the group's cohesiveness and resistance to the hated majority outside.

The generation gap is also present among ethnic groups. An individual may more readily find satisfying and intimate companionship with peers of similar ethnic origin than with primary family members of a different generation. This process has especially been noted among Mexican-Americans, where the ethnic peer group quickly replaces the primary family as a point of social reference.

Problems of ethnic identity can arise if self-affirmation signals that one is leaving the group. This decision leads to rejection or enforced isolation in the larger society and as such involves severe psychological strain. For example, former outcastes in Japan who have tried to pass for some time find the isolation intolerable and finally return to their own group, giving up promising professional careers bought at the cost of complete social estrangement (DeVos and Wagatsuma, 1966).

The whole topic of individualism and alienation is related to problems of ethnic maintenance. For some, a sense of group belonging is the ultimate meaning of life. An attempt to pass may completely strip away this meaning and cause total alienation.

NURTURANCE

The relationship between dependency and succorance can become highly complex when an ethnic minority is economically dependent on the majority culture. The welfare recipient, for example, may develop a peculiar form of hostility toward dependency on those outside his group.

When an ethnic group functions optimally, however, the group members are expected to care for, help, and comfort other members in times of need. For those who have an inner need to care for others and to see to their betterment, ethnic membership also provides a means for expressing their benevolent impulses.

When such care comes from outside the group, the problem of how to define the relationship becomes very complex. Very often, care is accepted only if a symbolic act that will negate the sense of dependency is possible. Welfare cheating, for example, may be an act of self-respect by those who otherwise feel helpless. Therefore, concerns with nurturance may overlap with problems of self-acceptance and depreciation.

In general, nurturance involves the transmission of care from one generation to another. It may be difficult for a sense of parental succor to go beyond the limits of one's ethnic group. Sometimes groups assuming some form of permanent parentalism over an ethnic minority can only do so with some sense of disdain for those who are permanently helpless and their charges. In contrast, within-group assistance may be formalized within given ethnic groups. American Jews, for example, have been pioneers in professional welfare agencies in the United States; these agencies originated from their need to provide care and assistance for the unfortunate among them. A major problem of public welfare programs in the United States has been the professionally trained workers' inability to reach across ethnic barriers. Similar problems hamper public health programs.

A recent interest in medical anthropology demonstrates the recognition that ethnic identity and differences in cultural traditions are important social issues in the United States in reaching and aiding the disadvantaged. The members of one's own ethnic group, when professionally trained, have the distinct advantage of reaching people with a sense of mutual identification. In all forms of medicine, including psychiatry, it may be well to consider that true assistance depends on some form of mutual trust and belief in the individual who brings succor.

The dependent role of being wards of the American government has forced a difficult relationship on American Indians and has helped to perpetuate their chronic identity problems.

APPRECIATION-DEGRADATION

As already indicated, ethnic identity is emotionally related to a basic sense of pride and self-esteem, or it can be related to a sense of shame and degradation. Each group seeks to create a positive image, a sense of dignity, respect, and properly appreciated status. Any human being becomes resentful and hostile when disparaged and depreciated by outsiders as well as by fellow members. Maintaining ethnic identity often involves a vulnerable feeling about self-respect or potential self-worthlessness. Some groups, more than others, are sensitive to outside opinion or public image. Perhaps the English (Gorer, 1975) or the Japanese (Wagatsuma, 1975) are extremes of a continuum in this regard. English self-sufficiency is related to a need for appreciation, developed only within and among members of the English class system. Outsiders are relatively unimportant. In contrast, the Japanese are deeply concerned with how others perceive them. The Japanese are particularly sensitive to possible depreciation in the attitudes of others and are very vulnerable to external criticism or inadvertent disparagement.

Some expressive feelings concerning appreciation or disparagement are central to understanding difficulties that arise either in intragroup or intergroup relationships. Culture traits cannot help but be evaluated ethnocentrically. What is seen as highly positive for one group may be disparaged by another. What was seen at one time in highly positive terms within a group may, with contact, come to lose its value, since a new way of seeing it in an acculturative situation may cause the trait, once appreciated, to take on a shameful quality. Such a change in evaluation may be a strong inducement to passing, since the trait in question may be seen as an attribute of one's ethnic group, to be avoided only by giving up one's identity.

Theodore Schwartz contends that one of the major reasons for the appearance of Cargo Cults (a religious movement) in Melanesia was the devaluation of their economic system (Schwartz, 1976). The Melanesians could no longer maintain their symbols of economic worth once they learned of a much superior alien technology which produced goods that the Melanesians could not produce. The resulting crises in the sense of self were felt acutely. Melanesians, proud of their skills as traders, could not countenance, without extreme self-devaluation, the idea that the superior material artifacts of the Westerners were simply the products of men like themselves.

Such a crisis in self-assessment is one of the great problems of culture contact. A group may be forced to recognize the relative merits, and sometimes the superior force, of an alien society. In the case of defeated groups, they must find a way of reestablishing their personal self-esteem. Groups such as the American Indians have suffered most from a sense of degradation. In recent times, American Blacks have been concerned with establishing a sense of black pride to overcome the effects of living in a society that has used contempt and degradation as a means of maintaining caste differentiations.

PLEASURE-SUFFERING

Belonging to any particular minority group is a mixed blessing—there are sufferings as well as pleasures. For many, the satisfactions of an integrated way of life demand forms of self-consistency. One cannot pick and choose what one wants to take from membership in a group. An ethnic identity gives savor to one's past; this sense of naturalness is derived only from experience going back into childhood. Individuals sometimes find modern life to be plastic since it has been stripped of a sense of past accumulations of meanings that have been husbanded carefully and passed with reverence to a new generation. Stripped of such continuity, the individual faces indifference, boredom, and, perhaps, a sense of normlessness or anomie, resulting not only from a lack of regulation governing life, but also from the heedless casting out of past custom. Emile Durkheim saw anomie as a threat of disillusion within society. When cohesiveness is lost, he stated, individuals become normless. In his description of American society in the early part of the nineteenth century, de Tocqueville noted many traits of Americans that might fit Durkheim's concept of anomie. As a consequence of their high geographic and social mobility, Americans have shown particular proneness to a sense of alienation. Americans hunger for belonging and, with all their energetic restlessness, find that should they falter they are faced with a loss of meaning. One answer to the dilemma of the American *Babbitt* is to return to one's past to seek out some meaning in ancestry, to assuage one's present sense of aimlessness with reassuring convictions. The passing of passing is an indication that in their avowal of past ethnicity many modern Americans are seeking, not only present satisfaction, but also a sense of continuing moral purpose for American society in general.

11

The Decline of Character: Socialization and Self-Consistency

KENNETH J. GERGEN

My analysis really begins in the hush of an early morning several years ago when I sat hunched over my desk in a moment of rapt anxiety. The evening had begun in leisure. It was one of those rare occasions in which professional matters were pushed aside in favor of writing to dear friends of other times and places. The writing itself was pure pleasure as I doted on memories and fantasized about my friends' reactions to my letters. It was not until I later began to read over the various letters that haunts began to fill the room. I stared with amazement as I began to realize what a different picture of myself each of the letters presented. In one, I seemed to be a pensive and soul-searching romantic, in another, a raucous libertine, in another, a responsible and dedicated professional, and in another, a somewhat witless athlete. Where, in this cluttered maze of discrepant appearances, was the "real me," the "true self" that has played such a central part in Western thinking ever since the Delphic oracle handed down the dictum "know thyself"? Had I somehow selected the inferior alternative to Hamlet's question, "To be or not to be"? Had I failed to achieve the major goal of adolescence, which according to Erik Erikson is the sense of a firm identity? Was it possible that my only identity was invested in a set of incoherent social masks, each donned for a particular audience upon a particular occasion? Was it possible that a searching look inward, into the core of my identity, would reveal only a gaping emptiness?

Convincing myself for the moment that I was not prepsychotic, I began to see that this condition of fragmented and evanescent identity might be explored more systematically. In fact, for the professional psychologist, there seemed to be some critical theoretical issues at stake in my condition. Since the days of William James, the literature on self-concept has treated normal identity as the coherent and enduring substratum of experience. The self-concept is molded throughout childhood and adolescence, it is argued, and, once crystallized (in the sense of personal identity), furnishes the individual with a baseline against which to judge the normalcy, adaptiveness, and self-benefiting qualities of his behavior. What if such assumptions had been misleading us all these years? What if normal identity were neither coherent nor enduring, but an unfixed buoy cast upon the tides of social circumstance?

With such thoughts in mind, and supporting funds from the National Science Foundation, a program of experimental inquiry was begun. Let me describe very briefty some of our experimental findings. In particular, we may concentrate on several studies employing measures of self-esteem. It is traditionally assumed in the field of self-psychology that the individual develops during the early formative years a basic and enduring sense of self-worth. Numerous assessment devices have been developed to tap this essential characteristic, and these devices (in the form of self-esteem tests) are typically used to make differential predictions about persons who are high, as opposed to low, in their self-evaluations. In the present studies we did not use scores of these measures to predict, but rather, we focused on various factors that may modify such scores.

In the first of these studies (Gergen, 1965), female undergraduates participated in an interview in which they talked at length about themselves. By special arrangement, each time one of the women said something positive about herself, the interviewer would smile, nod her head, or indicate some form of approval or agreement. Each time the woman evaluated herself negatively, the interviewer would subtly indicate disagreement. The results showed a steady increase in expressions of self-esteem as the interview progressed. This increase was not found in a control group not exposed to such approving feedback. Furthermore, these public expressions of esteem seemed to reflect actual change in the subjective feelings of the women. Their ratings on a standard self-esteem measure taken after the interview showed a markedly enhanced level of esteem, a level not reached by the control group. As one woman told me later in an informal conversation, "I don't know why, but I just felt great the whole day."

In a second study, undergraduates were to exchange information about themselves by written communication (Gergen and Wishnov, 1965). By special arrangement, one group received a message from an individual who seemed immensely egotistical. This individual had no problems, liked her college work, had marvelous family relations, and looked forward to the future. A second group received a message from someone who seemed very low in self-esteem. She felt she had many problems, had troubles in her family, found school work difficult, and so on. The persons receiving these different messages then had to write about themselves in return. One way in which they had to communicate was by rating themselves on a standardized self-esteem measure taken some weeks prior to the experiment. The results showed that the self-ratings of subjects communicating with the egotist underwent a marked increase in esteem from the previous period. Those faced with the self-derogating partner showed dramatic decreases in esteem ratings. How did they feel about their public expressions of esteem? Later evaluations showed that the vast majority of subjects in both conditions felt that their evaluations had been sincere, honest, and authentic expressions of their underlying feelings about themselves. Whether high or low in expressed esteem, they felt as if they were giving voice to "true self."

In a third study, subjects were applying for a highly tantalizing job (Gergen and Taylor, 1966). Before the job interview, they were allowed to sit for twenty minutes and to think over all the good points about themselves to present later in the interview. After the thinking period had taken place, and before the interview, they were given a self-esteem test in a situation completely disconnected with the interview. Scores on this test showed a marked increase in self-esteem over ratings taken some weeks before. Subjects in a control group showed no such increase. It appears that simple self-examination is sufficient to change feelings about self for brief periods.

In another study at the University of Michigan, undergraduates were given a chance to apply for a lucrative summer job (Morse and Gergen, 1970). During the application procedure, each applicant was placed in a room alone and filled out a variety of forms. One of the forms was a minor variant of the Coopersmith Self-Esteem Inventory.

When the applicant had completed half the test, the secretary entered with a second, especially prepared, applicant. For one group of subjects, the second applicant was impeccably dressed and carried an attaché case. After he was seated, he opened the case to take out a freshly sharpened pencil. Next to the pencils, and in plain sight of the subject, was a slide rule and a copy of Aristotle. This we called the *Mr. Clean* condition. Subjects in a contrasting condition were exposed to the same experience, with the exception that the incoming applicant appeared in a ripped sweat shirt, pants torn at the knees, two days' growth of beard, and a dog-eared copy of *The Carpetbaggers*, which he tossed onto the table before slouching into the chair across the table from the subject. No words were ever exchanged between the subject and either Mr. Clean or Mr. Dirty. The primary interest was, of course, in what effects these individuals would have on the self-esteem ratings of the subjects. The effects proved powerful: when faced with the impeccable Mr. Clean, self-esteem began to plummet; when Mr. Dirty was available for social comparison, self-esteem began to soar. In effect, who you are depends importantly on the attributes of those occupying the social surroundings.

Although these various studies are hardly conclusive, as a group they do suggest a radical revision in our thinking about normal self-conception or -identity. First, it appears that we carry with us numerous concepts of who or what we are. These concepts may be highly disparate and are quite often antithetical in their implications. We harbor conceptions of ourselves as strong and as weak, as loving and as hostile, as ambitious and as lazy, as expressive and as inhibited, and so on. There is little evidence to suggest that these concepts form a coherent whole. In fact, we are not normally required to face the antithetical views we have of self. This is so because these concepts have been learned in quite different circumstances, circumstances often separated from each other in both time and place.

How, in this light, can we explain the feelings people have of personal authenticity, of being true to self? The answer is that the presence of certain other people, of certain motives or needs, or of certain physical environments or information sources is sufficient to bring to mind relevant conceptions of self. Our father may cause us to think of ourselves as "not especially mature," while a younger brother may cause us to feel "very mature"; a victory on the athletic field may cause us to feel we are "truly talented," while a loss may confirm our suspicions that we are "second rate." As a student, a professor may cause us to think of ourselves as "unlearned," while those in the classes beneath us make us feel "highly knowledgeable." When thinking of ourselves as one type of person, we are not likely to be entertaining all those self-images discrepant or antithetical to the dominant image. Thus, within any given situation we may feel that our behavior is wholly authentic, a true indication of what we really are. However, we are quite capable of turning about and acting in precisely the opposite way, and again feeling truly authentic and that our behavior is a perfect indication of our underlying feelings of identity.

Traits and the Impact of Social Settings

At this point in the research, it seemed challenging to broaden the intellectual horizons, for on the horizon was the entire tradition of personality theory and research. This tradition repeats, in very bold letters, the message built into the traditional view of self-conception. Namely, the personality tradition holds that we develop over time an enduring style of relating to the world about us. Early socialization is said to be critical in this regard, and the results are often said to be reflected in our major traits or personal dispositions. We say that Jim is a very aggressive person, while John tends to be very unaggressive; Sue is a very talkative and affable sort who gets along well with others, while Connie is a shy and retiring person. Gandhi was a passive, loving, and gentle man, while Hitler was maniacal, aggressive, and without moral fiber. For the psychologist, such assumptions have given rise to the development of innumerable measures attempting to assess individual differences in various traits or personal dispositions. Once a person can be identified as high, medium, or low on a given trait, widespread predictions can be made regarding the behavior of the individual under many varying circumstances. The literature indicates, for example, that people who are high in need for social approval are more responsive to social cues than people who are low (Crowne and Marlowe, 1964), that people in an advanced state of moral development are less obedient to authority than those at lesser stages (Kohlberg, 1969), that people who are high in authoritarianism are more prejudiced against minority groups (Adorno, Frenkel-Brunswik, Levinson, and Sanford, 1950), and so on.

Now, it may be asked, what if the assumptions underlying almost all trait research and so common to social understanding are largely erroneous? As in the case of self-conception, is it possible that closer examination will reveal that people are capable of virtually any type or style of behavior along with its opposite? Is it possible that people are capable of both needing approval and eschewing it, of morally principled behavior and inconscience, of seeking achievement and avoiding it? At least three lines of converging research support this possibility.

The first comes from Walter Mischel's (1968) extensive review of the literature in which trait measures have been used to predict behavior. Here it must first be recognized that the literature itself favors highly significant results: that is, research failing to yield statistically significant results is not likely to be published. We have a literature, then, where the confirmations tend to appear while the failures to confirm are excluded. Second, when we look at the magnitude of the correlations, we find that they seldom exceed .35. That is, if a trait tendency is assessed and then correlated with some behavior of interest (like obedience to authority, conformity, or altruism), such correlations seldom exceed the .35 mark. Essentially, this means that one is very fortunate if he can account for as much as 13 percent of the variance in behavior. As Mischel concludes, trait measures have thus far served as trivial predictors of behavior. Endler, Hunt, and Rosenstein (1962:12) reached similar conclusions after an extensive examination of individual differences in anxiety. As they put it, "The fact that a sampling of situations can contribute over 11 times the amount of variance contributed by individual differences among a sampling of Ss should give pause to clinicians, personologists and psychometricians in general."

In addition to the fact that personality variables do not generally seem to account for much of the variability in human behavior, we must add the results of inquiries into consistency across varying circumstances. Do people whose behavior is marked by a given trait in one situation seem to display this same trait in other situations? Classic in this respect is Harthshorne and May's 1928 study of cheating among children. Six thousand children were given the opportunity to cheat in a variety of different settings. They were given a copying test, a speed test, an athletic test, and so on. In all cases, the children could make better scores by cheating and were given ample opportunity to do so without the apparent knowledge of the investigators. If there are general tendencies to be either dishonest or moral, you would expect to find some general tendency to cheat across tasks. Those lacking moral character should be more likely to cheat in the various settings. However, as Harthshorne and May found, there was only a minimal relationship in cheating across the tasks. None of the correlations between tasks exceeded .31, and the average correlation was only .21. Essentially, if there is a general moral tendency operating, it only seems to be accounting for 4 percent of the variance in behavior.

These findings are hardly unique. Research by Theodore Newcomb (1929) concentrated on the consistency of introversion-extroversion in the personalities of young boys. Newcomb kept daily records of fifty-one boys in a summer camp over a period of several weeks. He recorded their tendency to talk, to socialize, to take control of situations, and so on in over thirty different contexts. The data revealed virtually no consistency from situation to situation. Similarly, Dudycha (1936) made some 15,000 observations of conscientiousness among college students. Records were made of the students' time of arrival at early morning classes, meals, appointments, religious services, and so on. The relationship of conscientiousness across situations proved to be trivial.

We must add to the emerging picture still a third set of findings. These are studies that demonstrate the strong impact of situational variables on people's actions. To the extent that people have well-formed personalities and that their traits are truly dominant, they should display a resistance to many situational pressures. If behavior is primarily a product of the forces in the immediate social situation, the utility of trait theory is seriously jeopardized.

The data in this case are no less than several thousand studies in social psychology that demonstrate the effects of situational variables on interpersonal behavior. If present-day social psychology has one major lesson to teach us, it is that once you have gained control of the individual's social and physical surroundings you have largely mastered his behavior. Let me illustrate with a few interesting findings:

The first set of findings will be mentioned only in brief. The research is well known to anyone with a passing acquaintance of current psychology. Few of us think of ourselves as aggressive persons, and few of us would feel that we are capable of administering severe pain and suffering to a perfectly innocent human being. We just do not assume that it is part of our basic personality makeup to inflict exceptional pain on others. Yet, as the distressing studies of Stanley Milgram (1974) have shown, normal adults in society can be persuaded with relative ease to administer severe electric shock to another person. The vast majority of Milgram's subjects could be moved within less than an hour to deliver shock to an individual who was screaming in torment, and to continue delivering even greater dosages of shock when the silence of the victim indicated that he might have suffered a heart attack. Surely our cozy assumptions about our "basic personality" must be questioned by such findings.

Traversing the continuum of human potential, you might also consider the extent to which you would be likely to exchange physical intimacies with a perfect stranger. Few of us consider ourselves the kind of person who would melt into the arms of someone we had barely met. We feel ourselves to be more judicious or cautious, and we generally desire that another care for us as a person before having access to our bodies. In a study conducted at Swarthmore by Mary Gergen, Bill Barton, and myself (1973), an advertisement was posted in various locales throughout the surrounding county; subjects for research in environmental psychology were needed and substantial wages were offered for participation. It was so arranged that subjects arrived at the experiment at different times and from differing locales and, thus, had no opportunity to meet each other. After waiting for a suitable period in separate rooms, each was told that he or she would be taken to a room without any light. They would be left in the room for a period not exceeding an hour in the company of "some other people." There were no instructions as to what they should do, and they were free to do what they wished during the period. We were simply interested, it was said, in asking them questions about their reactions to the special environment when they returned to the original room. Participants were further told that they would have no opportunity to meet the other participants in the study after they were each taken from the room. In effect, the participants would be cut away from all social surveillance and were free to act in any way they wished. Subjects participated in groups of approximately eight each, half of either sex, and some fifty persons participated in the study.

Behavior in this setting proved most interesting. Over 90 percent of the participants later admitted to purposeful touching; only 20 percent indicated that they at any time stopped another from touching them.

Over 50 percent of the subjects also engaged in hugging, and 80 percent found themselves sexually aroused. As one participant wrote of the experience, "As I was sitting, Beth came up and we started to play touchy face and touchy body and started to neck. We expressed it as 'love to each other.' Shortly before I was taken out, we decided to pass our 'love' on, to share it with other people. So we split up and Laurie took her place. We had just started touchy face and touchy body and kissed a few times before I was tapped to leave." None of these results occurred in a contrasting condition where all factors were the same but the lights remained on. Apparently, our general perceptions of ourselves as cautious, judicious, and physically restrained with strangers does not apply to our behavior in the dark.

A third study will round out the present summary. Most of us know persons who seem shy and retiring. Their essential character is such that they are not likely to speak out in groups, nor are they likely to take a leadership role. Investigators at Stanford University (Hastorf, 1970) were interested in the matter, and began their investigations with the assumption that shifts in group reaction might be sufficient to produce dramatic changes in the behavior of the so-called quiet person. Male college students participated in the study in groups of four. During an initial ten-minute session, the four talked over a case that had been supplied by the experimenters. During this session, careful note was made from behind a one-way mirror of how much each person contributed to the discussion. That individual whose participation was next to the lowest in each group was selected as the target for the next phase of the procedure. During this phase, subjects were told that a shielded light placed before each of them would display either a red or green light. The lights would be controlled by human behavior experts in the adjoining room. The green light signaled encouragement to talk, while the red light suggested that silence might be more functional at just that time. By using the lights in this way, the observers were able to limit the contributions made by those who had previously been highly talkative. Even more important for our purposes, they were able to produce a highly significant increase in the participation of the previously quiet member.

After twenty minutes of discussion under these conditions, a further critical test occurred. The major question was whether the "mouse" who had been trained to "roar like a lion" would be able to maintain his new position. Thus, a new case was presented for discussion, and all participants were allowed to talk as they pleased. During this final discussion period, it was found that indeed the newly arrived leader did not relinquish his position. His volume of talking did not quite reach that found in the previous twenty-minute period, but it did not drop to its previously low level. When later asked to rank the contributions made by members of the group during the session, it was found that the selected targets had moved from a third-place to a second-place position in the eyes of their mates. The previously quiet one was seen as second highest in the group in the quality of his ideas and his ability to lead group discussion.

To be sure, none of these studies is without flaw. However, in light of the general pattern of results, what validity is retained in the traditional notion of personality as an enduring style or pattern of individualized behavior? What we seem to find, instead, is that the normal indiviudal is potentially capable of a myriad of varying and often discrepant behaviors. We seem to harbor the capacity to be rational or emotional, achieving or lazy, dominant or submissive, and so on, depending on the exigencies of the moment and what we may have learned is desirable in the situations we face. There may be faint traces of an enduring style, certain needs, or motives that can transcend situations, but their importance seems to have been vastly overstated. To be sure, others whom we encounter from day to day usually seem the same, but it would be unwise to generalize from such observations. Another's seeming consistency over time may, indeed, be the result of our own influence on the individual. We ourselves may form part of the other's "situation" and, as such, we probably have a constant and continuing effect on his behavior. If another seems to be superficial, retiring, and conservative, we may indeed be encouraging these characteristics in this person.

Childhood Socialization: Potent or Pallid?

At this point our analysis must take still a further turn. If the traditional view of identity as an enduring and coherent core is faulty, and if the traditional view of personality as an enduring style or pattern of individualized behavior is found lacking, then what does this say for our common assumptions about the impact of early socialization? After all, there is an intimate linkage between the assumption of enduring character in adulthood and the importance placed on early socialization. It is early experience that is said to stamp the individual with his or her differentiated character. If we do not generally find such differentiated character, then we must also call into question the assumption held so dear to the hearts of parents, so central to our many institutions concerned with proper molding of the child's values, morals, and motives, and so paramount to current understanding within many branches of psychology, sociology, cultural anthropology, and political science. In short, we must entertain the hypothesis that early socialization has very little to do with adult self-conception, personality, morality, political investments, values, and aspirations.

On what grounds can we entertain such a blasphemous question? After all, are there not hundreds, if not thousands, of empirical studies that lend strong support to what we may call the early impact hypothesis (that early socialization has an impact on adult character)? There is an immense volume of empirical evidence; yet, let us look a little more closely at it. First, we find that the major share of evidence is in the form of case studies. Psychoanalysts, psychiatrists, and clinical psychologists have all followed in Freud's footsteps in their attempts to show how adult disorders can be traced to events long-since removed. Can we trust such findings?

If the case study is a valid indicator of events in nature, it should be possible to use early case material to predict adult behavior. If we begin with the hypothesis that early socialization has a strong effect on adult character, it is very easy to discover validating evidence in anyone's life history. Life histories are very rich repositories, and it is possible in such circumstances to find support for virtually any hypothesis as well as its contradiction. The critical test is whether, if provided with the early life history material, one could predict the outcome. Knowing about an individual's childhood, could you tell whether he was likely to end up a criminal, a minister, a psychotic, or just an average bloke? Perhaps you would like to try your hand:

Consider the following account given by a gentleman of some note. "My father (was) a conscientious employee of the (government), my mother, occupied with the household, and above all was devoted to us children with loving care . . . How it happened, I cannot now say, but one day it was clear to me that I would be a painter, an artist . . . The only curious thing was that, as I grew older, I took an increasing interest in architecture . . . Along with music, I thought architecture the queen of the arts." This budding young lover of the arts later became perhaps the most despised human being of the century, Adolf Hitler. Alongside this account, we must consider a few details from the life of Charles Wilson. Wilson was a big, handsome boy who grew up in a small Texas town. He starred in football, basketball, and track, and managed at the same time to achieve high academic marks. He attended a Methodist church near his father's small grocery store and gas station. In his junior year of high school, he was voted outstanding member of his junior class. Yet within three years Charles Wilson had become one of the central members of the Manson gang. He and his friends slaughtered almost a dozen persons without any significant motive.

Let us consider another case. In this autobiography we find: "With a friend, I stole money to buy cigarettes . . . I recollect having been put to school. It was with some difficulty that I got through the multiplication tables. The incident of (encouraging students to cheat on a standardized exam) did not in the least diminish my respect for my teacher. I was, by nature, blind to the faults of elders." Most parents would wince at the thought of having such a son: most would never suspect that this young man of little promise grew up to be Mahatma Gandhi.

These various cases are not unusual; many others could have been supplied. Nor do these particular cases *prove* anything; they were, after all, selected for the occasion. The major point is that one must maintain extreme caution in generalizing from the case studies that crowd the literature of the field. They are subject to immense biases and form perhaps the poorest existing data base in the sciences. There is no theory, however outlandish, that cannot be supported by case study material.

More significant are those studies that have systematically examined individuals as they have developed over time. Such longitudinal studies are indeed rare as they are horrendously time consuming, arduous in execution, and difficult to fund. One of the most elaborate studies in existence was conducted at the Fels Institute in Yellow Springs, Ohio. In this study, some eighty individuals were followed from soon after their birth until after their thirtieth year of life. In each of four testing periods, 60 to 100 different tests were made. Assessments were made of tendencies toward passivity, aggression, dependency, achievement, sexuality, compulsivity, conformity, and so on. The major results of this work are published in Kagan and Moss' (1962) now famous work, *From Birth to Maturity*. These results have been widely heralded as providing the *essential* evidence that traits developed early in life persist into adulthood. Indeed, a number of intriguing correlations do emerge from the study. For example, there is a significant correlation of .39 between aggression shown by boys to their mothers between the ages of three and six and the aggression they display toward the mother in early adulthood. Further, girls who are least spontaneous in the early years tend to be more anxious in social situations as young adults.

Yet these results deserve more careful examination. Rather than concentrate only on those findings that support the early impact supposition, we must consider the entire data set, the confirming findings as well as the disconfirming. When we do this, several interesting facts emerge. First, looking at the various traits measured during the infancy to three-year-old period and the same traits as assessed during the thirty-year-old period, we discover *no* significant relationship. Of the 120 correlations computed, only six reached statistical significance; by chance alone, exactly six should have emerged. If we then look at the relationship between the traits as measured during the three-to-six period and early adulthood, we find almost no improvement in predictive ability. Out of the 200-odd such correlations, only twenty emerged as significant, and ten of these would have done so by chance. It is not until we examine the ten-to-fourteen-year-old group that we begin to find anything that approaches continuity. Here, some 25 percent of the correlations reach significance. However, at this point, we find that the average magnitude of correlation hovers at approximately .23. In effect, even when we can make reliable predictions from the early period (in this case, adolescence), we find that the predictions are generally trivial in the amount of adult behavior for which they account. When closely examined, the Kagan and Moss findings simply do not deliver as advertised.

The third major source of evidence supporting the early impact assumption comes from the study of early social or maternal deprivation. Strong research support exists, it is said, showing that the absence of other living beings, especially the mother, during the child's early stages of development has traumatic effects on his later behavior. How strong is this support? As it happens, the major findings cited in this case come from the Harlows' (1965) work with monkeys. As they have shown, infant monkeys raised in social isolation undergo severe difficulty when they are reintroduced into normal monkey populations. They display abnormal aggressive, sexual, play, and maternal behaviors, and these behaviors appear to be permanent. Of course, given our knowledge about the increasing plasticity of behavior in various species as the proportion of cortical mass is increased, one might well doubt whether the Harlows' results apply to the human condition (cf. Beach, 1965). Yet, even if they did, we find in a more recent paper by Suomi and Harlow (1972) that, if you know what you are doing, social rehabilitation of the isolated monkeys may be accomplished with relative ease. In this seldom-cited study, monkeys that spent the first six months of their lives in total isolation were completely rehabilitated if allowed to spend a subsequent six-month period with normal monkeys slightly younger than themselves. Six months were required to undo the damage produced by six months of total isolation during infancy.

Thus, we find that all three of the major bodies of data traditionally employed in support of the early impact supposition are in serious question. But what about evidence to the contrary, evidence suggesting a high degree of plasticity in human capacities? In one respect, we have already discussed such findings. The various social psychological experiments described earlier all lend credence to the plasticity characterization. In addition, however, we must add the following types of evidence:

First, we might consider the acquisition and loss of language ability. Language certainly represents the most overlearned set of behavior patterns ever acquired by the normal individual. Thousands of times a day, from approximately the age of two onward, the child is trained repetitively in using the language of his culture. What happens, however, if we take the child out of the original language culture and place him in a second culture where the initial language is of no use? To what extent is the initial ability retained? Although there is no exact data on this problem, we have now collected the observations of eight professional linguists, each of whom has made special note of the rapid *loss* of ability in the initial language after separation. As William Labov (1972) has noted, for example, "It is seldom that we can trace any permanent influence [of the initial language culture] on the children's speech." Saporta (1961) has even noted that adolescents may almost entirely lose their initial language capacity after several years' absence from the original culture. If such rapid decay takes place in the case of language, to what extent can we expect the unsystematic and inconsistent lessons in aggression, achievement, and so on to persist?

We must further take into consideration the literature on socialization in later life. It is becoming increasingly clear that highly significant shifts in motives, beliefs, sentiments, and proclivities can occur at virtually any point in the life span. Two other contributors to this volume have already made note of this fact. As Professor Suzman told us in Chapter 3, factors operative in the adult context in his study outweighed early socialization factors in their predictive power by two to one. In Chapter 7, Professor Levinson discussed in detail the significant shifts in the kinds of responses the individual needs for adaptation to later periods in life.

Finally, there is the rapidly developing literature on behavior modification techniques in psychotherapy. Theories of mental disorder that presuppose early socialization effects naturally assume that long periods of time are required in order to mitigate these effects. If one decides to be psychoanalyzed, he is automatically buying a hidden agenda which says that "revelation" will be a long time in coming—possibly years. If, on the other hand, we assume that in order for learned habits to persist, they must be continuously supported by environmental contingencies (or what the individual perceives as environmental contingencies), then it should be possible to alleviate problems once control can be gained over the contingencies. In the main, this is the position of the behavior modifiers. The conclusion follows that if one is discerning enough, cure may be a short-term process. But is it in fact?

At least with respect to sharply defined behavioral difficulties, the rapidly burgeoning literature in this area is certainly optimistic. For example, Lazarus (1963) reports one study in which eleven agrophobics, fifteen claustrophobics, four patients with mixed phobias, and five impotent men were treated with a systematic desensitization technique. The average age of the patients was 33.2 years. These various problems had persisted long enough to cause severe limitations in the patients' social mobility, interpersonal relationships, constructive abilities, and marriages. After an average of twenty treatments, in which subjects essentially practiced relaxing in the face of the feared stimulus, thirteen of the patients had accomplished complete neutrality to the stimulus. The majority of the others demonstrated marked improvement. In contrast, fifteen control patients suffering from similar difficulties were treated by traditional group therapy. *None* of these patients evidenced apparent benefits during the same period. They were then given ten desensitization treatments, as a result of which two-thirds indicated complete freedom from their initial fears. Although not a perfect piece of research by any means, the results of several hundred findings of similar import do much to reduce skepticism. Cure for difficulties of long standing can be had on a relatively short-term basis, provided the therapist can pinpoint relevant reinforcing agents.

Now we must be clear about what this analysis is and is not saying. It does not say that dispositions learned during the early years will not be found in adulthood. Indeed, they will often be found, but as in the case of language learning, whether they are found or not may primarily depend on whether the environment continues to support the habit. Change the environment and you are likely to alter the habit.

Nor does the analysis say that there are no individual differences among people. Certainly, people have different learning experiences, and their reactions to a given situation will largely reflect the meanings they import into the situation and the motives that happen to be operating at the moment. However, the analysis *does* say that these meanings and motives are highly malleable.

At the same time, not *everyone, at all times,* is so malleable. Some personal traits may persist for long periods unsupported by the environment. Yet, most of the available evidence does suggest that such enduring characteristics may be attributable either to genetic factors (as aggression, emotionality, and generalized activity levels may be) or to very severe, if not traumatic, learning experiences. It seems to be the abnormal individual, not the normal one, who is of fixed character.

The Emergence of the Repertory Culture

It is with this last statement that my analysis must take its final twist. I wish now to recast the entire line of reasoning in historical perspective. Again, I must begin meagerly, in this case, by recalling to mind elementary principles of learning. We know from the learning literature that whether a learned habit persists or not *all depends*. It depends not only on what we have been calling support conditions (the continuing contingencies in the environment), but also on such factors as the consistency of the early learning experiences, the intensity of reinforcement, the continuity of one's models, the affect associated with the learned response, and so on. It is my contention that as the culture has evolved, the character of childhood learning experience may have been altered as well. Thus, what we are detecting in our studies of the self, in our mediocre trait correlations, in our behavioral inconsistencies, in our rapid cure therapies, and so on may largely be an indicator of the times. That is, the plasticity that we are repeatedly encountering may largely be a function of the particular learning experiences encountered in present-day socialization. In this case, however, it is the lack of, rather than the presence of, strong and consistent learning experiences that is furnishing the plasticity.

It seems apparent that in contrast to the past, children of today are exposed to very few clear messages, strong or consistent reinforcements, or continuous models. The child may learn that aggression does not pay off in the home, but that it is a very effective strategy in the unsupervised peer group; he is told that fighting is bad in principle, but television tells him that fighting is good fun. Sexuality seems to breed long faces on the part of adults, but movies and books say "get it on"; television and movies all preach racial tolerance, your parents are ambivalent, and your friends are either intimidated by, or take pleasure in tormenting, those from other races. And so it goes.

And so it must go. How can early socialization be otherwise in a pluralistic society, a society composed of extremely heterogeneous populations whose elbows rub with increasing frequency? What consistency in learning can we anticipate in a society with highly complex role patterning, where many different styles of behavior are needed to get through the day successfully, where the mass media are furnishing continuously changing models and standards of comparison, where rapid transportation systems put us in touch with far more people than ever before, and where rapid economic mobility alters our living conditions with an unrhythmic wrenching? And how could we hope to provide strong learning experiences when we have learned the wisdom of ethical relativity, the danger in powerful leadership, and the joys of freedom? Would we really have it any other way?

I suggest that we are rapidly becoming a repertory culture in which we are each called upon to play an increasing number of roles each day. Most of these roles demand a performance that is convincing both to our audience and to ourselves. There is no room for the character actor of bygone days who drags his single style from theater to theater, or the one-part-man who just waits for his turn to come up. In the repertory culture, the modal type is to be both revered and feared. We cannot but be impressed at the ability of the contemporary American to participate fully in a rich variety of experiences. The fact that we can explore so many of our capacities, be in touch with such a wide range of feelings, see ourselves in multiple perspectives, and competently master many roles is indeed a marvelous thing. At the same time, we may be witnessing the demise of strong character in our society. The traditional virtues of honesty, loyalty, true grit, permanence, determination, and fidelity are becoming petty pieties, appropriate for commencement speeches, Sunday School, and parties to celebrate the old times.

What is the character of life in a repertory culture? Certainly, it is one in which we should place increasingly less trust in our public officials. For every value they espouse to the public, we must be aware that these same officials are quite capable of behavior to the contrary. We must anticipate an increasing incidence of divorce and a continued search for intimacy arrangements that are more adaptive for the multifaceted and ever-changing individual. We can expect a continued parade of social movements as the media can always find a pocket of enthusiasm for any cause. However, these movements may also be short-lived (unless they can continuously recruit) because of their typical demands for a one-dimensional commitment. I do not believe with Professor Hsu (see Chapter 5) that we are witnessing a vanishing of affect. Rather, if the vast encounter movement is any indication, it appears that we are learning how to express our sentiments more quickly, even in the most superficial relations. In the repertory culture, one learns to kiss and run, so that relations may be intimate but without responsibility. It also seems to me that social planning and long-term policy will become increasingly difficult. Because we are multifaceted, we are capable of moving in virtually any direction on rather short notice. Give us two years and we can make obsolescent all dire predictions about overpopulation. Give us another two and black is beautiful; two years later, black is invisible. And behind it all we must expect the unexpected. Who can be secure when he knows his social world is composed of disposable personalities? I greet tomorrow with dismayed fascination.

Basic Characterological Needs and Changing Social Systems

12

AMITAI ETZIONI

Social problems result when societies are unresponsive to the basic human needs of their members or to changes in the natural and social environments that surround these societies. That is to say, social problems arise (1) when forces within society prevent, rather than advance, the fulfillment of basic human needs (e.g., the early stages of industrialization typically require mass migration of persons from the country to the city, hindering the maintenance or formation of lasting, encompassing, positive, interpersonal relations, thus depriving these persons of satisfying a profound human need); or (2) when there are deficiencies in the collective capacity to respond appropriately and effectively to environmental challenges, ranging from world economic crisis to invasion (e.g., the inability to mobilize individuals and collectivities to commit themselves to make the sacrifices and adaptations required by a creative response, for example, to resource shortages).

The term *societal guidance*, rather than *societal management* or *social control*, is used to refer to the sum total of the collective efforts in order to stress that the capacity to render society responsive to internal needs and external challenges, and hence to overcome its problems, depends in part on the people's involvement and support. It is not only a matter of knowledge, strategies, and resources available to those in "command" positions.[1] Processes and structures that provide for "upward" consensus building (collective input from individuals and groups to the control mechanism) plus those that provide for "downward" control (the institutionalization of rules and procedures for individuals and groups by the control mechanism), are the mechanisms of societal guidance.

The study of societal guidance encompasses not only the analysis of specific programs, but the totality of the societal structure and process as well. That is, society—its rules, allocative patterns, power relations, and organizations—is itself viewed as society's chief product, the result of its previous acts. Hence, a responsive society, one which "solves" its problems, must be continually restructuring itself, or must be reconstructed by its collective and individual members. No utopian end result, such as attaining a fully responsive society, is expected since changes in the environment would repeatedly arise to pose new challenges, even if all internal problems were ever to be overcome. While perpetual revolution—in the sense of recurrent, sharp, violent acts of overthrowing the existing order—may well not be necessary, the task of reforming *and* transforming the society is a never-ending one. A highly responsive society would have to be internally organized so as to transform itself expeditiously and, with as little human and economic cost as possible, to cope with these challenges.

The societal reality is composed of three layers. The first is the world of *symbols,* including what we "label" various social phenomena, our rhetoric, and political promises and threats. This first layer is a primary concern of ethnomethodologists, symbolic interactionists, and consensus sociologists. The second is the realm of *objects,* including economic and technological resources. This second layer is of particular relevance to economists, engineers, and scientists. The third is the *action "space" of behavior,* interpersonal links, role-specifications, and collectivities. This layer is of special interest to structural-functional sociologists and is also studied by symbolic interactionists and conflict theorists.

The key point with respect to societal guidance is that these layers differ sharply according to the human capacity to affect their dynamics. For reasons that cannot be spelled out here, we cannot change the laws of *objects* at all; we can only learn to play along with them instead of being ignorantly subject to their whims (try to modify the second law of Newton). In contrast, *symbols,* as John Locke stressed, are extremely pliable. We can readily create a mental image of a winged horse out of the concept of wings and the picture of a horse. Presidential declarations, laws, and charters are rewritten by the stroke of a pen. The *action* space is intermediate from this viewpoint. We can reorganize a community, change race relations, or mobilize a dormant people, but to do so typically requires extensive and prolonged effort. As a result, when we aim to change the "world," to solve a social problem, or to abolish its root condition, an important question to ask is on what layer are we acting: symbols, objects, or action? The efforts needed and the results that can be expected will vary accordingly. Thus, we could remove outmoded laws in one day (e.g., decriminalize homosexual liaisons between consenting adults), only gradually change the social system of a school, and never change the laws of gravity.

Finally, and most relevant, the societal world is becoming gradually less object-bound and more responsive to symbols. The reasons are many and range from the growing importance of knowledge as compared to material resources—yearly expenditures on knowledge grew very rapidly until recently "stabilizing" at a high 29 percent of GNP (Machlup, 1962)—to the importance of education versus inherited wealth for social standing and mobility (although wealth still helps in getting well-educated). Computers, communication satellites, and television are all significant and relatively recent developments that work with symbols. The ratio of professionals to nonprofessionals in the labor force is changing in favor of the professionals, who work more with symbols than the nonprofessionals who work with objects. The tentativeness of social relations is growing, and with it the significance of symbolic links among persons. That is, society is gradually becoming more pliable, more guidable, and hence, in principle, more subject to our collective will and individual needs, and less a matter of fate.

Human Nature

It is fruitful to assume that there is a universal set of basic human needs with attributes of their own that are not determined by social structures, cultural patterns, or socialization processes. If this postulate is accepted, it follows that, since human needs are universal but societies differ in their cultural patterns, societies must also differ in the extent to which they are able to satisy their members' needs. The fact that human beings can adapt and are adapting to a very large variety of societal structures and cultural patterns is not sufficient evidence that their needs are highly malleable, as long as the frustrations they suffer, or satisfactions they gain, also co-vary. In other words, that people lived both in Athens and in Sparta is not proof that they found both kinds of societies equally responsive to their needs. Adaptation may have exacted much higher costs in Sparta than in Athens.

Attempts to operationalize how happy one is with one's society, or with one's position in it, proceed along both subjective and objective lines. N. M. Bradburn (1969) developed a happiness scale. He found a strong positive correlation between factors in social stratification, such as education and income, signaling a link between happiness and differential satisfaction of the lower needs, as well as opportunities for further satisfaction of needs. In addition, happily married persons were happier all around than either the unhappily married or the non-married. Social interaction and participation was found to be related to one component of happiness, positive feelings. Organizational membership was found to be positively related to happiness, especially among women and lower socioeconomic groups. The "negative feelings" component of the happiness index correlated positively with scores on an anxiety symptom checklist, as well as with having sought help for a mental or emotional problem.

A comparative study of five nations by Almond and Verba (1963) showed that the individuals' subjective "sense of civic competence" or belief that he could have a political impact was found to be highly correlated with political participation—that is, with membership in voluntary organizations—as well as with education and higher socioeconomic status.

Objective studies show a correlation between lack of satisfaction of certain needs and various forms of asocial or certain social behaviors as well as illness. For example, black persons who are more socially isolated, as well as feel more powerless and dissatisfied, are more violence prone.[2]

Following Maslow (1968) and other humanist psychologists, we see a tentative list of basic human needs as including a need for secure survival (food, shelter, protection), affection (or love), recognition (or dignity), and self-actualization.

The data in support of the thesis that there is a "specific" human nature, as distinct from a highly malleable one, are far from conclusive. The thesis has gained in plausibility, however, as a result of numerous studies showing that, contrary to popularly held beliefs, attempts to remold people on significant personality dimensions, as in psychoanalysis, rehabilitation of criminals, and "brainwashing," have little effect. Brainwashing, the most encompassing and intensive of these efforts, seems to have affected only a minority of those on whom it was tried, and this minority included people predisposed to the views they were "persuaded" to accept (see, e.g., Schein, 1961; Lifton, 1966). Moreover, many of those who were affected stayed this way only so long as they remained in the particular environment where the efforts had been made.

Communist countries are of particular interest here. The USSR, for instance, has now functioned more than fifty years as a society exercising tight control over its educational institutions and its media. This control is supplemented by well-regulated ideological machinery, such as Marxist reading sessions, and by a closely linked reward-structure in which party members, quota-breaking workers, and others who have proven themselves loyal gain various privileges. Nevertheless, the needs manifested in the behavior of the average Russian are surprisingly similar to those of the Westerner: first they focus on a quest for consumer goods, and then on more affection, recognition, *and* autonomy. The Russians' acceptance of the "party line" is often shallow and expeditious.[3]

Though the basic human needs are held to be universal, their foundation is not seen as biological. We are referring especially to the needs for affection, recognition, and self-actualization. These needs may exist in the animal world in a very primitive and marginal way but are central to human beings. How can such needs be universal but not biologically derived? The answer, in part, seems to be that having these needs is a functional prerequisite of human beings. That is, unless these needs are present and satisfied, at least to some extent, the animal-like newborn infant will not become a human being.

Studies of infants left locked in attics or otherwise subjected to extreme isolation established that, even though their physiological needs were met, without affection and recognition such children remained crawling, barking, seemingly nonhuman creatures. From a development viewpoint, it might be suggested that the processes that turn biological infants into members of society have certain universal features which, in turn, instill the basic human needs. For example, the link to the biological mother is generalized and abstracted and turned from a physiological dependence to a need for love. As all human beings must travel this route in order to become what we call "human," they all acquire the same markings.

Logically, the concept seems to us unavoidable. We find that societies differ in their capacity to satisfy the human needs, that is, in the general satisfaction or level of happiness they generate. One may argue that the sources of differences in the level of members' satisfaction a society generates is intrasocietal, as a result of "technical" difficulties. It might be said that frustration is generated by socialization to conflicting social norms, rather than by the discrepancy between the norms the society prescribes and the underlying basic human needs. But this argument also presumes a human need for consistency, a need frustrated by conflicting demands. If human nature is highly malleable, why can it not find satisfaction in the variety and tensions afforded by conflicting demands?

That there are some "limit" conditions under which societal demands become very frustrating to the members has been widely recognized. But the conception usually is one of a very large "box" in the confines of which more or less anything "goes" as long as the boundaries are not transgressed. Our position on this point is as different from the "box" image as a continuum is from a dichotomy. We hold that any two societal structures, polities, or roles that differ significantly from each other will also differ from each other in terms of their responsiveness to basic human needs. The "box" is full of gradations leading up to and away from the "limits." It is not only that a free society is more responsive to human needs than a totalitarian one, but also that totalitarian societies differ in their "tightness" (e.g., Stalin's versus Khrushchev's U.S.S.R.) and that free societies differ in their measure of liberties (e.g., the United States in the Joe McCarthy era versus the United States during John F. Kennedy's presidency).

The implication of this concept for formulating social problem interventions should be explicated. It cannot simply be assumed that the individual's subgroups or subcultures are "at fault," that therefore efforts must focus on these "deviants" who are unsatisfied and acting out their dissatisfaction by rebellion, retreat, or illegitimate innovation, and that the cure is to correct their attitudes via resocialization and social control. Rather, our approach, while it recognizes that all these malfunctions may take place, also sees it as equally possible that society may be the source of the problem. If its institutional structure does not provide opportunities for satisfying basic human needs, or does not provide them to all members, the individuals and groups so deprived will become disaffected and act on their disaffection. The nature of the need or needs neglected will suggest the nature of the problem. For example, economic deprivation, lack of deep interpersonal ties or opportunities for self-expression will generate *different* kinds of change-demanding behavior, though there is no simple one-to-one correlation between the nature of the deprivation and the reaction. Alienation occurs when a societal situation is beyond the control of an actor. Some societies are more responsive to human nature than others, but it is hard to envisage a fully responsive society, one totally free of alienation. Only if a limitless malleability of human nature is assumed can a fully "happy" society in which each member is fully socialized *and* fully satisfied with his or her social role exist. Otherwise, as Freud (1930) noted in "Civilization and Its Discontents," the individual's pleasure principle clashes with society's reality principle. If we assume a set of autonomous human needs, the tension between them is also an irreducible source of alienation as some needs are incompatible and as the deferment of gratification itself may be dissatisfying.

But most alienation results from sources that *are* reducible, from sociocultural patterns that could be made more responsive or from the distribution of resources, power, sexual freedoms, and knowledge which could be more egalitarian. Since a share of assets is an important source of control, a more egalitarian society should have less alienation.

It is not only those at the bottom of the societal pyramid that are alienated. If the society is an oppressive one, then the elites are as "free" of the consequences of oppression as are the guards of prisons. The elites may be the targets of hate (open or suppressed) and must experience anxiety, if not for their lives, then for their positions.

If the goal is to minimize alienation, then it is important that social change be structural and not superficial. There is a split between appearances and underlying realities. It is possible for a society to *seem* responsive to demands while in fact remaining immutable beneath the facade. Thus, democratic systems can maintain a participatory institutional shell of a multiplicity of parties and regular elections, while in reality there is great homogeneity in terms of policy and goals. The choice devolves to that of candidates who mainly share class background and represent similar ways of looking at the world.

Thus, a social condition may be called *inauthentic* when the underlying structure is unresponsive but an institutional or symbolic front of responsiveness is maintained (cf. Sartre). Marcuse (1964) developed the notion of "repressive tolerance" whereby a society may be open and allow freedom of speech, but so co-opts ideas as to castrate them and not allow the action followthroughs that are the logical consequences of certain ideas. Post-World War II industrialized societies have spent a large amount of money and energy actively promoting certain "front" activities—via advertising, escapist entertainment, PR work, and the use of social science notions—to manipulate taste in choosing products, politicians, or even spouses.

A society is *authentic* only when both the appearance and the underlying structure are responsive to basic human needs.

Thus, what needs changing is not necessarily the person or group, but society—its rules, norms, polity, economics, stratification, and other relevant features. Each problem area must be examined as to its sources: a deficient socialization and social control, or an unresponsive societal structure, or what combination of the two? If the problem is chiefly of the first kind, then improved schooling, rehabilitation, and policing should be helpful. If they are more of the second kind, then greater reliance on changing laws (e.g., replacing laws prescribing racial segregation with laws that ban it), more tolerance (e.g., acceptance of homosexual liaison between consenting adults), reallocation of wealth (e.g., to reduce lower-class mental illness), and total transformation of the central project and pattern toward less emphasis on material objects and greater emphasis on the quality of life are called for.

Theories about societies, however formalized and "neutral" in their terminology, tend to have a normative impact on those who draw upon them for tools of social analysis. Theories that lack a conception of human needs, or that see these needs as lacking specific attributes and thus being highly pliable, are open to a conservative interpretation, which expects individuals and groups to adapt to the society as it is. Theories that assume autonomous human needs provide an independent basis for comparing societies to each other, as more versus less consonant with basic human needs. Such theories lead to a systematic consideration of the need to change existing societies and cultures toward more responsive ones, rather than to the employment of correctives that adapt people to roles as the main approach to the resolution of social problems.

Dynamics

The concept of societal responsiveness means, of course, that the question of how yielding the social world is to our understanding and control is central to the guidance approach. Our view of the malleability of the social world, its accessibility to guidance according to human purpose, is rooted in a synthesis of two opposing philosophical traditions that have separately inspired sociological theory in the past: voluntarism and determinism.

The voluntaristic world view posits an actor who, at least in principle if not always in practice, "can do," who is able to recognize the sources of a problem and deal effectively with them. Of course, restrictions on our ability to change the world are recognized, but these are viewed as nonpermanent, "lower level" limitations. Given more knowledge (which this approach assumes can be gained), a serious political commitment or "will," sufficient funds, or more intensive personal efforts by the people involved, even unusually difficult problems can be overcome.

Voluntarism, the image of a person writ large, standing over a problem like a driver over his stalled car, is at the core of several major schools of thought. The scientific approach to the world, for example, assumes that the world is inherently ordered and subject to laws, which we can unveil and learn to use. Science recognizes that there may be many things we do not now know. Its inherent voluntarism reveals itself in the suggestion that a greater investment of resources, man and woman power, and time in the social sciences would surely lead, as it has in the study of nature, to greater understanding, opening the door to a capacity to manage.

Then there is the technological-engineering approach, which, while less rationalistic than the scientific approach in that it does not tie action so closely to understanding, is at least as voluntaristic. Focusing on tools and techniques of molding and remolding the world, it discovered that we can often fix things even if we do not fully understand what we are doing or how they work. Thus, for instance, during the 1960s American society became even more concerned about the illicit use of narcotics, particularly heroin. A large variety of methods was tried, from the psychotherapeutic to the custodial. The one method which was widely held to "work best" in the early 1970s was methadone. It seemed to be successful in getting thousands of addicts off heroin, out of crime, and back to work or study and normal family and interpersonal relationships. *How* it worked, whether by replacing the physiological deficiencies which heroin created, by blocking the pleasurable effects of heroin, by serving as a tranquilizer, or by factors having to do with the treatment programs and not the drug itself, was not known. In a sense, the societal engineers did not care. The main thing was that it "worked" better than other societal tools available at the time.

Voluntarism also underlies a large variety of psychotherapeutic approaches. While they differ significantly in their conceptions of the roots of personal, interpersonal, and social problems, they tend to assume that these can be laid bare and uprooted. Individual psychotherapy, group therapy, transactional analysis, sensitivity training, and behavior modification all assume that with varying amounts of time and dedicated help a committed person can overcome his childhood traumas, or his sexual inhibitions, or previously learned patterns of response, or his interpersonal communications blocks. Much of the philosophy that lies behind social work practice, theories of education, planning, and administration, as well as law, is also voluntaristic.

In traditional philosophy, voluntarism is contrasted with determinism, the idea that the world is "set" and will not yield to the mental or physical efforts of humankind. Supernatural forces, from God to Satan, to abstract principles of Good and Evil, to sheer randomness or the impotence of man, are all listed as causes.

In social sciences, determinism appears, among those biologically inclined, in the attribution of dominant causality to genetic inheritance. Indeed, from differences in educational and status attainment to alcoholism and homosexuality, more and more social problems have recently been reassigned genetic causes.

Whatever the verdict on the role of these forces, they are given for any specific person, or even population, at any given time. The genetic pool of the next generation may be subject to influence, but persons alive now must live out their lives with fixed genetic traits (see Etzioni, 1973).

Determinism appears in individual psychology among those who believe in unavoidable urges or instincts that govern behavior, e.g., erotic or acquisitive. The notion of a "basic personality" more or less set in concrete during the formative first years of a child's life is also deterministic. Thus, if the personality is distorted during formation, the resulting deviant population is more or less "given." Basic personalities are said to be very resistant to change.

In its more purely sociological form, first, determinism appears among those to whom history is unfolding according to a largely fixed script that can be marginally edited but not replaced; those who see, in technological and economic developments that we neither understand nor control, the forces that define both our problems and our capacities (or incapacities) to cope with them. Second, determinism appears among collectivists who see societies basically as oversized tribes or communities that hang together according to structural patterns or "gestalts," that change or "differentiate" according to their own internal logic and not by the will of persons, groups, or the collectivity as a whole. Max Weber (1946) assumed that charismatic movements, such as religious, labor, minority, and other liberation movements, would *inevitably* routinize. That is, they would become institutionalized and inflexibly bureaucratized the way early Christianity turned into the Roman Catholic church, and the way movements of national liberation became the contemporary African and Asian states. The movements' leaders or members ultimately have no choice in the matter. Similarly, the pioneer American sociologists Robert E. Park and Ernest W. Burgess (1924) saw a "natural history" of relations between ethnic groups and races, traversing through four phases: from conflict, through competition and cooperation, to assimilation. Park identified reasons for the process; for example, conflict brought people of different groups into contact and hence changed their views of each other. But he considered the process to be basically given. Similarly, Parsons' (1951) discussion of structural differentiation is basically deterministic—virtually automatically independent of the will of the members of society. It is an adaptive process societies go through. Thus, the determinist believes that our social problems will be with us and cannot be changed by our own hand; only the inherent principles of social process can change them. What of the future? Such a deterministic vision has meant a swing from an optimistic view of man's capabilities and a continual abundance of material goods to a fatalistic pessimism regarding man's inability to respond adequately to current and imminent crises, including the population explosion, limited food and resource supplies, and environmental pollution.

Almost the only certain thing about the future is that it will be different from whatever is expected. It is possible, however, to envisage a different scenario from that of the relentless pursuit of materialism and an aggressive, individualistic struggle to preserve one's current standard of living. Following a Maslowian perspective, it is possible to see Americans living in a situation of comparative plenty and moving towards attempts to realize the higher orders of needs—love, dignity, and self-actualization.

The 1960s saw various attempts at "alternative" life-styles that necessitated a total break with and rejection of "normal" existence. Hippydom and communes are such examples. Such notions did not die with that decade. In the 1970s, they are being slowly integrated into ordinary, everyday life. Thus, there is a greater development of group consciousness and attempts to gain greater control over one's life, as reflected in the formation of block associations and a variety of community organizations. There is a widespread desire to know oneself and others better and to communicate more fully through sensitivity and encounter groups. A range of psychical and physical therapies, and analyses, are all very popular. There is greater concern to preserve one's leisure time intact and to develop interesting pursuits for the sheer, intrinsic pleasures these give.

Such developments are growing very rapidly in the United States as part of a recognition by many that the pursuit of materialism alone cannot inherently satisfy the full range of human needs.

Thus, a shift in focus from material production and consumption to various forms of nonmaterialistic pursuits is underway, though the material must necessarily continue but at a less frantic pace. Such a focus may also necessitate a greater degree of social justice and better material distribution than before, so that *all* Americans can enjoy a reasonable level of material existence and *all* can then attend to the fulfillment of their higher needs.

NOTES

1. For more discussion, see Etzioni (1967) and Etzioni (1968, especially Chapter 5).

2. For a review of several studies, see Davies (1963:6ff); on drinking, see Brenner (1967); and on self-actualization, see Maslow (1968).

3. For Eastern Europe, this is reported by Czeslaw (1953).

Theoretical and Methodological Perspectives on the Study of Social Character

13

GORDON J. DiRENZO

A little more than 140 years ago, the distinguished social theorist Alexis de Tocqueville, in his classic assessment (1840) on the political institutions of our nation concluded that:

> The manners [character] of the Americans of the United States are, then, the *real* cause which renders that people the only one of the American nations that is able to support a democratic government . . . the physical circumstances are less efficient than the laws, and the laws very subordinate to the manners [character] of the American people.[1]

De Tocqueville's assertion that the maintenance of democracy depends upon the primacy of certain elements of character or what he called manners—meaning thereby "various notions or opinions current among men . . . the mass of those ideas which constitute their character of mind . . . the whole moral and intellectual condition of a people"—often has been reaffirmed by numerous political and social authorities. Indeed, as Inkeles (1961:195) has suggested, even a casual content analysis of any sampling of opinions on democratic society reveals an extraordinary degree of agreement in regard to those values, attitudes, opinions, and other traits of character that are thought to be important to the maintenance of democracy.

However much we may wish to accept de Tocqueville's thesis at face value, either really or ideally, the fact of the matter is that his contention has not been empirically verified—nor is this to say that attempts at confirmation have failed.

Historical Dimensions

Much has been written, and much more has been said, about the character of the American people. Articles and books describing the American character number well into the thousands—if under the label of "national character" we also include impressionistic, introspective, and loosely evaluative works. On the other hand, if we insist on rigorous standards of empirical social science—considering only systematic investigations based on representative samples and utilizing standard psychological tools—perhaps not more than a half-dozen studies could qualify for mention.

The pioneer examination of American character is found in the writings of a French immigrant, J. Hector de Crèvecoeur (1782). Shortly after the birth of American independence, he posed what since has become a classic question in this field of study: "What, then," he asked, "is the American, this new man?" Much of the basis for this concern lay in the fact that allegedly the political elite among the early American colonists were very conscious of developing a distinctively American character out of the regional and generational polarities and contradictions that understandably marked a new nation of immigrants and migrants.

Fascination with Crèvecoeur's query[2] has not been diminished by its reiteration. For nearly two centuries Americans have been trying to explain themselves to themselves—not to mention the attempts of foreigners (e.g., Bryce, 1910; Gorer, 1948)—and they are still actively engaged in this undertaking.[3] Indeed, this concern has so preoccupied the American people that not too long ago the literary figure John Kouwenhoven (1961), in his essay on "The Depraising of America," concluded that Americans may be distinctively characterized in one respect: by their self-consciousness about their Americanness.

Of course, the evidence from social psychology suggests that it is natural for the human psyche to explore its self-image, but one might wonder in more technical terms whether Kouwenhoven may be suggesting that there is an identity-crisis in the American character. Indeed, the very phenomenon of identity-crisis may be distinctively American. Erikson (1974) contends that the concept of identity-crisis now seems almost native to the United States, and he asks whether there is any other country that continually asks itself: "Who are we anyway?"

Despite the fact that his own contentions have been challenged, and indeed even modified by later students, Crèvecoeur's major themes continue to control the analyses of American character. The objectives in this task remain essentially the same today, namely, to trace whatever characterological patterns may exist within the national population, to examine the ways in which Americans may differ from the people of other nations in these respects, and to inquire into the factors and forces that have conditioned the experiences by which the social character has been formed and may be altered.

Yet, the skeptic may ask: Are we able to show in a sufficiently convincing way that indeed there are significant patterns of psychological differences between populations?[4] That there are great variations in patterns of institutionalized behavior—for example, beliefs and values—from one culture to another is not disputed. But does it follow that there are corresponding differences in the organization of the human personality?

It is easy to assume that any given personality type may be found in any given society, and it is equally as easy to get allegiance for such an assertion. On the other hand, it is much more difficult to obtain allegiance to a thesis that might be equally easy to assume, namely, that the frequencies of different personality types vary tremendously within different societies or given populations. This underlying assumption dominates the study of national character today.

The idea that members of various nations have, or could have, different personality or psychological norms is probably as old as recorded history. We could mention, for example, the recollection of Thucydides of the famous speech by Pericles on the characterological differences between Athenians and Spartans. Similar concerns, of course, can be cited in the writings of Plato and Aristotle as well. Aristotle, for example, in his *Politics*, remarked on the necessity of fitting the constitution of a city-state to the character of its people. For somewhat more recent history, even from a different civilization and cultural tradition, references to the psychological character of nations can be found even in the works of that unofficial hero of all students of social thought—the incomparable ibn Khalduhn. Hence, it seems to be nearly as natural for mankind to observe, and to reflect on, the psychological character of national bodies of people as it has been for them to interact.

Nonetheless, even though it may be conceived as an important dimension of the study of human behavior, the scientific analysis of social character, as with most endeavors in the social and behavioral sciences, is of very recent origin. As an empirical enterprise of these disciplines, the analysis of social character rests on the foundations of culture-and-personality studies—an area of investigation that has been the nearly exclusive domain of the anthropologists.

The initial impetus for this particular work usually is credited to the anthropologist Franz Boas, who back in the 1920s initiated a series of seminars at Columbia University on the theme of "Individual and Society." Among the students in those seminars were the well-known anthropologists Ruth Benedict and Margaret Mead. The publication of Benedict's celebrated work, *Patterns of Culture*, in 1934 traditionally marks the formal beginnings of the field of culture-and-personality studies. In this work, Benedict offered a psychological typology of American Indian societies in terms of their major cultural configurations, and from it came her well-known dichotomy of Apollonian and Dionysian forms. Without deprecating the catalytic value of Benedict's work—particularly in providing impetus to the field of culture-and-personality studies—it can be said that this initial effort, as with most such efforts, was much too simplistic to reflect in a conceptually meaningful manner the complexity of the phenomena to which it was addressed.

Benedict's work was paralleled, although in a somewhat different dimension, by the work of Margaret Mead, whose extensive field studies in the South Pacific (1928; 1930) culminated in the introduction of the concept "national character." She proposed this concept as an analytical tool to describe those regularities common to the individuals who live in a politically defined nation, even though that may represent a cluster of cultures. Mead's term, as well as her work, has become a notable contribution not only in the field of anthropology, but in several other related areas as well.

The 1930s and the 1940s were the heydays for the culture-and-personality studies. Tremendous impetus was given to this new field during and immediately after World War II when a number of anthropologists attempted explorations into the psychology of various nations, especially the United States and its wartime allies and enemies. During this same period, a number of highly creative psychoanalysts—among them, Abram Kardiner, Karen Horney, Franz Alexander, Erich Fromm, Theodore Reich, Erik Erikson, Theodore Reik, and Harry Stack Sullivan—turned to anthropology and other social sciences in search of more comprehensive perspectives for the formulation of their respective explanations of human behavior.

Unfortunately, nearly all of the work in this area—up to very recent times, at least—has been the lot of anthropologists and psychoanalysts. For example, psychologists by and large have neglected this field of investigation as though it were inundated with massive populations of diseased white rats.[5] And, sociologists—laboring, and in our judgment suffering, under the anti-psychological dicta of Emile Durkheim (1897) and Max Weber (1922)—have shown only limited interest in this field of analysis. One towering exception, of course, is the notable work of David Riesman (1950) and his collaborators in the well-known study *The Lonely Crowd* and its related works. Particular mention too should be made here of the enormous, and profound, sociological contributions made by Alex Inkeles in terms of conceptual and theoretical specifications.[6]

Since the early 1950s, however, psychoanalysts have played a less prominent role in the study of cultural psychology. Indeed, during the past decade or so, even the anthropologists have withdrawn greatly from this area of investigation.[7] This turn of events may be in part the result of the negative reception given to much of the early work in the field of culture-and-personality studies, which was seen as grossly atheoretical, as well as of many of the empirical studies of national character that appeared during and in the period immediately following World War II. Yet, by no means have these negative evaluations diminished the significance and the challenge of the basic questions in the study of social character.

The study of social and national character has been a resistant and compelling problem primarily because of the historians, political scientists, and other humanists who have been greatly responsible for perpetuating the speculative—if not the empirical—research on this question. Of late, however, there are increasing glimmers of a rebirth of interest and work in this area of human social analysis. The study of social and national character, however slowly, is being restored to its former respectability as a legitimate subject of scientific inquiry by all the forces of the behavioral disciplines. These developments in great part are being made by the many methodological and theoretical advances in psychology, sociology, and anthropology, which have provided the basis for a renaissance in the field of national character.

Indeed, it is our hope that this volume itself may be taken as one modest effort in the reconstruction of this area of study, which in many respects may yet become one of the principal theoretical crossroads of the social and behavioral sciences. For, as Erich Fromm (1941:278) has told us, if we want to understand how human energy is channeled and operates as a productive force in a given social order, then social character deserves our main interest.[8]

Methodological Problems

The study of social character, as with most other areas of investigation in the social and behavioral sciences, has been burdened by a number of methodological problems. Some of these problems are common to all of the social and behavioral sciences, and others are unique to this particular sphere of inquiry.

There is, first of all, the obstacle presented by those who deny the legitimacy of this field of study, particularly through their contention that "national character" is a vacuous, catchall construct—a composite of stereotype and myth—and hence useless for understanding human behavior.[9] There has been a persistent confusion regarding the nature of national character. Others, obviously including ourselves, prefer to side with G. K. Chesterton, who is alleged to have remarked that "national character is as hard to define as smell, but surely it exists."[10] Herein lies the fundamental problem for the study of social and national character—the problem of conceptual specification.

Conceptual Specification

The problem of conceptual specification has come to be the haunting ghost of the behavioral sciences.[11] Herein are issues that, admittedly or not, constitute the initial basis of all inquiry in our various disciplines. Hence, it seems most plausible, however methodical, to suggest that one of our first concerns here must be to provide some clarification for the pivotal concepts of our inquiry. What then is meant by social character and national character?

The term *national character* has been used quite specifically, but in a variety of ways, in the social and behavioral sciences. At the same time, it has received extensive, although more general and somewhat less precise, popular usage. Perhaps in the light of this situation one would be inclined to conclude with Terhune (1970:207) in his recent assessment that national character is a protean and prescientific term—not amenable to simple definition. In any event, over the years, or so it appears from surveying the literature, the term has acquired a vast progeny of meanings which in turn have multiplied the number of relevant constructs as well. These various meanings have been usefully categorized by Daniel Bell (1968). Among his classifications for this term are the following:

(1) *National creed*—which refers to an implicitly or explicitly approved set of values that legitimate social behavior and define its purpose. Bell suggests that in the United States this category might include such values as individualism, achievement, equality of opportunity, a belief that "nothing is sacred," and positive orientations toward social change.

(2) *National imagoes*—which refer to the diverse folk, historical, and literary characters who embody modes of response to life situations (e.g., Huckleberry Finn and Daniel Boone).

(3) *National consciousness*—which refers to a kind of symbolic attachment for national identity and/or we-feeling, which in the terms of Franklin H. Giddings (1896), the late American sociologist, would be known as a "consciousness of kind."

(4) *National style*—which refers to the political style or type of leadership that characterizes a given country.

The above categorical meanings,[12] by and large, share a central denotation that accentuates the national or societal aspects of the term *national character*. In these broad senses, the term is used as more or less synonymous with learned patterns of cultural behavior, such as customs and folkways. Hence, these conceptions stress attributes of the collectivity and its output rather than individuals and their performance. Yet, if such a definition applies, as Inkeles and Levinson (1969) point out, then to relate character to culture is largely to relate character to itself. Accordingly, we subscribe to the position that the viability of the term must involve its being distinguished from cultural behavior by restricting its reference to actual psychological attributes of people.

The more technical meanings of national character, however, avoid the tautological problem. They emphasize the personal, individual, or psychological dimensions of the term. Social character in these respects is not a simple human microcosm of culture.[13] Rather, it is a complex phenomenon that has its own laws and principles—psychological ones, if you will. Indeed, it is this emphasis that the concept of national character has received in the behavioral sciences—that is, in anthropology, sociology, and psychology—during the past forty years or so. On the basis of these considerations, Bell offers a fifth category of conceptual reference under the term *modal personality* about which we shall have more to say subsequently. But, first, let us mention very briefly some of the principal constructs for the study of social character that have emerged in the psychological or characterological dimension of the term *national character.*

The bulk of the initial work in the empirical study of social character focused on the experiences and the psychological residues of the early processes of socialization and enculturation. It was in this context, beginning with the work of Margaret Mead, that the principal theoretical specifications of national character evolved. One notable refinement of the concept was that proposed with the formulation of the construct of "basic personality structure" which was suggested by Abram Kardiner, a psychoanalyst collaborating with the anthropologist Ralph Linton at Columbia University during the 1930s in joint seminars on the effects of common child-rearing practices on adult personalities. Basic personality structure referred to that personality configuration which is shared by the bulk of society's members as a result of the early experiences they have in common (Kardiner, 1939). This construct, however, as the label implies, did not correspond to one's total personality; rather, it represented, as the common denominator, a series of fundamental characteristics upon which other and more variable elements of personality content are superimposed. Yet, despite its methodological value, the concept of basic personality structure has not been as theoretically useful or as durable as its formulators had hoped.

A more recent conceptual specification in the cultural assessment of personality is that of "modal personality"—also suggested by Kardiner, but originally utilized by the anthropologist Cora DuBois

(1944)—to discern the central tendency of personality typology within a given society or culture. This concept rests on the postulate that within a given sociocultural milieu there may be a range of diverse personality types, but that one type, possibly two or three or even more, would be found so extensively as to constitute the typical or characteristic psychological expression for that particular population.

More recently, Terhune (1970) has preferred to make an analytical distinction between two kinds or aspects of modal personality: (1) social personality,[14] which is limited to systems of beliefs, values, and attitudes that are modal in a national population, and (2) core personality, which refers to "deeper variables" such as traits, needs, and defense mechanisms, and which incorporates the conception of personality types that are modal in a national population. Such a distinction seems to be an important one for the following reasons. The more general concept of modal personality would include many personality characteristics that originate from early childhood experiences. Social personality refers to attributes resulting mainly from enculturation to orientations that are socially sanctioned, and therefore legitimate, within a nation. Such influences, as Inkeles (1953) and Frijda and Jahoda (1966) note, may substantially modify adult character away from the patterns established in early childhood. Hence, the utility of modal personality data for the production and/or prediction of human behavior is dependent in part on the distinction of these two levels of the personality system.

Other related constructs are those of "national syntality" suggested by Cattell (1949), "national identities" used by Erikson (1950), and "mentality expressed in cultural products" (e.g., attitudes, values, beliefs, and styles of thought expressed in language, literature, art, and philosophy) offered by Duijker and Frijda (1960). More detailed conceptual analysis of these specifications—which have culture rather than personality as their central focus—is provided by Terhune (1970) in his excellent analytical review of the study of national character.

The current status of research on national character, as well as other social-systemic conceptions of personality, has culminated in the approach of modal personality. This conceptual perspective is being utilized in the analysis not only of entire sociocultural systems, but also of subsystems, such as organizations, institutions, groups, and roles. Such a conceptualization of social and national character is clearly more compatible with the expectations created by the size and diversity of populations in many contemporary societies and various segments thereof.

The authoritative definition of national character in this perspective today is that offered by Inkeles and Levinson (1969:428) whereby national character—or, more specifically, national modal character—refers to the "relatively enduring personality characteristics and patterns that are modal among the adult members of society."

As Inkeles and Levinson point out, however, national character is not a phenotypic phenomenon; it does not refer to regularities of social behavior; and hence it cannot be described in concrete behavioral terms. Rather, as a high-level abstraction, the construct refers to stable, general dispositions or modes of psychological function (e.g., attitudes, beliefs, ideologies, motives, values, and self-concepts) that may assume a variety of concrete behavioral forms. As determinants of behavior, these predispositions are subject to the modifying influence of a host of other factors, including in particular the structure of the social situation in which behavior occurs.[15] The implicit reference for the causative factors remains primarily to basic experiences and modes of life that are relatively common to a particular society.

Frequency is not the only defining criterion that has been used for national character—although there is much less agreement on other criteria. Of the greatest importance here are the conceptual formulations for the term *social character*, which was introduced by Erich Fromm (1941) and later adopted by David Riesman (1950). For Fromm and Riesman social character represents only one segment of the human character, which itself is only part of the human personality. It is that aspect which is shared among significant social groups, and which at the same time is the product of the experience of these groups. Their respective conceptions of social character in this sense are very similar to those of basic personality structure. The common collective properties of both formulations are structural in nature rather than analytical and have "culture-in-personality" as their central focus.

For Fromm, more particularly, the focus and primary criterion of social character is not necessarily its frequency or modality, but rather its prerequisite quality or strategic imperativeness for the social organization. It consists, says Fromm, of those psychological characteristics that lead the individual to "*desire* to act as he *has* to act" (1941:283) in the existing social milieu.

This essential notion of conformity for social character is continued by Riesman, with perhaps less emphasis on the dimension of societal requirement. For Riesman, the dominant aspect of social character is synonymous with the psychological mode of conformity and refers to the kind of mental "set" by which a person relates to the world and its people.[16] Hence, for Riesman conformity itself is not all of social character; mode of conformity is as much a part of it.

At any rate, for the moment, we are concerned here with matters of definition and not of analytical consequences.[17] Formulations of both types are theoretically indispensable, but each of them is conceptually distinct. Ideal types of character for a given society are not necessarily the modal ones, and vice versa. Accordingly, among the principal conceptions of national character, we need to distinguish: (1) the *actual*, modal patterns of personality structure that may be found in a given society, (2) the *socially congenial* personality structures that may be assumed to perform optimally in a given society, and (3) the *socially required* personality structures that are strategically necessary for the function of the corresponding social system.

In this respect, we contend with Inkeles and Levinson (1969:425) that the concept of national character should not be equated with that of social character as defined by Fromm and Riesman. We have no great brief otherwise for any of the terms or concepts that have emerged within this field of study. Each should stand or fall on its own methodological or theoretical merits. As Inkeles (1961:178) states: "It is in the nature of science and the inevitable path of its advance that concepts are replaced as empirical research advances. If for sentimental reasons we are unable to abandon the old familiar concepts, we may do ourselves honor as classicists, but we disqualify ourselves as scientists." Hence, we hope that the allusions to these questions of conceptual definition and theoretical specifications in some of the chapters of this volume will culminate in a refinement of these central concepts. For example, in Chapter 9 Professor Yinger offers some clarification of the definition of social character under conditions of rapid social change, namely, that it can be based on a similarity of adaptations to significant aspects of a current social situation, as well as being based more usually on shared experiences of enculturation. On this basis, then, Yinger distinguishes between "traditional social character" and "adaptive social character," both of which are described as modal tendencies founded in common experiences. The traditional is a product of a set of cultural experiences, while the adaptive reflects the efforts to deal with changes in the traditional arrangements that are shared among the members of a collectivity. Such attempts at continual refinement and conceptualization are endemic to any effort directed at the precision of theoretical analysis and explanation.

It is therefore within the spirit of scientific objectivity that we have adopted *social character* as our working term for these analyses of American character and social change. In this volume, however, *social character*, or references to it, have somewhat different meanings for the individual contributors. For example, as regards the specific distinctions made above, social character here encompasses both "core" and "social" personality as defined by Terhune. Social character in any case is used in this volume as a somewhat comprehensive concept, and refers fundamentally to those structures and contents of psychological disposition that are modal in a given population.

These matters of definition aside, the next question concerns the ontological and epistemological nature of such a phenomenon as social character. Do we have here, correspondingly, a real or nominal concept?[18]

Empirical Measurement

The issues and problems of measurement for social character have generated perhaps as much confusion and malaise in the respective fields of study as have questions of definition. However, there is much more to be encouraged about here.

The existence of distinctive personality norms for relatively small, simple, and culturally homogeneous societies seems to be rather well established. Modern societies, however, invariably include a variety of "cultures," each with its own distinctive patterns, such as those involved with child rearing, the processes of enculturation, and the various other experiences that relate to personality development, and which as such constitute the bases of social character. Of course, a considerable number of cultural patterns and experiences (e.g., government), and hence whatever residual effects they might have, are shared—but in significantly varying ways—by all of the members of any modern nation, regardless of class, ethnic, racial, regional, or other such distinctions. Nonetheless, one fundamental problem of methodology that has troubled scholars during the past thirty to forty years concerns the feasibility of applying the conceptualizations and the considerations of social character to relatively large, complex, and heterogenous societies such as the United States. When de Tocqueville undertook his comparative study of democracy in the 1830s, the United States was a much smaller nation than it is today (twenty-four states and 13 million people). Hence, from a methodological perspective, such a study was far more manageable than it might be today. On the contrary, some would object—as apparently even Crèvecoeur (1782) did in his time—that many of the allegedly methodological obstacles confronting us today appeared no less insurmountable nearly two hundred years ago.[19]

Nonetheless, it cannot be denied that the pivotal concepts in the study of social character, such as national character, basic personality structure, and modal personality, were developed out of the research that had been conducted nearly exclusively in so-called primitive societies where the control of relevant variables—however difficult in any circumstances—was quite manageable. And, despite whatever encouraging success such studies may have had in the early years, the existence of distinctive personality norms for modern, complex, and heterogeneous societies has not been as well demonstrated.

Many interested scholars, nevertheless, share the view that the same approaches—with appropriate modifications in some techniques, and perhaps an acceptance of a lower level of generality or precision—can be applied just as effectively to the study of culturally homogeneous societies in modern nations.[20] The basic assumption is that for large, complex, and heterogeneous societies fewer elements of personality would normally be involved in the delineation of social character than would be the case in smaller, simpler, and more homogeneous societies. Given the greater complexity and variety of elements in the corresponding and producing social system, it should be expected that any individual would be exposed to and experience only a small portion of his sociocultural system, and thereby have relatively less in common with other people from the same society.

One of the fundamental problems in applying the perspectives of social character to relatively large, complex, and heterogeneous societies is the fallacy of hypothesizing the existence of a monolithic social character for all segments of the society in question. Even though the complex problems of studying social character are recognized, especially in heterogeneous societies, and our conceptual specifications notwithstanding, still we frequently find people searching for and trying to describe *the* social character of a given population or society. The search for the social character of a particular society is not necessarily a search for unique characterological distinctions, however desirable that may be. Rather, it refers to the delimitation of significant differences in traits, patterns, or configurations of personality that may distinguish national populations. Indeed, to treat social character, as frequently is done, in terms of a uniqueness of psychological attributes would preclude some nations or societies from having one.

Of related significance are the equally sterile attempts to provide monistic, or single causal-factor, explanations for distinctive patterns of national character in a given society. Witness such contentions as can be found in the frontier hypothesis of Turner (1920), the M-factor thesis proposed by Pierson (1962), and the principle of abundancy which Potter advocated (1954). It seems unlikely, as Inkeles and Levinson (1969:427) state, that any particular personality or character type will be found in as much as 60 to 70 percent of any modern national population. Rather, they suggest, it is more likely that such a population, in order to accommodate its subcultural variations, will be marked by a limited number of modes, for example, five to six, some of which may apply to 10 to 15 percent, or even to as much as 30 percent, of the total population.[21] A multimodal conception of social character would seem to be, both theoretically and empirically, more realistic and more meaningful for modern, complex, industrial societies.

Critics nonetheless point to the enormous amount of time and resources that would be required to assess the norms of social character in relatively large, complex, and heterogeneous societies by scientifically valid techniques, tools, and procedures. Among the many requirements would be precise and extensive sampling, refined psychological measurements, and elaborate statistical treatments. Such prospects have not been very attractive to many modern scholars—and they have had even less appeal to funding agencies and foundations. Even so, the study of social character in large, modern societies is no longer impossible, however arduous an undertaking it may continue to be. Great strides have been made during the past twenty-five years in our understanding of personality dynamics, and the development of apparently valid and reliable tools and techniques for their assessment (e.g., TAT, Rorschach, sentence completion tests, and measures of individual modernity) that can be administered rather easily and effectively to large samples. Indeed, totally new methods for the rather exclusive study of social character have been proposed for the analysis of different types or patterns of psychodynamic structures and processes. Terhune (1970), for example, suggests that the new technique of Q-type factor analysis and the linear discriminant function seem most appropriate for such tasks. Other specialized techniques have been suggested by Spindler and Spindler (1961) and Smith (1966); Smith in particular critically argues that research on social character has been viewed exclusively in personality terms. In addition to the standard data collection techniques of interviews and questionnaires, the administration of personality tests, and field observations, there are various methods for the content analysis of personal and collective documents, rituals and customs, beliefs and value systems, and social institutions.

All of these accomplishments have been accompanied by extensive refinements in survey research which now make it comparatively easy and economical to draw adequate statistical samples of enormous populations. Moreover, the facility of electronic computation for rapid and intricate data analysis, combined with innovative statistical techniques, such as path analysis, have revolutionized the complex analysis and sophisticated interpretation of massive sets of empirical findings. While more work needs to be done in all of the relevant areas of empirical methodology, the many advancements to date have opened new doors for making possible today the impossible research of yesterday.[22]

Another basic problem in this area of research is that the bulk of the work, the early as well as the contemporary, is based on the still greatly empirically problematic theories of psychoanalysis—as is nearly all of the work in other areas of social science where personality has been one of the foci of analysis. Conceptual contributions and empirical findings based on these theoretical orientations have led to considerable skepticism and even outright rejection of much of the work in the field of social character studies. While the validity of certain psychoanalytic postulates has been established, many remain as simply unverified assumptions. Such a situation has not been conducive in many quarters to the acceptance of studies that have been based on psychoanalytic principles. The great accomplishments in other personality or psychological theories, such as field theory or self-theory, with the exception of learning theory, have been little employed or explored in this area of investigation.[23] Of late, however, recent work has brought to bear the concepts, methods, and perspectives of other theoretical orientations that are quite promising of fruitful consequences.

We advocate no particular theory of personality or psychology; instead we prefer to proceed within the perspectives of an eclectic approach to the problems of investigation. Many theoretical formulations have been offered to explain the origin and dynamics of personality,[24] and nearly all current theories with the exception of a few, such as that of the constitutional school, are potentially useful for the analysis and explanation of social character.

In any case, research of this type requires that we know, if only in a rather broad sense, which particular dimensions or variables of personality are relevant for social analysis in general and the analysis of social character in particular. Not all aspects of personality have the same value or utility as far as durability, consistency, or comparability in behavior is concerned. The crucial task is to delimit and to select those levels, dimensions, variables, and other aspects of personality that are most conceptually appropriate, methodologically amenable, and theoretically meaningful for the particular kinds of theoretical questions presented in the study of social character. In a much broader perspective, we need to address ourselves to this question in terms of personality *content* (e.g., motives, values, attitudes, and beliefs) versus personality *structure* (e.g., cohesion, integration, and complexity).[25] A related and more fundamental question on this issue is that of durability: which aspects or elements of personality are the more stable elements. Much controversy has existed on this particular question, for example, in terms of motives versus values as the more viable variable for studies of social character.

We share the view (see, e.g., Terhune, 1970) that the relevant variables for the study of social character should be determined not by assessing modes of specific and single characteristics or traits of personality—however valuable and methodologically necessary they may be—but rather by delineating personality configurations, or types, as we would call them. In these perspectives, Terhune (1970) suggests two general categories of variables: (1) cognitive patterns (the structure or style of cognitive systems rather than the specific content), and (2) conative patterns (action-tendencies and goal-orientations). He argues that motives, values, and value-orientations are the most useful variables for studies of social character because, in addition to being relevant and accessible, they (1) are relatively few in number, (2) are hierarchically organized, which facilitates the determination of patterns, (3) get at "deeper" (more basic and fundamental) personality phenomena, and (4) may be the most, or some of the most, stable and durable elements of personality, evolving slowly over time.[26] These questions constitute one of the focal dimensions of inquiry into the entire issue of social character, and indeed, of the relationship of personality to sociological and anthropological analyses more generally.

Another principal methodological problem to be resolved concerns the clarification of the appropriate segments of a population for the study for social character. Where is the social or social-categorical locus of social character for a given society? Terhune (1970) distinguishes, in politically relevant terms, four principal loci for social character: masses, elites, leaders, and significant minorities. He contends that social character ought not be sought in the psychological attributes of the overall population, but that it would be more productive to concentrate on elites and leaders who, in his view, are primarily responsible for making policy. This issue is a crucial one because social character is usually typified in terms of the lower class, since, representing the majority, its character is thought to be more typical in a given population. The matter is voided, however, with the idea of dominant and variant modes.

Another procedural problem that deserves mention in an era when ethical considerations of research are becoming more and more paramount is the contention that the search for distinctive social or national characters is personally pernicious and socially dysfunctional.[27] The study of social character has been severely attacked in some quarters for being another version of the discredited theories of racial psychology. Such studies, it is contended, impede the realization of an international or supranational community. Responses such as these, unfortunately, border on naivete. As McGiffert (1970) has stated so well, such remonstrances, however well intended, appear to be misdirected: national differences cannot be wished away by refusal to examine them, let alone by denying that they exist. On the contrary, quite aside from national strategies of survival, the general interests of humanity are better served by candid assessments of differences to the end that erroneous stereotypes may be corrected and avenues of international communication may be improved.

The study of social character is based on two legitimate, scientific questions for the social and behavioral disciplines. We cannot afford to ignore these questions: Are there significant differences among the various national and subnational populations in the distribution of discrete personality types or psychological characteristics? And, if so, how do these distinctive patterns affect the functioning of the corresponding social systems? We need not—and indeed should not—be making value-judgments either in asking, or, more especially, in answering these questions. Truth should be the only value that is neither arbitrary nor compromisable.

Can we really assume that a given social system will function in much the same way regardless of the set of personalities that are placed in that context? Furthermore, assuming a lack of congruence, or even compatibility, between the personality needs of individuals and the functional requirements of the social system, what kinds of stimuli to social or personal change might be expected to follow? And what kinds of limitations on social change might follow from the lack of certain values and motivations in the population? In both cases, we have questions of fundamentally theoretical and practical significance.

These are but a few of the more crucial methodological problems that are related to the study of social character. Unique or common as they may be, we need to bear in mind that methodological problems are the name of the game in empirical science. We need not be daunted by them, however insurmountable they may appear to be. And no longer can we afford to surrender our efforts to the echoes of, or with cries of, "impossible research." As scholars and scientists, we have no other fundamental method than to do our utmost. It is not only the well-popularized sociological imagination—lest I sound too provincialistic—that is required, but rather the broader, and more synthetic, methodological creativity of all of the social and behavioral sciences. Our orientation must be one of optimism and expectation, not fatalism and futility. For, as we have said elsewhere (DiRenzo, 1966:288), the resolution of the theoretical viability of these issues is an empirical question that must be approached with conviction and determination.

Scientific Relevance

The question that remains for the more theoretically oriented scholar, and for the policy-oriented activist as well, is the question of why social character should be studied. What, if anything, is the social impact of characterological modalities in a given population?

Social character is not only the product of sociocultural processes and systems, but also one of their producers. Studies of social character, in this perspective, offer the possibility of providing a more thorough and comprehensive explanation for both individual and collective behavior. Of more specific significance is the opportunity which such studies provide for understanding the development of the human organism in both its social and psychological dimensions, and correspondingly for assessing the structure and function of the processes of socialization and enculturation.

Hence, no analysis of social behavior may be considered complete without a psychological examination of the actors who are the agents of that behavior. Correspondingly, we might add that no understanding of individual human behavior can be complete without a consideration of the nature and structure of the social situation in which human behavior takes place. While it may be argued that the study of individual personality is a psychological consideration that has little value for understanding the structure and dynamics of the collectivity, social character—concretely in the forms of modal personality—is a property of the collectivity. As such, social character is a sociological variable that is not only relevant for sociocultural explanation, but indeed indispensable for many analytical problems. Thus, considerations of the impact of characterological modalities in a given population can serve a tremendously valuable function in enriching the assessment of its social systems and processes when integrated with other established modes of social analysis.

The concept of social character is a key one for understanding social processes.[28] Specifically, in maintaining social equilibrium or producing social change, characterological dynamics play an instrumental role. In this regard we submit Fromm's assertion that the character types of a given society can serve either as a cement holding the system together or as an explosive tearing it apart—depending upon the degree to which a given character type fits the demands of the system and finds satisfaction within it. "Character in the dynamic sense of analytic psychology," says Fromm (1941:278), "is the specific form in which human energy is shaped by the dynamic adaptation of human needs to the particular mode of existence in a given society."

The social character, in these perspectives, is adapted to—and must be adapted to—the objective tasks which the individual has to perform in society. For, again, as Fromm (1944:380-384) states: "In order that any society may function well, its members must acquire the kind of character which makes them want to act in a way they *have* to act as members of the society . . . they have to desire what objectively is necessary for them to do." Indeed, this was de Tocqueville's message with his idea of the "democratic social character" as a functional prerequisite of democratic sociopolitical systems.[29] Hence we subscribe to Fromm's thesis (1941) that the disparity between socially required behavior and characterologically compatible or available behavior can be a great source of social change—and indeed of individual, psychological change as well.

In other respects, the study of social character should lead to an understanding not only of what is distinctive about single nations, but also of the relatively universal, psychological phenomena in human society. In our particular considerations of social character in this volume, we are concerned only indirectly with determining the uniqueness of American social character. Many of the components of social character may be shared with other nations, particularly those with similar histories and sociocultural structures (for example, industrialized Western societies). As some have contended,[30] all contemporary Western societies may contain essentially the same range of personality types. Contrary to the inference of this contention, to search for *the* social character of a country in terms of distinctive psychological attributes of a national population does not mean that each national or social character must be unique, any more than each personality is expected to be totally unlike any other. Rather, in a much more fundamental perspective, we seek to characterize the national population in terms that are both categorically socioculturally relevant and psychologically standard.

Here we refer in particular to what might be called the universal nature of human character. Human society—or rather social engineering—seems to go forward on the assumption that the human organism is infinitely malleable. Such a conception may not only be erroneous but also disastrous. However variable and plastic the human organism in general and human character in particular, it seems more logical, and—as a consequence of social and behavioral research—more empirically founded that there may be, at any given point in the evolutionary process, a fixed, delimited human psychological nature, one with its own inherent structure, laws, functional requisites, and dynamism. Again, as Fromm (1941:289) tells us: "Even if we are not able to state clearly in psychological terms what the exact nature of this human dynamism is, we must recognize its existence. In trying to avoid the errors of biological and metaphysical concepts we must not succumb to an equally grave error, that of a sociological relativism in which man is nothing but a puppet, directed by the strings of social circumstance." We have labored in vain too long with the "over-socialized conception of man" (Wrong, 1961), and we now need to broaden our conceptions in a more realistic sense.

Of relevance in this context is the idea of basic human or characterological needs which Professor Etzioni discusses in Chapter 12. Many of the motivations that distinguish human beings, and classes or categories of them, such as national ones, have their origin in, and are products of, social interaction. But other, nonbiological drives which appear to be socially acquired may be in fact characterological needs inherent in human nature. Fromm (1941:289), for example, argues: "Man's inalienable rights of freedom and happiness are founded in inherent human qualities: his striving to love, to expand and express the potentialities that have developed in him in the process of historical evolution." We need to put this thesis to an empirically exhaustive test, and the cross-cultural assessment of social character is but one indispensable step in this process.

Here we have another, but rather obvious, example of the value of studies of social character, namely, the importance which such studies have for facilitating comparative studies of a cross-cultural or cross-national nature, and comparative analyses of groups from different national populations that occupy comparable positions in their respective social systems. Inkeles and Levinson (1969:447-448), for example, offer some approaches to "standard analytical issues" in studies of social character that would enable cross-cultural comparisons. They delineate criteria for selecting issues which they suggest might be of universal psychosocial relevance in terms of the functional significance for both personality and social systems. One example would be the question of personal authority. There are enough data on this question, say Inkeles and Levinson, for the beginnings of a "comparative national character approach." Terhune (1970) describes, in more concrete and elaborate terms, the potential utility and functional significance of the study of social character in terms of the assessment and prediction of national, and even international, behavior—and, moreover, in facilitating the formation of policy in these respects. Indeed, the analysis and understanding of the social character of various countries as a guide to more enlightened national policies have been proposed repeatedly.[31]

The theoretical significance of characterological modalities for social systems are, of course, multifold.[32] We have tried within the limits of space to include only a few of the more macroscopic and salient considerations. We share the fundamental thesis, however, that the study and assessment of social character—when integrated with other established modes of social investigation—serve to enrich the analysis of sociocultural systems and processes. Such studies, of course, are by their very nature multidisciplinary in perspective. Usually, this requirement constitutes the grounds, as it has so often in the past, for another methodological problem of major proportions. Unfortunately, in many quarters of the social and behavioral sciences, provincialism remains a salient characteristic. Interdisciplinary studies pose a threat to the purity and independence—however fallaciously construed—of the individual disciplines. Such a situation invariably will continue to prove to be a serious handicap to a more complete and comprehensive, distortion-free, and hence error-free explanation of human and social behavior. But the common, though not necessarily exclusive, subject matter of the diversified fields of the social and behavioral sciences is "socially relevant human behavior" (Inkeles and Levinson, 1969:422). Accordingly, we must work to dispel the lingering myth that human beings, and human society, either have been created or have evolved in the image and perspectives of any one academic discipline.

The road of science is an eclectic one. It is constructed not only of the individual blocks of knowledge that come from the separate disciplines, but more especially of the complementary mortarization of their specialized perspectives. Hence, the hope of the social and behavioral sciences—indeed of all sciences—rests upon scientific convergence in the formulation of both methodology and theory. Such synthetic perspectives, if we are to succeed to any effective degree, need to become the axis of our individual disciplinary enterprises. Encouragingly, such prospects seem to be more promising today than they did a decade or two ago. Here, then, in the study of social character is an opportunity for contributing to the integration of the various disciplines of the behavioral sciences. The particular problem before us clearly requires the multidisciplinary perspectives of scholastic and scientific convergence. However valid these hypothetical assumptions and theoretical speculations may be, we first of all need to ask more concretely about when and how it makes sense to talk about social character. Contributing to the specification of these questions has been one of the cardinal dimensions of our analysis.

NOTES

1. While de Tocqueville admired our system of justice and our independence, there was much about America that displeased him. For example, he thought us "the most prosaic of all peoples on earth," and in this respect we clearly bored him to death. He considered Americans to be in mortal fear of being different from their neighbors, as well as being very frightened of having a deviant opinion (see Henry, 1963:5). Have we changed much? Riesman (1950) came to the same conclusion more than one hundred years later, although several of the contributors to this volume argue for marked individualism as a modal characteristic of Americans today.

2. See, e.g., Schlesinger (1949).

3. Among the well-known attempts of this half-century to describe American character, the following deserve particular mention: "the neurotic personality of our times" (Horney, 1937); "the authoritarian personality" (Adorno et al., 1950); "the inner-, other-, and tradition-directed" types (Riesman, 1950); "the organizational man" (Whyte, 1956); "one-dimensional man" (Marcuse, 1964); "consciousness III" (Reich, 1970); and "protean man" (Lifton, 1970).

4. The exhaustive survey by Duijker and Frijda (1960), already dated, offers ample empirical evidence of distinctive patterns of national character in several countries.

5. Some notable exceptions of psychologists who have contributed to the study of national character are the following: Klineberg (1944), Eysenck and Crown (1948), Cattell (1949), and Farber (1950, 1955).

6. See the bibliography provided at the end of this volume.

7. Inkeles and Levinson (1969) provide some explanation for these disciplinary perspectives in terms of their respective historical development. This view, however, is not shared in all quarters. Levine (1963), for example,

argues for extensive increase and expansion of activity in the field of culture-and-personality studies.

8. It should be pointed out that Fromm was referring to a very specific conception of social character which we shall describe subsequently.

9. See, e.g., Bendix (1951) and Shafer (1955).

10. Cited by Northedge in a lecture at the London School of Economics, October 1962.

11. For a discussion of this question, see DiRenzo (1966).

12. A similar classification, utilizing a somewhat different focus, is presented by Inkeles (1961).

13. Anthropologists frequently advocate this position. For example, personality for Benedict (1934:251-252) was "culture writ small." Other arguments of similar perspective may be found in Spiro (1951).

14. This construct supposedly was introduced by Inkeles in 1951.

15. This formulation is not intended to sound reductionistic. Social character is only one of several sets of factors that, conjointly, may determine behavior.

16. The dominant type of social character in metropolitan America, according to Riesman (1950), is that of the "other-directed" person—one for whom the chief source of direction, and the principal area of sensitivity, is located in other people. This type of social character is similar to Fromm's (1947:67) "marketing orientation."

17. An interesting and thorough discussion of the various conceptions of national character, particularly as we have discussed them here, may be found in Terhune (1970:207-211). His analysis is in the perspectives of the typology of collective properties (analytic, structural, and global) delineated by Lazarsfeld and Menzel (1961).

18. For a discussion of the theoretical and methodological implications of this distinction, see DiRenzo (1966), especially Chapters 1 and 9.

19. Crèvecoeur (1782) said in this regard: "The difficulty consists in the manner of viewing so extensive a scene." His reference was not only to the formidable spaciousness of the country, but essentially to the problem of procedure and perspective for assessing the cultural heterogeneity of its inhabitants.

20. Inkeles (1961) offers some useful commentary on the problems of methodology for the study of national character in modern societies.

21. See Inkeles and Levinson (1969) for a discussion of the methodological and theoretical advantages in using the multimodal conception of social character.

22. For a review and assessment of methods for the study of social character, see Duijker and Frijda (1960), Inkeles (1961), and Terhune (1970), who describe a number of tools and techniques that have produced a reasonable degree of success.

23. For a discussion of how personality theory has been, and may be, used in the empirical delineation of social character, see Inkeles and Levinson (1969:428-452).

24. See, e.g., Hall and Lindzey (1970).

25. We have treated these questions to some extent elsewhere. (DiRenzo, 1974).

26. Murray (1938), e.g., has delineated about two dozen needs (motives), Morris (1956) describes thirteen basic value-orientations; and Rokeach (1968) enumerates eighteen instrumental and goal values. McClelland (1961), incidentally, is the only one who has studied social character in terms of motives.

27. See, e.g., Shafer (1955).

28. See Martindale (1967) for a discussion of the relevance of social character for sociological studies and explanation.

29. See Inkeles (1961) for a discussion of the democratic social character as a functional prerequisite for democratic sociopolitical systems.

30. See, e.g., Bendix (1951).

31. For a discussion on the utility of national character studies in the fields of diplomacy, foreign relations, and intelligence, see, e.g., Klineberg (1944), Mead (1952), Platt (1961), Smith (1966), and Terhune (1970). A negative view in these respects is offered by Hennessy (1962).

32. See Inkeles (1953:585-588) for a more extended discussion of the significance of psychological regularities in the function of social systems.

Bibliography

Adelman, Irma, and Morris, Cynthia Taft. *Society, Politics, and Economic Development*. Baltimore: John Hopkins Press, 1971.

Adorno, T. W.; Frenkel-Brunswik, Else; Levinson, Daniel J.; Sanford, R. Nevitt. *The Authoritarian Personality*. New York: Harper and Bros. 1950.

Almond, Gabriel A., and Verba, S. *The Civic Culture*. Princeton: Princeton University Press, 1963.

———; Flanagan, Scott C.; and Mundt, Robert J. (eds.). *Crisis, Choice and Change*. Boston: Little, Brown and Company, 1973.

Appelbaum, Richard P. *Theories of Social Change*. Chicago: Markham Publishing Company, 1970.

Armer, Michael, and Schnaiberg, Allan. "Measuring Individual Modernity." *American Sociological Review* (1972):301-316.

Aschenbrenner, Joyce S. "Lifelines: Black Families in Chicago." *Case Studies in Anthropology*. New York: Holt, Rinehart and Winston, 1974.

Astin, Helen S., and Bisconti, Ann A. *Trends in Academic and Career Plans of College Freshman*, Report No. 1. The CPC Foundation, 1974.

Banfield, Edward. *The Moral Basis of a Backward Society*. New York: The Free Press, 1958.

———. *The Unheavenly City: The Nature and Future of Our Urban Crisis*. Boston: Little, Brown and Company, 1968.

Beach, F. A. *Sex and Behavior*. New York: Wiley, 1965.

Bell, Daniel. *The End of Ideology*. New York: The Free Press, 1960.

———. "National Character Revisited: A Proposal for Renegotiating the Concept." In *The Study of Personality*, edited by Edward Norbeck, Douglas Price-Williams, and William M. McCord. New York: Holt, Rinehart and Winston, 1968.

———. *The Coming of the Post Industrial Society*. New York: Basic Books, 1973.

Bendix, Reinhard. "Images of Man in the Social Sciences." *Commentary* II (1951):187-192.

Benedict, Ruth. *Patterns of Culture*. Boston: Houghton Mifflin Company, 1934.

Benson, George; Benson, C.S.; and Engeman, Thomas S. *Amoral America*. Stanford, Calif.: Hoover Institution Press, 1975.

Berreman, Gerald D. "Structure and Function of Caste Systems." In *Japan's Invisible Race*, edited by George A. DeVos and Hiroshi Wagatsuma. Berkeley: University of California Press, 1966.

Black, Cyril. *The Dynamics of Modernization*. New York: Harper and Row, 1966.

Block, Jeanne H.; Haan, Norma; and Smith, M. Brewster. "Socialization Correlates of Student Activism." *Journal of Social Issues* 25 (1969): 143-176.

Bonjean, C. M., and Vance, G. G. "A Short Measure of Self 'Actualization'." *Journal of Applied Behavioral Science* 4 (1968): 299-312.

Bradburn, Norman M. *The Structure of Psychological Well-Being*. Chicago: Aldine, 1969.

Breneman, David. "The Ph.D. Production Process: A Study of Departmental Behavior." Ph.D. dissertation, University of California, 1970.

Brenner, B. "Patterns of Alcohol Use, Happiness and the Satisfaction of Wants." *Quarterly Journal of Studies on Alcohol* 28 (1967): 667-675.

Brenner, M. Harvey. *Mental Illness and the Economy*. Cambridge, Mass.: Harvard University Press, 1973.

Brody, Eugene B. (ed.). *Behavior in New Environments: Adaptation of Migrant Populations*. Beverly Hills, Calif.: Saga Publications, 1970.

Brogan, D.W. *The American Character*. New York: Alfred A. Knopf, 1944.

Bryce, James, *The American Commonwealth*. New York: Macmillan Company, 1910.

Campbell, Angus. *White Attitudes Toward Black People*. Ann Arbor: University of Michigan, Institute for Social Research, 1971.

———; and Converse, Phillip E.; Miller, Warren E.; and Stokes, Donald E. *The SRC American Panel Study: 1956, 1958, 1960*. Ann Arbor: University of Michigan, Inter-University Consortium for Political Research, 1971.

Campbell, Jospeh. *The Portable Jung*. New York: Viking Press, 1971.

Cancian, Francesca. "Functional Analysis of Change." *American Sociological Review* 25 (1960):818-827.

Caplan, Nathan. "The New Ghetto Man: A Review of Recent Empirical Studies." *Journal of Social Issues* 26 (1970): 59-73.

Cattell, Raymond B. "The Dimensions of Culture Patterns by Factorization of National Character." *Journal of Abnormal and Social Psychology* 44 (1949):443-469.

Christie, Richard, and Jahoda, Marie (eds.). *Studies in the Scope and Method of "The Authoritarian Personality": Continuities in Social Research*. Glencoe, Ill.: The Free Press, 1954.

Clark, Kenneth. *Dark Ghetto: Dilemmas of Social Power*. New York: Harper and Row, 1965.

Clinton, Charles. "The Social Organization of an Occupational Subsociety:

An Ecological Approach to the Carpenters of Local 1281." Ph.D. dissertation, Washington State University, 1973.
Coles, Robert. *Children of Crisis: A Study of Courage and Fear.* Boston: Little, Brown and Company, 1967.
Comstock, C., and Duckles, R. "Swing Voters: A Comparison of Attitudes on Leadership Style and on the War in Viet Nam, Expressed by Undecided Voters and by Supporters of McGovern and of Nixon." Unpublished paper. Berkeley, Calif.: The Wright Institute, 1972.
Coser, Lewis. *The Functions of Social Conflict.* New York: The Free Press, 1956.
———. "Unanticipated Conservative Consequences of Liberal Theorizing." *Social Problems* 16 (1969): 263-272.
Crain, Robert, and Weisman, Carol S. *Discrimination, Personality and Achievement: A Survey of Northern Blacks.* New York: Seminar Press, 1972.
Crowne, D. P., and Marlowe, D. *The Approval Motive.* New York: Wiley, 1964.
Cuber, John F., and Harper, Robert A. *Problems of American Society: Values in Conflict.* New York: Henry Holt and Company, 1948.
Czeslaw, Milosz. *The Captive Mind.* New York: Alfred A. Knopf, 1953.
Daner, Francine. *Children of Krsna.* New York: Holt, Rinehart and Winston, 1976.
Davidson, Theodore. *Chicano Prisoners: The Key to San Quentin.* New York: Holt, Rinehart and Winston, 1974.
Davies, J. C. *Human Nature in Politics.* New York: Wiley, 1963.
Davis, James A. *National Data Program for the Social Sciences Spring 1973 General Social Survey.* Ann Arbor: University of Michigan, Inter-University Consortium for Political Research, 1973.
Davis, Kingsley. *Human Society.* New York: Macmillan, 1948.
DeVos, George A. "Social Stratification and Ethnic Pluralism: An Overview from the Perspective of Psychological Anthropology." *Race* 13 (1972):435-460.
——— (ed.). *Responses to Change.* New York: D. Van Nostrand Company, 1976.
———. "Urbanization: Adaptation and Adjustment." In *Responses to Change,* edited by George A. DeVos. New York: D. Van Nostrand Company, 1976.
———, and Wagatsuma, Hiroshi. "Socialization, Self-Perception, and Burakumin Status," and "Group Solidarity and Individual Mobility." In *Japan's Invisible Race,* edited by George A. DeVos and Hiroshi Wagatsuma. Berkeley: University of California Press, 1966.
DeVos, George A., and Romanucci-Ross, Lola (eds.). *Ethnic Identity.* Palo

Alto, Calif.: Mayfield Publishing Company, 1975.

DeVries, Egbert. *Man in Rapid Social Change*. Garden City, N.Y.: Doubleday, 1961.

Dillon, Wilton S. (ed.). *The Cultural Drama*. Washington, D.C.: Smithsonian Institution Press, 1974.

DiRenzo, Gordon J. (ed.). *Concepts, Theory and Explanation in the Behavioral Sciences.* New York: Random House, 1966.

———. *Personality, Power, and Politics.* Notre Dame, Ind.: University of Notre Dame Press, 1967.

———. *Personality and Politics.* New York: Doubleday and Company, Inc., 1974.

Dougherty, Molly Crocker. *Maturation and Motherhood in a Black Rural Southern Community.* Case Studies in Cultural Anthropology. New York: Holt, Rinehart, and Winston, 1977.

DuBois, Cora. *The People of Alor.* Minneapolis: University of Minnesota Press, 1944.

DuBois, Linda. "A Jewish Subculture at Stanford University." Unpublished paper. Stanford University, 1972.

Dudycha, G. J. "An Objective Study of Punctuality in Relation to Personality and Achievement." *Archives of Psychology* 204 (1936): 1-319.

Duijker, H. C. J., and Frijda, N. H. *National Character and National Stereotypes: A Trend Report Prepared for the International Union of Scientific Psychology.* Amsterdam: North Holland Publishing Company, 1960.

Duncan, Otis D. "Social Organization and the Ecosystem." In *Handbook of Modern Sociology,* edited by Robert E. L. Faris. New York: Rand McNally, 1966.

———; Schuman, Howard; and Duncan, Beverly. *Social Change in a Metropolitan Community.* New York: Russell Sage Foundation, 1973.

Durkheim, Emile. *Suicide.* New York: The Free Press, 1951. Originally published, 1897.

Eisenstadt, S. N. *Modernization: Protest and Change.* Englewood Cliffs, N.J.: Prentice-Hall, 1966.

Elder, Glen H., Jr. "Democratic Parent-Youth Relations in Cross-National Perspective," *Social Science Quarterly* 49 (1968): 216-228.

———. *Children of the Great Depression.* Chicago: University of Chicago Press, 1974.

Elkins, Stanley. *Slavery: A Problem in American Institutional and Intellectual Life.* Chicago: University of Chicago Press, 1959.

Endler, N. S.; Hunt, J. M.; and Rosenstein, A. J. "An S-R Inventory of Anxiousness." *Psychological Monographs* 76, No. 536 (1962). Entire issue.

Erikson, Erik H. *Childhood and Society.* New York: W. W. Norton and Company, 1950.

———. *Insight and Freedom.* Ninth T. B. Davie Memorial Lecture, University of Capetown, South Africa, 1968.
———. *Gandhi's Truth.* New York: W. W. Norton and Company, 1969.
———. "Thomas Jefferson—Protean Man." *New York Times,* April 13, 1974.
Etzioni, Amitai. *Studies in Social Change.* New York: Holt, Rinehart and Winston, 1966.
———. "Toward a Theory of Societal Guidance." *American Journal of Sociology* 73 (1967): 173-187.
———. *The Active Society.* New York: The Free Press, 1968.
———. *Genetic Fix.* New York: Macmillan, 1973.
———, and Etzioni, Eva (eds.). *Social Change: Source, Patterns, and Consequences.* New York: Basic Books, 1964.
Eulau, Heinz. *Micro-Macro Political Analysis.* Chicago: Aldine, 1969.
Eysenck, Hans J., and Crown, S. "National Stereotypes: An Experimental and Methodological Study." *International Journal of Opinion and Attitude Research* #2 (1948): 26-39.
Farber, Maurice L. "The Problem of National Character: A Methodological Analysis." *Journal of Psychology* 30 (1950): 307-311.
———. "The Study of National Character." *Journal of Social Issues* 11 (1955): 52-56.
Feuer, Lewis. *The Conflict of Generations.* New York: Basic Books, 1969.
Fogel, Robert W., and Engerman, Stanley L. *Time on the Cross: The Economics of American Negro Slavery.* Boston: Little, Brown and Company, 1974.
Forward, John, and Williams, Jay. "Internal-External Control and Black Militancy." *Journal of Social Issues* 26 (1970): 75-92.
Frazier, E. Franklin. *Black Bourgeoisie.* New York: The free Press, 1957.
Freud, S. "Civilization and Its Discontents." In *The Standard Edition of the Complete Psychological Works of Sigmund Freud,* edited by G. Strachey. Vol. 21. London: Hogarth Press, 1961 (1st German ed., 1930).
Fried, Morton H. "Chinese Culture, Society, and Personality in Transition." In *Responses to Change,* edited by George A. DeVos. New York: D. Van Nostrand Company, 1976.
Frijda, Nico, and Jahoda, Gustav. "On the Scope and Methods of Cross-Cultural Research." *International Journal of Psychology* 1 (1966): 109-127.
Fromm, Erich. *Autoritat und Familie.* Alcan, 1936.
———. *Escape from Freedom.* New York: Holt, Rinehart and Winston, 1941.
———. "The Individual and Social Origins of Neurosis." *American Sociological Review* 9 (1944): 380-384.
———. Man for Himself: *An Inquiry into the Psychology of Ethics.* New York: Rinehart and Company, Inc., 1947.
———, and Maccoby, M. *Social Character in a Mexican Village.* Englewood

Cliffs, N.J.: Prentice-Hall, 1970.

Gallup, George H. *The Gallup Poll.* New York: Random House, 1972.

Geertz, Clifford. *Peddlers and Princes.* Chicago: University of Chicago Press, 1963.

Genovese, Eugene D. "American Slaves and Their History." *New York Times Review of Books,* December 3, 1970, pp. 34-43.

———. *Roll, Jordan, Roll: The World the Slaves Made.* New York: Pantheon, 1974.

Geredes, Theodore. "A Study of Values in a Stanford Student Sample." Unpublished paper. Stanford University, 1969.

Gergen, Kenneth J. "Interaction Goals and Personalistic Feedback as Factors Affecting the Presentation of Self." *Journal of Personality and Social Psychology* 1 (1965): 413-424.

———. "Multiple Identity." *Psychology Today,* May 1972, pp. 31ff.

———; Gergen, Mary M.; and Barton, William. "Deviance in the Dark." *Psychology Today,* October 1973, pp. 129-130.

———, and Gordon, Chad (eds.). *The Self in Social Interaction.* New York: Wiley, 1968.

———, and Marlowe, David (eds.). *Personality and Social Behavior.* Reading, Mass.: Addison-Wesley Publishing Company, 1966.

———, and Taylor, M. G. "Role-Playing and Modifying and Self Concept." Paper presented at annual meetings of the Eastern Psychological Association, New York City, 1966.

———, and Wishnov, B. "Others' Self-evaluations and Interaction Anticipation as Determinants of Self-Presentation." *Journal of Personality and Social Psychology* 2 (1965): 348-358.

Gerth, Hans, and Mills, C. Wright. *Character and Social Structure.* New York: Harcourt, Brace and Company, 1953.

Giddings, Franklin H. *Principles of Sociology.* New York: Macmillan Company, 1896.

Glenn, Norval D. "Trend Studies with Available Survey Data: Opportunities and Pitfalls." In *Survey Data for Trend Analysis,* edited by Philip K. Hastings. Roper Public Opinion Research Center and Social Science Research Council, 1974.

Gold, M. "The Brief Interlude: Federal Intervention in American Education, 1944-1974." Paper presented at annual meetings of the American Educational Research Association, Chicago, 1974.

Goldstein, Rhoda L. "Comments on the January, 1971 Issue, 'American Sociology and Black Americans'." *American Journal of Sociology* 77 (1971): 574-579.

Gorer, Geoffrey. *The American People: A Study in National Character.* New York: W. W. Norton and Company, 1948.

———. "English Identity Over Time and Space." In *Ethnic Identity*, edited by George A. DeVos and Lola Romanucci-Ross. Palo Alto, Calif.: Mayfield Publishing Company, 1975.

Gough, Harrison G. "A Measure of Individual Modernity." *Journal of Personality Assessment* 40 (1976): 3-9.

———, and Lazzari, R. "A 15-Item Form of the F Scale and a Cross-Cultural Application." *Journal of Psychology* 88 (1974): 39-46.

Gouldner, Alvin. *The Coming Crisis of Western Sociology*. New York: Basic Books, 1970.

———, and Peterson, Richard A. *Technology and the Moral Order*. Indianapolis, Ind.: Bobbs-Merrill, 1962.

Graves, Theodore. "Urban Indian Personality and the 'Culture of Poverty'." *American Ethnologist* 1 (1974): 65-86.

Greer, C. *The Great School Legend: A Revisionist Interpretation of Public Education*. New York: Basic Books, 1972.

Grier, William, and Cobbs, Price. *Black Rage*. New York: Basic Books, 1968.

Gruenfeld, Leopold W., and MacEachron, Ann E. "The Relation of Socio-economic Status to Field Articulation." Ithaca: Cornell University, New York State School of Industrial and Labor Relations, no date.

Gump, P. "Anti-Democratic Trends and Student Reaction to President Truman's Dismissal of General MacArthur." Lawrence, Kans.: Kansas University, Psychology Department, 1951.

Gurin, Gerald; Veroff, Joseph; and Feld, Sheila. *Americans View Their Mental Health*. New York: Basic Books, 1960.

Guterman, Stanley S. (ed.). *Black Psyche: Modal Personality Patterns of Black Americans*. Berkeley, Calif.: Glendessary Press, 1972.

Hagen, Everett E. *On the Theory of Social Change: How Economic Growth Begins*. Homewood, Ill.: Dorsey Press, 1962.

Hall, Calvin S., and Lindzey, Gardner. *Theories of Personality*. New York: Wiley, 1970.

Hampden-Turner, C. "The Search for an Institutional Ethic." Mimeographed. Berkeley, Calif.: The Wright Institute, 1974.

Han, Wan Sang. "Two Conflicting Themes: Common Values Versus Class Differential Values." *American Sociological Review* 34 (1969): 679-690.

Harlow, H. F., and Harlow, M. K. "The Affectional Systems." In *Behavior of Nonhuman Primates*, edited by A. M. Schrier, H. F. Harlow, and F. Stollnitz. New York: Academic Press, 1965.

Harrington, Charles, and Whiting, John W. M. "Socialization Process and Personality." In *Psychological Anthropology*, edited by Francis L. K. Hsu. Cambridge, Mass.: Schenkman Publishing Company, 1972.

Harris Survey. "Report on White Stereotypes." *Cleveland Plain Dealer*, October 4, 1971, p. 5-B.

———. "Report on Perceived Discrimination." *Cleveland Plain Dealer,* January 15, 1973, p. 9-A.

Hartshorne, H., and May, M. A. *Studies in the Nature of Character.* New York: Macmillan, 1928.

Haskell, Thomas L. "Were Slaves More Efficient? Some Doubts About 'Time on the Cross'." *New York Times Review of Books,* September 19, 1974, pp. 38.42.

Hastorf, A. H. "The 'Reinforcement' of Individual Actions in a Group Situation." In *Personality and Social Behavior,* edited by Kenneth J. Gergen and D. Marlowe. Reading, Mass.: Addison-Wesley, 1970.

Heizer, Robert Fleming. *The Other Californians: Prejudice and Discrimination Under Spain, Mexico, and the United States to 1920.* Berkeley: University of California Press, 1971.

Heller, Joseph. *Something Happened.* New York: Alfred A. Knopf, 1975.

Hennessy, Bernard C. "Psycho-cultural Studies of National Character: Relevances for International Relations." *Background* 6 (1962): 27-49.

Henry, Jules. *Culture Against Man.* New York: Random House, 1963.

Hermalin, Albert, and Farley, Reynolds. "The Potential for Residential Integration in Cities and Suburbs: Implications for the Busing Controversy." *American Sociological Review* 38 (1973): 595-610.

Hicks, George L. *Appalachian Valley.* New York: Holt, Rinehart and Winston, 1976.

Hillman, James. "Puer and Senex." *Eranos jahrbuch* 36 (1968): 301-359.

Horney, Karen. *The Neurotic Personality of Our Times.* New York: W. W. Norton and Company, 1937.

Hoselitz, Bert F., and Moore, Wilbert E. (eds.). *Industrialization and Society.* Paris: UNESCO and Mouton, 1963.

Howard, J. M., and Somers, R. H. "Resisting Institutional Evil from Within." In *Sanctions for Evil,* edited by Nevitt Sanford and Craig Comstock. San Francisco: Jossey-Bass, 1971.

Hsu, Francis L. K. *Psychological Anthropology: Approaches to Culture and Personality.* Homewood, Ill.: Dorsey Press, 1961.

———. *Americans and Chinese: Purpose and Fulfillment in Great Civilizations.* New York: Doubleday and Company, 1970.

———. *Kinship and Culture.* Chicago: Aldine Publishing Company, 1971a.

———. "Psychosocial Homeostasis (PSH) and Jen: Concepts for Advancing Psychological Anthropology." *American Anthropologist* 73 (1971b): 23-44.

———. "Prejudice and Its Intellectual Effect in American Anthropology: An Ethnographic Report." *American Anthropologist* 75 (1973a): 1-19.

———. "Kinship Is the Key." *Center Magazine* 6, No. 6 (November-December 1973b): 4-14.

———. "Kinship Is the Key." *Center Magazine* 6, No. 6 (November-Decem-
ral Factors in Learning and Education.* Fifth Western Symposium on Learning, Western Washington State College, Bellingham, Wash., 1974.

———. *Iemoto: The Heart of Japan.* Cambridge, Mass.: Schenkman Publishing Company, 1975.

———. (ed.). *Aspects of Culture and Personality: A Symposium.* New York: Abelard-Schuman, 1954.

Hyman, Herbert H.; Wright, Charles R.; and Reed, John Shelton. *The Enduring Effects of Education.* Chicago: University of Chicago Press, 1975.

Hymes, Dell (ed.). *Reinventing Anthropology.* New York: Random House, 1972.

Ike, Nobutake. "Economic Growth and Intergenerational Change in Japan." *American Political Science Review* 67 (1973): 1194-1203.

Inglehart, Ronald. "The Silent Revolution in Europe: Intergenerational Change in Post-Industrial Societies." *American Political Science Review* 69 (December 1971): 991-1017.

———. *The Silent Revolution.* Princeton, N.J.: Princeton University Press, 1976.

Inkeles, Alex. "National Character and Social Structure." *Antioch Review* 9 (1949): 155-162.

———. "Some Sociological Observations on Culture and Personality Studies." In *Personality in Nature, Society and Culture,* edited by C. Kluckhohn, H. A. Murray, and D. M. Schneider. New York: Alfred A. Knopf, 1953.

———. "Personality and Social Structure." In *Sociology Today: Problems and Prospects,* edited by Robert K. Merton, Leonard Bloom, and Leonard S. Cottrell, Jr. New York: Basic Books, 1959.

———. "Industrial Man: The Relation of Status to Experience, Perception and Value." *The American Journal of Sociology* 66 (1960): 1-31.

———. "National Character and Modern Political Systems." In *Psychological Anthropology,* edited by Francis L. K. Hsu. Homewood, Ill.: Dorsey Press, 1961.

———. "The Modernization of Man." In *Modernization,* edited by M. Weiner. New York: Basic Books, 1966.

———. "Society, Social Structure, and Child Socialization." In *Socialization and Society,* edited by J. A. Clausen. Boston: Little, Brown and Company, 1968.

———. "Continuity and Change in the Interaction of the Personal and Sociocultural Systems." In *Stability and Social Change,* edited by Bernard Barber and Alex Inkeles. Boston: Little, Brown and Company, 1971.

———, and Levinson, Daniel J. "The Personal System and Social Structure in

Large Scale Organizations." *Sociometry* 26 (1963): 217-230.

———, and Levinson, Daniel J. "National Character: The Study of Modal Personality and Sociocultural Systems." In *The Handbook of Social Psychology, IV,* edited by G. Lindzey and E. Aronson. Reading, Mass.: Addison-Wesley, 1969. First edition published, 1954.

———, and Smith, David H., *Becoming Modern: Individual Change in Six Developing Countries.* Cambridge, Mass.: Harvard University Press, 1974.

———, and Smith, David H. "Personal Adjustment and Modernization." In *Responses to Change,* edited by George A. DeVos. New York: D. Van Nostrand Company, 1976.

Janis, Irving. *Victims of Groupthink: 14-49.* Boston: Houghton Mifflin Company, 1972.

Jaques, Elliott. "Death and the Mid-life Crisis." *International Journal of Psychoanalysis* 56 (1965): 502-514.

Jencks, Christopher, et al. *Inequality: A Reassessment of the Effect of Family and Schooling in America.* New York: Basic Books, 1972.

Johnson, Charles S. *Patterns of Negro Segregation.* New York: Harper and Row, 1943.

Johnson, Neil H. "The Real People: A Rural New York Community." Unpublished manuscript, 1973.

Jung, Carl G. *The Archetypes and the Collective Unconscious.* Bolligen Series XX (2d ed.). Princeton, N.J.: Princeton University Press, 1968.

Kagan, J., and Moss, H. A. *Birth to Maturity: A Study in Psychological Development.* New York: Wiley, 1962.

Kahn, Roger. *Boys of Summer.* New York: Harper and Row, 1973.

Kardiner, Abram. *The Individual and His Society: The Psychodynamics of Primitive Social Organization.* New York: Columbia University Press, 1939.

———; DuBois, C.; Linton, R.; and West, J. *The Psychological Frontiers of Society.* New York: Columbia University Press, 1950.

———; and Linton, R. *The Individual and His Society: The Psychodynamics of Primitive Social Organization.* New York: Columbia University Press, 1949.

———, and Ovesey, Lionel. *The Mark of Oppression: A Psychological Study of the Black American.* New York: W. W. Norton and Company, 1951.

Karon, Bertram. *The Negro Personality.* New York: Springer, 1958.

Katz, J.; Korn, H.; Lozoff, M.; et al. *No Time for Youth: Growth and Constraint in College Students.* San Francisco: Jossey-Bass, 1968.

Katz, M. *The Irony of Early School Reform: Educational Innovation in Mid-Nineteenth Century Massachusetts.* Boston: Harvard University Press, 1968.

Kavolis, Vytautas. "Post-Modern Man: Psycho-Cultural Responses to Social Trends." *Social Problems* 17 (1970): 435-448.

Kerr, Clark; Dunlop, John T.; Harbison, Frederick H.; and Myers, Charles H. *Industrialism and Industrial Man.* Cambridge, Mass.: Harvard University Press, 1960.

Klapp, Orrin E. *Heroes, Villains, and Fools: The Changing American Character.* Englewood Cliffs, N.J.: Prentice Hall, 1962.

Klineberg, Otto. "A Science of National Character." *Journal of Social Psychology* 19 (1944): 147-162.

Kohlberg, Laurence. *Stages in the Development of Moral Thought and Action.* New York: Holt, Rinehart and Winston, 1969.

———, and Gilligan, Carol. "The Adolescent as a Philosopher: The Discovery of the Self in a Post-Conventional World." *Daedalus* 100 (1971): 1051-1086.

Kohn, Melvin. *Class and Conformity: A Study of Values.* Homewood, Ill.: Dorsey Press, 1969.

Kouwenhoven, John. *The Beer Can by the Highway: Essays on What's "American" About America.* Garden City, N.J.: Doubleday, 1961.

Kroeber, Alfred K. *Configurations of Cultural Growth.* Berkeley: University of California Press, 1944.

Kronus, Sidney. *The Black Middle Class.* Columbus, Ohio: Merrill, 1971.

Kunkel, Peter, and Kennard, Sara S. *Spout Spring: A Black Community.* New York: Holt, Rinehart and Winston, 1971.

LaBarre, Weston. "They Shall Take Up Serpents: The Psychology of the Southern Snake Handling Cult." Minneapolis: University of Minnesota Press, 1962.

Labov, William. *Sociolinguistic Patterns.* Philadelphia: University of Pennsylvania Press, 1972.

Land, Kenneth C., and Spilerman, Seymour (eds.). *Social Indicator Models.* New York: Russell Sage Foundation, 1975.

Lane, Robert E. *Political Life.* Glencoe, Ill.: The Free Press, 1959.

Laski, Harold J. *The American Democracy.* New York: Viking Press, 1948.

Lauer, Robert H. *Perspectives on Social Change.* Boston: Allyn and Bacon, 1973.

Lazarsfeld, Paul F., and Menzel, Herbert. "On the Relation Between Individual and Collective Properties." In *Complex Organizations: A Sociological Reader,* edited by Amitai Etzioni. New York: Holt, Rinehart and Winston, 1961.

Lazarus, A. A. "The Results of Behavior Therapy in 126 Cases of Severe Neurosis." *Behavior Research and Therapy* 1 (1963): 69-79.

Lennox, Robert S. "Cultural Transvaluation." Unpublished paper. Stanford University, 1969.

LeVine, Robert. "Culture and Personality." *Biennial Review of Anthropology*. Stanford, Calif.: Stanford University Press, 1963.

———. *Culture, Behavior, and Personality*. Chicago: Aldine Press, 1973.

Levinson, Daniel J. "The Mid-life Transition: A Period in Adult Psychosocial Development." *Psychiatry* 40 (1977) (in press).

———; Darrow, Charlotte M.; Klein, Edward B.; Levinson, Maria H.; and McKee, Braxton. "The Psychosocial Development of Men in Early Adulthood and the Mid-Life Transition." In *Life History Research in Psychopathology*, edited by D. F. Ricks, A. Thomas, and M. Roff. Minneapolis: University of Minnesota Press, 1974.

———. *Seasons of a Man's Life*. New York: Alfred A. Knopf, 1977 (in press).

Lewis, Oscar. *Five Families*. New York: Basic Books, 1959.

———. *The Children of Sanchez*. New York: Random House, 1961.

———. "The Culture of Poverty." *Scientific American* 215 (1966a): 19-25.

———. *La Vida: A Puerto Rican Family in the Culture of Poverty*. New York: Random House, 1966b.

Liebow, Elliott. *Tally's Corner: A Study of Negro Streetcorner Men*. Boston: Little, Brown and Company, 1967.

Lifton, Robert Jay. "Thought Reform of Chinese Intellectuals." In *Attitudes*, edited by Marie Jahoda and Neil Warren. Baltimore: Penguin Books, 1966.

———. *History and Human Survival: Essays on the Young and Old Survivors and the Dead, Peace and War, and on Contemporary Psychohistory*. New York: Random House, 1970.

Lipset, Seymour Martin. "A Changing American Character?" In *The First New Nation*, edited by Seymour M. Lipset. New York: Basic Books, 1963.

———, and Lowenthal, Leo (eds.). *Culture and Social Character: The Work of David Riesman Reviewed*. Glencoe, Ill.: The Free Press, 1961.

———, and Schaflander, Gerald M. *Passion in Politics*. Boston: Little, Brown and Company, 1971.

Livson, Norman. "Developmental Dimensions of Personality: A Life-Span Formulation." In *Life-Span Developmental Psychology*, edited by P. B. Baltes and K. W. Schaie. New York: Academic Press, 1973.

Loevinger, Jane, and Wesster, Ruth. *Measuring Ego Development*. San Francisco: Jossey-Bass, 1971.

Lowi, Theodore. *The End of Liberalism*. New York: Holt, Rinehart and Winston, 1969.

Maccoby, Michael. "Technology and the American Character." Unpublished paper. Cambridge, Mass.: Institute for Policy Studies, Harvard Program on Technology and Society, 1970.

———. *The Gamesman: The New Corporate Leaders*. New York: Simon and Shuster, 1977.

Machlup, Fritz. *The Production and Distribution of Knowledge in the U.S.* Princeton, N.J.: Princeton University Press, 1962.

Madsen, William. *The Mexican-Americans of South Texas.* New York: Holt, Rinehart and Winston, 1973.

Marcuse, Herbert. *One Dimensional Man: Studies in the Ideology of Advanced Industrial Society.* Boston: Beacon Press, 1964.

Marsh, Alan. "Explorations in Unorthodox Political Behavior." *European Journal of Political Research* 2 (1974): 107-131.

———. "The Silent Revolution, Value Priorities and the Quality of Life in Britain." *American Political Science Review* 69 (1975): 21-30.

Martindale, Don. "The Sociology of National Character." *Annals of the American Academy of Political and Social Science* 370 (1967): 30-35.

Marx, Gary. *Protest and Prejudice.* New York: Harper and Row, 1967.

Marx, Karl. *Das Kapital.* New York: International Publishers, 1967.

Maslow, Abraham H. "A Theory of Human Motivation." *Psychology Review* 50 (1943): 370-396.

———. *Motivation and Personality.* New York: Harper, 1954.

———. *Toward a Psychology of Being.* New York: Van Nostrand Reinhold, 1968.

McAllister, Bernice J. S. "Educator's Status-Roles, Social Antecedents, and Perceptions Related to a Continuum of Traditional-Emergent Values." Ph.D. dissertation, Stanford University, 1967.

McClelland, David C. *The Achieving Society.* New York: D. Van Nostrand Company, 1961.

McGiffert, Michael (ed.). *The Character of Americans.* Homewood, Ill.: Dorsey Press, 1970.

Mead, Margaret. *Coming of Age in Samoa.* New York: Blue Ribbon Books, 1932; Mentor Books, 1949. Originaly published, 1928.

———. *Growing Up in New Guinea.* New York: Mentor Books, 1953. Originally published, 1930.

———. *Sex and Temperament in Three Primitive Societies.* New York: Mentor Books, 1950.

———. "National Character." In *An Appraisal of Anthropology Today,* edited by Sol Tax. Chicago: University of Chicago Press, 1952.

———. "The Idea of National Character." In *The Search for Identity: Essays on the American Character,* edited by Roger L. Shinn. New York: Institute for Religious and Social Studies, 1964.

Merton, Robert K. "Insiders and Outsiders: A Chapter in the Sociology of Knowledge." *American Journal of Sociology* 78 (1972): 9-47.

Metzger, Paul L. "Reply to Goldstein and Washington on Metzger." *American Journal of Sociology* 77 (1971): 587-590.

Milbrath, Lester W. *Political Participation.* Chicago: Rand McNally, 1965.

Milgram, Stanley. *Obedience to Authority.* New York: Harper and Row, 1974.

Miller, Arthur. "Political Issues and Trust in Government: 1964-1970." *American Political Science Review* 68 (1974): 951-972.

Miller, Walter B. "Lower Class Culture as a Generating Milieu of Gang Delinquency." *Journal of Social Issues* 14 (1958): 5-19.

Milton, O. "Presidental Choice and Performance on a Scale of Authoritarianism." *American Psychologist* (abstract) 7 (1952): 597-598.

Mischel, Walter. *Personality and Assessment.* New York: Wiley, 1968.

Mitchell, John D. and Schwartz, Emanuel K. "A Psychological Approach to the Peking Opera." In *Leonardo*. New York: Pergamon Press, 1974.

Morris, C. W. *Varieties of Human Value*. Chicago: University of Chicago Press, 1956.

Morse, S. J., and Gergen, K. J. "Social Comparison, Self-Consistency and the Presentation of Self." *Journal of Personality and Social Psychology* 16 (1970): 148-156.

Muraskin, William. "The Moral Basis of a Backward Sociologist: Edward Banfield, the Italians, and the Italian-Americans." *American Journal of Sociology* 79 (1974): 1484-1496.

Murray, Henry A. *Explorations in Personality*. New York: Oxford University Press, 1938.

Myrdal, Gunnar. *The Challange to Affluence.* New York: Random House, 1963.

Nakane, Chie. *Japanese Society.* Suffolk, Great Britain: The Chaucer Press, 1970.

Nay, Barbara. "American Values: An Anthropological Analysis." Senior Honors Thesis, Stanford University, 1974.

Neugarten, Bernice L. "A Developmental View of Adult Personality." In *Relations of Development and Aging,* edited by James E. Birren. Springfield, Ill.: Charles C. Thomas, 1965.

Newcomb, Theodore M. *Consistency of Certain Extrovert-Introvert Behavior Patterns in 51 Problem Boys.* New York: Columbia University, Teachers' College, Bureau of Publications, 1929.

Nicolson, Harold. *National Character and National Policy.* Nottingham, England: University College, 1938.

Nie, Norman H.; Verba, Sidney; and Kim, Jae-on. "Political Participation and the Life Cycle." *Comparative Politics* (1974): 319-340.

Nisbet, Robert A. *Tradition and Revolt.* New York: Random House, 1968.

Ogburn, William F. *Social Change.* New York: B. W. Huesbsch, 1922.

Ortega y Gasset, Jose. *Man and Crisis.* New York: W. W. Norton and Company, 1958.

Ozane, H. "Social Character as a Sociological Concept." *American Sociological Review* 8 (1943): 519-524.

Park, Robert E., and Burgess, Ernest W. *Introduction to The Science of Sociology.* Chicago: University of Chicago Press, 1924.

Parker, Seymour, and Kleiner, Robert. "The Culture of Poverty: An Adjustive Dimension." *American Anthropologist* 72 (1970): 516-527.
Parsons, Talcott. *The Social System*. New York: The Free Press, 1951.
———. *Social Structure and Personality*. Glencoe, Ill.: The Free Press, 1964.
———. "Basic Personality Structure: Modal Clustering and Diversity." In his *The Social System*. New York: Macmillan and Company, 1951.
Partridge, William. *Hippie Ghetto*. New York: Holt, Rinehart and Winston, 1973.
Phillips, U. B. *American Negro Slavery*. New York: Appleton, 1918.
———. *Life and Labor in the Old South*. Boston: Little, Brown and Company, 1929.
Pierson, George W. "The M-Factor in American History." *American Quarterly* 14 (1962): 275-289.
Pilcher, William W. *The Portland Longshoremen: A Dispersed Urban Community*. New York: Holt, Rinehart and Winston, 1972.
Platt, Washington. *National Character in Action: Intelligence Factors in Foreign Relations*. New Brunswick, N.J.: Rutgers University Press, 1961.
Portes, Alejandro. "Modernity and Development: A Critique." *Comparative International Development* 8 (1973): 247-277.
Potter, David M. *People of Plenty: Economic Abundance and the American Character*. Chicago: University of Chicago Press, 1954.
Powdermaker, Hortense. "The Channeling of Negro Aggression by the Cultural Process." *American Journal of Sociology* 49 (1943): 750-758.
Rainwater, Lee. "The Problem of Lower Class Culture." *Journal of Social Issues* 26 (1970): 133-148.
Reich, Charles. *The Greening of America*. New York: Bantam Books, 1970.
Riesman, David. "Some Observations on the Study of American Character." *Psychiatry* 15 (1952): 333-338.
———. "Psychological Types and National Character." *American Quarterly* 5 (1953): 325-343.
———. "Some Questions About the Study of American Character in the Twentieth Century." *Annals of the American Academy of Political and Social Science* 370 (1967): 36-47.
———, et al. *The Lonely Crowd*. New Haven, Conn.: Yale University Press, 1950.
———, and Glazer, Nathan. "The Lonely Crowd: A Reconsideration in 1960." In *Culture and Social Character*, edited by Seymour Lipset and Leo Lowenthal. New York: The Free Press, 1961.
Roach, Jack, and Gursslin, Orville. "An Evaluation of the Concept 'Culture of Poverty'." *Social Forces* 45 (1967): 383-392.
Robinson, Jackie. *I Never Had It Made*. New York: Putnam, 1972.
Rodman, Hyman. "The Lower-Class Value Stretch." *Social Forces* 42 (1963): 205-215.

Rodriguez, Richard. "Memories and the Graduate Student Who Became a Chicano." *Saturday Review World* (February 1975): 46-48.

Rohrer, John; Edmonson, Munro, et al. *The Eighth Generation: Cultures and Personalities of New Orleans Negroes.* New York: Harper and Row, 1960.

Rokeach, Milton. *Beliefs, Attitudes, and Values.* San Francisco: Jossey-Bass, Inc., Publishers, 1968.

Rosengarten, Theodore. *All God's Dangers: The Life of Nate Shaw.* New York: Alfred A. Knopf, 1974.

Roszak, Theodore. *The Coming of the Counter-Culture.* Garden City, N.Y.: Doubleday, 1969.

Rudolph, Lloyd I., and Rudolph, Susan Hoeber. *The Modernity Tradition.* Chicago: University of Chicago Press, 1967.

Russett, Bruce M., et al. *World Handbook of Political and Social Indicators.* New Haven, Conn.: Yale University Press, 1964.

Sahlins, Marshall D., and Service, Elmer R. *Evolution and Change.* Ann Arbor: University of Michigan Press, 1960.

Sanford, R. Nevitt. "Personality Development During the College Years." *Personnel and Guidance Journal* 35 (1956): 74-80.

———. *The American College: A Psychological and Social Interpretation of Higher Learning*. New York: Wiley, 1962.

———. "Developmental Status of the Entering Freshmen." In *The American College: A Psychological and Social Interpretation of Higher Learning,* edited by R. Nevitt Sanford. New York: Wiley, 1962.

———. *Self and Society: Social Change and Individual Development.* New York: Atherton Press, 1966.

———. *Where Colleges Fail: A Study of the Student as a Person.* San Francisco: Jossey-Bass, 1967.

———. "Whatever Happened to Action Research?" *Journal of Social Issues* 26 (1970): 3-23.

———. *Issues in Personality Theory.* San Francisco: Jossey-Bass, 1970.

———. "Notes Toward a General Theory of Personality Development—at 80 or Any Old Age." Mimeographed. Berkeley, Calif.: The Wright Institute, 1973.

———. "Authoritarian Personality in Contemporary Perspective." In *Handbook of Political Psychology,* edited by J. N. Knutsen. San Francisco: Jossey-Bass, 1973.

———. "Morality and Education for the Enjoyment of Life." Mimeographed. Berkeley, Calif.: The Wright Institute, 1974.

———, and Comstock, Craig (eds.). *Sanctions for Evil.* San Francisco: Jossey-Bass, 1971.

Sapir, Edward. *Selected Writings in Language, Culture, and Personality.* Berkeley: University of California Press, 1948.

Saporta, R. *Readings in Psycholinguistics.* New York: Holt, Rinehart, 1961.

Schein, Edgar H. *Coercive Persuasion: A Socio-Psychological Analysis of the "Brainwashing" of American Civilian Prisoners by the Chinese Communists.* New York: W. W. Norton and Company, 1961.

Schlesinger, Arthur M. *Paths to the Present.* New York: Macmillan Company, 1949.

Schumacher, E. G. *Small Is Beautiful: Economics As If People Mattered.* New York: Harper and Row, 1973.

Schuman, Howard, and Hatchett, Shirley. *Black Racial Attitudes: Trends and Complexities.* Ann Arbor: University of Michigan, Survey Research Center, 1974.

Schwartz, Theodore. "The Cargo Cult: A Melanesian Type-Response to Change." In *Responses to Change,* edited by George A. DeVos. New York: D. Van Nostrand Company, 1976.

Selznick, G., and Steinberg, P. *The Tenacity of Prejudice.* New York: Harper and Row, 1969.

Sewall, Richard. *The Vision of Tragedy.* New Haven, Conn.: Yale University Press, 1959.

Shafer, Boyd. *Nationalism: Myth and Reality.* New York: Harcourt, Brace and World, 1955.

Shannon, Lyle and Magdaline. *Minority Migrants in the Urban Community: Mexican-American and Negro Adjustment to Industrial Society.* Beverly Hills, Calif.: Sage Publications, 1973.

Silverman, Sydel. "Agricultural Organization, Social Structure, and Values in Italy: Amoral Familism Reconsidered." *American Anthropologist* 70 (1968): 1-20.

Simpson, George E, and Yinger, J. Milton. *Racial and Cultural Minorities: An Analysis of Prejudice and Discrimination.* New York: Harper and Row, 1972.

Slater, Phillip. *The Pursuit of Loneliness.* Boston: Beacon Press, 1970.

Smelser, Neil J. "Growth, Structural Change, and Conflict in California Public Education, 1950-1970." In *Public Higher Education in California,* edited by Neil Smelser and Gabriel Almond. Berkeley: University of California Press, 1974.

Smith, David H., and Inkeles, Alex. "The OM Scale: A Comparative Socio-Psychological Measure of Individual Modernity." *Sociometry* 29 (1966): 353-377.

Smith, Don D. "Modal Attitude Clusters: A Supplement for the Study of National Character." *Social Forces* 44 (1966): 526-533.

Smith, M. B. "Peasant Characterology: Method versus Insight," review of E. Fromm and M. Maccoby, *Social Character in a Mexican Village." Contemporary Psychology* 16 (1971): 635-637.

Sorokin, Pitirim A. *Society, Culture, and Personality.* New York: Harper and Row, 1947.

Spencer, Herbert. *Principles of Sociology.* New York: D. Appleton, 1892.

Spengler, Oswald. *The Decline of the West.* New York: Alfred A. Knopf, 1926.

Spindler, George D. "The Military—A Systematic Analysis." *Social Forces* 27 (1948a): 83-88.

———. "American Character as Revealed by the Military." *Psychiatry: Journal for the Operational Statement of Interpersonal Relations* 11 (1948b): 275-281.

———. "The Doolittle Board and Cooptation in the Army." *Social Forces* 29: 305-310.

———. "Education in a Transforming American Culture." *Harvard Educational Review* 25 (1955): 145-156.

——— (ed.). *The Making of Psychological Anthropology.* Berkeley, Calif.: University of California Press, 1977.

———, and Spindler, Louise. "Psychology in Anthropology: Application to Culture Change." In *Psychology: A Study of a Science,* edited by S. Koch. New York: McGraw-Hill, 1963.

Spindler, Louise, and Spindler, George. "A Modal Personality Technique in the Study of Menomini Acculturation." In *Studying Personality Cross-Culturally,* edited by B. Kaplan. New York: Harper and Row, 1961.

Spiro, Melford E. "The Natural History of a False Dichotomy." *Psychiatry* 15 (1951): 19-47.

Spring, J. H. *Education and the Rise of the Corporate State.* Boston: Beacon Press, 1972.

Spuhler, James N. (ed.). *Genetic Diversity and Human Behavior.* Chicago: Aldine Publishing Company, 1967.

Stampp, Kenneth. *The Peculiar Institution: Slavery in the Ante-Bellum South.* New York: Alfred A. Knopf, 1965.

Steele, Edward D. "The Rhetorical Use of the 'American Value System' in the 1952 Presidential Campaign Addresses." Ph.D. dissertation, Stanford University, 1957.

Stern, George G. *People in Context.* New York: Wiley, 1970.

Steward, Julian H. *Theory of Culture Change.* Urbana: University of Illinois Press, 1959.

Stewart, Wendy A. "The Formation of the Early Adult Life Structure in Women." Ph.D. dissertation, Teachers College, Columbia University, 1977.

Suomi, S. J., and Harlow, H. F., "Social Rehabilitation of Isolate-Reared Monkeys." *Developmental Psychology* 6 (1972): 487-496.

Suzman, Richard M. "The Modernization of Personality." Ph.D. dissertation, Harvard University, 1973.

———. "Psychological Modernity." *International Journal of Comparative Sociology* 14 (1974): 3-4.

———. "Ego Development, Modernity and the Social Structure." Paper presented at annual meetings of the American Sociological Association, Montreal, Canada, September 1974.

Tadao, Maruoka. "Let Come the Day to Say 'Once It Was So'." In *Japan's Invisible Race*, edited by George A. DeVos and Hiroshi Wagatsuma. Berkeley: University of California Press, 1966.

Terhune, Kenneth W. "From National Character to National Behavior: A Reformulation." *Journal of Conflict Resolution* 14 (1970): 203-263.

Terkel, Studs. *Working*. New York: Pantheon, 1972.

Thomas, William I. *Social Behavior and Personality: Contributions of W. I. Thomas*. New York: Social Science Research Council, 1951.

Tocqueville, Alexis de. *Democracy in America*. Garden City, N.Y.: Doubleday, 1969. Originally published 1835.

Toynbee, Arnold J. *A Study of History*. New York: Oxford University Press, 1939.

Unamuno, Miguel de. *Tragic Sense of Life*. New York: Dover, 1954.

U.S.A., The Permanent Revolution. Edited by the Editors of *Fortune*. Englewood Cliffs, N.J.: Prentice-Hall, 1951.

U.S. Bureau of the Census. *Historical Statistics of the United States, Colonial Times to 1970*. Bicentennial Edition. Washington, D.C.: U.S. Government Printing Office, 1975.

U.S. Department of Commerce, Bureau of the Census. *Social and Economic Status of the Black Population in the United States*. Washington, D.C.: U.S. Government Printing Office, 1972.

U.S. Office of Management and Budget. *Social Indicators*. Washington, D.C.: U.S. Government Printing Office, 1973.

Valentine, Charles. *Culture and Poverty*. Chicago: University of Chicago Press, 1968.

Wagatsuma, Hiroshi. "Problems of Cultural Identity in Modern Japan." In *Ethnic Identity*, edited by George A. DeVos and Lola Romanucci-Ross. Palo Alto, Calif.: Mayfield Publishing Company, 1975.

Warner, Lloyd W. (ed.). *Yankee City*. New Haven and London: Yale University Press, 1963.

———; Havighurst, R. J.; and Loeb, M. B. *Who Shall Be Educated?* New York: Harper, 1944.

Warth, Peggy. "A Study of Values in a Mexican-American Junior High School Sample." Unpublished paper for Education 315, Stanford University, 1972.

Washington, Robert. "Further Comments on 'American Sociology and Black Americans'." *American Journal of Sociology* 77 (1971: 580-587.

Weber, Max. Translated by Talcott Parsons. *The Protestant Ethnic and the Spirit of Capitalism*. New York: Charles Scribner's Sons, 1930.

———. *From Max Weber: Essays in Sociology*. Translated and edited by

Hans H. Gerth and C. W. Mills. New York: Oxford University Press, 1946.

———. *The Theory of Social and Economic Organization.* Translated by Talcott Parsons. New York: The Free Press, 1964. Originally published, 1922.

Webster, H.; Freedman, M. B.; and Heist, P. "Personality Changes in College Students." In *The American College: A Psychological and Social Interpretation of Higher Learning,* edited by R. Nevitt Sanford. New York: Wiley, 1962.

Weilenmann, Hermann, "The Interlocking of Nation and Personality Structure." In *Nation-Building,* edited by Karl W. Deutsch and William J. Foltz. New York: Atherton Press, 1963.

Weiner J. S. *The Natural History of Man.* New York: Universe Books, 1971.

Weinstein, Fred, and Platt, Gerald M. *The Wish to Be Free.* Berkeley: University of California Press, 1969.

White, Leslie. *The Science of Culture.* New York: Grove Press, 1949.

White, Robert W. *Lives in Progress.* New York: Dryden, 1952.

Whyte, William H., Jr. *The Organization Man.* New York: Simon and Schuster, 1956.

Wilensky, Harold. "Life Cycle, Work Situation and Participation in Formal Associations." In *Aging and Leisure,* edited by R. Kleemeier. New York: Oxford University Press, 1961.

Winnicott, D. W. *The Maturational Processes and the Facilitating Environment.* New York: International Universities Press, 1965.

Witkin, Herman A., et al. *Psychological Differentiation.* New York: Wiley, 1962.

Wright Institute, The Bulletin of the Wright Institute Graduate School. Berkeley, Calif., 1974.

Wrong, Dennis. "The Oversocialized Conception of Man in Modern Sociology." *American Sociological Review* 26 (1961): 183-193.

Yankelovich, Daniel. *The Changing Values on Campus.* New York: Washington Square Press, 1972.

———. *The New Morality: A Profile of Youth Values in the 70s.* New York: McGraw-Hill, 1974.

Yinger, J. Milton. *Toward a Field Theory of Behavior.* New York: McGraw-Hill, 1965.

———, and Simpson, George E. *Racial and Cultural Minorities: An Analysis of Prejudice and Discrimination.* New York: Holt, Rinehart and Winston, 1972.

Index

NOTES ON THE CONTRIBUTORS

GABRIEL A. ALMOND is Professor and Executive Head of the Department of Political Science at Stanford University and was previously a member of the faculty at the City University of New York, Yale University, and Princeton University. He is co-author of *The Civic Culture,* a widely known volume concerned with the interaction of political culture and political character. His most recent work is *Crisis, Choice, and Change.*

GEORGE A. DeVOS is Professor of Anthropology at the University of California at Berkeley and was formerly Professor of Psychology at the University of Michigan. With his extensive academic background in both psychology and anthropology he has become a recognized authority in the field of culture-and-personality studies. He is co-author and editor of the recently published volume *Responses to Change.*

GORDON J. DiRENZO is Professor of Sociology at the University of Delaware and formerly held appointments at several other universities. His principal research interests involve the functional relationships between personality systems and social systems. He is the author of *Personality, Power and Politics,* and the co-author and editor of *Concepts, Theory and Explanation in the Behavioral Sciences* and *Personality and Politics.*

AMITAI ETZIONI is Professor of Sociology at Columbia University and Director of the Center for Policy Research in New York City. He has been concerned primarily with the character of responses which the American society is making to the basic psychological needs of its members. He has written extensively for scientific journals and numerous other publications. His books include *Studies in Social Change* and *The Active Society.*

KENNETH J. GERGEN is Professor and Chairman of Psychology at Swarthmore College in Pennsylvania, and previously held appointments at Duke, Harvard, Yale, and other American, as well as foreign, universities. He has conducted extensive studies in the fields of personality theory and social psychology. He is the co-author of *The Self in Social Interaction* and has published many other books and articles.

FRANCIS L.K. HSU is Professor and Chairman of the Department of Anthropology at Northwestern University where he has served for more than twenty-five years following appointments at Columbia University and Cornell University. His principal research efforts have been directed to defining a theoretical link between the psychological needs of the individual and the patterns of social and cultural development. He is the author of *Psychological Anthropology* and several other volumes.

DANIEL J. LEVINSON is Professor of Psychology in the Department of Psychiatry at Yale Medical School and Director of the Research Unit in Social Psychology at the Connecticut Mental Health Center. He previously held similar appointments at Harvard Medical School and the Massachusetts Mental Health Center. He is an author of the classic study of *The Authoritarian Personality* and of many other books and articles. He has contributed authoritatively to the conceptual and theoretical issues involved in national character studies.

MICHAEL MACCOBY is Psychologist and Resident Fellow of the Institute on Policy Studies in Washington, D.C., as well as Director of the Project on Technology, Work and Character sponsored by the Harvard Seminar on Science, Technology, and Public Policy. He is also a member of the faculty at the Mexican Institute of Psychoanalysis. With Erich Fromm he co-authored the interdisciplinary work, *Social Character of a Mexican Village.*

NEVITT SANFORD is President of The Wright Institute in California, and formerly served as Professor of Psychology at the University of California in Berkeley, and more recently as a member of the faculty at Stanford University. He is one of the authors of *The Authoritarian Personality.* Among his numerous other publications in the fields of psychology and education are *Self and Society: Social Change and Individual Development* and *Issues in Personality Theory.*

GEORGE D. SPINDLER is Professor of Anthropology and Education at Stanford University. He is a pioneer in the application of anthropology to the analysis of educational processes. He is the author of several books and articles on the psychology of adaptation to cultural change and other anthropological topics. His latest work is *The Making of Psychological Anthropology.*

RICHARD M. SUZMAN is an Assistant Professor of Sociology in the Department of Psychiatry at the University of California Medical School in San Francisco, and also serves as a faculty associate in the School of Education at Stanford University. He has done a series of studies on the relationship of modernity, socialization, and personality development during late adolescence and early adulthood.

J. MILTON YINGER is Professor and Chairman of the Department of Sociology and Anthropology at Oberlin College in Ohio. He is an authority in the field of culture-and-personality studies and on racial minorities in the United States. His numerous publications include *Toward a Field Theory of Behavior* and the award-winning *Racial and Cultural Minorities: An Analysis of Prejudice and Discrimination.* He currently serves as president of the American Sociological Association.